Readings in the
CRUDE OIL WINDFALL PROFIT TAX

Readings in the CRUDE OIL WINDFALL PROFIT TAX

D. Larry Crumbley, CPA
Professor of Accounting
Texas A&M University

Craig E. Reese
Assistant Professor
University of Texas

PennWell Books
PennWell Publishing Company
Tulsa, Oklahoma 74101

PennWell Publishing Company
1421 South Sheridan Road/P.O. Box 1260
Tulsa, Oklahoma 74101

Library of Congress cataloging in publication data

Main entry under title:

Readings in the crude oil windfall profit tax.

1. Excess profits tax — United States —
Addresses, essays, lectures. 2. Petroleum —
Taxation — United States — Addresses, essays,
lectures. I. Crumbley, D. Larry. II. Reese,
Craig E.
KF6475.A2R4 343.7305′582282 81-19968
ISBN 0-87814-185-5 347.3035582282 AACR2

Printed in the United States of America

1 2 3 4 5 86 85 84 83 82

Table of Contents

Preface

When Congress enacted the Crude Oil Windfall Profit Tax Act of 1980, only a few sophisticated tax professionals were cognizant of the technical problems that would ensue in implementing the windfall profit tax (WPT). In the 18 months since the law was enacted, there has been a wealth of technical literature published on compliance problems related to the implementation of the WPT. Some of the literature also includes planning ideas and suggestions for minimizing the WPT. We have collected what we consider to be a comprehensive set of technical articles on the WPT. If one were to read all of the articles selected for this volume, he would notice some duplication in the content. Such duplication may actually be advantageous to the reader for at least two reasons. Where there are two or more articles that cover the same WPT issue or problem, one should read the most recent explanation thereof insofar as changes in the regulations and law have occurred over the past 18 months. In addition, reading two or more explanations of the same problem or issue often facilitates the reader's comprehension, even though one analysis is more timely than the other. In respect to the most recent changes in the WPT law and prospective changes in the law and regulations related thereto, one should read the Postscript chapter and, of course, monitor changes in the law and regulations by reading weekly or monthly tax newsletters.

D. Larry Crumbley
College Station, Texas

Craig E. Reese
Austin, Texas

Part I

Overview of the WINDFALL PROFIT TAX

The Windfall Profit Tax is a federal excise tax on the difference between the removal price and specified base price of a taxable barrel of crude oil. This difference between the removal price and the base price is the so-called windfall profit. The removal price is the actual or constructive sales price of a barrel of crude at the wellhead. The base price is generally the predecontrol price at which the oil would have been sold.

The tax is imposed on the producer but, depending upon the situation and certain elections, the *first purchaser* (the operator) or another person called a *qualified disburser* may be liable for payment of the tax.

Property under the WPT is defined for the entire tax, except the net income limitation, as it is defined under DOE (Department of Energy) regulations. In most cases, the property unit will be the same for DOE and federal tax purposes.

The windfall profit on a barrel of crude oil is limited to 90 percent of the net income attributable to that barrel; however, net income for WPT purposes is based on taxable income and not on financial accounting income.

The WPT will phase out with a 3-percent reduction in rates over a 33-month period. This phase-out period will begin the later of (1) January 1, 1988, or (2) when it is estimated that aggregate net WPT revenues will exceed $227.3 billion. This aggregate net figure takes into account refunds, credits and the reduction in income taxes as a result of the WPT deductibility. The phased decontrol cannot begin until after January 1981.

Calculating the WPT may be summarized as follows:

removal price (taxable oil production)
– [base price + severance tax adjustment]
= windfall profit (not to exceed 90 percent net income)
x applicable tax rate
= windfall profit tax

For an explanation of the expansion of categories of oil exempt from the WPT, see the postscript chapter.

PLANNING FOR THE CRUDE OIL WINDFALL PROFIT TAX

Robert D. Shattuck, Jr., Esq.*

The windfall profit provisions of the Crude Oil Windfall Profit Tax Act of 1980, Pub. L. No. 96-223 ("COWPTA"), impose, effective March 1, 1980, an excise tax on the "windfall profit" derived from the initial removal and sale of most domestically produced crude oil. The tax is imposed on the producer and only on the first removal and sale of the oil. The "windfall profit" is the initial selling price (removal price) of a barrel of oil minus the sum of a base price for the barrel of oil, which is adjusted for inflation, plus state severance taxes imposed with respect to the barrel to the extent attributable to the excess of the selling price over the adjusted base price. (Base prices and, to a lesser extent, the inflation adjustment vary according to different categories of oil; base prices within a single category are not one fixed price, but are dependent on the grade, quality, and location of the oil.) The amount of the windfall profit is lim-

* Robert D. Shattuck, Jr. is associated with the law firm of North, Haskell, Slaughter, Young & Lewis in Birmingham, Alabama.

Article reprinted courtesy of *Oil & Gas Tax Quarterly*, June 1980, pp. 387–418

ited to 90% of a specially computed "net income" amount which is attributable to the barrel of oil. The percentage tax rate which is applied to the windfall profit varies according to different categories of oil.

The tax will be phased out over a 34-month period beginning sometime between 1987 and 1990. The windfall profit tax is deductible for federal income tax purposes.

Crude Oil; Domestic

COWPTA defines crude oil by incorporating the definition thereof in the regulations prescribed under Section 4(a) of the Emergency Petroleum Allocation Act of 1973 (the "energy regulations"), as those regulations existed on June 1, 1979 (the "June 1979 energy regulations"). The June 1979 energy regulations define crude oil as a mixture of hydrocarbons that existed in liquid phase in underground reservoirs and remain liquid at atmospheric pressure after passing through surface separating facilities. This includes condensate recovered in associated or nonassociated production by mechanical separators. 10 C.F.R. § 212.31 (1979). H.R. Rep. No. 96-817, 96th Cong., 2d Sess. (1980) (the "Conference Report") states that only natural crude oil is included and not synthetic petroleum, such as oil from shale or tar sands.

Domestic crude oil which is generally subject to the windfall profit tax is oil produced from an oil well located in the United States or in a possession of the United States. Continental shelf areas are included per Section 638 of the Internal Revenue Code. The COWPTA definition of "possession of the United States" makes an incomplete cross-reference to Internal Revenue Code Section 638(2).

Exemptions; Tier Categories

All domestic oil is subject to the windfall profit tax; however, there is a complete exemption for certain oil owned by governmental bodies and charities, certain Indian oil, certain Alaskan oil, and certain "front-end oil." All remaining domestic crude oil which is subject to the tax is divided into three numbered tier categories. Tier 3 oil includes "newly discovered oil," "heavy oil," and "incremental tertiary oil." Tier 2 oil includes oil which is not Tier 3 oil and which is either from a "stripper well property" or from an economic interest in a National Petroleum Reserve held by the United States. Tier 1 oil is all other taxable crude oil.

Elements of Computation

The unadjusted base price for Tier 1 oil is the upper-tier ceiling price under the energy regulations, as those regulations were in effect on March 1, 1979 (the "March 1979 energy regulations"), for oil sold in May 1979, minus $.21. The energy regulations allowed for variation of ceiling prices according to the grade, quality, and field of oil, and hence the base price is not a single, fixed number. The Conference Report estimates that the *average* upper tier ceiling price for oil sold in May 1979 was $13.02 per barrel.

The base prices for Tier 2 oil and Tier 3 oil will be determined by the Secretary of the Treasury as the price such oil (subject to variation to take into account grade, quality, and field) would have sold for in December 1979 if prices had been decontrolled at such time, and the removal price for all domestic oil had been, respectively, $15.20 a barrel in the case of the Tier 2 determination and $16.55 in the case of the Tier 3 determination.

An unadjusted base price for a particular calendar quarter is adjusted for inflation by increasing the base price by the percentage by which the implicit price deflator for the gross national product for the second preceding calendar quarter exceeds the implicit price deflator for the calendar quarter ended June 30, 1979. Tier 3 oil gets an additional special inflation adjustment which is computed by multiplying the regular adjustment by 1.005 raised to the Nth power where N is the number of calendar quarters which have elapsed since September 1979.

State severance taxes attributable to the excess of the selling price over the adjusted base price are added to the adjusted base price. The sum is subtracted from the selling price to obtain the "windfall profit." The "windfall profit" (limited to 90% of "net income" attributable to the barrel of oil) is then taxed at rates which vary according to the tier categories, including special Tier 1 and Tier 2 rates for "independent producer oil." The tax rate for all Tier 3 oil is 30%. The tax rate for Tier 1 oil which qualifies as "independent producer oil" is 50% and the tax rate for Tier 2 oil which qualifies as "independent producer oil" is 30%. Otherwise, the tax rate for Tier 1 oil is 70% and the tax rate for Tier 2 oil is 60%.

Methodology to Compute Tax

To summarize, a step-by-step methology for calculating the windfall profit tax on a barrel of oil is (1) determine what category the oil is in, (2) determine the base price, (3) adjust the base price, (4) add the state severance tax adjustment, (5) subtract the sum from the selling price, (6) test for the 90% of "net income" limitation, (7) apply the appropriate percentage tax rate to the windfall profit, and (8) make the phaseout reduction of the tax, if the phaseout period for the windfall profit tax has begun.

Categories of Oil

To determine the windfall profit tax on a barrel of oil, the first step is to determine the category of oil. Oil is either in the completely exempt category or else placed in one of three tier categories.

Exempt Oil

There are four types of oil which are completely exempt from the tax.

Qualified Governmental Interest or Qualified Charitable Interest

The first type of completely exempt oil is oil from a qualified governmental interest or from a qualified charitable interest. The term "qualified governmental interest" means an economic interest in crude oil if such interest is held by a state or political subdivision or by an agency or instrumentality of a state or political subdivision, and, under applicable state or local law, all of the net income (gross income minus production costs minus generally applicable severance taxes) received from the interest is dedicated to a public purpose. COWPTA contemplates that permanent funds may be established to meet the latter requirement. (The Conference Report states that federal royalty oil, including production from a National Petroleum Reserve and royalties from federal leases, is subject to the windfall profit tax.)

The term "qualified charitable interest" means an economic interest in crude oil if the interest either is (1) held by an educational or medical organization described in clauses (ii), (iii), or (iv) of I.R.C. § 170(b)(1)(A), which is also described in I.R.C. § 170(c)(2), or (2) is held by a church organization described in clause (i) of I.R.C. § 170(b)(1)(A), which is also described in I.R.C. § 170(c)(2) but is held for the benefit of an educational or medical organization referred to in the (1) clause of this sentence. In either case, however, the exemption is available only if the interest was so held by the organization in question on January 21, 1980, and at all times thereafter until the end of the calendar quarter in which the oil is removed. A provision in the Senate version of COWPTA (the "Senate bill") that the exemption should be available for bequests of interests in the future to educational or medical organizations was deleted in conference.

Exempt Indian Oil

The second type of completely exempt oil is "exempt Indian oil." This consists of oil from mineral interests held in trust by the United States for an Indian tribe or member thereof or an Indian tribal organization or held directly by the tribe, member, or organization subject to a restriction on alienation imposed by the United States by reason of being so held. However, for the exemption to apply, the producer of the oil must be the Indian tribe or the member or organization, and the economic interest must have been held by the tribe, member, or organization on January 21, 1980. ("Indian tribe" has the meaning provided in Section 106(b)(2)(C)(ii) of the Natural Gas Policy Act of 1978.) Additionally, oil from mineral interests received and held by a native corporation organized under the Alaska Native Claims Settlement Act and which is produced by the native corporation is classified as exempt Indian oil, but this exemption will terminate in 1992. Also, proceeds from the sale of oil deposited with the United States Treasury to the credit of tribal or native trust funds pursuant to law as of January 21, 1980, also get the exemption.

Alaskan Oil

Oil which is produced from a reservoir through a well located north of the Arctic Circle (provided the production is in commercial quantities) or from a well located on the northerly side of the divide of the Alaska-Aleutian Range and at least 75 miles from the nearest point on the Trans-Alaska Pipeline System is completely exempt from the tax, except the exemption does not extend to any oil produced from the Sadlerochit Reservoir in the Prudhoe Bay oil field ("Sadlerochit oil").

Exempt Front-End Oil

There is a complete exemption for oil removed before October 1, 1981, where such oil is not subject to the ceiling price limitations under the energy regulations solely by reason of the provisions of 10 C.F.R. § 212.78 (as such provisions took effect on October 1, 1979), provided 50% or more of the operating mineral interest in the property (see definition of "property," *infra*) was, on January 1, 1980, held by persons who were "independent producers" for the last quarter of 1979. If the 50% ownership test is not met, certain refunds of the windfall profit tax are allowed. These provisions require some explanation.

Under energy regulations promulgated in August of 1979, effective October 1, 1979, 44 Fed. Reg. 51148-58 (COWPTA calls these the "front-end tertiary provisions"), a producer who undertakes a specific type of enhanced oil recovery project is allowed to deregulate the price of limited quantities of oil sold by the producer and thereby obtain additional revenue to finance the costs and expenses of the enhanced recovery project. The additional revenue from the deregulated oil (called "tertiary incentive revenue" by the energy regulations) is measured by the excess of the market-clearing price of the deregulated sales over the otherwise applicable ceiling price, less any ad valorem or severance taxes attributable to the excess. Deregulated sales are permitted until "tertiary incentive revenue" equals 75% of specified costs and expenses (costs of the hydrocarbons are excluded, according to S. Rep. No. 96-394, 96th Cong., 1st Sess. (1979) (the "Senate Report")) incurred in the enhanced recovery project, subject to an absolute ceiling of $20,000,000 of costs and expenses with respect to a particular property. Under the energy regulations, according to the Senate Report, producers may deregulate oil produced from property other than the one on which the project is located, and a producer is not limited in the number of projects the producer undertakes.

If oil has been deregulated under the front-end tertiary provisions (COWPTA calls this deregulated oil "front-end oil"), in the case of an enhanced recovery project on property, 50% or more of the operating mineral interest of which, on January 1, 1980, was owned by persons who were "independent producers" for the last quarter of 1979, the "front-end oil" related to such project and removed before October 1, 1981, is also completely exempt from the windfall profit tax by COWPTA. For this purpose, however, COWPTA does not allow costs and expenses attributable to periods after September 30, 1981, to be taken into account in determining the quantity of deregulated and ultimately exempt front-end oil. An item is attributable to periods before October 1, 1981, only to the extent that, under I.R.C. Chapter 1, deductions for such item (including depreciation) are properly allocable to periods before October 1, 1981; except any injectant and any fuel are treated as attributable to periods before October 1, 1981, if the injectant is injected, or the fuel is used, before October 1, 1981. (For purposes of what is attributable to a period, an act will be treated as taken before a particular date if it would have been taken before such date but for an act of God, a severe mechanical breakdown, or an injunction.) Independent producers, whose 50% ownership is required, are producers who are not substantial retailers or refiners per the definition in I.R.C. § 613A discussed *infra.*

In the case of a front-end tertiary project (COWPTA's name for a project under the front-end tertiary provisions) on property which fails the test of 50% ownership by independent producers, all front-end oil related to the project (including any produced by an independent producer), says the Conference Report, is subject to the windfall profit tax. However, the producer is allowed the benefit of a deemed payment of the windfall profit tax as of September 30, 1981. The amount of the deemed payment is the amount of the shortfall of the tertiary incentive revenue the producer has received below the costs and expenses the producer could have recovered as tertiary incentive revenue under the front-end tertiary provisions (excluding, as above, costs and expenses attributable to periods after September 30, 1981). The amount of the deemed payment is further limited to the amount of the windfall profit tax on the nonexempt front-end oil of the producer removed after February 1980 and before October 1981. According to the Conference Report, the deemed payment is subject to a refund to the producer or the producer may adjust his windfall tax withholding for periods after September 30, 1981, in a manner provided by regulation.

If a producer has some front-end oil which qualifies for exemption from the windfall profit tax and some which does not, COWPTA has an ordering rule that front-end oil is first deemed to be the front-end oil which is exempt from the windfall profit tax.

Tier 3 Oil

In describing the three tier categories for oil, it is easiest to list and discuss the tiers in reverse order. There are three types of oil which are put in the Tier 3 category.

Newly Discovered Oil

The first type of oil in the Tier 3 category is "newly discovered oil." COWPTA, for this purpose, incorporates the definition of "newly discovered crude oil" provided in the June 1979 energy regulations. Those regulations define "newly discovered crude oil" to mean domestic crude oil which is (1) produced from a new lease on the Outer Continental Shelf (a new lease is a lease entered into on or after January 1, 1979, of an area from which there was no production in 1978), or (2) produced (other than from the Outer Continental Shelf) from a property (see definition of "property" *infra*) from which no crude oil was produced in calendar year 1978. 10 C.F.R. § 212.79. The Conference Report states that production incident to the drilling of exploratory or test wells and not part of continuous or commercial production from the property during 1978 does not count. The Senate Report states that the definition includes property which was previously developed but which had no production in 1978.

If any portion of a property is transferred after December 31, 1978, crude oil produced from the property may not be classified as newly discovered crude oil if the oil would not have been so classified if the property had not been transferred. See definition of "property" *infra*.

Heavy Oil

"Heavy oil" is the second type of Tier 3 oil. "Heavy oil" is defined to mean all crude oil which is produced from a property if the crude oil produced and sold from such property either during the last month before July 1979 in which crude oil was produced and sold from such property, or during the current taxable period, had a weighted average gravity of 16° API or less (corrected to 60° Farenheit). According to the Conference Report, oil from a particular property may be heavy oil for one taxable period and not for another taxable period. Also, according to the Conference Report, if production can satisfy the requirements of the energy regulations pertaining to production from a single well with multiple completions which constitutes separate properties, oil from one of the completion locations which satisfies the gravity requirements can qualify as heavy oil.

If any portion of a property is transferred after December 31, 1978, crude oil produced from the property may not be classified as heavy oil if the oil would not be so classified if the property had not been transferred. See definition of "property" *infra.*

Incremental Tertiary Oil

Incremental tertiary oil is the third and final type of oil placed in the Tier 3 category. Incremental tertiary oil is determined by reference to a "qualified tertiary recovery project" (which may be an expansion of an existing project) and by reference to the excess of production over a decline curve of production from the property.

Qualified Tertiary Recovery Project

Qualified tertiary recovery projects are of two types. The first type is a "qualified tertiary enhanced recovery project" certified under the June 1979 energy regulations. 10 C.F.R. § 212.78. These provisions were in effect prior to, and continued in effect subsequent to, the promulgation of the front-end tertiary provisions discussed *supra.* A little explanation of the provisions is helpful. Under the provisions, sales of "incremental crude oil" resulting from the implementation or expansion of a "qualified tertiary enhanced recovery project" are free from price regulation. A "qualified tertiary enhanced recovery project" is a project utilizing one of nine listed tertiary recovery techniques. A project is certified by the Department of Energy pursuant to application or, after promulgation of the front-end tertiary provisions, may be self-certified in some cases. The "incremental crude oil" is the amount of crude oil which is or will be produced as a result of the implementation or expansion of the qualified tertiary enhanced recovery project in excess of the amount of crude oil which could have been produced from the property or project area through continued maximum feasible production from methods of production employed prior to the implementation or expansion of the project. The certification itself expressly determines the amount of the "incremental crude oil" on an overall basis and during particular time periods.

The second type of qualified tertiary recovery project under COWPTA is a project involving self-certification or certification by a state agency or the United States Geological Survey. For projects on lands not under federal jurisdiction, the governor of a state may designate an appropriate state agency to certify projects. (The Senate Report states that an appropriate state agency is one authorized to administer generally applicable regulatory or taxing provisions related to mineral interests.) The United States Geological Survey will certify projects on lands under federal jurisdiction or where the governor of a state has not made a designation of an appropriate state agency. The requirements for a self-certified project or a project certified by a state agency or the United States Geological Survey are the following:

1) The project must involve the application (in accordance with sound engineering principles) of one or more tertiary recovery methods which "can reasonably be expected to result in more than an insignificant increase in the amount of crude oil which will ultimately be recovered." There are nine types of tertiary recovery methods which are expressly authorized and these are the methods listed as subparagraphs (1) through (9) of Section 212.78(c) of the June 1979 energy regulations. The Secretary of the Treasury may approve additional methods.

2) The project has a beginning date after May 1979.

3) The portion of the property to be affected by the project must be adequately delineated.

4) The operator must submit to the Secretary of the Treasury either a certification from a petroleum engineer that the project meets the foregoing requirements or else a certification of a designated state agency or the United States Geological Survey that the agency has approved the project as meeting the foregoing requirements.

5) The operator must submit from time to time as the Secretary of the Treasury may require an ongoing certification from a petroleum engineer that the project continues to meet the requirements in question.

The Production Decline Curve

The "incremental tertiary oil" which qualifies for the Tier 3 category is the excess of the amount of crude oil which is removed from a property during any month after the beginning date of the qualified tertiary recovery project over a base level amount which declines from month to month. The base level amount starts out as the average monthly amount of crude oil removed from the property during the six-month period ending March 31, 1979 (determined under rules similar to the rules used in determining the base production control level under the June 1979 energy regulations). The base level amount is then reduced by 1% for each month from and including January 1979 through and including the month of the project beginning date and is additionally reduced by 2.5% for each month thereafter through and including the month immediately prior to the month for which the base level is being determined. The excess of the amount of crude oil which is removed from a property over the base level for such property for such month is the amount of the incremental tertiary oil for the month.

In the case of a qualified tertiary enhanced recovery project which has been certified and approved under 10 C.F.R. § 212.78, the amount of the incremental tertiary oil for purposes of the windfall profit tax is subject to a lower limit that it shall not be less than the incremental crude oil determined in the certification.

For purposes of determining which barrels of oil from a property are incremental tertiary oil (and therefore put in the Tier 3 category) and which barrels of oil are not (since only part of the oil will be incremental tertiary oil), the rule is that first the total number of barrels of oil which are incremental tertiary oil are allocated between oil which (but for the incremental tertiary oil provisions) would be Tier 1 oil and oil which (but for the incremental tertiary oil provisions) would be Tier 2 oil, in proportion to the respective amounts of each. Then, the highest-priced barrels within such Tier 1 oil and Tier 2 oil are deemed to be the incremental tertiary oil barrels.

Miscellaneous

The incremental tertiary oil provisions apply only so long as the project continues in effect—a matter which the Conference Report states is largely to be determined on a case-by-case basis, depending on factors such as the size of the project, the characteristics of the reservoir, and the particular process involved. If a regulatory agency revokes a certification, the Conference Report indicates that the project would continue to qualify if it can meet the requirements for self-certified projects.

In the case of certification by a designated state agency or the United States Geological Survey, the taxpayer may request from the Secretary of the Treasury a ruling concerning whether the project is a qualified tertiary recovery project. The Secretary is required to issue such ruling within 180 days of the date after which he receives the request and such information as may be necessary to make a determination. Moreover, the certification by a designated state agency or the United States Geological Survey of a qualified tertiary recovery project must be accepted by the Secretary of the Treasury unless the Secretary determines that the certification was not supported by substantial evidence on the record upon which such certification was based or additional evidence not contained in the record upon which such certification was based demonstrates that such project does not meet the requirements in question.

If a qualified tertiary recovery project affects only a portion of a property, the portion of a property is supposed to be treated as a separate property for purposes of the incremental tertiary oil provisions. See definition of "property" *infra*. Similarly, a significant expansion of a project is supposed to be treated as a separate project.

A project beginning date is the later of the date on which injection of the tertiary injectant begins and the date the applicable certification is given.

The Senate Report states that generally a tertiary project that has not been preceded by a secondary project cannot qualify without adequate explanation of the sound engineering principles involved. The Senate Report states that mere acceleration of production as opposed to increasing the total production will not qualify. The Senate Report otherwise has useful additional discussion of the topic.

Tier 2 Oil

There are two types of oil in the Tier 2 category.

Stripper Well Property

Oil from stripper well property is put in the category of Tier 2 oil. Stripper well property is defined by reference to the June 1979 energy regulations. The June 1979 energy regulations define "stripper well property" as a property whose average daily production of crude oil (excluding condensate recovered in nonassociated production) per well producing crude oil from the property did not exceed 10 barrels per day per well during any preceding consecutive 12-month period beginning after December 31, 1972. For purposes of the definitional test, each well must have been maintained at the maximum feasible rate of production during the 12 months, subject to recognized conservation practices, and not curtailed by disruptions. 10 C.F.R. § 212.54. In referring to the energy regulations definition, the Senate Report mentions that once a property is classified as a stripper well property, it retains that status regardless of future increases in production. See definition of term "property" *infra.*

If any portion of a property is transferred after December 31, 1978, crude oil from the property will not be considered oil from stripper well property unless the oil would have been so classified if the property had not been transferred. The Senate Report makes clear that the foregoing applies to both transferred and retained portions.

National Petroleum Reserve Oil

Oil from an economic interest in a National Petroleum Reserve held by the United States is put in the category of Tier 2 oil.

Tier 3 Oil Is Not Tier 2 Oil

If oil falls into the Tier 3 category it is and remains Tier 3 oil notwithstanding that it comes within either of the two foregoing Tier 2 categories.

High Water-Cut Crude Oil

The Senate bill would have put "high water-cut oil" in an earlier version of the Tier 2 category. (High water-cut oil refers to the ratio of water to oil in a property.) The conference committee omitted any special treatment of high water-cut oil. However, the Conference Report suggests that the Department of Energy should give special price treatment to high water-cut oil.

Tier 1 Oil

All other domestic crude oil which is not exempt oil or in the Tier 2 or Tier 3 categories is Tier 1 oil.

Base Prices

Tier 1 Oil

The base price for Tier 1 oil is the ceiling price which would have applied to such oil under the March 1979 energy regulations if it had been produced and sold in May 1979 as upper-tier oil, reduced by $.21. Under the March 1979 energy regulations, the initial upper-tier ceiling price for a particular grade of domestic crude oil in a particular field is defined as the highest posted price on September 30, 1975, for transactions in such grade of crude oil in such field in September 1975, or if there was no posted price in such field for such grade of domestic crude oil, the related price for that grade of domestic crude oil which is most similar in kind and quality in the nearest field for which prices were posted, less $1.32 per barrel. 10 C.F.R. § 212.74. Upper-tier ceiling prices have been subject to monthly adjustment for inflation since 1975 by the Department of Energy. (The Energy Policy and Conservation Act of 1975 required a rollback of the upper-tier ceiling price.) The adjustments have been published as Appendix A to Subpart D of Part 212 of 10 C.F.R. The adjustment for May 1979 is an increase of $.39 over the September 30, 1975, prices. The Tier 1 base price for any particular oil would be computed accordingly. For informational purposes, and as an average number, the Conference Report estimates that the May 1979 upper-tier ceiling prices averaged about $13.02 per barrel, which, reduced by $.21, yields an average Tier 1 base price of $12.81.

Tier 2 and Tier 3 Oil

The base prices for Tier 2 oil and Tier 3 oil are supposed to be determined pursuant to methods prescribed by the Secretary of the Treasury, which will yield, with respect to oil of any grade, quality, and field, a base price which approximates the price at which such oil would have sold in December 1979 if all domestic crude oil were uncontrolled and the average removal price for all domestic crude oil (other than Sadlerochit oil) was $15.20 a barrel for purposes of determining base prices for Tier 2 oil and was $16.55 a barrel for purposes of determining base prices for Tier 3 oil. In effect, the Conference Report indicates that this is supposed to yield an average base price of $15.20 for Tier 2 oil and an average base price of $16.55 for Tier 3 oil, subject to variation according to grade, quality, and location.

Pending regulatory determination of base prices for Tier 2 and Tier 3 oil, COWPTA has on interim provision that for months beginning before October 1980 (or such earlier cutoff as the Secretary of the Treasury may decide), the base prices for Tier 2 oil and Tier 3 oil, respectively, are to be the product of the highest posted price for December 31, 1979, for uncontrolled crude oil of the same grade, quality, and field (or if there is no posted price, the highest posted price for such date for uncontrolled crude oil at the nearest domestic field for which prices for oil of the same grade and quality were posted) multiplied by a fraction the denominator of which is $35.00 and the numerator of which is $15.20 for purposes of determining base prices for Tier 2 oil and $16.55 for purposes of determining base prices for Tier 3 oil. Prices posted after January 14, 1980, are not to be taken into account. The interim rule is subject to a lower limit that the base price for Tier 2 oil or Tier 3 oil shall not be less than the May 1979 upper-tier ceiling price under the March 1979 energy regulations which would have applied to such oil, plus, in the case of Tier 2 oil, $1.00, and, in the case of Tier 3 oil, $2.00

Inflation Adjustment to Base Price

A base price determined as stated above is adjusted for a particular calendar quarter in which the windfall profit tax is being applied by adding to the base price an amount equal to the base price multiplied by the "inflation adjustment" for the calendar quarter in which the crude oil is removed from the premises. The inflation adjustment for any calendar quarter is the percentage by which the implicit price deflator for the gross national product for the second preceding calendar quarter before the calendar quarter of removal exceeds such deflator for the calendar quarter ending June 30, 1979.

In the case of Tier 3 oil, the inflation adjustment is determined by substituting for the implicit price deflator for the second preceding calendar quarter such implicit price deflator multiplied by 1.005 to the Nth power where N equals the number of calendar quarters from and including the fourth quarter of 1979 through and including the calendar quarter immediately before the calendar quarter in which the oil is removed from the premises.

The first revision of the price deflator is used for the foregoing adjustments.

In the case of oil produced from the Sadlerochit Reservoir in the Prudhoe Bay oil field, the base price as adjusted in accordance with the foregoing rules receives a further special adjustment by increasing it to the extent that the average Trans-Alaska Pipeline System tariff for the preceding calendar quarter fell below $6.26 a barrel.

State Severance Taxes

State severance taxes, subject to limitations, are allowed to be added on to the adjusted base price prior to the making of the subtraction from the selling price in order to compute the windfall profit. This allowance is limited to the severance tax attributable to the excess of the selling price over the adjusted base price, or more precisely, the allowance is the amount by which any severance tax imposed with respect to a barrel of oil exceeds the severance tax which would have been imposed if the barrel had been valued at its adjusted base price.

A severance tax is defined as a tax imposed by a state with respect to the extraction of oil and determined on the basis of the gross value of the extracted oil. A severance tax is not taken into account to the extent that the rate thereof exceeds 15%. Further, the amount of the severance tax taken into account shall not exceed the amount which would have been imposed under a state severance tax in effect on March 31, 1979, unless such excess is attributable to an increase in the rate of the severance tax (or to the imposition of a severance tax) which applies equally to all portions of the gross value of each barrel of oil subject to the tax.

Removal Price; Subtraction of Adjusted Base Price and State Severance Tax Adjustment

The windfall profit (subject to the 90% of "net income" limit) is the excess of the removal price of a barrel of crude oil over the sum of the adjusted base price and the amount of the severance tax adjustment with respect to such barrel, as described *supra.*

The removal price of a barrel of oil is the amount for which the barrel is sold. In the case of a sale between related persons (within the meaning of I.R.C. § 103(b)(6)(C)), the removal price is not less than the constructive sales price for purposes of determining gross income from the property under I.R.C. § 613. If crude oil is removed from the premises before it is sold, the removal price is the constructive sales price for purposes of determining gross income from the property under I.R.C. § 613. If conversion of the crude oil into refined products is begun before it is removed from the premises, the crude oil is treated as removed on the day the refining begins and the removal price is the constructive sales price for purposes of determining gross income from the property under I.R.C. § 613. The terms "premises" and "refined product" have the same meaning as used under I.R.C. § 613.

In the case of crude oil produced from the Sadlerochit Reservoir in the Prudhoe Bay oil field, there is a special rule that the removal price of a barrel of oil removed during any calendar month is the average of the producer's removal prices for the month. (The Senate Report states that the purpose of this rule is to eliminate wellhead price differentials attributable only to the final destination of the barrel of oil.)

The windfall profit to which the tax is applied is the excess of the removal price over the sum of the adjusted base price plus the state severance tax adjustment, subject to the 90% of "net income" limitation.

90% of Net Income Limitation

The windfall profit on any barrel of crude oil may not exceed 90% of the net income attributable to the barrel. The net income attributable to a barrel is determined by dividing the taxable income from the property for the taxable year attributable to taxable crude oil by the number of barrels of taxable crude oil from such property taken into account for such taxable year. For these purposes, taxable income from a property is generally determined under I.R.C. § 613(a), except no deduction is allowed for depletion, the windfall profit tax, or I.R.C. § 263(c) costs. Also, no deduction is allowed for qualified tertiary injectant expenses which the taxpayer elects to capitalize for the special purpose described in the next sentence. While the foregoing deductions are disallowed, the taxable income is, however, reduced by the cost depletion which would have been allowable for the taxable year with respect to the property if all I.R.C. § 263(c) costs, and also (if the taxpayer specially elects for this purpose) qualified tertiary injectant expenses (i.e., deductible under I.R.C. § 193) allocable to the property, had been capitalized and as if cost depletion had been used by the taxpayer for all taxable periods. (I.R.C. § 263(c) costs are intangible drilling and development costs incurred by the taxpayer which by reason of an election under I.R.C. § 263(c) may be deducted as expenses for purposes of federal income taxes, but costs incurred in drilling a nonproductive well are not included.) The Senate Report states that if intangible drilling and development costs are actually capitalized for income tax purposes by the producer, the producer may reduce taxable income from the property by the amount deductible under I.R.C. § 611 (either as cost depletion or depreciation) rather than assuming that all those costs were deducted as cost depletion.

For purposes of the 90% of net income limitation, in the case of a proven oil or gas property (that is, a property whose principal value has been demonstrated by prospecting or exploration or discovery work per I.R.C. § 613A(c)(9)(A)), if there is a transfer (including by sublease or the creation of a production payment) giving the transferee an economic interest in the property, the transferee, in reducing his taxable income as aforesaid, may not reduce it by more than the amounts which would have been allowable with respect to the transferor plus amounts attributable to costs incurred by the transferee during periods after the transfer. The rule applies only to post-1978 transfers and it can apply to a transfer of a partnership or trust interest.

The Senate Report states that for purposes of the net income limitation, the term "property" has the meaning given to it in § 614, rather than the meaning in the energy regulations. See definition of term "property" *infra.*

For purposes of the 90% of net income limitation, a production payment is treated as income of both the transferor and the transferee of the economic interests in the property. Thus, the Senate Report states, the gross income will be taken into account in computing the 90% of net income limitation of two persons: the creator of the production payment and the owner.

Rate of Tax

The percentage tax which is applied to the windfall profit varies according to the tier category, with special rates for "independent producer oil" in the Tier 1 and Tier 2 categories.

Tier 3 Oil

The windfall profit tax rate is 30% of the windfall profit in case of all Tier 3 oil.

Tier 1 and Tier 2

For oil other than "independent producer oil," the rates for Tier 1 oil and Tier 2 oil are 70% and 60%, respectively, of the windfall profit.

Tier 1 and Tier 2; Independent Producer Oil

In the case of Tier 1 oil and Tier 2 oil, the rates are 50% and 30%, respectively, if the oil is "independent producer oil."

An "independent producer" is allowed to have up to 1,000 barrels per day taxed at "independent producer oil" rates, provided certain conditions are met. (The 1,000-barrels-per-day amount is determined for each calendar quarter and equals 1,000 multiplied by the number of days in the calendar quarter (31 days in the case of the first quarter of 1980).)

First, an independent producer, which is defined by reference to I.R.C. § 613A(d)(2) and (4), is generally a taxpayer who does not, directly or through related persons, sell oil (or natural gas (see Senate Report)) products at retail or to any retailer who is obligated to sell under the taxpayer's name or who uses a retail outlet owned or controlled by the taxpayer, where the gross receipts for a calendar quarter from the retailing exceed $1,250,000 and who also does not, directly or through any related person, engage in the refining of crude oil, where the refinery runs of the taxpayer and related persons exceed 50,000 barrels on any one day during the calendar quarter.

Further, to qualify for the independent producer oil rates, the independent producer must be the producer of the oil (i.e., he must be the holder of the economic interest with respect to the crude oil); the oil must be removed during the calendar quarter in question; the oil must be Tier 1 oil or Tier 2 oil; and the oil must be attributable to the independent producer's working interest in a property. Working interest is defined to mean an operating mineral interest (within the meaning of I.R.C. § 614(d), which, states the Senate Report, generally means an interest that must pay the costs of production) which was in existence as such an interest on January 1, 1980, except an overriding royalty interest may also qualify if the overriding royalty interest was in existence as such an interest on January 1, 1980, and no later than February 20, 1980, there was in existence a binding contract under which such interest was to be converted into an operating mineral interest.

In the case of a related group of persons, the 1,000-barrels-per-day amount is allocated among such persons in proportion to the number of barrels produced by each which could otherwise qualify for the independent producer oil rates (except for the 1,000-barrels-per-day limit). For purposes of this allocation, persons will be treated as members of a related group if they are members of a family, a controlled group of corporations, a group of entities under common control, or if 50% or more of the beneficial interest in one or more corporations, trusts, or estates is owned by the same family, all such entities, and such family. A controlled group of corporations has the meaning given the term given by I.R.C. § 613A(c)(8)(D)(i). The Secretary of the Treasury is given authority to define by regulations the term "group of entities under common control." "Family" means an individual and the spouse and minor children of such individual. There are constructive ownership rules that an interest owned by or for a corporation, partnership, trust, or estate shall be considered as owned directly by the entity and proportionately by its shareholders, partners, or beneficiaries, as the case may be. Finally, if a person is a member of more than one related group, his allocation is the least possible allocation.

If the number of barrels produced for a calendar quarter exceeds the 1,000-barrels-per-day amount (or a lesser allocated amount for a member of a related group), a rule is given for determining which barrels are taxed at the special independent producer oil rates and which are not. The rule is that the 1,000-barrels-per-day amount (or lesser amount) is allocated between all the producer's Tier 1 oil which could be independent producer oil (but for the limit) and all the producer's Tier 2 oil which could be independent producer oil (but for the limit), in proportion to the amounts thereof. The highest priced barrels of oil in such Tier 1 oil and such Tier 2 oil are then deemed to be the independent producer oil barrels.

If an interest in a property is transferred (including by sublease or through transfer of a partnership or trust interest) on or after January 1, 1980, production attributable to such an interest generally will not qualify for the independent producer oil rates unless it can be established, pursuant to regulations to be prescribed, that at no time after December 31, 1979, was the property held by a person who at any time after September 30, 1979, and prior to the time of the transfer had production of oil which could qualify for the independent producer oil rates in excess of his 1,000-barrels-per-day amount (or lesser allocated amount) for a quarter, or was not an independent producer for the quarter. For purposes of this transfer rule, property held by a partnership is treated as owned proportionately by the partners and property held by a trust or estate is treated as owned both by the trust or estate and proportionately by its beneficiaries. The rule does not apply to a transfer of property at death, or to a change of beneficiaries of a trust which qualifies under clause (iii) of I.R.C. § 613(A)(c)(9)(B) (determined without regard to the exception at the end of such clause), or to any transfer if the transferor and transferee are required to share the 1,000-barrels-per-day amount.

Fractional Barrels

In the case of a fraction of a barrel, the tax is the same fraction of the amount of such tax imposed on the whole barrel.

Phaseout of Tax

There will be a 34-month phaseout period for the tax. The phaseout period will begin as of the later of December 1987 or as of such month that the Secretary of the Treasury estimates that $227,300,000,000 of windfall profit taxes (net of lost income tax revenues) will have been collected, but in no event will the phaseout begin later than December 1990. During the 34-month phaseout period, the tax is the amount of the tax which would have been imposed multiplied by 100% reduced by three percentage points for each month which has elapsed in the 34-month phaseout period.

Administration

Withholding

The windfall profit tax is imposed on the producer, but it is to be collected by withholding by the first purchaser of the oil (unless the Secretary of the Treasury prescribes otherwise). The purchaser determines the amount to withhold on the basis of certified information supplied to the purchaser, which the purchaser may rely on unless he has reason to believe that it is incorrect. The information is supplied by the operator of a property, who is the person primarily responsible for the management and operation of the property. The information includes the adjusted base price, the tier and category of the oil, any certification by the producer to the operator that the oil is exempt or independent producer oil, and the amount of the oil. (The 90% of net income limitation does not apply for purposes of determining the amount of the withholding and is not contained in the certified information. A refund procedure is followed if the limitation is applicable.) In lieu of withholding by the purchaser, the purchaser and the operator of a property may agree that the operator shall be substituted for the purchaser for purposes of withholding.

If the Secretary of the Treasury prescribes no withholding, the operator certifies to the producer the information otherwise certified to the purchaser (except regarding exemptions or independent producer oil).

If the purchaser makes an incorrect withholding, the purchaser, pursuant to regulations, is supposed to make adjustments in subsequent withholding with respect to the same producer.

Returns; Deposits of Withheld Amounts

The first purchaser is required to file quarterly returns (with information statements to the producers). Producers are generally not required to file windfall profit tax returns.

Integrated oil companies are required to make estimated payments twice a month. (An integrated oil company is a taxpayer described in I.R.C. § 613A(d)(2) or

(4) who is not an independent refiner as defined in the Emergency Petroleum Allocation Act of 1973.) Persons who are not integrated oil companies make deposit of amounts required to be withheld 45 days after the close of the month in which the oil was removed, except where an independent refiner is the purchaser and he is not required to make any payment of the purchase price before the 46th day after the close of the month in which the oil is purchased, then the deposit must be made before the first day of the third month which begins after the close of the month in which such oil was removed. When the producer and operator have agreed that the operator will be substituted for the purchaser, the operator makes estimated payments or deposits in accordance with the purchaser's status as an integrated oil company or not, unless the operator is an integrated oil company.

If there has been no withholding, producers make estimated payments or deposits of the tax on their own oil under the foregoing rules in accordance with their status as an integrated oil company or not.

Court Jurisdiction

The respective courts will exercise jurisdiction over cases involving the windfall profit tax in the same manner that jurisdiction is exercised with respect to income, estate, and gift taxes. The Tax Court will have prepayment jurisdiction over deficiencies and the United States District Courts and the Court of Claims will have jurisdiction over refund suits. The taxable period is a calendar quarter, and the scope of a deficiency suit or a refund suit is the tax for the entire quarter. The United States District Courts and the Court of Claims have jurisdiction with respect to withholding liabilities.

Definitions; Miscellaneous

"Property"

The Senate Report states that the term "property" as used by COWPTA generally has the meaning given in 10 C.F.R. § 212.72(a). "Property" is defined there as a right to produce oil that arises from a lease or fee interest. A producer may treat as a separate property each separate and distinct producing reservoir that is subject to the same right to produce, provided that such reservoir is recognized by the appropriate government regulatory authority as a producing formation that is separate and distinct from, and not in communication with, any other producing formation. However, for purposes of the 90% of net income limitation, the Senate Report says that the definition of property in I.R.C. § 614 applies.

"Producer"

A producer means the holder of an economic interest with respect to the crude oil.

Property Unitization

The Senate Report indicates that the Secretary of Treasury may make regulations pursuant to which producers will not suffer increased or adverse windfall profit tax consequences if they enter into "unitization" agreements for the joint operation of interests in a property. These could be applicable to "newly discovered oil" or "stripper well property" under COWPTA, as finally enacted.

Taxable Period

The windfall profit tax is generally imposed with respect to a calendar quarter, with March 1980 constituting its own taxable period.

Production Payments

The Conference Report states that the only case in which the original House bill imposed the tax on a person other than a holder of an economic interest in the oil was that of a production payment which was measured in a fixed number of dollars as opposed to a fixed number of barrels. This provision was deleted in conference.

TEMPORARY WINDFALL PROFIT TAX REGULATIONS: MUCH ADO ABOUT NOTHING?

Prof. Craig E. Reese*

Although it took the Congress nearly a year to formulate the windfall-profit excise tax on domestic crude oil, the Internal Revenue Service took little time in promulgating temporary or proposed regulations for the new Chapter 45 exaction. In what must have been record time, the IRS published T.D. 7690 in the April 4, 1980, issue of the *Federal Register.*[1] Thus, the temporary regulations were made public only two days after President Carter signed the act into law and less than a month after the Conference Committee had decided upon the final language of the law.

As one might expect, the hastily written regulations do not add much to the explanation of the statutory language provided in the House, Senate, and Conference Committee reports. In fact, IRS Commissioner Jerome Kurtz expedited the promulgation of regulations because the new excise tax is retroactive to March 1, 1980, but

* Dr. Craig E. Reese is an Assistant Professor of Tax Accounting at the University of Texas, Austin, Texas.

1 45 Fed. Reg. 23384, April 4, 1980.

Article reprinted courtesy of *Oil & Gas Tax Quarterly*, September 1980, pp. 1-65

taxpayers and their representatives may have been better off if they only had the statute and committee reports upon which to rely, especially in those cases where there seems to be an inconsistency between Congressional intent as explained in the congressional committee reports and the temporary regulations. In defense of the Service, they did promulgate amendatory temporary regulations on April 25 in T.D. 7694 to clear up confusion created by T.D. 7690 in respect to the withholding and depositing of the windfall profit tax where the producer is an integrated oil company.[2] However, identification of the "first purchaser," who generally is liable for both withholding and depositing the windfall profit tax continues to be a difficult problem in many situations. There are, of course, many other compliance problems that can not be definitively resolved by relying on the IRS interpretation of Congressional intent as provided in the temporary regulations.[3]

The IRS scheduled a public hearing for the proposed (temporary) regulations of T.D. 7690 and T.D. 7694 for July 16, 1980. It is hoped the commentary—oral and written—on the temporary regulations received before and at that hearing will inspire the IRS to rewrite and expand the proposed regulations so that the final regulations are more helpful in resolving the complex problems that arise in complying with the windfall profit tax law. During the interim, taxpayers and their representatives must comply therewith in good faith by relying on the statute, congressional committee reports and the temporary regulations; and therefore, the following text is primarily an analysis of the temporary

---

2 45 Fed. Reg. 27929, April 25, 1980.

3 Charles J. DiBona, "Comments Concerning Proposed Excise Tax Regulations Under the Crude Oil Windfall Profit Tax Act of 1980," submitted by the American Petroleum Institute, Mid-Continent Oil & Gas Association, Rocky Mountain Oil and Gas Association and Western Oil and Gas Association to the Internal Revenue Service, June 3, 1980.

regulations as they complement the statute and the Congressional intent thereof.

Taxing Windfall Profits

In effect, the windfall-profit excise tax recently enacted by the Congress and signed into law[4] by President Carter is not a tax on profits. The exaction is on a portion of the revenue derived from the production and sale of specified categories of domestic crude oil after February 28, 1980. Accordingly, to the extent that President Carter's announced schedule for decontrol of the prices for all categories of domestic crude oil results in increases in the revenue derived from the production and sale thereof, a portion—30 to 70 percent—of the marginal revenue for each category of crude oil will be taxed as a "windfall profit." Although the base price, which depends on the DOE (Department of Energy) controlled price, to be used for determining marginal revenue is "indexed" or adjusted for inflation, there is no provision for adjusting the "windfall profit" for any increases in the cost of production (except for a "net income limitation") or for the increased cost of exploration for, and development of, replacement crude oil reserves within the United States.

Decontrol of Crude Oil Prices

Although a lengthy discourse on the development of domestic oil and gas price controls is beyond the scope of this article, a cursory review of the history of price controls is integral to one's understanding of the decontrol thereof, and to the determination of the windfall profit tax. Crude oil price controls began in 1971 as part of the Nixon Administration's anti-inflation program wherein general wage and price controls authorized by the Economic Stabilization Act of 1970 were imposed throughout

---

4 *The Crude Oil Windfall Profit Tax Act,* P.L. 96-223, April 2, 1980.

the economy. Ironically, the decade of the 1960s was characterized by import quotas for cheaper foreign crude oil.[5] This facet of federal energy policy, which was rationalized as integral to our "national security," was instituted by President Eisenhower in 1959, under authority first provided to the executive branch in the Trade Agreements Extension Act of 1955, and later in the Trade Expansion Act of 1962.

In 1973, President Nixon replaced the quota system with import license fees or tariffs.[6] In 1975, the Federal Court of Appeals for the Fourth Circuit upheld a decision of the Federal District Court for the District of Columbia that Congress had not given the President the authority to use such indirect methods as taxing power to control crude oil imports; however, President Ford succeeded in pursuading the Supreme Court to reverse the appellate court's ruling by upholding the President's power to use tariffs to control the importing of crude oil and petroleum products to regulate the level of such imports.[7]

On March 14, 1980, President Carter decided to reimpose as of May 15, a tariff on imported oil—$4.62 per barrel—until Congress enacted a ten-cent increase in the current Federal gasoline tax of four-cents per gallon. The President's proposal to levy an import fee was not only designed to reduce the consumption of foreign crude oil, thereby conserving energy and reducing our balance-of-payments deficit, but it was also part of the Carter Administration's spring economic program for controlling inflation. The President's plan included a revised fiscal 1981 Federal budget with no deficit, credit controls, a

---

5 Margaret Thompson, editor, *Energy Policy* (Washington: Congressional Quarterly, Inc., 1979), p. 61.

6 *Ibid.*, p. 37A.

7 Federal Energy Administration v. Algonquin SNG, Inc., et al., 426 U.S. 548 (1976).

Federal hiring freeze, the oil import fee revenue, and withholding taxes on dividends and interest, but it did not include revenues from the new windfall profit excise tax, which had not been enacted at that time. The President used his executive authority as alledgedly provided in the Trade Expansion Act of 1962, and the Emergency Petroleum Allocation Act of 1973, to impose the duty on imported oil.[8] Although a legal battle over President Carter's authority to impose a gasoline tax through reinstatement of an oil import fee ensued, the Congress rendered the debate "moot" when the House and Senate voted overwhelmingly on June 5 and June 6, 1980, respectively, to override President Carter's veto of a debt-ceiling bill which included a resolution disapproving of the President's oil import fee, which had never taken effect. Coincidently, Section 401 of the Crude Oil Windfall Profit Tax Act of 1980 amends the Trade Expansion Act of 1962 to explicitly authorize the Congress to rescind any Presidential action under Section 232(b) of the latter Act to regulate imports of petroleum products.

Before the aforementioned discretionary general wage and price controls expired (in 1974),[9] Congress mandated price controls for domestic crude oil, natural gas, and petroleum products through enactment of the Emergency Petroleum Allocation Act of 1973 (EPAA/P.L. 93-159). EPAA was proposed after the midwinter fuel shortages of early 1973 and when supplies of gasoline were inadequate during the following summer, but was not enacted until the Arab oil embargo of late 1973. In announcing his intention to decontrol the price of domestic oil and gas and the products derived therefrom during his 1975 State-of-the-Union message to Congress, Presi-

---

8 Richard J. Levine, et al., "Carter's Prescription to Ease Inflation Fails to Impress Economists, Congress or Business," *Wall Street Journal,* March 17, 1980, pp. 1-4.

9 Thompson, *Energy Policy,* pp. 11A-12A.

dent Ford aligned his Administration with the "conservation-by-price" forces of which there were few Congressional constituents; however, the battle to return to the market mechanism as the primary determinant of the allocation and price for oil, gas, and petroleum products had begun.

After several months of fighting over the Ford Administration's proposed plan for decontrol of oil prices, a compromise was reached in the form of the Energy Policy and Conservation Act of 1975 (EPCA/P.L. 94-163). EPCA not only amended the EPAA in respect to domestic crude oil pricing, but it also established fuel economy standards and authorized establishment of a "strategic petroleum reserve" as insurance in the event of future embargos.

More specifically, the law effected a relatively complex system for holding down the price of "old" oil, i.e., that oil which had already been discovered and was under production, while allowing higher prices for newly discovered or "new" oil in an effort to stimulate exploration and production.[10] "Old" oil is that produced from wells existing in 1973, but at a rate equal to 1972 base production levels; whereas "new" oil is that produced from wells drilled after 1972, or from old wells to the extent that production exceeds 1972 base production levels.[11] However, EPCA also instituted a "composite" price, i.e., the weighted average of prices for "new" and "old" oil. The composite price was used as the basis for limiting overall price increases for both the inflation adjustment factor and the new production incentives to 10 percent annually.

In 1976, Congress enacted a third law which affected prices—the Energy Conservation and Production Act (ECPA/P.L. 94-385). ECPA modified the pricing sys-

---

10 *Ibid.*, p. 61.
11 *Ibid.*, p. 44A.

tem by exempting from controls the crude oil produced by "stripper" wells, i.e., wells from which it is difficult and expensive to extract the oil, such as the oil "stripped" from the bottom of an old well. In practice, "stripper" oil is oil from wells producing less than ten barrels per day (after 1972). Although the mandatory price controls inherent in the three laws above expired on May 31, 1979, the President's decision to phase out price controls between June 1, 1979, and September 30, 1981—when price controls would automatically expire without Congressional action—was voluntary and required changes in existing regulations, which were subject to public hearing and judicial review.[12]

Although President Carter has exercised his discretionary power to phase out crude oil price controls, there is still a three-tier pricing system for domestic crude. The three tiers—"lower tier" for old oil, "upper tier" for new oil or oil discovered and produced after 1972, and world market or "uncontrolled" prices for stripper, Alaskan North Slope (ANS), and Naval Petroleum Reserve oil—are a legacy from the 1973, 1975, and 1976 price control legislation explained above.[13] In addition, five other categories of crude oil production have been established through Department of Energy (DOE) regulations—newly discovered, heavy, incremental tertiary, marginal and tertiary incentive (front-end) crude oil production.

As of June 1, 1979, a "newly discovered" crude oil production is eligible for world market or "uncontrolled" prices.[14] This category of oil is defined as follows: production sold on or after June 1, 1979, either from an onshore property in respect to which there had been no produc-

---

12 *Ibid.*, p. 61.

13 Marianne S. Kah, "The Merits of Oil Price Decontrol," *GAO Review*, Summer, 1979, p. 23.

14 Jamie Replogle, "DOE Update: The Decontrol Strategy," *Petroleum Independent*, August, 1979, p. 60.

tion during calendar year 1978, or from an outer continental shelf property for which a lease was consumated after December 31, 1978, and in respect to which there had been no production during calendar year 1978.[15]

Earlier, at the end of the summer of 1978, "tertiary" crude oil production became eligible for world market or "uncontrolled" prices. As of September 1, 1978, the incremental production from a "qualified" tertiary recovery project was eligible for world market prices; however, eligibility for such prices is contingent upon application to and certification from the DOE that the producer's incremental oil production results from a tertiary recovery project.[16] With the intent of stimulating even more tertiary production, the DOE issued proposed regulations in March of 1979, which took effect in October 1979, wherein "front-end" financing for producers initiating or expanding "qualified" tertiary recovery projects is provided by allowing specified volumes of a producer's lower and/or upper tier oil to receive world market prices as of January 1, 1980. Thus, the category of "front-end" or "tertiary incentive" crude oil receives world market prices and thereby generates additional revenue to finance tertiary projects when limited amounts of lower and upper tier production are reclassified as world market.[17]

The fourth new category of oil—marginal oil—was established by DOE regulations in April of 1979. Most of this type of oil qualified for upper tier prices on June 1, 1979, inasmuch as the base production control level (BPCL) of a marginal oil property was reduced to 20 percent of its average monthly production (and sale) of "old" oil in calendar year 1978. Originally, the remaining 20 percent of a marginal oil property was to qualify

---

15 44 Fed. Reg. 25828, May 2, 1979.

16 43 Fed. Reg. 33679, August 1, 1978.

17 44 Fed. Reg. 18677, March 29, 1979, as amended.

for upper-tier process on January 1, 1980,[18] but late in 1979, President Carter issued an executive order to defer decontrol of the remaining twenty percent of a marginal property's production of crude oil until an acceptable "windfall profits" tax bill was forwarded to him for signing.[19] Oil properties with wells producing "old" oil and meeting the following criteria qualify for marginal status:

Average Completion Depth (Feet)	Average Daily Production
2,000 or more up to 4,000	20 barrels or less
4,000 or more up to 6,000	25 barrels or less
6,000 or more up to 8,000	30 barrels or less
8,000 or more	35 barrels or less

The qualifying period for applying the above criteria to determine marginal property status is, as noted above, calendar year 1978.[20]

The decontrol of upper tier (or new) crude oil prices is being effected through equal monthly increments in prices from January 1, 1980, to October 1, 1981, at which time world price levels should be attained. The "phaseout" rate is 4.6 percent for the month of October, 1981. In other words, all production remaining in the lower and upper tier categories on October 1, 1981, will be reclassified as "free-market" oil.

As of August, 1979, the price for a category of oil referred to as "heavy oil" was deregulated so that it could be sold at "free-market" or world prices. Heavy oil was originally designated as that oil which had a weighted average of sixteen degrees API (gravity class) or less for

18 44 Fed. Reg. 22010, April 12, 1979, as amended in 44 Fed. Reg. 25160, April 27, 1979.

19 Ernest Holsendolph, "Carter Slows Decontrol to Prod Oil Profits Tax," *New York Times*, December 23, 1979.

20 44 Fed. Reg. 22010, April 12, 1979, as amended in 44 Fed. Reg. 25160, April 27, 1979.

the last month prior to July, 1979, in which crude oil was produced and sold. In December of 1979, the designation was amended by raising the sixteen degrees or less gravity classification to twenty degrees or less.[21]

The decontrol of lower tier (or old) crude oil prices is being effected through a downward adjustment of the BPCL—the base production control level established in 1973 on the basis of 1972 production or the BPCL for 1978-79 if elected—so that the volume of lower tier (or old) oil is systematically "converted" into upper tier (or new) oil. An imputed monthly production decline rate is used to adjust the BPCL volume of lower tier oil, resulting in a commensurate increase in the volume of upper tier oil.

As of June 1, 1979, DOE regulations allow producers the option of using their original BPCL or an updated version thereof. The latter is computed by determining the average monthly production (and sale) of crude oil during the six-month period, October 1, 1978, through March 31, 1979. In addition, this updated BPCL may be reduced at a rate of 1½ percent per month during 1979, i.e., January 1 through December 31, 1979. Accordingly, the updated BPCL could be reduced by 9 percent for the period January 1 to June 1. However, only the crude oil production after June 1, 1979, can be used to determine the volume of oil production "converted" from lower tier to upper tier pricing. The election to use an updated BPCL had to be made by filing with the DOE by August 31, 1979.

As of January 1, 1980, the 1½ percent per month decline factor is doubled to 3 percent. Moreover, both producers using the updated BPCL and producers relying on their original BPCL may reduce their volume of lower

---

21 W.A. Bachman, "Phase-out Under Way for U.S. Crude Price Controls," *Oil and Gas Journal*, January 14, 1980, pp. 27-31.

tier oil production by three percent per month beginning January 1, 1980, but none of the above percentage volume reductions are applicable to the pricing of oil produced by "marginal" properties. Finally, "old" oil properties were permitted a one-time elimination of cumulative deficiencies regardless of the BPCL option elected by the producer.[22]

About two-thirds of domestic crude oil produced before President Carter initiated the decontrol of prices was regulated as either "old" or "new" oil. In 1978, the prices of lower tier, upper tier and "free-market" oil were $6.00, $13.00, and $14.50 per barrel respectively,[23] whereas, the average price was $10.45 and the world price, $14.50. About a year later (May, 1979) the lower tier, upper tier, and world market prices were $6.60, $1420, and $19.00 per barrel respectively. By December, 1979, the world market price had increased to about $29.00 while the lower tier, upper tier, and average domestic prices were at $6.90, $15.15, and $18.84.[24]

In summary, the above explanation of the pricing system for domestic crude oil is admittedly over-simplified. Hopefully, however, the following description of the windfall profit tax will be easier to understand inasmuch as the reader thereof will have at least a rudimentary knowledge of price controls that have evolved over six years. It is noteworthy that the administration of the windfall profit tax should be similar to that which has occurred in the case of the Pension Reform Act (ERISA) of 1974, where both the Treasury and the Labor Department have been responsible for promulgating regulations. Because of the need for coordination in the control

---

22 Replogle, "The Decontrol Strategy," pp. 60-62.

23 Kah, "Merits of Decontrol," p.23.

24 U.S., Department of Energy, *Monthly Energy Review,* March, 1980, pp. 73-76.

of energy prices and the taxation of profits from price decontrol, the Congress has provided for overlapping administrative authority for the Departments of Treasury and Energy; however, practical considerations necessitate that the assignment of primary responsibility for administering any Federal tax law be made to the U.S. Treasury. Nevertheless, the oil industry, like any institution with a "qualified" retirement plan, is forced to deal with two Federal agencies, which often treat crude oil production somewhat differently for pricing and excise tax purposes.

Synopsis of the Windfall Profit Tax

As noted above, the windfall profit tax is intended to transfer a significant proportion, 30 percent to 70 percent of the difference between the crude oil base price—lower tier, upper tier, and "free market" or uncontrolled—and the higher prices at which domestic crude oil has and will be selling as a result of the gradual decontrol that began on June 1, 1979. In general, no deduction for costs or expenses (except severance taxes) incurred in producing the crude oil are allowed, although the base price is "indexed," *i.e.,* adjusted for inflation. Thus, the base or "windfall profit" is the marginal revenue received upon the sale of domestic crude oil at decontrolled prices, but the amount of the "windfall profit" tax base per barrel may never be greater than 90 percent of the "net income" per barrel. For purposes of determining this limitation, "net income" is rather restrictively defined. A general formula for determining the windfall profit tax is as follows:

Gross receipts from production and sale of crude oil

LESS

Gross receipts from foreign and selected domestic production and sale of crude oil.

EQUALS

Gross taxable receipts

LESS

Adjusted base price (base price per DOE controlled price adjusted) and incremental state severance tax

EQUALS

Windfall profit (limited to 90 percent of the "net income" from each category)

MULTIPLIED BY

Rate of tax (depends on category of oil)

EQUALS

Gross windfall profit tax

LESS

Overpayment and prepayment of taxes

EQUALS

Net windfall profit tax liability.

The determination of the base for each category of domestic crude significantly complicates the calculation process. Delineating the type or category of crude oil produced is also a complicating factor because of the overlapping of price-control and tax law taxonomies for classifying domestically produced crude oil. In contrast, once the domestically produced crude oil has been properly classified, the determination of the appropriate tax rate has also been made, insofar as there is only one tax rate for each category of taxable crude oil. In essence, there are five different categories of oil and rates of taxation under Section 4987(b) which can be summarized as follows:

Category of Oil	Tax Rate
Regular Tier One	70%
Independent Producer Tier One	50%
Regular Tier Two	60%
Independent Producer Tier Two	30%
Tier Three	30%

In the case of a fractional barrel of taxable crude oil, Section 4987(c) and the temporary Regulations provide that the tax imposed is the same fraction of the amount of tax imposed on the whole barrel.

As indicated in the general formula above, the tax base or "windfall profit" is the excess of the removal price of a barrel of crude oil over the sum of the base price of such a barrel adjusted for inflation (i.e., the adjusted base price) and the amount of the state severance tax which exceeds the severance tax that would have been imposed if the barrel had been valued at the adjusted base price. However, the "windfall profit" on any barrel of oil can not exceed 90 percent of the "net income" attributable to that barrel—the "net income limitation" of Section 4988.

The crude oil which is subject to taxation includes all domestically produced crude oil except any crude oil from a "qualified" governmental interest or a "qualified" charitable interest, exempt Indian oil, exempt Alaskan oil, and exempt "front-end" oil. There are essentially three categories of taxable crude oil defined in Section 4991. Tier Three oil includes "newly discovered oil," "heavy oil," and "incremental tertiary oil." Tier Two oil encompasses both "stripper oil" and oil from an economic interest in a National (Naval) Petroleum Reserve held by the Federal government, but does not include Tier Three oil. Accordingly, Tier One oil encompasses all taxable crude oil excepting Tier Two and Tier Three oil.[25]

25 Craig E. Reese, "New Windfall Profit Tax on Crude Oil: How It Works and Whom It Affects," *Taxation for Accountants*, May, 1980, p. 292.

The following summary is a comparative analysis of the price control and windfall profit tax classification systems for domestic crude oil:

DOE Price Control Category	Windfall Profits Tax Category
Lower tier or old oil	Tier One
Upper tier or new oil	Tier One
Alaskan North Slope	Tier One
Marginal oil	Tier One
Stripper oil	Tier Two
Naval Petroleum Reserve oil	Tier Two
Newly discovered oil	Tier Three
Heavy oil	Tier Three
Incremental tertiary oil	Tier Three

The reduced rate of taxation for two types—Tier One and Tier Two—of independent producer oil has the effect of creating two additional tax categories of oil. "Independent producer oil" is that portion of an independent producer's "qualified production," for a quarter that does not exceed the independent producer amount, i.e., 1,000 barrels per day for the quarter. The "qualified production" of an independent producer is the number of barrels of taxable crude oil of which such person is the producer, which is produced during a quarter, which is Tier One and Tier Two oil, and which is attributable to the independent producer's working interest in an oil property.[26] For a more detailed explanation of the windfall profit tax based on the statute and congressional committee reports, see the June, 1980 issue of the *Quarterly.*[27]

26 Reg. Sec. 150.4992-1.

27 See Robert D. Shattuck, Jr., "The Crude Oil Windfall Profit Tax Act of 1980," *Oil and Gas Tax Quarterly,* June 1980, pp. 387-417; and "Analysis of the Crude Oil Windfall Profit Tax: With an Emphasis on the Independent Producer," *Oil and Gas Tax Quarterly,* June 1980, pp. 418-449.

Liability for the Windfall Profit Tax

Although the windfall profit tax is imposed on the crude oil producer,[28] which is defined as the holder of an economic interest in oil property—as defined in DOE Regulation 212.72(a),[29] the first purchaser of any domestic crude oil is liable for this new Chapter 45 excise tax. Accordingly, the first purchaser of domestic crude must withhold from his payment to the producer of such crude an amount equal to the excise tax imposed thereon.[30] Thus, the purchaser must file tax returns, keep records related thereto and furnish such other information as prescribed in the Treasury Regulations. In addition, each partnership or fiduciary producing domestic crude oil, each operator of a well from which domestic crude oil was produced and any other person liable for the Section 4986 excise must file such tax returns, maintain such records and provide such other information prescribed by the Treasury Secretary in Chapter 45 regulations.[31]

There are several important exceptions to the general rule that first purchasers are liable for and must withhold the windfall profit tax imposed on producers of domestic crude. In the case of domestic crude oil produced, processed and sold (or used) by "integrated oil companies" (as defined in Section 613A (d) (2) and (4) for depletion purposes) there would be no purchaser and no withholding; and therefore, the integrated-oil-company producer is liable for tax on its own domestic production, as well as on any domestic crude oil it purchases from other producers.[32] If the purchaser of domestic crude and the operator of the oil property from which the crude is produced

---

28 Reg. Sec. 150.4986-1.

29 Reg. Sec. 150.4996-1(b).

30 Reg. Sec. 150.4995-1(a).

31 Reg. Sec. 150.4997-1.

32 Reg. Sec. 150.4995-3(a).

jointly elect in respect to such property, the operator may be substituted for the purchaser for purposes of withholding and the payment of the excise tax on windfall profits.[33] In the case of domestic crude produced and either processed and sold (or used) or removed from the premises for processing and sale (or use) by a person which is not an "integrated oil company," there would also be no first purchaser and no withholding; and consequently, the producer is liable for the tax on both its own domestic production and the crude it purchases from other producers.[34]

As noted above, a "producer" is generally defined as the holder of an economic interest (*i.e.,* either a working interest or a royalty interest) in an oil property. Moreover, if a partnership holds an economic interest in an oil property, the domestic crude produced therefrom is allocated among the partners in accordance with their pro rata share of profits and each partner is treated as the producer of his (her or its) proportionate share of the total production.[35] For purposes of the windfall profit tax, an "operator" is generally defined as the person (or persons) primarily responsible for the management and operation of the production of crude oil from a property. However, persons (or person) holding operating mineral interests in a property may designate another person (or persons) as the "operator" of a crude oil producing property for purposes of windfall profit tax.[36]

Production Excluded From Windfall Profit Taxation

First purchasers of "exempt oil" do not have to withhold the windfall profit tax from payments to producers

---

33 Reg. Sec. 150.4995-2(f).

34 Reg. Sec. 150.4995-3(f).

35 Reg. Sec. 150.4996-1(b).

36 Reg. Sec. 150.4996-1(c).

thereof. "Exempt oil" implicitly includes foreign crude oil insofar as the windfall profit tax is only applicable to domestic crude oil,[37] which is defined as crude oil produced from an oil well located in the United States or a U.S. possession (as defined in Section 638).[38] As noted above, "exempt oil" explicitly encompasses crude oil from both a qualified governmental interest and a qualified charitable interest, exempt Indian oil, exempt Alaskan oil, and exempt "front-end" (or tertiary incentive) oil, all of which are defined in Section 4994.[39]

A "qualified governmental interest" means an economic interest in crude oil if such interest is held by a state or political subdivision thereof and if, under the applicable state or local law, all of the net income received pursuant to such interest is dedicated to a public purpose. In respect to a qualified governmental interest, "net income" means gross income reduced by production costs and severance taxes of general application to the extent they are allocable to the governmental interest. In addition, any net income which, under applicable state or local law, is placed in a permanent fund of which the earnings are dedicated to public purposes, meets the requirement that net income be dedicated to a public purpose.[40]

A "qualified charitable interest" is defined as an economic interest in crude oil if such interest is held by a Section 170(c) (2) institution organized and operated exclusively for religious, charitable, scientific, literary, or educational purposes or for prevention of cruelty to children or animals. Moreover, the interest must be held either by an educational, medical, or charitable organization as provided in Section 170(b) (1) (A) or for the benefit of an

---

37 Reg. Sec. 150.4991-1(a).

38 IRC Sec. 4996(b).

39 Reg. Sec. 150.4994-1.

40 IRC Sec. 4994(a).

educational organization if held by a church or convention of churches. Finally, the oil property must have been held by the "public charity" (or certain private foundations) on January 21, 1980, and at all times thereafter, before the last day of the taxable period. Thus, an interest is treated as "held by or for the benefit of a public charity" only if all the proceeds from such interest were dedicated on January 21, 1980, and at all times thereafter, before the last day of the taxable period to a public charity.[41]

There are several circumstances under which domestic crude oil production would be classified as "exempt Indian oil." In general, domestic crude oil is excluded from taxation where the producer is an Indian tribe, an individual member of an Indian tribe, or an Indian tribal organization on January 21, 1980, and where the mineral interests from which the oil is produced are either held in trust by the U.S. government for the tribe, member, or organization, or held by the tribe, member, or organization subject to a restriction on alienation imposed by the U.S. government because the interest is held by an Indian tribe, an individual member of an Indian tribe or an Indian tribal organization. Exempt Indian oil also includes domestic crude oil which is produced by a native corporation organized under the the Alaskan Native Claims Settlement Act (as in effect on January 21, 1980), which is produced from mineral interests held by the corporation, which were received under the aforementioned Act, and which is removed from the prmsises by 1992. Finally, exempt Indian oil includes domestic crude oil production from which the proceeds of sale are deposited in the U.S. Treasury to the credit of tribal or native trust funds pursuant to a provision of law in effect on January 21, 1980.[42]

---

41 IRC Sec. 4994(b).

42 IRC Sec. 4994(d).

In order for domestic crude oil production to qualify as "exempt Alaskan oil," it must be produced from a reservoir from which oil is being produced in commercial quantities through a well located north of the Arctic Circle, or from a well located on the northerly side of the divide of the Alaskan-Aleutian Range, and at least seventy-five miles from the nearest point on the Trans-Alaska Pipeline System. Notwithstanding the above definition, exempt Alaskan oil does not include production from the Sadlerochit reservoir on the Alaskan North Slope,[43] which is technically classified as "upper tier" oil, although it sells at below-ceiling market prices to accommodate high transportations costs, *i.e.,* the Trans-Alaska Pipeline System, (TAPS) tariff.[44] Thus, ANS oil actually sold at world market prices when TAPS was included in 1978–79.

By far the most complex exclusion provisions are those applicable to "exempt front-end tertiary oil," which is defined as any domestic crude oil which is removed from the premises before October 1, 1981 and which is treated as "front-end oil" by reason of a "front-end tertiary project" on one or more properties each of which is a "qualified project." The latter term means any oil property if on January 1, 1980, 50 percent or more of the operating mineral interest in such property is held by persons who were "independent producers" per Section 613A (as amended for windfall profit tax purposes by Section 4992(b)) for the last quarter of 1979.

"Front-end oil" is defined as any domestic crude which is not subject to a first-sale ceiling price under DOE regulations solely by reason of the front-end tertiary provisions of such regulations. Similarly, "front-end tertiary project" means any project which qualifies under

---

43 IRC Sec. 4994(e).

44 Replogle, "The Decontrol Strategy," pp. 60-62.

the front-end tertiary provisions of the DOE regulations Finally, "front-end tertiary provisions" are the provisions of Section 212.78 of the DOE regulations which exempt crude oil from ceiling price limitations to provide financing for tertiary projects (as such provisions took effect on October 1, 1979) and any amendments of such regulations to the extent such amending is for purposes of coordinating DOE and Treasury regulations.[45] The "front-end tertiary incentive crude oil" provisions were succinctly described above in the context of the decontrol of crude oil prices as "lower" and/or "upper" tier oil which may be sold at "free market" or uncontrolled prices so that the additional revenues can be used to finance tertiary recovery projects.[46]

In respect to any front-end tertiary project which is not on qualified property, the excess of the "allowed expenses" of the taxpayer related to such project over the "tertiary incentive revenue" will be treated as a payment of the windfall profit tax made on September 30, 1981. However, the amount of the payment or credit for windfall profit taxes can not exceed the aggregate windfall profit tax imposed by Section 4986 in respect to the front-end oil of that producer removed after February 1980, and before October 1981. For purposes of this refund (or credit) for the tertiary projects of integrated producers, "tertiary incentive revenue" has the meaning given such term by the front-end tertiary provisions of DOE regulations.

In some cases, a taxpayer may be liable for taxes on production from a tertiary project encompassing both qualified and non-qualified property. In such cases, the taxpayer must treat the front-end oil related thereto as attributable first to tertiary projects of independents, *i.e.*, qualified.

---

45 IRC Sec. 4994(c).

46 44 Fed. Reg. 18677, March 29, 1979, as amended.

For purposes of the exemption and credit (refund) for front-end tertiary oil, including the application of the DOE front-end tertiary provisions, there are limitations on the deduction of "prepaid expenses." In general, the "allowed expenses" are determined under front-end tertiary provisions, *i.e.,* DOE regulations, but such expenses can not include any amount attributable to periods after September 30, 1981. Moreover, any other expenditures should be treated as attributable to periods before October 1, 1981, only to the extent that as provided in Chapter 1 (income tax) deductions for such expenditures (including depreciation of related capital expenditures) are properly allocable to periods before October 1, 1981. Finally, an act should be treated as taken before October 1, 1981, or any other date if it would have been taken before such date but for an Act of God, a severe mechanical breakdown, or an injunction.[47]

Taxable Categories of Crude Oil Production

As illustrated in the table above, the DOE price-control classification system for crude oil may be readily converted to the three tier taxonomy used for windfall profit tax purposes. Thus, Tier One includes "old" oil, "new" oil, Alaskan North Slope oil, and "marginal" oil; Tier Two encompasses "stripper" oil and oil production from the Federal government's National Petroleum Reserves; and Tier Three consists of "newly discovered" oil, "heavy" oil, and "incremental tertiary" oil. Although it is not apparent from reviewing the aforementioned "comparative analysis" table, the definitions of heavy crude oil and incremental tertiary crude oil for tax purposes are not identical to the definitions thereof established by the DOE for price control purposes.

---

47 IRC Sec. 4994(c).

When its price was decontrolled last August (1979), "heavy oil" was defined as crude oil produced from a property which had a maximum weighted average of sixteen degrees API (gravity classification) for the last month prior to July 1979, in which oil was produced and sold from the property; and therefore, the windfall profit tax law definition of heavy oil is consistent therewith. However, in late December of 1979, the DOE reclassified heavy oil by increasing the gravity classification from sixteen to twenty degrees.[48] For tax purposes, the term "heavy oil" means all crude oil which is produced from a property if crude oil produced and sold from that property during either the last month before July, 1979 in which crude oil was produced and sold from that property, or the taxable period, had a weighted average of sixteen degrees API or less (corrected to sixty degrees Fahrenheit).[49]

In contrast to the more restrictive tax law definition for "heavy oil," there is a more liberal definition for "incremental tertiary oil" for windfall profit tax purposes. When the price thereof was decontrolled, on September 1, 1978, incremental tertiary oil was defined as crude oil produced from a property on which a qualifying tertiary method is used in excess of the property's estimated production in absence of tertiary recovery; moreover, a producer must apply for and receive certification from the Department of Energy. The tax definition which follows relies to some extent on the DOE regulations, but it is generally broader in its scope than that found in price control regulations.[50]

For windfall profit tax purposes, "incremental tertiary oil" is the excess of the amount of crude oil which is

---

48 Bachman, "Phase-Out for Crude Oil Prices," p. 31.

49 Reg. Sec. 150.4991-1(b).

50 U.S. Congress, Staff of the Joint Committee on Taxation, *Conference Comparison on H.R. 3919—Crude Oil Windfall Profit Tax Act of 1979,* December 18, 1979, pp. 4-6.

removed from a property during any month and which is produced on or after the project beginning date and during the period for which a "qualified tertiary recovery project" is in effect on the property over the "base level" for such property for a month. The "base level" for any property for any month is the average monthly amount—which is determined under rules similar to rules used in determining the base production control level under the June, 1979 DOE regulations—of crude oil removed from such property during the six-month period ending March 31, 1979, reduced (but not below zero) by the sum of 1 percent of the average monthly amount for each month which begins after 1978 and before the first calendar month beginning after the project beginning date and 2½ percent of such amount for each month which begins after the project beginning date (or after 1978 if the project beginning date is before 1979) and before the month for which the base level is being determined. However; in the case of a project that is certified by the DOE, the amount of incremental tertiary oil can not be less than the incremental production determined under the June, 1979 DOE regulations.

To determine from which category of taxable crude the incremental tertiary should be converted or transferred, there are allocation rules. The determination of which barrels of crude oil removed during any month are incremental tertiary oil should be made first by allocating the amount of incremental tertiary oil between oil which, but for this allocation would be Tier One oil, and oil which, but for this allocation would be Tier Two oil, in proportion to the respective amounts of each type of oil removed from the property during a month, and then by taking into account barrels of crude oil so removed in the order of their respective removal prices beginning with the highest of such prices.[51]

---

51 Reg. Sec. 150.4993-1(a).

A qualified tertiary recovery project includes both a qualified tertiary enhanced recovery project in respect to which DOE certification has been obtained and any project for enhancing recovery of crude oil which meets the following four requirements:

(1) The project involves the application (in accordance with sound engineering principles) of one or more tertiary recovery methods which can reasonably be expected to result in more than an insignificant increase in the amount of crude oil which will ultimately be recovered; (2) The project beginning date is after May 1979; (3) The portion of the property to be affected by the project must be adequately delineated; and (4) The operator submits (to the Secretary of Treasury) either a certification from a petroleum engineer that the project meets the three requirements enumerated above, or a certification that a jurisdictional agency (as defined in Section 4993 (d) (5)) has approved the project as meeting the three requirements and that such approval is still in effect.[52]

In respect to this expanded tax definition of a qualified tertiary recovery project, there are several definitions and special rules, including definitions for tertiary method, project beginning date, and jurisdictional agency, and special rules on partial and separate tertiary projects, for rulings on tertiary projects and on the basis for review of projects.[53] Finally, the temporary regulations prescribe specific procedures that must be followed by any petroleum engineer who certifies that a project meets the aforementioned requirements for "tertiary recovery" status.[54]

---

52 Reg. Sec. 150.4993-1(b).

53 Reg. Sec. 150.4993-1(c).

54 Reg. Sec. 150.4993-2.

Computing the Windfall Profit

In general, the base for the windfall profit tax is the removal price of a barrel reduced by its adjusted base price and the state severance tax adjustment, but the windfall profit can never be greater than 90 percent of the net income attributable to such barrel. The "removal price" is the amount for which the barrel is sold, including any adjustments to the sales price made after the sale. However, in the case of a sale between related persons as defined in Section 103(b) (6) (C), the removal price may not be less than the "constructive sales price" used for determining gross income from property under Section 613. The constructive sales price is also used when crude oil is either removed from premises before it is sold or deemed removed therefrom per Section 4988 (c) (4). The removal price for oil removed during any calendar month from the Sadlerochit reservoir on the Alaskan North Slope is the average of the producer's removal prices for such month. Finally, a district director may adjust the removal price in the case of any transaction to clearly reflect the fair market value of the oil removed.[55]

The "adjusted base price" is the base price for the barrel of crude oil plus an amount equal to such base price multiplied by the inflation adjustment for the calendar quarter in which the crude oil is removed from the premises, rounded to the nearest cent.[56] The inflation adjustment for any calendar quarter is the percentage by which the implicit price deflator for the gross national product for the second preceding calendar quarter exceeds such deflator for the calendar quarter ending June 30, 1979. There is an additional inflation adjustment for Tier Three oil. The first revision of the price deflator should be used in calculating the inflation adjustment.[57]

55 Reg. Sec. 150.4988-1.

56 Reg. Sec. 150.4989-1(a).

57 IRC Sec. 4989(b).

For March 1980, the inflation adjustment is 1.0195 in respect to Tier One and Tier Two oil; whereas, the adjustment for Tier Three oil is 1.0246. The IRS will publish future inflation adjustments periodically.[58]

The base price for Tier One oil under Section 4989 is twenty-one cents less than the ceiling price that would have applied to such oil under March, 1979 DOE regulations if it had been produced and sold in May 1979, as "upper tier" oil. For purposes of this determination, the grade and quality of the oil produced from the property in May 1979 is used.[59] Inasmuch as the May 1979 "upper tier" ceiling price averaged $13.02, the base price for Tier One oil is $12.81 per barrel,[60] adjusted for grade, quality, and location.

In general, the base prices for Tier Two oil and Tier Three oil are to be determined by the Secretary of the Treasury. The method prescribed by Regulations is to be designed so as to yield, with respect to oil of any grade, quality, and field, a base price which approximates the price at which such oil should have sold in December 1979, if all domestic crude oil were uncontrolled and the average removal price for all domestic crude oil (other than Sadlerochit oil) were $15.20 per barrel for Tier Two oil and $16.55 per barrel for Tier Three oil. In addition, there is a special rule for determining base prices from March 1 to September, 1980 (or earlier if Treasury Regulations so prescribe).[61]

The interim rule provides that the base price is the product of the highest posted price for December 31,

---

58 Reg. Sec. 150.4989-1(a).

59 Reg. Sec. 150.4989-1(b).

60 U.S. Congress, Conference Committee, *Conference Report (No. 96-817) On The Crude Oil Windfall Profit Tax Act of 1980*, 96th Congress, 2d Sess., March 7, 1980, p. 28.

61 IRC Sec. 4989(b).

1979, for uncontrolled crude oil of the same grade, quality, and field, multiplied by a fraction, the denominator of which is $35 and the numerator of which is $15.20 for Tier Two oil (or $16.55 for Tier Three oil). If there is no posted price, the highest posted price for such date for uncontrolled crude oil at the nearest domestic field for which prices for oil of the same grade and quality were posted for date, multiplied by 15.20/35.00 (or 16.50/35.00). However, the interim base price may not be less than the sum of ceiling price which would have applied to such oil under March 1979 DOE regulations if it had been produced and sold in May 1979 as "upper tier" oil, plus $1 in the case of Tier Two oil or $2 in the case of Tier Three oil.[62] In summary, the base price for Tier Two oil is $15.20 adjusted for grade, quality, and location, while the base price for Tier Three oil is $16.55 adjusted for grade, quality, and location.

Once the base price is determined, it is not to be adjusted for later changes in grade or quality. Where the production from a property in May or December of 1979 varied in grade or quality during the month, the per barrel average grade and quality for the month is used to determine the base price. Finally, where there was no commercial production in May or December of 1979, the grade and quality of the oil produced in the first month of commercial production after May or December is used to determine the base price.[63]

There is also an adjustment to the adjusted base price of Alaskan North Slope oil from the Sadlerochit reservoir in the Prudhoe Bay oilfield. The adjusted base price of such oil is increased by any TAPS (Trans-Alaskan Pipeline System) adjustment, which is defined as the excess for any calendar quarter of $6.26 over the TAPS tariff

---

62 Reg. Sec. 150.4989-1(c).

63 Reg. Sec. 150.4989-1(d).

(transportation cost) for the preceding calendar quarter. Thus, as the average per barrel amount for transporting crude oil through the TAPS decreases below $6.26, the adjusted base price for a barrel of such Alaskan North Slope oil is increased an equal amount.[64]

Finally, an amount approximately equal to the marginal increase in state severance taxes resulting from oil price decontrol should be added to the adjusted base price to determine the total deductions from the removal price in arriving at the windfall profit. Thus, one can deduct that portion of the state severance tax paid which is attributable to difference between the removal price and the adjusted base price, i.e., incremental price or value.

For purposes of this adjustment for state excise taxes on the increase in crude oil prices, state severance tax is defined as any tax imposed by a State, but not including a political subdivision thereof, in respect to the extraction of crude oil that is determined on the basis of the gross value of the oil extracted. Neither an exaction levied on the value of crude oil reserves in the ground, nor an impost levied on the net proceeds from the production of crude oil are considered state severance taxes. Moreover, a tax on the production of crude oil that is levied at a fixed amount per barrel is not a severance tax.

There are two limitations on the severance tax deduction. One limits the deductible severance tax to 15 percent of the incremental price or value. The other requires that any future increases in the severance tax must apply uniformly to all portions of the gross value of the oil.

In situations where the rate of state severance tax exceeds 15 percent, the portion of the tax in excess of 15 percent on the "incremental" price or value of the crude oil can not be deducted in determining the windfall profit.

---

64 IRC Sec. 4996(d).

In respect to increases in the state severance tax after March 31, 1979, there must be an equal increase in such taxes on all categories of oil. Thus, any amount of severance tax that exceeds the amount imposed under the state law in effect on March 31, 1979, is only deductible if such excess is attributable to an increase in the rate of tax (or imposition of a severance tax) that applies equally to all portions of the gross value of each barrel of oil subject to such tax.[65]

Congressional Intent in Respect to Base Prices for Tiers Two and Three

As explained above, regulations establishing base prices for Tier Two and Tier Three oil are to be promulgated by October 1, 1980 (or earlier if the Treasury so prescribes) at which time the interim pricing rules will no longer be applicable. Under the interim rule, the Tier Two base price on any property is the highest posted price for December 31, 1979, for uncontrolled oil of the same grade, quality, and field multiplied by the fraction 15.20/35.00. If there was no December posting for such oil, the producer is to use the December 1979 posting for oil of the same grade and quality in the nearest domestic oil field for which prices for oil of that grade and quality were posted for December 1979. No postings made after January 14, 1980, are to be taken into account. This cut-off prevents purchasers from raising base prices artificially by increasing posted prices retroactively for December.

This formula is intended to achieve an array of base prices such that oil of national average grade, quality, and location (excluding North Slope Alaskan oil, whose wellhead price is affected by the extraordinary transportation costs) would have a base price of $15.20 and oil of above-or below-average grade, quality, and location will have a

---

65 Reg. Sec. 150.4996-2.

proportionately higher or lower base price. The data on December 1979 prices for uncontrolled oil posted as of January 14, 1980, suggest that thirty-five is the proper denominator in the fraction to achieve this result.

To ensure that this formula does not unduly penalize producers in fields where December 1979 posted prices are unusually low, there is a minimum Tier Two base price equal to the property's May 1979 upper tier ceiling price plus $1.00. Without this minimum base price, some properties would have a Tier Two base price less than their May 1979 upper tier ceiling price.

For a posted price to qualify for use in determining a producer's base price, the price has to be published in writing by a purchaser of a substantial volume of crude oil in the field. A posted price does not, for example, include a price offered by a purchaser who simply offers to buy oil at a figure (say) $1.00 higher than whatever prices are posted by the purchasers who are purchasing most of the oil in a particular oil field.

The Treasury Regulations prescribing the permanent method of determining Tier Two base prices must estimate the price at which oil from a particular property would have sold in December 1979 if all domestic oil had been uncontrolled and the average price for domestic crude oil, other than North Slope Alaskan oil, had been $15.20. Thus, if oil from a particular property typically sells for 80 percent of the price of oil of national average grade, quality, and location, based on market price differentials prevailing in December 1979, its Tier Two base price should generally be 80 percent of $15.20, or $12.16.

The conferees did not simply adopt the interim rule as the permanent rule because the interim rule may not lead to a situation in which the Tier Two base price for oil of national average grade, quality, and location equals $15.20 and because the interim rule may not be equitable for all categories of oil. The $35.00 price used in the denominator is based on preliminary data for prices for December 1979 posted as of January 15, 1980, and better data available later in 1980 will permit the Secretary to make a better estimate. The Secretary may want to take into account the increase in December postings which occurred in late January and February, although this may require raising the denominator above $35.00. Also, the Secretary may determine, after analyzing the data, that a formula based on actual selling prices, not posted prices, would be more accurate.

The conferees were aware that the interim rule might lead to inequities in the case of oil produced in California and certain other areas, because its December 1979 price was much lower, relative to the national average, than it had been in prior years and is likely to be in the future. That is why the conferees included the minimum interim base price. The guidelines in the conference agreement give the Secretary enough flexibility to devise a permanent solution to this problem.

Similarly, the base price for Tier Three oil—newly discovered oil, incremental tertiary oil, and heavy oil—is dependent upon Treasury Regulations to be promulgated by the October, 1980 expiration date for the interim pricing rule. Consequently, the Tier Three base price on a specific property will be formulated exactly like the Tier Two base price determination explained above.[66]

Net Income Limitation

Inasmuch as the "windfall profit" is limited to 90 percent of the net income attributable to a barrel of oil, the determination of "net income" is integral to the computation of the windfall profit tax. "Net income" is determined

---

[66] Conference Committee, *Report on Windfall Profit Tax,* pp. 96-97.

by dividing the "taxable income from property" for the taxable year attributable to taxable crude oil by the number of barrels of taxable crude oil from such property taken into account for such taxable year. The "taxable income from property" is determined under Section 613(a) except that no deduction is allowed for depletion, the windfall profit tax, Section 263(c) intangible drilling and development costs except those incurred in drilling a nonproductive well, or Section 193 tertiary injectant expenses if capitalized for windfall profit tax purposes. However, cost depletion may be deducted where all intangible drilling and development costs (excepting those incurred in drilling nonproductive wells) and "qualified tertiary injectant expenses" incurred by the taxpayer have been capitalized and taken into account in computing cost depletion and cost depletion has been used by the taxpayer in respect to such property for all taxable periods.

There are two special rules that are applicable to the net income limitation. One provision limits the benefits of certain transfers of proven oil and gas property by taxpayers where the property qualifies for the cost depletion deduction for windfall tax purposes. The second rule, which only applies where there are production payments, provides that where any portion of the taxable crude oil removed from a property is applied in discharge of a production payment, the gross income from such portions must be included in the gross incomes from the property of both the person holding such production payment and the person holding the economic interest from which such production payment was created.[67]

The Independent Producer

Although the independent producers were unable to effect an exemption from the windfall profit tax as they

67 IRC Sec. 4988(b).

had done when percentage depletion was repealed for only the integrated oil companies in the Tax Reduction Act of 1975, the lower tax rates on the Tier One and the Tier Two oil of independents was a significant victory in view of the paucity of political support from the major, integrated oil companies. However, the cost of these preferential rates has been a set of complicated provisions applicable to the determination of "independent producer oil" i.e., the amount of production from Tier One oil and Tier Two oil for which the "independent producer" tax rates can be used.

As noted above, the definition of an "independent producer" for windfall profit tax purposes is based on the Section 613A definition thereof for percentage depletion eligibility. More specifically, an independent producer is defined with respect to any quarter as any person other than a person to whom Section 613A(c) does not apply by reason of Section 613A(d)(2) relating to retailers and Section 613A(d)(4) relating to refiners except that "quarter" and "$1,250,000" should be substituted for "taxable year" and "$5,000,000" respectively. In summary, an independent producer or related party may only realize gross receipts of up to $1,250,000 from the retail sale of crude oil or petroleum products or refine up to 50,000 barrels of crude oil during any calendar quarter.[68]

To review: "independent producer oil" is that portion of an independent producer's "qualified production" for the calendar quarter which does not exceed such person's "independent producer amount" for such quarter.[69] As noted above, "qualified production" is defined for any calendar quarter as the number of barrels of taxable crude oil of which an independent producer is the producer, which is removed during such quarter, which is Tier One

---

68 Reg. Sec. 150.4992-1(b).

69 Reg. Sec. 150.4992-1(a).

or Tier Two oil, and which is attributable to the independent producer's "working interest" in an oil property. The term "working interest" means a Section 613(d) operating mineral interest which was in existence as such an interest on January 1, 1980, or which is attributable to a "qualified overriding royalty interest." The latter term is defined as an overriding royalty interest, in existence as such an interest on January 1, 1980, but only if on February 20, 1980, there was in existence a binding contract under which such interest was to be converted into an operating mineral interest (within the meaning of Section 614(d)).[70]

As one might expect, the "independent producer amount" can not exceed 1,000 barrels of crude oil production per day. Thus, we note the similarity to the maximum amount of production for which an independent producer can elect to deduct percentage depletion. More precisely, the independent producer amount is defined as the product of 1,000 barrels multiplied by the number of days in a calendar quarter—thirty-one in the case of the first quarter of 1980. However, when a person's qualified production for any calendar quarter exceeds his independent producer amount for that quarter, the independent producer amount shall be allocated between Tiers One and Two, in proportion to his production for that quarter of domestic crude oil in each tier; and within any tier, on the basis of the removal prices for his domestic crude oil in that tier removed during the quarter, beginning with the highest of the removal prices.[71]

In respect to persons who are members of the same related group at any time during a calendar quarter, there must be an allocation of the 1,000 barrels per day maximum independent producer amount within the group in

---

70 Reg. Sec. 150.4992-1(d).

71 Reg. Sec. 150.4992-1(c).

proportion to their respective qualified production for such quarter. Special rules for and/or definitions of related group, controlled group of corporations, group of entities under common control, family, constructive ownership and members of more than one related group can be found in Section 4992(e). The final regulations should also include an extensive explanation of the special rules and definitions found in Section 4992(e).[72]

In order to discourage the sale of interest in oil properties to create independent producers, transfers on or after January 1, 1980, of an interest in any property generally are not included in the qualified production of the transferee for purposes of determining independent producer oil. There is a major exception to the non-transferability of independent producer oil in the case of small producers, *i.e.,* the "small producer transfer exemption." If a transferee can establish to the satisfaction of the district director (for the district in which the property is situated) that at no time after December 31, 1979, has the property transferred been held by a person who was a "disqualified transferor" for any quarter ending after September 30, 1979, and ending before the date such person transferred the interest, then such transferee qualifies for the "small producer transfer exemption" and such person can consider the property acquired in determining qualified production for purposes of calculating the independent producer amount. For purposes of the "small producer transfer exemption," there are special rules applicable to property held by partnerships and property held by fiduciaries. In general, partnership property is treated as owned proportionately by the partners; and fiduciary property, proportionately by beneficiaries.

Other exceptions to the general rule of non-transferability apply in the case of a transfer of property at

---

72 Reg. Sec. 150.4992-1(e).

death, certain changes of beneficiaries of trusts, and any transfer between related parties who are required by Section 4992(e) to share the "independent producer's amount." Other special rules apply to subleases, which should be treated as property transfers, and an interest in a partnership or trust, which should be treated as an interest in property held by the partnership or trust.[73]

Withholding Requirements

In general, the "purchaser" of domestic crude oil is required to deduct and withhold the windfall profit tax from amounts payable by that purchaser for the oil. The term "purchaser" includes only the first person purchasing domestic crude oil where person is defined in Section 7701(a)(1) to include an individual, a trust, estate, partnership, association, company, or corporation. There are three major exceptions to this general rule. If crude oil is "removed from the premises" before it is sold, then the producer is generally liable for paying (and thus depositing) the tax. Moreover, where the manufacture or conversion of crude oil into refined products begins before the oil is removed from the premises, then the producer is usually liable for paying the tax. Similarly, if the producer of the oil is an "integrated oil company," there usually is neither a "first purchaser," nor a witholding requirement; and therefore, the integrated oil company must pay the windfall profit tax on its own behalf. Finally, an "integrated oil company" must pay the tax in respect to many sales of its crude oil production to first purchasers.[74]

In addition, crude oil production (accounting) records, tax returns and other related information generally may be required of each taxpayer liable for the windfall profit tax, each partnership and fiduciary (trust or estate) pro-

---

73 Reg. Sec. 150.4992-1(d)(3).

74 Reg. Sec. 150.4995-1(a).

ducing domestic crude oil, each purchaser of domestic crude oil, and each operator of a well from which domestic crude oil is produced. Such records, returns and information may have to be furnished to the Treasury or to other persons with an interest in oil.[75] These accounting requirements are explained in greater detail below, along with the election to allow certain operators to substitute for the purchaser.

If a purchaser has received an operator's certification and if the purchaser has no reason to believe that any information contained therein that affects the windfall profit tax computation is incorrect, then the amount of tax to be deducted and withheld is the amount of tax imposed by Section 4986 based on the information provided in the aforementioned certification. In determining the amount to be deducted and withheld, the "net income limitation" is ignored.

The operator of a property from which domestic crude oil is produced must certify (as prescribed in Regulation 150.6050C-1) to the purchaser the adjusted base price of the crude oil purchased, the tier and category of such crude oil for tax purposes, the amount of such crude oil, a copy of any certification by the producer in respect to whether such oil is exempt or independent producer oil and such other information as may be required by Treasury Regulations. However, the operator of an oil property and the purchaser of crude oil therefrom may agree (as prescribed in Regulation 150.4995-4) that the operator is relieved of the duty to furnish some or all of the information required above, as well as withholding and depositary requirements.

In situations where the purchaser has not received the operator's certification or where the purchaser has reason to believe that any information contained therein is

---

75 Reg. Sec. 150.4996-2.

incorrect, there are special rules for determining the amount of windfall profit tax a purchaser must deduct. If the purchaser pays the lower tier (or "old oil") ceiling price for oil, he (she or it) need not deduct and withhold any windfall profit tax from the purchase price of that oil. If either the upper tier (or "new oil") ceiling price or the uncontrolled (or "world market") price is paid for oil, the purchaser must deduct and withhold from the purchase price of each barrel of such oil an amount equal to 70 percent of the excess of the removal price over the amount equal to the sum of $11.01, plus $11.01 multiplied by the Section 4989(b)(1) inflation adjustment for the calendar quarter in which the oil was removed, plus the Section 4996(c) state severance tax adjustment if the amount of the adjustment is known by the purchaser.

If a purchaser receives an operator's certification that a producer's share of production from a property qualifies as either "exempt oil" or "independent producer oil" and if that purchaser has no reason to believe that the certification includes an incorrect statement pertinent to such qualification, the purchaser should not withhold tax from amounts payable for any share of production that has been certified as "exempt oil;" whereas, in respect to certified "independent producer oil," the purchaser should generally apply the Section 4987(b)(2) independent producer rates, but should substitute 50 percent for 70 percent when no operator's certification has been received. If a payment by a purchaser is made to an operator or partnership, rather than directly to the producer, the amount of exempt oil and independent producer oil is determined on the basis of information provided by the operator or partnership.[76]

Although the "first purchaser" is generally liable for withholding and depositing the windfall profit tax, three

---

76 Reg. Sec. 150.4995-1(b).

major exceptions to this requirement were noted above. Both in the case of crude oil which is not sold until after it is removed from the premises and where the manufacture or conversion of crude oil into refined products begins before the oil is removed from the premises, the producer is liable for the tax. Oil is "removed from the premises" when it is physically transported off the "premises," which means " a tract or parcel of land" as defined in Regulation 1.614-1(a)(3). If oil is used on the premises or if the manufacture or conversion of crude oil into refined products begins on the premises, the oil is treated as removed on the day the use, manufacture, or conversion begins. However, oil that is produced and then reinjected into the reservior or used on the same tract or parcel of land to power a production process or production equipment is not removed from the premises so long as the oil is at no time transported off the tract or parcel of land from which it was produced. Moreover, oil used to power a production process or production equipment will not be considered removed from the premises if it is transported from one tract or parcel of land to a contiguous tract or parcel of land, provided that 100 percent of the economic interest in the oil produced from both tracts or parcels of land is held by the same persons.[77]

The third exception to the general rule that first purchasers must withhold and deposit the windfall profit tax applies to an "integrated oil company" which is liable for the tax on its own production used in producing and distributing petroleum products and to an "integrated oil company" that has furnished an "integrated oil company's certificate" to a first purchaser as provided in Regulation 150.4995-2(c)(2) wherein the purchaser is relieved of the liability for withholding the tax. An "integrated oil company" is a taxpayer that both produces oil and is either a "retailer" or a "refiner."

---

77 Reg. Sec. 150.4996-1(d).

The term "retailer" means any taxpayer described in Section 613A(d)(2). Thus, a retailer is one who directly, or through a related person, sells oil or natural gas (excluding bulk sales to commercial or industrial users) or any product derived from oil or natural gas either through any retail outlet operated by the taxpayer or a related person; or to any entity either obligated under an agreement or contract with the taxpayer or related person to use a trademark, trade name, or service mark or name owned by such taxpayer or related person, in marketing or distributing oil or natural gas or any product derived from oil or natural gas, or given authority, pursuant to an agreement or contract with the person or related person, to occupy any retail outlet owned, leased or in any way controlled by the taxpayer or related person. However, a "retailer" is not considered an "integrated oil company" for windfall profit tax purposes where the combined gross receipts from the sale of such oil, natural gas, or any product derived therefrom, for the taxable period (calendar quarter) of all retail outlets do not exceed $1,250,000. For purposes of this exception, sales of oil, natural gas, or any product derived from oil or natural gas does not include sales made of such items outside the United States, if no domestic production of the person or a related person is exported during the calendar year or immediately preceding calendar year.

The term "refiner" means any taxpayer described in Section 613A(d)(4). Thus, a refiner is one who is engaged in the refining of crude oil or is related to a person so engaged, provided that on any day during the taxable period (calendar quarter) the refinery runs of the person and any related persons exceed 50,000 barrels, where the term "related person" has the same meaning as prescribed in Section 613A(d)(2) and (4).[78]

---

78 Reg. Sec. 150.4996-1(g).

In addition to the regular withholding requirements, there are interim withholding rules. Because these interim rules were optional and applied to a period from April 18, 1980, through June 4, 1980, they have not been included herein. Furthermore, the interim rules do not differ materially from the regular rules for withholding.[79]

Every purchaser required to deduct and withhold the windfall profit tax is liable for the tax required to be withheld, whether or not it is actually withheld by the purchaser. However, in no event should the purchaser's liability for the tax required to be withheld exceed the producer's liability for the tax in respect to oil sold to that purchaser, and the purchaser's liability is abated to the extent that the producer's liability for the tax is paid (including payments by the producer or by the purchaser through adjustments in amounts later withheld). The producer from whom the correct amount was not withheld is liable to any purchaser for the amount of the producer's tax liability paid by the purchaser. The purchaser is relieved of liability to any other person for the amount of any tax withheld and paid to the Internal Revenue Service or deposited with a duly designated depositary of the United States.[80]

Depositary Requirements

In general, purchasers must make deposits for each calendar month not later than forty-five days after the close of that month. The amount to be deposited for each month is the amount required to be withheld from payments that have been, or will be made, for oil removed from the premises during that month.[81] However, where a purchaser of crude oil and the operator of the property

79 Reg. Sec. 150.4995-1(d).

80 Reg. Sec. 150.4995-1(e).

81 Reg. Sec. 150.4995-3(c).

from which the crude oil is produced make a Section 4994(a)(7) election to substitute the operator for a purchaser, the operator must withhold and deposit the tax in lieu of that purchaser. While such an election is in effect, all the requirements otherwise imposed on the purchaser are imposed on the operator. Substitution of the operator for a purchaser may only be elected in respect to a property when the operator is otherwise required to make deposits as a purchaser of oil produced from a different oil reservoir.[82] Except in the case of certain "integrated oil companies," a producer who is liable for the windfall profit tax because the oil it produces is not subject to withholding must, for each calendar month, deposit the tax imposed on the removal of oil in that month of oil that is not subject to withholding. The deposits must be made no later than forty-five days after the close of the month in which the oil was removed or deemed removed.

With respect to estimated deposits of a producer, these depositary requirements will be considered to have been met for a month only if one of the four following conditions is satisfied: (1) The producer's aggregate deposit liability for the three months of a taxable period is less than $100 and the producer deposits the amount of tax owed on, or before the last day for filing the required return for that taxable period or remits the tax owed with that return; or (2) The producer's deposit for the month is not less than 90 percent of the total amount otherwise required to be deposited by it for the month, and the producer complies with the special requirements of Regulation 150.4995-3(f)(2); or (3) The producer's deposit for each month of the taxable period is not less than 30 percent of the total amount otherwise required to be deposited by it for the three months of the taxable period, and the producer complies with the special requirements of Regulation 150.4995-3(f)(2); or (4) The producer's de-

82 Reg. Sec. 150.4995-4(a).

posit for the month is not less than 100 percent of the amount required to be deposited by it for the third preceding month (determined without regard to this and the three previous conditions), and the producer complies with the special requirements of Regulation 150.4995-3(f)(2). However, the third and fourth conditions do not apply to any producer that normally incurs in the first month in each taxable period (calendar quarter) more than 45 percent of its total liability for deposit for the taxable period (determined without regard to the second, third and fourth conditions). Finally, the special requirement referred to in the second, third, and fourth conditions mandates that the producer deposit any underpayment of the windfall profit tax liability for a taxable period not later than forty-five days after the close of the last month in that taxable period.[83]

In the case of an integrated oil company other than an independent refiner (as defined in Regulation 150.4996-1(h)) that is either liable as a producer for the windfall profit tax (unless such tax is required to be deducted and withheld by the purchaser), or is required as a purchaser to deduct and withhold the tax, deposits must be made semimonthly, where a semimonthly period is defined in Regulation 150.4995-3(a)(3) as the first fifteen days of a calendar month or the portion of a calendar month following the fifteenth day of such month. The amount to be deposited for each semimonthly period is the amount of tax imposed by Section 4986 that is not required to be withheld on oil removed from the premises during that semimonthly period for which the company is liable as a producer, plus the amount required to be withheld by the company as a purchaser from payments that have been or will be made, for oil removed from the premises during that semimonthly period. The deposits must be made on, or before the depositary date, which is defined in Regula-

83 Reg. Sec. 150.4995-3(f).

tion 150.4995-3(a)(3) as the ninth day of the semimonthly period following the semimonthly period in which the oil was removed.

These depositary requirements will be considered to have been met for a semimonthly period in respect to estimated deposits only if one of the four following conditions are satisfied by the integrated oil company: (1) The company's deposit for such semimonthly period is not less than 90 percent of the total amount otherwise required to be deposited by it for such period, and if such period occurs in a month other than the last month in a taxable period, it deposits any underpayment for such month by the ninth day of the second month following such month; or (2) Its deposit for each semimonthly period in the month is not less than 45 percent of the total amount otherwise required to be deposited by it for the month, and if such month is other than the last month in a taxable period, it deposits any underpayment for such month by the ninth day of the second month following such month; or (3) Its deposit for each semimonthly period in the month is not less than 50 percent of the total amount required to be deposited by it for the second preceding calendar month (determined without regard to conditions one through four), and if such month is other than the last month in a calendar quarter, it deposits any underpayment for such month by the ninth day of the second month following such month; or (4) The requirements of any of the above three conditions are satisfied for the first semimonthly period of a calendar month, and the company's deposit for the second semimonthly period of that calendar month is, when added to the deposit for the first semimonthly period, not less than 90 percent of the total amount otherwise required to be deposited by it for that month, and if such period occurs in a month other than the last month in a calendar quarter, the company deposits any underpayment for such month by the ninth day of the second month following such month. However, conditions two and three do not apply to any company that normally incurs in the first semimonthly period in each month more than 75 percent of its total liability for deposit for the month (determined without regard to conditions one through four). Finally, if the aggregate amount of deposit liability for a taxable period (determined without regard to conditions one through four) exceeds the total amount deposited by an integrated oil company for such taxable period (calendar quarter), then the company is required, on or before the last day of the first month following the close of the taxable period, to deposit an amount equal to the amount by which the deposit liability exceeds the total deposits made for the taxable period.[84]

As implied above, independent refiners—including those who purchase oil pursuant to a delayed payment contract—are not required to comply with the depositary requirements for integrated oil companies. An "independent refiner" is defined in Regulation 150.4996-1(h) as a refiner who obtained, directly or indirectly, in the second preceding calendar quarter, more than 70 percent of his refinery input of domestic crude oil (or 70 percent of his refinery input of domestic and imported crude oil) from producers who do not control, are not controlled by, and are not under common control with such refiner, and marketed or distributed in such quarter and continues to market or distribute a substantial volume of gasoline refined by him through branded independent marketers or nonbranded independent marketers. In general, purchasers who are independent refiners must withhold taxes and make deposits thereof for each calendar month in accordance with the depositary requirements explained above for the first purchasers that are required to withhold and deposit the windfall profit tax. In the case of oil purchased under a contract therefor under which no pay-

84 Reg. Sec. 150.4995-3(a).

ment is required to be made by the purchaser before the forty-sixth day after the close of the month in which the oil is purchased, the deposits must be made for each calendar month not later than the last day of the second month which begins after the month in which the oil was removed. The amount to be deposited for each month is the same amount required to be withheld by other purchasers (as explained above).[85]

Tax deposits must be made with a Federal Reserve Bank or, at the depositor's election, with a financial institution authorized in accordance with Treasury Department Circular No. 1079. Each deposit must be accompanied by a federal tax deposit form for excise taxes (FTD Form 504), and the timeliness of the deposit is determined by the deposit received (or deemed received under Section 7502(e)) by a Federal Reserve Bank, or by an authorized financial institution, whichever is earlier.[86]

If the amount of tax withheld from a producer for a calendar year is less than the total liability of the producer for the windfall profit tax in respect to oil removed during the calendar year and subject to withholding as prescribed by Regulation 150.4995-1, the producer must remit the difference with a timely return as required by Regulation 150.4997-1. Alternatively, the producer may, on or before the last day for filing a tax return under Regulation 150.4997-1, deposit such difference.[87]

Tax Accounting Requirements: Returns and Recordkeeping

In general, a person (purchaser or operator) required to withhold the windfall profit tax for any taxable period

---

85 Reg. Sec. 150.4995-3(b).

86 Reg. Sec. 150.4995-3(h).

87 Reg. Sec. 150.4995-3(e).

(calendar quarter) must file a tax return (Form 720, with Form 6047 attached thereto) not later than the last day of the second month following the close of a taxable period. The same filing requirement is applicable where oil production is not subject to withholding, as in the case of selected producers and integrated oil companies. Thus, the producers of crude oil in respect to which withholding is required are not required to file a windfall profit tax return in respect to such oil. However, an annual tax return must be filed by each producer whose liability for tax in respect to oil that was removed during the four taxable periods (calendar year), exceeds the amount of tax withheld in respect to that oil. Such annual returns must be filed not later than the last day of the first February following the close of the calendar year in which the oil giving rise to the underpayment was removed.[88]

As indicated above, each taxpayer liable for the windfall profit tax, each producer or purchaser of domestic crude oil, each operator of a property producing domestic crude oil, and each partnership or other person either receiving information on behalf of, or providing information to producers is subject to recordkeeping requirements. In general, such producers, purchasers, operators, partnerships, and other persons must keep records of all documents, material, and information necessary for either determining the windfall profit tax or records that affect his (her or its) administrative obligations under Chapter 45 or the regulations related thereto. This recordkeeping requirement includes material furnished to other persons, as well as information received from other persons. These records must be available at all times for inspection by authorized officers or employees of the Internal Revenue Service and must be retained as long as the con-

88 Reg. Sec. 150.4997-1(a) and Reg. Sec. 150.6076-1.

tents thereof may be pertinent to the administration of the Internal Revenue Code.[89]

If a purchaser either is subject to the rules for withholding and depositing the windfall profit tax in respect to any crude oil purchase or would be subject thereto in the absence of an exemption certificate, such purchaser must furnish both monthly statements and an annual statement (on Form 6248) to each producer of the crude oil purchased. However, if payment for the oil purchased is made to the operator, rather than to the producer or to a partnership, rather than to the partners, the statements must be furnished to the operator or the partnership, respectively. Such purchaser must also file the annual information return with the Internal Revenue Service. Any person who receives a statement with respect to oil of which such person is not the producer must, within fifteen days of receipt of the statement, furnish to each producer or partnership of producers (and the Internal Revenue Service in the case of an annual statement) the information relating to that producer's or partnership's share of the oil purchased.

Each purchaser must furnish statements for each calendar month showing the total amount of windfall profit tax withheld by the purchaser from payments made to the producer, operator, or partnership with respect to oil removed during that month. Where the purchaser did not withhold tax from payments to that person because of the receipt of an exemption certificate, the monthly statement need only state the reason for the absence of withholding. Each monthly statement should be furnished before the first day of the second month that begins after the close of the month to which the statement is applicable.

---

89 Reg. Sec. 150.4997-1(b).

For each calendar year, the purchaser must furnish statements and must file information returns with the Internal Revenue Service. A separate statement must be furnished to, and a separate information return must be filed for each producer, operator, or partnership to whom the purchaser made payments for oil purchased during the calendar year.

Each statement and information return should contain the following information with respect to oil for which that person received payment:

(1) The quantity, removal price, severance tax adjustment, TAPS adjustment (if any), adjusted base price, and windfall profit tax liability (computed without regard to the net income limitation) for oil in each tier that was removed during that calendar year; (2) The total quantity of the taxable crude oil that was removed during that year; (3) The total amount of the windfall profit tax liability in respect to the oil incurred during that year; and (4) The amount of windfall profit tax withheld by the purchaser in respect to the oil removed during each month of that year and the total tax withheld in respect to oil removed during the year. For purposes of the preceding sentence, each category of Tier Three oil, independent producer oil withheld upon at a 50 percent rate, and independent producer oil withheld upon at a 30 percent rate should be treated as a separate tier. Where the purchaser did not withhold tax from payments to that person because of the receipt of an exemption certificate, the annual statement and information return should state that fact and should set forth the above information clearly identified as relevant to tax consequences that would have occurred had the exemption certificate not been received.

When the withholding adjustments mandated by Regulation 150.4995-1(c) are not completed during the calendar year, the purchaser must provide supplemental information in the annual statement and information return in respect to the person subject to the adjustment. The statement and information return should set forth the amount that has been underwithheld or overwithheld, the amount actually adjusted, and the amount remaining unadjusted. Where the adjustment was due to underwithholding, the statement must also inform the recipient that the producer is liable for the amount of the windfall profit tax in excess of the amount of such tax withheld by the purchaser and that this information is being supplied to the Internal Revenue Service. Where the withholding adjustment was due to overwithholding, the statement should inform the recipient that the purchaser was unable to fully adjust the overpayment as required by Regulation 150.4995-1(c) and that the producer is eligible for a credit or refund which he (she or it) may claim on his (her or its) federal income tax return in accordance with the rules provided in Regulation 150.6402-1.

The annual statement and information return required for each person should also set forth as the amount deductible for federal income tax purposes the total amount of windfall profit tax withheld from payments made to the producer, operator, or partnership during the calendar year without regard to when the oil was removed. The annual statements required to be furnished by a purchaser (as provided above) for any calendar year should be furnished on or before January 31 of the year immediately following the calendar year to which the statement is applicable, and the annual information returns required to be filed by a purchaser should be filed on or before the due date for the windfall profit tax return (Forms 720 and 6047) for the last taxable period of the calendar year.[90]

---

[90] Reg. Sec. 150.4997-2.

Certification of Production and Exemption

The operator of any property from which domestic crude oil is removed during a calendar month must furnish a monthly statement, signed under the penalties of perjury, certifying the amount, category, adjusted base price, severance tax adjustment, etc., of each type of oil produced therefrom to either the purchaser of the oil, if the purchaser is required to withhold tax from payments for the oil, or the producer, in any other case. However, if the producer of oil is a partner in a partnership, the statement may be furnished to the partnership if the producer and the partnership so agree. In that case, the partnership must furnish the information to the producer in respect to that producer's share of the oil within fifteen days of receipt.

In the case of exempt Alaskan oil or exempt front-end oil, the statement must certify that the oil is exempt from tax. In all statements not certifying exemption, the following information is required: the tier, for purposes of the tax imposed by Section 4986, of the oil removed during the month, and if the oil is Tier Three oil, whether the oil constitutes newly discovered oil, heavy oil, or incremental tertiary oil; and the amount of the oil removed and, if the oil removed includes oil of different tiers or categories, the amount of oil removed from each tier or category. The following additional information must also be included in any statement not certifying exemption: the adjusted base price for each tier of oil removed; the severance tax adjustment (if any) with respect to each tier of oil removed; the TAPS adjustment (if any) and the average removal price for the month in the case of oil from the Sadlerochit Reservoir; and the property from which the oil was removed.

In the case of a statement furnished to a purchaser, the operator must provide the information with respect to the aggregate amount of oil sold to that purchaser and removed during the month. In the case of a statement furnished to a producer or partnership, the operator must provide the information with respect to that person's allocable share of all oil removed from the premises during the month (including any oil delivered in kind to that producer). The operator must furnish the required statement to each purchaser or producer (as the case may be) no later than the fifteenth day of the month following the calendar month in which the oil was removed.

If the purchaser or producer agrees in a signed statement that the operator is relieved of the duty of furnishing to such purchaser or producer the statement otherwise required (as explained above), or some or all of the information required therein, the operator will be relieved of such duty, provided that the purchaser or producer has the information necessary to comply with all of the requirements of the windfall profit tax without such statement or information. Such an agreement immediately ceases to have effect when the operator, purchaser, or producer, by a written statement signed by an authorized person, notifies the other party that it is terminating the agreement. Moreover, where the operator and purchaser have elected pursuant to Regulation 150.4995-4 to have the operator assume the purchaser's obligation (as explained above) to withhold, deposit, etc., then the statement otherwise required of the operator in respect to the purchaser is no longer necessary.

Where the operator receives a producer's certificate (as explained above) certifying a share of production to be exempt from tax, subject to a lower rate of tax, or not to be withheld upon, the operator should furnish a copy of that certificate to each purchaser of oil from that property by the fifteenth day of the month following the month in which the certificate was received. However, if payment is to be received by the operator on behalf of the producers, the former should furnish a certificate that summarizes the contents of the producers' certificates and states that the operator has received such certificates and has them available for inspection.[91]

In general, the producer of exempt Indian oil, or the holder of any interest in crude oil that is a qualified governmental interest or is a qualified charitable interest may furnish an exemption certificate in respect to such oil to the purchaser of the oil or to the operator of the property from which the oil is produced (or, if the producer is a partner, to the partnership). Any producer of independent producer oil may furnish a certificate in respect to such oil to the purchaser of the oil or to the operator of the property from which the oil is produced (or, if the producer is a partner, to the partnership). However, there are both mandatory and optional withholding "exemption certificates" in the case of integrated oil companies.

An exemption certificate is a written statement certifying that the producer's oil is exempt from the windfall profit tax because the oil constitutes exempt Indian oil or the oil is from a qualified governmental interest or a qualified charitable interest. Any producer who furnishes an exemption certificate to an operator, purchaser, or partnership must also file an exemption certificate with the Internal Revenue Service Center for the region in which the producer's income tax return is filed. Only one such certificate need be filed with the IRS although the producer may furnish certificates to more than one operator or purchaser.

Similarly, an independent producer's certificate is a written statement certifying that the entire amount of the producer's oil expected to be sold to the purchaser is subject to the lower rates of tax provided in Section 4987(b)(2), because the oil constitutes independent pro-

---

91 Reg. Sec. 150.6050C-1.

ducer oil. No certificate may be furnished, however, in respect to oil if it is reasonable to believe that the number of barrels to be affected by the certificate, taken together with all other oil in respect to which a certificate has been furnished by the producer to any operator, purchaser, or partnership, will exceed the producer's independent producer amount.

Every integrated oil company that is a producer of oil from a property of which that company is the operator (or would be the operator in the absence of a designation under Regulation 150.4996-1(c)) must furnish a statement to each purchaser of oil from that property no later than the date by which the first statement by the operator to the purchaser (under Regulation 150.6050C-1 as explained above) is required to be furnished (or May 12, 1980, if later). Furthermore, any integrated oil company that is a producer of oil from a property of which that company is not the operator may, at its option, furnish such a statement with respect to such oil to the purchaser of the oil or to the operator of the property from which the oil is produced (or, if the producer is a partner, to the partnership). Any certificate furnished by an integrated oil company must state that the producer is an integrated oil company, that the producer will deposit its own windfall profit tax liability, and that the producer's share of production is not to be withheld upon. Finally, any certificate of an integrated oil company will apply to all payments for oil of which that integrated oil company is the producer made after the date on which the purchaser received the certificate.

In general, each certificate must set forth the facts that establish entitlement to the exemption or lower rates claimed. The certificate (or any revocation of a certificate) must identify the producer by name, address, and employer identification (or social security) number and must be signed by the producer (under the penalties of perjury except in the case of a revocation). Where a producer who has furnished certification with respect to oil subsequently discovers that the oil is not, or has ceased to be, eligible for certification for exemption or lower tax rates, the producer must furnish notice thereof within ten days to the person to whom the certificate was originally furnished.

In situations where the purchaser of crude oil and the operator of the property from which crude oil is produced have elected to substitute the operator for the purchaser in respect to withholding, tax deposits, etc., the purchaser should forward to the operator, at the time of the election, any exemption certificate or notice of revocation received after the election. Thus, any operator can treat any exemption certificate or notice of revocation forwarded by a purchaser as a producer's exemption certificate or revocation notice.[92]

Substitution of an Operator for a Purchaser

As indicated above, the substitution of the operator (as defined in Regulation 150.4996-1(c)) for the purchaser will make the administration of the windfall profit tax more practicable only when the operator is otherwise required by Regulation 150.4995-3 to make deposits as a purchaser of oil produced from a different oil reservoir. Consequently, a purported election to have an operator substitute for a purchaser is invalid unless such substitution meets the aforementioned requirement.

Where allowed, the operator of the property and a purchaser of crude oil produced from that property may make a joint election with respect to oil produced from the entire property or any portion thereof. While the election is in effect, all the requirements otherwise imposed upon

---

92 Reg. Sec. 150.4995-2.

the purchaser are imposed upon the operator, and the purchaser will not be held responsible for failing to meet those requirements. The operator must promptly notify all producers of oil from that property (or portion thereof) that a joint election has been made, and that all information otherwise required to be sent to the purchaser should be sent to the operator. If the operator makes payments for oil produced from the property to a partnership rather than directly to the producers, the notice should be sent to the partnership. The operator and the purchaser must agree to transfer responsibility for meeting all the requirements otherwise imposed upon the purchaser to the operator in order for the agreement to constitute an effective election.

The joint election must be made by the execution of a document, signed and dated by both the purchaser and operator, that states that both parties have agreed that the operator of the property shall be responsible for all the requirements otherwise imposed upon the purchaser by Chapter 45 (or related provisions of Subtitle F) of the Code, or pertinent regulations. The purchaser and operator must, within ten days of the execution of the document, each forward a copy of the document to the Internal Revenue Service Center for the region in which it files its income tax return. The election will remain in effect from the date of its execution (or later effective date specified in the election document) until either of the parties executes a document, signed, dated, and delivered to the other party, that declares that the joint election is to be terminated. There are also special procedures for terminating the election. Finally, both the purchaser and operator must retain in their records, for as long as they may be material in the administration of any internal revenue law, a copy of the joint election and any subsequent termination.[93]

---

93 Reg. Sec. 150.4995-4.

Withholding Adjustments and Overpayments

A purchaser who determines that the amount of tax withheld from any payment for crude oil was more or less than the amount of tax imposed by Section 4986 (computed without regard to the net income limitation) with respect to that crude oil should make adjustments in the amount to be withheld from subsequent payments to the same person. Adjustments are generally required when the purchaser has made an incorrect calculation in respect to a prior payment, when the purchaser has withheld in accordance with the special rules of Regulation 150.4995-1(b) (2) because of the absence of an effective operator's certification and the purchaser later receives an effective certification, when an earlier certification is corrected, or when the purchaser has withheld tax from a producer at generally applicable rates and the purchaser subsequently receives a retroactively effective independent producer's certificate. Every adjustment should be reflected on the federal excise tax return (Form 720 along with Form 6047) prescribed for use in reporting windfall profit tax withholding.

If the entire adjustment could be reported in the return for the same taxable period (calendar quarter) as the withholding giving rise to the adjustment, the return for that period should reflect only the amount withheld as adjusted. Otherwise, every return on which an overpayment or underpayment is adjusted must include a statement explaining the adjustment, designating the return period to which the adjustment relates, and setting forth such other information as may be required by the instructions to the return.

In general, the purchaser must make a full adjustment by underwithholding or overwithholding in subsequent payments to the same person (whether or not from the same property) so that the total amount withheld is equal to the windfall profit tax thereon (computed without regard to the net income limitation) as soon as possible. The full adjustment must be made, if possible, in the next payment. If it is not possible to complete the adjustment in the next payment, the purchaser should adjust by underwithholding or overwithholding to the fullest extent possible in each subsequent payment until the adjustment is completed.

No adjustment is to be made, however, in the amount withheld from payments made for oil removed in a later calendar year or from payments made after the annual statement required by Regulation 150.4997-2(c) is furnished. Where the error is one of underwithholding that cannot be fully adjusted by the purchaser, *e.g.,* where the relationship between the producer and the purchaser has terminated, or where the next payment is for oil removed in the following calendar year, the producer is required to file a return at the end of the year unless the producer's windfall profit tax liability has been completely satisfied by reason of overwithholding with another purchaser. Where the error is one of overwithholding that cannot be fully adjusted by the purchaser, the rules of Regulation 150.6402-1 with respect to claims for credit or refund, are applicable to the producer (as explained below).

If the need for an adjustment arises in respect to a payment for oil removed in a calendar year prior to the year within which the purchaser determines the need for an adjustment, no adjustment should be made unless the adjustment can be made in a payment for oil removed in the prior year and unless that payment is made prior to the furnishing of the required annual statement. However, Regulation 150.4997-2(c)(2) (as explained above) requires that withholding adjustment information be furnished by purchaser to producer, where under- and over-withholding carries over to a subsequent year. Finally, no amount should be deducted or withheld from any payment in excess of the windfall profit (without regard to the net income limitation) in respect to the oil giving rise to that payment; however, if the producer and purchaser have agreed to additional withholding as provided in Section 4995(a)(3)(D), any amount withheld pursuant to the agreement should be treated as an amount required to be withheld.[94]

In general, any producer who pays, or is deemed to have paid, more than the correct amount of the crude oil windfall profit tax for a taxable period may file for a refund of the overpayment or may claim credit for such overpayment, in the manner and subject to the conditions explained below, as well as those prescribed by Regulation 301.6402-2. As provided in Section 4995(a)(4), the producer of oil is treated as having paid any amount withheld on the last day of the first February after the calendar year in which the oil was removed from the premises. Therefore, if the sum of the producer's liability for the tax on oil subject to withholding for all taxable periods of a calendar year is less than the amount deducted and withheld from the producer in respect to oil removed during the calendar year, the producer may file a claim for a credit or refund of the overpayment after such last day of February. However, in the case of an overpayment due to the application of the net income limitation, the claim for credit or refund should not be filed until the income tax return is filed for the taxable year that includes the last day of the last taxable period of such calendar year.

The producer may file a claim for refund of the overpayment or may claim credit for the overpayment against any liability in respect to the income tax in accordance with the form and instructions provided for that purpose. The producer should also attach to the claim a copy of all Forms 6248 furnished to the producer by the purchaser or operator.

---

94 Reg. Sec. 150.4995-3(c).

In the case of any overpayment of the windfall profit tax attributable *solely* to tax paid on crude oil not subject to withholding, the producer may file a claim for refund of the overpayment on or after the date for filing the return of such tax for such taxable period under Section 6076, or may claim credit for such overpayment by making an adjustment on the return of windfall profit tax for the current or subsequent taxable periods, in accordance with Form 720 and the instructions for such adjustment.

A producer who, because of the application of the net income limitation on windfall profit provided in Section 4988(b), has overpaid the windfall profit tax for any taxable period should not file a claim for credit or refund of that overpayment until the income tax return is filed for the taxable year that includes the last day of the taxable period. The producer may file a claim for refund of the overpayment or claim credit for the overpayment against any liability for the income tax in accordance with the form and instructions provided for that purpose.

If a producer of any crude oil from a qualified governmental interest or a qualified charitable interest, or a producer of exempt Indian oil has had tax withheld from payments made for oil removed before July 1, 1980, the producer may file a claim for refund on or after July 1, 1980. The claim should be filed on Form 843 and should have attached a copy of each monthly statement received from a purchaser (or operator).[95]

Phasing Out the Tax

The windfall profit excise tax imposed by the new Chapter 45, Subtitle D of the Internal Revenue Code is only a temporary tax designed, as its name suggests, to tax the "windfall" resulting from the decontrol of domes-

95 Reg. Sec. 150.6402-1.

tic crude oil prices between June 1, 1979, and October, 1981. This latest energy tax is the price the petroleum industry must pay for the continued decontrol of prices for domestically produced crude oil. When President Carter announced on April 5, 1979 a phase-out of price controls, he also proposed that a windfall profit tax be imposed on crude oil producers because they would allegedly reap unconscionable profits from decontrol.

In his treatise on the history of the western frontier, Walter Prescott Webb defined a "windfall" as unexpected or unanticipated benefits such as the good fortune which befalls a passerby when the wind blows a branch from a tree.[96] The need for a "windfall profits" tax during the energy crisis is just the latest use by the federal government of an excess-profits type of tax mechanism. Previously, the excess-profits-tax mechanism has been relied on during wars and other major crises when price controls and shortages of consumer goods created temporary distortions in the American economy. The excess-profits-tax mechanism is, like the distortions in a wartime crisis economy, only a temporary exaction that has historically been phased out as the economy returned to peace-time operation.[97]

Two interrelated issues are implicit in the concept and history of "excess" or "windfall" profits taxation. First, will the oil producers experience "windfall profits" from decontrol in an era of rapidly increasing costs for exploration and development of new domestic crude oil? Secondly, assuming "windfall profits" do exist, how long will they last once the domestic and international markets for crude oil become one, assuming that they are

---

96 Walter P. Webb, *The Great Frontier* (Austin: University of Texas Press, 1975), pp. 180-181.

97 See J.S. Seidman, *Legislative History of Federal Income Tax 1938-1861* and *Excess Profits Tax Laws 1953-1939.* Englewood Cliffs, NJ: Prentice-Hall, Inc. (out of print).

not one now. Both of these questions are not only beyond the scope of this text, but also "moot" now that the "Crude Oil Windfall Profit Tax Act of 1980" has been enacted for a period of at least a decade. Only time will tell if this new tax is on "windfall profits" or is simply an excise tax on crude oil.

As a result of public skepticism, it has been easier for a concerned Congress[98] facing reelection to enact an increase in the tax on gasoline and diesel fuel used for transportation, and on fuel oil used for home heating and by industry under the guise of a "windfall profits" tax on oil producers. Carter's 1977 legislative proposals for a national energy policy included an ill-fated gasoline tax increase of five cents per gallon per year for more than a decade (as well as a crude oil equalization tax).[99] Carter's spring proposals (March 14, 1980) for fighting inflation and balancing the budget included a ten-cent-per-gallon increase in the federal gas tax. A recently-released study by the International Monetary Fund (IMF) recommends a substantial increase in national motor fuel taxes in the major industrial nations,[100] but the Conservative Party government of former Canadian Prime Minister Joe Clark was toppled in 1979 because of his proposals to significantly increase excise taxes on motor fuels and to balance the Federal budget, although our North American neighbor is one of the most energy profligate nations in the world.[101] Conversely, the decision by many major oil-producing companies to diversify their business by investing both in other energy resources and energy-

---

98 Barry Sussman, "Poll Shows House Believes Energy Crisis Real," *Washington Post,* November 7, 1979.

99 Thompson, *Energy Policy,* pp. 38-39.

100 "IMF Study Says U.S., Other Nations Should Try Higher Taxes to Cut Fuel Use," *Daily Tax Report,* March 7, 1980, p. G1.

101 John Urquhart, "Liberals' Victory in Canada Could Mean More Activity By Government in Economy," *Wall Street Journal,* February 20, 1980, p. 16.

related industries, and in industries that are unrelated to energy,[102] along with the significant increase in the profits of major oil companies during the second half of 1979[103] (and first half of 1980) has further eroded their credibility with the public and the Congress.

Notwithstanding serious Congressional proposals to make the Chapter 45 exaction permanent, Section 4990 provides for a phase-out of the tax over a 33-month period beginning with the month following the "target month," which is the later of December, 1987 or the first month for which the Treasury publishes an estimate of net windfall profit tax revenue that exceeds $227.3 billion. The phase-out percentage for any month is 100% reduced by 3% for each month after the target month and before the month following the month for which the phase-out percentage is being determined. Thus, once the phase-out period begins, a person responsible for withholding or paying the windfall profit tax will determine the actual liability by multiplying the regular tax by the phase-out percentage. The earliest termination of the windfall profit tax will be October, 1990

Post Script

In conclusion, the above commentary on the temporary regulations for the statutory provisions of the windfall profit tax could have been (and for the most part was) written without the benefit of the proposed regulations. In addition, portions of the first set of temporary regula-

---

102 Alice L. Priest, et. al., "The New Diversification Oil Game," *Business Week*, April 24, 1978, pp. 76-88; and John Love and Michael G. Sheldrick, "Exxon: Searching for Another Game That Equals Oil in Size," *Business Week*, July 16, 1979, pp. 80-82.

103 Paul Blustein, "An Embarrassment of Riches: A Look at Big Profits in Petroleum for Third Period," *Wall Street Journal*, October 25, 1979, p. 6; and "More Oil Firms Report Records For 1979 Earnings," *Wall Street Journal*, January 25, 1980, p. 5.

tions created so much confusion that it was necessary for the Treasury to issue a second set of temporary regulations that amended or superseded the first set as they pertained to the withholding requirements for integrated oil companies.

While the windfall profit tax will affect the pocketbooks of all Americans who consume petroleum products, only those tax professionals with clients or employers who have an economic interest in crude oil production, who purchase crude oil, who are operators of oil producing property, or who are integrated oil companies will have to become proficient in the performance of the complex tax accounting inherent in the new Section 4986 excise tax. Although the above explanation should serve as an introduction to the subject of windfall profit taxation for any tax professional, the solution of all but the simplest compliance and planning problems effected by this excise tax on domestic crude oil will necessitate reliance on the new Chapter 45 Code Sections, the Congressional Committee reports, and the Internal Revenue Service Regulations, and the editorial commentary published commercially, both in periodicals and through the loose-leaf, technical services for excise taxes. Hopefully, the final regulations will be available in October 1980, inasmuch as the public hearings on the temporary regulations were scheduled for July 16, 1980. Ideally, publishing of final regulations in October would make them available for the year-end tax planning in November and December.

Part II

Independent Producer Provisions

Independent producers are allowed reduced tax rates on up to 1,000 barrels per day production of tiers I and II oil. For these purposes, an independent producer is one who does not engage in retail sales or refining activities above specified limits. Sales from retail activities must not exceed $1,250,000 for the calendar quarter, and refinery runs must not exceed 50,000 barrels throughput for the quarter.

The *independent producer amount* is simply 1,000 barrels multiplied by the actual number of days in the quarter. An independent producer's qualified production is his Tier I and Tier II production attributable to his working interest.

That portion of an independent producer's qualified production that does not exceed his independent producer amount is eligible for the reduced rates. Beginning in 1983, the stripper oil production (Tier II) of independent producers is exempt from the WPT, as provided in the Economic Recovery Act of 1981.

The rates for independent producers and all others are:

	Independent Producers	*Nonindependent Producers*
Tier I	50%	70%
Tier II	30%	60%
Tier III	30%	30%

If an independent producer's qualified production exceeds his independent producer amount, the excess is taxed at the higher nonindependent producer rates. If qualified production exceeds the independent producer amount and consists of tiers I and II oil, the independent producer amount is allocated between the tiers in proportion to that producer's qualified production.

The independent producer amount may be less than 1,000 barrels per day if the producer is a member of a related group. In that instance, the independent producer amount is allocated to the members of the related group in proportion to their qualified production percentage of the total qualified production of the related group.

Generally, if a party who was not eligible for the lower rates with respect to any portion of his production transfers a property or portion thereof, none of the production from the property will constitute qualified production to the transferee. Hence, the transferee would not be eligible for the reduced tax rates on the production from the property transferred to him.

For an explanation of the stripper oil exemption for independent producers, see the postscript chapter at the end of the textbook where the Economic Recovery Act of 1981 is analyzed as it affects the WPT.

ANALYSIS OF THE CRUDE OIL WINDFALL PROFIT TAX: WITH AN EMPHASIS ON THE INDEPENDENT PRODUCER

Main Hurdman & Cranstoun*

In April 1979, the President announced his intention to use his discretionary authority to decontrol oil prices. The President's program involves the immediate decontrol of newly discovered oil (oil produced from a property which had no production in 1978) and the gradual phaseout of controls on other oil. The oil price decontrol will result in a significant increase in revenues received by oil producers and royalty owners.

The President and the Congress have both concluded that profits to be realized from these price increases should be subject to additional taxes. Therefore, the President proposed, and the Congress has enacted, the Crude Oil Windfall Profit Tax Act of 1980, which imposes a temporary excise tax (windfall profit tax) on domestic oil producers and royalty owners with respect to their increased revenues attributable to oil price decontrol.

The provision that has been ultimately approved represents a compromise between the Administration and both Houses of Congress with respect to how the tax burden should fall on the various types of oil covered by the tax. Generally, the Act places the higher tax burden on oil discovered prior to 1979, while providing for lower rates on newly discovered oil. Certain oil production and certain producers and royalty owners are

---

*** This article is reprinted with the permission of Main Hurdman & Cranstoun and is based on a booklet prepared by that firm's Oil and Gas Committee.**

Article reprinted courtesy of *Oil & Gas Tax Quarterly*, June 1980, pp. 418–449

entirely exempt from the tax. Finally, special treatment has been afforded to independent producers (their special treatment is considered in a separate section of this article).

CRUDE OIL WINDFALL PROFIT TAX ACT OF 1980

Overview of the Windfall Profit Tax

The windfall profit tax is a temporary excise, or severance, tax applying to taxable crude oil produced in the United States according to its classification in one of three tiers. Generally, Tier 1 consists of oil which would have been lower- or upper-tier oil had price controls been continued. Tier 2 consists primarily of stripper well production, i.e., wells producing 10 barrels or less per day. Tier 3 oil consists of newly discovered oil, certain heavy oil, and incremental tertiary oil.

For each tier, the taxable windfall profit is measured by the difference between the selling price of the oil and the adjusted base price for that tier, minus an additional adjustment for any state severance tax imposed on the windfall profit element. The base prices average $12.81 per barrel for Tier 1 oil, $15.20 for Tier 2 oil, and $16.55 for Tier 3 oil. All base prices will be adjusted for inflation and the adjusted base price for Tier 3 oil will receive an additional adjustment of 2% per year.

The tax rates that will be applied to the windfall profit are 70% for Tier 1 oil, 60% for Tier 2 oil, and 30% for Tier 3 oil. However, producers who qualify as *independent producers* are permitted reduced rates on 1,000 barrels per day on their combined production of Tier 1 and Tier 2 oil. These reduced rates are 50% for Tier 1 oil production and 30% for Tier 2 oil production.

The Act exempts oil produced by state and local governments, certain charitable medical facilities and educational institutions, as well as Indian tribes and Indians over whom the United States exercises trust responsibilities. Also exempted is most oil produced in Alaska other than from the Sadlerochit Reservoir and certain oil used to finance investments in tertiary recovery projects.

The entire windfall profit tax phases out over a 33-month period after the later of December 31, 1987, or when the cumulative revenues raised by the windfall profit tax reach $227.3 billion. However, in any event, the phaseout will begin no later than January 1991. The tax applies beginning with production after February 29, 1980.

A Technical Analysis of the Windfall Profit Tax

In General

The windfall profit tax is an excise, or severance, tax on domestic oil producers or royalty owners, which is determined by multiplying the windfall profit tax rate by the *windfall profit*. The amount of the tax depends on the category of oil, the identity of the producer, and other factors. Furthermore, certain types of oil are exempted from the tax, and the tax, in certain cases, is specifically limited by reference to the taxable income produced.

The Definition of the Windfall Profit

The *windfall profit* with respect to a barrel of taxable crude oil is the excess of (1) the *removal price* of a barrel of oil over (2) the *adjusted base price* plus (3) the *severance tax adjustment* with respect to such barrel.

The Removal Price

The *removal price* usually equals the sales price of the barrel of oil. However, when oil is removed from the premises prior to sale, or when refining is begun prior to the oil's removal from the premises, the removal price equals the constructive sales price used in determining gross income from the property for percentage depletion purposes.

Sales of crude oil between related persons are subject to the determination of a constructive sales price as described above. Persons are considered to be related if either Section 267 or Section 707(b) of the Internal Revenue Code of 1954 (Code) operates to disallow losses on exchanges between them. Related persons also include members of the same controlled group of corporations under Section 1563(a) of the Code, except that a *more-than-50%* test is substituted for the *at-least-80%* test in determining common ownership of voting control or value.

The Adjusted Base Price

The *adjusted base price* for a barrel of oil depends upon its classification in one of three tiers:

Category	Base Price*
Tier 1	$12.81
Tier 2	15.20
Tier 3	16.55

The base prices of all of the categories of oil are to be adjusted by an inflation factor. The inflation adjustment is to be computed by using the Gross National Product (GNP) deflator, which measures inflation in domestically produced goods and services. The inflation adjustment for Tier 1 and Tier 2 oil for any calendar

* The adjusted base prices set out above are averages and will be adjusted to reflect quality and location differentials. These adjustments will be made on a field-by-field basis, considering the grade and quality of oil in each field. A special interim rule for Tier 2 and Tier 3 oil has been provided for months prior to October 1980.

quarter would be the percentage by which the GNP deflator for the second preceding calendar quarter exceeds the GNP deflator for the second calendar quarter of 1979. The first adjustment under this method would occur for the first quarter of 1980. The revisions of the price deflator become available in the third week of the second month following the close of the quarter and it is to be used in all cases in determining the inflation adjustment.

The inflation adjustment for Tier 3 oil, which includes newly discovered oil, is computed in the same manner as outlined above for Tier 1 and Tier 2 oil. However, in the case of Tier 3 oil, an additional 2% annual *kicker* adjustment is allowed. This adjustment is intended to provide an additional incentive for producers to explore for and develop Tier 3 oil. The 2% increase is spread ratably through the year on the quarterly adjustments for inflation. The *kicker* would amount to an additional 0.5% over the quarterly adjustments for inflation, compounded quarterly.

The Severance Tax Adjustment

The *severance tax adjustment* for a barrel of oil equals the state severance or production tax imposed on the excess of sales price of a barrel of oil over the adjusted base price for that barrel. To discourage states from imposing additional severance taxes only on the additional sales price resulting from crude oil price decontrol, state tax increases after March 1979 would be only deductible if they apply equally to the entire price of oil. In any event, the severance tax adjustment will not be available for taxes levied at rates in excess of 15%.

Example of the Windfall Profit Computation

The computation of the *windfall profit* is illustrated by the following example. Assume a producer sells a barrel of Tier 1 oil for $30.00 and a state severance tax is imposed at the rate of 10%. The windfall profit of $15.47 is computed as follows:

Removal Price		$ 30.00
Less: Adjusted base price	($12.81)	
Severance tax adjustment [10% ($30.00 — $12.81)]	(1.72)	(14.53)
Windfall Profit		$ 15.47

The Categories of Oil

The House and Senate versions of the bill created several categories or tiers of oil which resulted in different treatment and different tax rates. In an attempt at simplification, the Conference Committee agreed to merge the separate categories of oil that had been created under both the Senate and the House versions of the bill into three tiers as well as to effect other modifications. As a result, the final categories of oil are as follows:

1. *Tier 1 Oil*

   Tier 1 oil includes the following categories of oil:

   - Already flowing oil—a category consisting basically of all oil produced from properties where production began prior to 1979. (Excluded from this category would be oil production from properties where production began prior to 1979 that would qualify as incremental and front-end tertiary oil, stripper oil, or heavy oil.)
   - Oil production from the Sadlerochit Reservoir in Alaska.
   - Production from marginal properties.
   - Production from high water-cut properties.

2. *Tier 2 Oil*

Tier 2 oil includes stripper oil production and oil produced from a National Petroleum Reserve in which the United States has an economic interest.

Stripper oil is oil produced from stripper well properties, i.e., those properties where the average daily production per well during any consecutive 12-month period after 1972 has been 10 barrels or less per day. To qualify for the stripper oil category, a property must be operated in accordance with recognized conservation practices and at its *maximum* feasible rate of production. Once a property qualifies for the stripper oil category, it retains that category regardless of any future increases in the production level.

3. *Tier 3 Oil*

Tier 3 oil includes newly discovered oil, incremental tertiary oil, and heavy oil.

a. *Newly Discovered Oil*

Newly discovered oil is defined as oil which was sold after May 31, 1979, *and* that was produced from either (i) an outer continental shelf area for which the lease was entered into on or after January 1, 1979, and from which there was no production in calendar year 1978, or (ii) an onshore property from which no crude oil was produced in calendar year 1978.

It appears that oil production from a property which was developed prior to 1978 but from which there was no production in 1978 would qualify as newly discovered oil. This would eliminate the *behind the pipe* exclusion from the newly discovered oil category which was proposed by the House. This *behind the pipe* exclusion would have served to remove from the newly discovered oil category production on proven properties where there had been no commercial production prior to 1979.

Production from a property transferred after 1978 does not qualify as newly discovered oil unless production from the property prior to the transfer would have qualified as newly discovered oil.

b. *Heavy Oil*

Heavy oil is defined as oil with a specific gravity of 16° or less (corrected to 60° Fahrenheit) for the last month prior to July 1979 for which the property had production, or which has such a specific gravity in the taxable period.

If a portion of a property is transferred after 1978, the production from the transferred portion of the property does not qualify as heavy oil after the transfer unless it qualified as heavy oil in the absence of the transfer. This is intended to prevent a taxpayer from obtaining the more favorable Tier 3 windfall tax rate through the acquisition of a portion of a property.

c. *Incremental Tertiary Oil*

Incremental tertiary oil is oil production from a project area on which an operator (the person primarily responsible for the management of the property) utilizes a qualified tertiary recovery method to increase production to a level in excess of the statutory base level for the project. The base level is the average daily amount of oil removed from the project area during the six-month period ending March 31, 1979, reduced by a decline curve, i.e., the sum of 1% for each post-1978 month up to the month following the project beginning date and 2.5% for each subsequent month. The amount of production below the base level as reduced by the decline curve is taxed in its appropriate category, i.e., already flowing oil, stripper oil, newly discovered oil, etc. The incremental tertiary oil category is the only windfall profit category for which it is necessary to establish base production control levels and to determine the production in excess of the base production control level as adjusted for the statutory decline curves.

In order for a project to qualify production from a property for incremental tertiary oil status, the operator must show that the project utilized one or more of the following tertiary recovery methods:

- Miscible fluid displacement
- Steam drive injection
- Microemulsion or miscellar emulsion flooding
- In situ combustion
- Polymer augmented flooding
- Cyclic steam injection
- Alkaline or caustic flooding
- Carbon dioxide augmented water flooding
- Immiscible carbon dioxide displacement
- Any other method approved by the Secretary of the Treasury.

In addition, the operator must be able to certify that the recovery methods employed are applied in accordance with sound engineering principles and could reasonably be expected to result in a significant increase in the amount of oil that ultimately will be recovered from the property or the project area above the amount that reasonably could be expected to be recovered in the absence of the project. Also, the operator must establish that the project's beginning date was after May 1979 and submit to the Secretary of the Treasury any information, forms, and certification as may be required by subsequent regulations. As an alternative to this self-certification procedure, operators may have a competent governmental body certify the tertiary project in advance. The advance certification would establish that the project meets all of the requirements for qualification.

If a qualified tertiary recovery project affected only a portion of the property, a property would have to be segregated into more than one property. The portion of the property affected by the project must be segregated from the unaffected portion of the property and the base level of production allocated between the two properties. Similarly, a project affecting more than one property necessitates the allocation of the base level production for the project to all of the affected properties. A significant expansion of a preexisting tertiary recovery project also requires a separate property allocation.

The operator must keep records to establish the beginning date of the project, which is normally the point at which the tertiary method significantly affected the reservoir. This requires use of the relevant tertiary process for a significant period of time to establish that it was not merely operated on a pilot or test basis. As a result, the beginning date of the project could be a few months before any significant increase in production was in evidence.

If the tertiary project merely accelerates the rate of recovery of oil and does not increase the total amount of oil to be recovered from the project area, production under that project does not qualify as incremental tertiary oil. It may be possible for the operator to establish that the tertiary project actually enhanced the total recovery of oil even though there was no evidence of increased rate of production. In this case, it would be necessary for the operator to establish that the tertiary project actually reduced the decline in production significantly below what it would have been in absence of the project.

In determining which barrels of oil will be treated as incremental tertiary production, the operator must first determine under which tier the oil would be classified in the absence of special treatment for the incremental tertiary production. If, absent the special treatment for incremental tertiary production, the oil production from the property would fall into more than one category, the amount of production which will be treated as incremental tertiary production must come pro rata from each category of oil. The specific barrels of production treated as incremental tertiary production will come from each category of production in the order of its removal price. Thus, the first barrel treated as incremental tertiary production will be the barrel with the highest selling price.

The Tax Rates

The tax rate on the windfall profit depends on both the identity of the producer and the category of oil involved. Production arising from a royalty interest or other nonoperating interests is not eligible to receive the special reduced rates which have been granted to *independent producers*. Only production arising from working interests owned by *independent producers* qualifies for the reduced rate treatment. The special rules governing *independent producers* are discussed later in this article.

The following table sets forth the windfall profit tax rates and shows the substantial tax savings available to *independent producers* for Tier 1 and 2 oil:

	Tax Rates	
Category	Integrated Oil Companies and Royalty Owners	Independent* Producers
Tier 1 Oil (already flowing oil)	70%	50%
Tier 2 Oil (stripper oil)	60%	30%
Tier 3 Oil (newly discovered, etc.)	30%	30%

* These reduced rates apply to the first 1,000 barrels per day of average daily production of Tier 1 and Tier 2 oil. Production in excess of 1,000 barrels per day is subject to the rates applicable to integrated oil companies and royalty owners.

The Limitation Based on Net Income

The windfall profit on a barrel of oil cannot exceed 90% of the net income attributable to such barrel. The net income attributable to a barrel of oil is determined for each taxable year by dividing the taxable income from the property, which is attributable to taxable oil, by the number of barrels of that oil produced from the property during the taxable year. The taxable income from the property is gross income less all applicable expenses other than percentage depletion, intangible drilling costs (other than cost of drilling a nonproductive well) and the windfall profit tax. If a property produces both oil and gas, the taxable income from the property must be allocated between the oil and gas production in proportion to the gross income of each during the taxable year.

For federal income tax purposes, a deduction for the cost of tertiary injectants is now permitted under a provision of the Act which is discussed later in this article. However, for purposes of computing the net income limitation on the windfall profit, a producer may elect to capitalize the cost of tertiary injectants and recover it over its effective life. This allows producers to spread the cost of tertiary injectants over a number of taxable periods, better enabling them to utilize the cost of the injectants as a reduction of the windfall profit.

The property unit used to determine the net income limitation is the property unit as defined in Section 614 of the Code, rather than the definition of the property unit that is used for price control purposes. Therefore, in the absence of valid separate property elections under Section 614 of the Code, it appears that the net income limitation computation could be made on a property unit (as defined in Section 614) that included oil that was priced under the pricing regulations in different categories.

In computing the net income limitation, a producer is allowed to deduct cost depletion on a property. The cost depletion computation is based on the assumption that all intangible drilling costs were capitalized and taken into account and that only cost depletion was deducted with respect to that property for all taxable periods. This hypothetical cost depletion computation can be made even if the producer has actually deducted percentage depletion with respect to the property. A producer may deduct the actual cost depletion if intangible drilling costs are capitalized for income tax purposes.

Effect of Property Transfers on the Limitation

If a proven oil or gas property is transferred after 1978, there is a special rule for determining the net income limitation. This special rule is retroactive since it presumably encompasses transfers of proven oil and gas properties effected during 1979 and 1980 prior to the effective date of the Act. *Proven properties* has the same meaning that it has under the percentage depletion rules in Section 613A(c)(9) of the Code and related proposed regulations.

Under the special rule for post-1978 transfers, transferees are allowed to compute their imputed cost depletion deduction on only those costs incurred during periods after the transfer of the property. However, transferees would also be allowed to utilize the transferor's remaining undepleted cost basis in the transferred property in addition to their own cost incurred after the transfer when computing imputed cost depletion. Thus, the consideration paid by transferees in post-1978 transfers *would not* be included in the basis when computing imputed cost depletion. For the foregoing purposes, a transfer includes any transfer of an economic interest in a property including leases, subleases and a transfer of an interest in a partnership or a trust.

Production Payments

If a property is burdened by a production payment, the gross income from the property used to discharge the production payment liability is included in the gross income of both the producer (creator of the production payment) and the owner of the production payment for purposes of computing the taxable income limit.

Example of the Net Income Limitation

The following example illustrates the effect of the 90% of net income limitation. In this example (1) intangible drilling and development costs incurred in prior years were $130,000 and in the taxable year, 15% of the estimated reserves of the property were produced, resulting in a hypothetical depletion of the intangible drilling and development costs of $19,500; (2) 1,000 barrels of Tier 1 oil were produced from the property at a gross sales price of $26 per barrel; and (3) state severance taxes (5% rate) were $1,300 and operating expenses were $3,000. The limitation is calculated as follows:

Net Income Computation:		
Gross income from property (1,000 barrels at $26)		$26,000.00
Less: Severance taxes	($ 1,300.00)	
Operating expenses	(3,000.00)	
Cost depletion assuming IDC's were capitalized	(19,500.00)	(23,800.00)
Net Income		$ 2,200.00
Windfall Profit Computation:		
Gross income		$26,000.00
Less: Adjusted base price ($12.81 per barrel)	($12,810.00)	
Severance tax adjustment [($26,000—$12,810) x 5%]	(659.50)	(13,469.50)
Windfall Profit:		$12,530.50
Net Income Limit on Windfall Profit: (90% x $2,200)		$ 1,980.00
Windfall Profit Tax: (70% x $1,980)		$ 1,386.00

The above example illustrates the importance of making the 90% of net income limitation calculation for each property.

Impact of Post-1978 Property Transfers

Generally, the classification of production from a property that was transferred after 1978 is determined in part by reference to its classification in the hands of the transferor-producer. For example, production from a property would not qualify as newly discovered oil or heavy oil after the transfer unless the property so qualified prior to the transfer. However, if a producer implemented a qualified tertiary recovery project on property transferred after 1978, the production from the property could qualify as incremental tertiary oil subsequent to the transfer.

Once the production from a property has qualified as stripper oil, it retains that category regardless of any future increase in the level of its production. Therefore, it appears that production qualifying as stripper oil production property prior to the transfer would continue to so qualify after the transfer in the hands of the transferee.

A special transfer provision was also enacted to reduce the attractiveness of property transfers from integrated oil companies to *independent producers* made after December 31, 1979. Under this special provision, the portion of the first 1,000 barrels of an independent producer's production per day attributable to a property interest owned by an integrated oil company on December 31, 1979, does not qualify for the reduced rates.

Exemption From the Windfall Profit Tax

The Act exempts from the windfall profit tax production owned by certain types of producers and production from certain geographical areas.

Front-End Tertiary Oil

Oil that the Department of Energy deregulates as front-end tertiary oil is generally exempt from the windfall profit tax if the project is controlled by producers who are *independent producers* for the fourth quarter of 1979. For these projects, all of the front-end tertiary oil deregulated in connection with the project (including any produced by a major company) is exempt with two exceptions. First, oil which could have been released from crude oil price controls under any other part of the Department of Energy pricing regulations cannot qualify for this exemption. Second, oil deregulated to finance prepaid expenses cannot qualify.

If the tertiary project for which front-end oil is being deregulated is controlled by a major oil company, all front-end tertiary oil related to that project is subject to tax (including any produced by an *independent producer*). Tax refunds are available for the windfall profit tax paid on the front-end tertiary oil to the extent the producers of the front-end tertiary oil incur qualifying expenditures in excess of the amount recouped under the front-end program.

The special exemption for front-end tertiary oil applies only with respect to oil which could *not* have been released from price controls under any other provision, and it terminates on September 30, 1981.

State-Owned Property Interests

The production from an economic interest in crude oil owned by a state or its political subdivisions, or by any of their agencies or instrumentalities, including an educational institution, is exempt if all of the net income received pursuant to such interest is dedicated to public education or any other public purpose. Ownership of a partial interest in a property by an exempt state or political subdivision thereof would not exempt the entire production from the property, only that production owned by the exempt taxpayer.

Production from an economic interest in a property owned by charitable medical facilities or educational institutions is also exempt from the windfall profit tax to the extent that the organization owned that economic interest on January 21, 1980. This exemption also applies to oil produced from an interest owned by a church on January 21, 1980, if the church, prior to January 22, 1980, had taken an appropriate official action to dedicate the net proceeds from the production of the property to the support of a charitable medical facility or an educational institution.

Indian-Owned Interests

Production from economic interests owned on January 21, 1980, by certain Indian tribes, tribal organizations, individual Indians over whom the United States exercises trust responsibilities, and production received by Indian tribes and individual Indians from Tribal Trust Lands is exempt from the tax. Exempt oil from Indian-owned interests also includes oil produced before 1992 by a native corporation organized under the Alaskan Native Claims Settlement Act from interests held by such corporation.

This provision exempts the production from economic interests owned by the qualified Indian tribe. It does not exempt the entire production from a property.

Alaskan Oil

Oil produced north of the Arctic Circle is exempt from the tax, as is any oil produced from a well located north of the Alaskan-Aleutian mountain range and more than 75 miles from the Alaskan pipeline. However, oil produced from the Sadlerochit Reservoir is Tier 1 oil and is subject to the tax.

Administrative Provisions

The Act provides that the first purchaser (normally a refiner) of the crude oil is responsible for (1) collecting the tax by withholding it from the purchase price, (2) depositing the tax, and (3) filing quarterly tax returns with respect to the windfall profit tax. In the event that the producer processes its own oil production, the producer is required to deposit the tax due on its own production and to file quarterly tax returns in the same manner as if it were the first purchaser.

Withholding and Deposit Requirements

Unless the operator, i.e., the person responsible for the management of the oil production, and the first purchaser elect to have the operator assume the first purchaser's responsibilities, the first purchaser is required to pay over withheld windfall profit taxes. The depository requirements are different for integrated oil companies and for independent refiners. Integrated oil companies are required to make estimated deposits of the tax semimonthly. Integrated oil companies are those companies that are ineligible for percentage depletion under Section 613A of the Code, i.e., companies with retailing and refining activities in excess of the limitations set forth in that section. Generally, nonintegrated oil companies who are first purchasers are required to make deposits of the tax within 45 days after the end of the month of purchase.

Independent refiners would be allowed to make deposits of the tax up to as much as 60 days after the end of the month of purchase if the oil is purchased pursuant to a delayed payment contract under which the refiner has more than 45 days from the end of the month of purchase to pay for the oil. If an independent refiner did not purchase its oil under a delayed payment contract as set out above, it would be required to make deposits of the withheld tax within 45 days after the end of the month of purchase.

An *independent refiner* is a refiner who (a) obtained, directly or indirectly, in the preceding taxable period, more than 70% of its refinery input of domestic crude oil (or 70% of its refinery input of domestic and imported crude oil), from producers who do not control, and are not controlled by, and are not under common control with, such refiner; and (b) marketed or distributed in such preceding period, and continues to market or distribute, a substantial volume of its refined gasoline through branded, independent marketers or nonbranded, independent marketers.

Information to Be Provided to First Purchaser

The operator must certify and provide certain information to the first purchaser to permit the computation of the amount to be withheld. If the first purchaser withholds an incorrect amount of tax, adjustments in withholding are required to correct the aggregate amount withheld on all oil purchased by that purchaser from that producer on oil removed during that calendar year. However, the amount of any mandatory withholding adjustment may not exceed the amount of the windfall profit on any barrel of oil. These required withholding adjustments only apply to transactions between the same purchaser and producer. In addition to mandatory adjustments, a producer may voluntarily authorize any purchaser to withhold additional amounts with respect to oil removed later in the calendar year to correct earlier withholding errors.

The information is required to be furnished to the first purchaser at such time and in such manner as prescribed by regulations to be issued by the Secretary of the Treasury. This includes the following:

- The tax tier or category into which the production falls;
- The adjusted base price;
- For incremental tertiary production, the property's base production control level, and the amount of incremental tertiary production subject to the reduced rate;
- A copy of any certification furnished to the operator by the producer with respect to whether such oil is exempt oil or *independent producer* oil;
- The amount of such oil;
- Any other information which the Secretary of the Treasury prescribes by regulations.

The Secretary of the Treasury may by regulations provide that if the operator and purchaser agree, the operator will be relieved of the duty of furnishing some or all of the information required above.

There is no specific requirement for either the operator or the first purchaser to furnish information to the producer, except as noted in the discussion below on return requirements. However, the Act grants the Secretary of the Treasury authority to require appropriate exchanges of information consistent with the specific provisions of the windfall profit tax.

When withholding is required, the producer will have no information or deposit requirements with respect to the windfall profit tax. However, when withholding is not required, producers are required to deposit the tax due on their own production as if they were first purchasers. In other words, integrated oil companies make deposits of their estimated tax liability semi-monthly and all other producers deposit the tax within 45 days after the month of removal.

Return Requirements

The first purchaser is required to file quarterly returns showing the amount of tax withheld, together with any other information required under regulations to be issued by the Secretary of the Treasury. The quarterly tax returns are due by the last day of the second month following the end of the quarter. In the quarterly return for the fourth calendar quarter, the first purchaser must provide a producer-by-producer summary of the amount of oil purchased for the year, the windfall profit tax withheld, and the amounts of tax deposited.

The first purchaser will provide each producer with information indicating the amounts of oil purchased and the tax withheld thereon. In the case of oil purchased from a partnership, the purchaser will provide this information with respect to the partnership's production, and the partnership is required on its return to provide information with respect to each partner's share of the production.

Refunds of Overpayments

When an overpayment of the windfall profit tax results from (1) a misclassification of the category of oil; (2) the net income limitation; (3) a withholding at improperly applied rates; or (4) any other reason, the producer may file a claim for refund of the overpayment. In the alternative, an excess withholding with respect to a producer is creditable for federal income tax purposes. In this case, the Secretary of the Treasury will issue regulations setting forth procedures for crediting overpayments against a federal income tax liability.

Generally, the claim for refund may be filed by the producer within three years from the time the return was filed, or two years from the time the tax was paid, whichever of such periods expires later, or if no return was filed by the producer, within two years from the time the tax was paid. In the case of oil subject to withholding, the producer is deemed to have paid, on the last day of February of the year following that in which the oil was removed, the amount of tax withheld by the purchaser.

The above rule is similar to the rule applicable to claiming refunds of income taxes. However, for windfall profit tax purposes, special rules have been added. First, in the case of oil subject to withholding for which no return is required to be filed by the producer, the statute of limitations for purposes of claiming a refund runs with respect to the producer's annual income tax return for the taxable year in which the calendar year of the oil's removal ends. Second, in the event that the Department of Energy makes a final determination reclassifying oil for price control purposes, a claim for refund for any overpayment attributable to such reclassification may be filed within one year from the date on which the reclassification becomes effective.

Refunds of Overpayments

Generally, the Internal Revenue Service can assess additional taxes within three years after the windfall profit tax return was filed. In the case of a producer who is not required to file a return, the return will be deemed to be the producer's income tax return for the taxable year in which ends the calendar year of the oil's removal from the premises. However, if, for price control purposes, a property is reclassified from one category of oil to another and additional tax with respect to that property is due, the tax may be assessed at any time before one year after the date on which the reclassification becomes effective.

Effective Date and Termination of the Tax

The tax applies to oil produced after February 29, 1980. The tax will phase out over a 33-month period starting in January 1988, or one month after the month for which the Secretary of the Treasury estimates that $227.3 billion has been raised by the tax, whichever is later. Even if $227.3 billion has not been raised, the phaseout will begin on January 1, 1991.

Taxation of the Independent Producer

In General

Since *independent producers* account for a substantial portion of domestic exploratory drilling in the United States, Congress concluded that special consideration should be given to these producers so as to encourage them to further increase their drilling activities. To accomplish this, the Act provides for reduced tax rates on the first 1,000 barrels per day of production incurred by an *independent producer* with respect to Tier 1 and Tier 2 oil. The application of these reduced rates and related problems are considered below.

The Definition of an Independent Producer

Independent producers include all taxpayers other than integrated oil companies. For windfall profit tax purposes, the term *integrated oil company* has the same meaning as it has for the purposes of the percentage depletion rules of Section 613A of the Code, except that the rules are applied on a quarterly rather than annual basis. Under those rules, a taxpayer is denied the percentage depletion deduction if the taxpayer was a *retailer* or a *refiner*. A *retailer* is defined as any taxpayer who directly, or through related persons, sells oil or natural gas or any product derived from oil or natural gas directly or indirectly through retail outlets. The taxpayer is not considered to be a retailer if the combined sales of oil and natural gas or products derived therefrom do not exceed $1,250,000 in a taxable quarter.

A *refiner* is defined as any taxpayer engaged in the refining of crude oil directly or indirectly and has total refinery runs exceeding 50,000 barrels on any day in the taxable year.

To qualify as an *independent producer,* a producer must take into account the retailing and refinery activities of certain related persons.

Rates of Taxation

The rate applicable to *independent producers* on Tier 1 oil is 50% of the windfall profit compared to the 70% rate applicable to royalty owners and integrated oil companies. The rate to be applied to Tier 2 oil (stripper production) is 30% for the *independent producer,* rather than the 60% rate imposed on integrated oil companies and royalty owners. On Tier 3 oil, the *independent producer* is taxed at the same 30% rate applicable to integrated oil companies and royalty owners.

How the Reduced Rates Are Applied

The special reduced rates are applied to the first 1,000 barrels of production classified as Tier 1 oil and Tier 2 oil. If the *independent producer's* total production exceeds 1,000 barrels of Tier 1 and Tier 2 oil per day, the 1,000-barrels-per-day limitation must be apportioned between the two categories on the basis of relative barrel production, and the amount in excess of 1,000 barrels per day for each class is subject to the higher rate categories. This calculation is made on a quarterly basis.

The allocation of the 1,000-barrels-per-day limitation is explained by the following example. An *independent producer* has 1,200 barrels per day of production attributable to Tier 1 and Tier 2 oil. Nine hundred barrels of Tier 1 oil are produced and 300 barrels of Tier 2 oil are produced. Each category would be allocated 10/12 or (1000/1200) to the lower rate. Thus, 750 barrels of Tier 1 oil would be taxed at the *independent producer's* reduced rate of 50% and 250 barrels of Tier 2 oil would be taxed at the *independent producer's* reduced rate of 30%. The remaining oil would be taxed at the higher rate in each category.

Related *independent producers* are limited to a single 1,000 barrels per day of production subject to the reduced rates. This 1,000-barrels-per-day limitation must be allocated among the related producers in proportion to their respective oil production during the applicable period. The related persons who share a single 1,000-barrels-per-day limitation include the following:

(1) A parent and subsidiary corporate group in which more than 50% of the stock is owned by the common parent organization;

(2) Business entities under common control, including corporations, trusts, and estates, if 50% or more of the beneficial interest is owned by the same or related persons;

(3) Certain family members, including an individual's spouse and minor child; and

(4) Family members and one or more corporations, trusts, or estates, in which such family members own 50% or more of the beneficial interest.

The Interests Which Qualify for Reduced Rates

The reduced rates apply only to working interests that were held on January 1, 1980, by persons qualifying as *independent producers.* Also, the reduced rates are not available for production from properties transferred after 1979 if the transferor is an integrated oil company, a royalty owner, or a producer whose production at any time between 1979 and the date of transfer exceeded 1,000 barrels a day. Even though a royalty owner might be defined as an *independent producer,* the special rates allowed to an *independent producer* are not allowable on production attributable to those royalties. Royalty owners include any owners of economic interests in oil properties that are defined as royalties for income tax purposes. This will include owners of overriding royalties (royalties which are paid out of working interests in properties), net profits interests, and royalties paid to landowners. This effectively penalizes taxpayers engaged in the oil and gas business who do not normally participate in working interests. Owners of overriding royalties in existence on January 1, 1980, which convert to working interests may qualify for reduced rates; however, they qualify only from the time that such interests convert into working interests pursuant to contracts in existence on February 20, 1980.

The transfer rules disallowing special rates to *independent producers* for transfers from integrated oil companies could have an especially adverse effect on some *independent producers.* These rules apparently also apply to carried interests which are transferred to *independent producers* after 1979, as a result of contractual payout provisions. For example, an *independent producer* farmed out his interest in a property to an integrated oil company prior to 1979. The property was drilled and producing prior to December 31, 1978. Under the farmout agreement, the integrated oil company is to own the property until it reaches payout, at which time the *independent producer* is to receive a 25% working interest in the property. If the payout of the well occurs after 1979, the *independent producer* is apparently required to pay a higher windfall profit tax rate for the production from the property, since the transfer could be treated as a disqualifying transfer from an integrated oil company.

Newly Discovered Oil

There is no special rate for *independent producers'* Tier 3 oil, which includes newly discovered oil. Production from transferred property does not qualify as newly discovered oil unless it would have been so classified if the property had not been transferred. Therefore, prospective purchasers of oil properties should ascertain before acquiring a property that production from the property has qualified as newly discovered oil.

How the Windfall Profit Tax Affects Partnerships and Royalty Owners

Partnerships

Partnerships are subject to special rules under the windfall profit tax that apply to the following:

(1) The production which qualifies for the reduced tax rates.

(2) The 90% of net income limitation.

The special rules are provided because the production amount is applied at the partner level rather than at the partnership level, and the net income limitation is applied at the partnership level.

Qualified Production

The amount of the production of the partnership that qualifies for the reduced tax rates must first be allocated between eligible and noneligible partners. Eligible partners are those partners who qualify as *independent producers.* All others are noneligible partners. The allocation between eligible partners and noneligible partners is based on the ratio that the interests of the noneligible partners in the production bear to the interests of all partners. Once the qualified production of the eligible partners has been determined, it is allocated to them in the proportion that their individual partnership interest bears to the total partnership interests of all eligible partners.

The eligible partners are treated as having produced and paid the windfall profit tax on their individual share of the qualified partnership production. Therefore, the partners are individually responsible for filing claims for refund due to excess withholding.

In order for a partner to file a claim for refund, the partnership must supply the partners with a substantial amount of information. The information supplied to the partner must cover the qualified production in addition to the 90% of net income limitation, which is discussed below. The partnership should consider providing the partners, as part of this information, with two *as if* calculations based on two assumptions: one calculation would be based on the premise that the partner is eligible for the *independent producer* reduced rates, and the second on the premise that the partner is not eligible for the reduced rates. These calculations would provide a partner with the starting point from which any overpayment or underpayment attributable to his partnership interest could be determined.

90% of Net Income Limitation

For partnerships, the Report of the Senate Finance Committee states that the determination of the 90% of net income limitation is made at the partnership level. In making the determination at the partnership level, it is not clear whether any disproportionate sharing of revenue and expenses by the partners can be considered. For example, in limited partnerships, it is common for 99 to 100% of the intangible drilling and development costs attributable to the property to be allocated to the limited partners. On the other hand, the tangible costs, i.e., the leasehold and equipment costs, are allocated to the general partner. These tangible costs carry with them depreciation expense and regular cost depletion attributable to these properties. In other partnership situations, certain partners may be allocated a disproportionate share of intangible drilling and development costs (e.g., in *promoted interests* certain partners pay and are allocated more intangible drilling and development costs than are attributable to their permanent interests).

The determination of the net income limitation at the partnership level is inconsistent with other provisions affecting partnerships, which require computations to be made at the partner's level. If the net income limitation is applied at the partnership level, it may still be possible to recognize the disproportionate sharing of revenue and expenses by the partners through a provision in the partnership agreement. However, it is anticipated that future regulations will address the manner in which the computation is to be made, including whether a disproportionate sharing of revenue and expenses can be recognized in the determination of the net income limitation.

Royalty Owners

Generally, royalty owners are subject to the provisions of the windfall profit tax in the same manner as integrated oil companies. Royalty owners include any owners of economic interests in oil properties that are defined as royalties for income tax purposes. This includes landowner royalties, overriding royalties and net profits interests. The following tax rates will apply to royalty owners:

Category	Rate
Tier 1 Oil	70%
Tier 2 Oil	60%
Tier 3 Oil	30%

The 90% of net income limitation also applies to royalty owners; however, it is unlikely that the limitation could benefit many royalty owners. The reduced rates on the first 1,000 barrels per day production of Tier 1 and Tier 2 oil that is available to *independent producers* do not apply to royalty owners.

The Act provides one benefit to royalty owners that is not available to integrated oil companies. For those royalty owners who qualify for the percentage depletion deduction, that deduction is computed by royalty owners on the full price of the oil *including* the windfall profit element. However, the windfall profit tax is taken into account in determining the 50% of net income limitation with respect to percentage depletion. For most royalty owners, the limitation should not limit the depletion expense computed at 22% of gross income which includes the windfall profit element. Therefore, the ability to claim the percentage depletion on the full price of oil should help to lessen the impact of the windfall profit tax for the royalty owner in comparison to the integrated oil companies, which do not qualify for percentage depletion.

Income Tax Provisions

In addition to the windfall profit tax, the Act contains a number of income tax provisions unrelated to oil production. However, Congress did enact three income tax provisions related to oil production.

The Deduction for Tertiary Injectant Costs

The Act allows a taxpayer a deduction in any taxable year for the cost of the taxpayer's qualified tertiary injectants used during the taxable year. The term *qualified tertiary injectant expenses* includes any cost paid or incurred during the taxable year for any tertiary injectant (other than a hydrocarbon injectant that is recoverable) that is used as a part of a tertiary recovery process. The term *hydrocarbon injectant* includes natural gas, crude oil, and any other injectant consisting of *more* than an insignificant amount of natural gas or crude oil. Any portion of a hydrocarbon injectant that is not a hydrocarbon is not treated as a hydrocarbon injectant.

A deduction is not available for any cost that is subject to the intangible drilling costs election under Section 263 of the Code, or to any other expenditure which otherwise is deductible under the Code. Therefore, any tertiary injectant cost or expense (hydrocarbon or otherwise) necessary for the preparation of wells for production that qualifies as an intangible drilling and development cost is currently deductible only if the taxpayer has made the election under Section 263 of the Code to deduct these costs. This election extends to any intangible drilling costs incurred in drilling nonproductive injection wells necessary for the primary development of a property.

The deduction of tertiary injectant costs under the Act is *not* elective. Also, the deduction is applicable to expenditures made after December 31, 1979.

In the event of the disposition of a property on which expenses have been claimed for tertiary injectant costs, the amount of the expenses deducted are subject to recapture as ordinary income under Section 1245 of the Code to the extent of any gain recognized on the disposition. However, tertiary injectant costs deducted under the Act are not considered to be preference items for purposes of the 15% add-on minimum tax.

LIFO Inventory Reductions

A new provision affects the recognition of LIFO inventory profits in the event that LIFO inventories are reduced and not currently replaced. Under the Act, at the taxpayer's election, the taxes paid on these LIFO profits may be refunded if the inventory is sold and not currently replaced due to any Department of Energy regulation or request with respect to energy supplies, or a major interruption of foreign trade. To obtain the refund, the taxpayer must replace the inventory within three years, or such shorter period as specified by the Secretary of the Treasury. This provision is effective for tax years ending after October 31, 1979.

Percentage Depletion Rules

Taxpayers qualifying for percentage depletion under the *independent producers* and royalty owners exemption will be allowed to calculate depletion using the full sales price before the application of the windfall profit tax. All other limitations would, of course, apply as before.

Planning for the windfall profits tax

JAMES L. HOUGHTON
Arthur Young & Co.
Tulsa

CONFUSION resulting from initial efforts to implement and administer the complex crude oil "windfall profit" tax continues as the Treasury Department attempts to respond to the lashing by industry representatives in hearings on the proposed regulations (OGJ, Aug. 4, p. 34).

The initial shock of this legislation related to withholding depository requirements. The ambiguity and uncertainty of such basic problems as form of producer certification, base prices, and withholding responsibilities continue to await Treasury's response.

Indeed, if Treasury's response is no more definitive on these problems than the proposed regulation, their ultimate judicial resolution may approach the scheduled date for phaseout of the tax.

While the wait for Treasury drags on, producers are mounting a two-pronged attack. First, several pieces of legislation have been introduced to exempt various levels of production of royalty owners, independent producers, and stripper well oil. Since Senator Long supports certain of these efforts, the possibility of some success must be taken seriously.

Secondly, judicial attacks—apparently aimed primarily at the constitutionality of the Act—led by the IPAA are developing but much slower than had been hoped (OGJ, Aug. 25, p. 51). Only the most optimistic see this as a means of substantive relief.

Rates of tax. What then can oil producers do to effectively counter the impact of the tax?

Certain strategies are immediately apparent.

The windfall profit tax rates are 60% and 70% respectively for Tier 2 oil (stripper well oil) and Tier 1 oil (generally other pre-1979 oil) for other than 1,000 b/d of average production of "independent producer oil." The rates are 30% and 50% for other Tier 1 and Tier 2 oil production.

Taxpayers must therefore attempt to avoid or minimize the amount of Tier 1 and Tier 2 oil production falling into the higher rates. Since the tests for qualifying for "independent producer oil" are made for each calendar quarter, there is a relatively quick economic response to a taxpayer's action.

A producer approaching or exceeding 1,000 b/d of average production of Tier 1 and Tier 2 must evaluate the impact of the higher windfall profit tax rates on any acquisitions of Tier 1 and Tier 2 oil production. To the extent that the acquired Tier 1 and Tier 2 production exceeds 1,000 b/d average production for a calendar quarter, the excess is subject to the higher tax rates.

These adverse tax rate consequences suggest that the producer may want to consider having such an acquisition made by an "unrelated" person such as a less than 50%-owned corporation or an adult child.

All Tier 1 and Tier 2 oil production acquired from a person who is not an independent producer or who is an independent producer but has exceeded the 1,000 b/d average for any calendar quarter ending after Sept. 30, 1979—and ending before the date of sale—is subject to the higher tax rates regardless of the acquiring person's status.

For example, assume that in 1980 a purchaser who had never before been involved in the oil business acquires 100% of the production of an independent producer who averaged 1,100 b/d of Tier 1 and Tier 2 oil production for the calendar quarter ending Dec. 31, 1979. The entire amount of such production would be subject to the higher tax rates even though only the Tier 1 and Tier 2 production in excess of 1,000 b/d would have been subject to the higher rates in the hands of the independent producers.

Since the 1,000-b/d amount is based on calendar quarter production, without regard to sales or the producer's accounting method, there is some confusion in determining the source of the production number. The definition of "qualified production" includes only oil that has been "removed" which suggests that crude oil in lease tanks is to be ignored for this purpose and could further invite "end of the calendar quarter" planning in some cases.

There is a special problem for oil producers who are classified as "retailers" or "refiners" and therefore subject to the higher tax rates on their total production. They must consider the feasibility of curing this tainted status so that up to 1,000 b/d of their existing Tier 1 and Tier 2 production can qualify for the lower rates. In the retailing situation, some persons are of the opinion that this can be done in some circumstances by organizing a holding company for the retailing activities.

The problem can obviously be cured prospectively by disposing of the disqualifying activity to appropriate "unrelated" parties. The windfall profit tax savings may far outweigh any economic benefits from the disqualifying activity.

Net income limitation. The most apparent planning opportunity for minimizing the windfall profit tax is the net income limitation.

In general, the law limits the "windfall profit" against which the appropriate tax rate is applied to 90% of the net income attributable to each barrel.

This computation of net income is made by dividing the net income from the property as defined by the number of barrels of taxable crude oil otherwise taken into account for the year. This computation gives the somewhat incongruous result that every barrel of production from a property for the taxable year has the identical net income regardless of perhaps significant differences in removal price.

This incongruity is most apparent in the case of lower tier oil which is being simultaneously phased to upper tier pricing and finally market level pricing. In such cases there are three quite disparate prices per barrel, but each barrel is deemed to have the identical net income for windfall profit tax purposes. The net effect of this is to generate substantial reductions in the windfall profit tax which would have been assessed on those barrels

Article reprinted courtesy of *Oil & Gas Journal*, 13 October 1980, pp. 141–142

entitled to market level pricing.

This benefit is particularly pronounced in the earlier stages of the phasing out of price controls when a substantial portion of the property's production is lower tier oil.

In a yet-unpublished case study by Robert E. Stathem and Ken L. Keenum of Threshold Development Co., Ft. Worth, the authors conclude that there will be dramatic overwithholding in 1980 on all lower tier oil production (including royalty production).

Since the net income limitation is computed on the basis of the taxpayer's taxable year, it is apparent that there may be opportunities for shifting deductions (and perhaps income) between taxable years in order to maximize the relief afforded by the limitation. In many instances this may require projections that are at best speculative.

Nevertheless, to the extent that a major workover or significant maintenance of equipment, lease roads, etc. can be shifted from a year where there is no windfall profit tax benefit to a year where there is such a benefit, there is a one time opportunity for permanent savings.

In computing net income, the taxpayer is not permitted to deduct intangible drilling costs (exclusive of costs in drilling a non-productive well). Rather, the taxpayer is entitled to deduct the cost depletion which would have been allowable if such costs had been capitalized and taken into account in computing cost depletion. For many taxpayers this information is not readily available and will need to be reconstructed where there may be some future benefit from the net-income limitation.

This problem is further compounded by existing uncertainties in the law regarding the correct classification of certain costs. In reconstructing prior years, it will be to the taxpayer's benefit to maximize the classification of costs to intangible drilling costs vis-a-vis operating expenses due to the prospective net-income limitation benefit of such classification. It seems clear that a prior misclassification should be corrected in reconstructing these costs.

For taxable years subject to the windfall profit tax the taxpayer may be tempted to take a different view of classifying expenditures. If there is immediate benefit from the net-income limitation by classifying an expenditure as an operating expense, such classification would clearly be more desirable than the speculative nature of a future benefit from increased cost depletion.

On the other hand, if there is no present benefit to the operating expense classification, there may be nothing to lose by classifying the expenditure as intangible drilling costs with a corresponding increase in future cost depletion.

The possible adverse tax affect of increasing the tax preference amount relating to intangible drilling costs should also be evaluated before making a final classification decision.

A similar problem or opportunity may be encountered in computing the "cost depletion" on intangible drilling costs for prior years. The more optimistic the recoverable reserves in prior years, the greater the prospective benefit of the cost depletion deduction.

Theoretically the recoverable reserves would be determined at the end of each prior taxable year based upon the facts known at that time and therefore without the benefit of hindsight. This theoretical principle could either help or hurt the taxpayer.

For proven property transfers after 1978 the acquiring person computes his cost depletion using the lower of his basis for cost depletion or the amount of cost depletion the transferor could have claimed. In these cases the transferee will be required to secure the necessary historical data from the transferor or forego any benefit for cost depletion.

This provision eliminates attempts to frustrate the law by selling properties but also has the effect of discouraging certain gifts and tax free transfers. In these latter situations a transferee will not be able to take into consideration the intangible drilling costs incurred by the transferor. Such transaction should be avoided if future net-income limitation benefits are anticipated.

The author . . .

James L. Houghton

James L. Houghton is the lead specialist in oil and gas taxation for Arthur Young & Co. in Tulsa. He joined the tax department of Arthur Young in 1956. In 1963 he transferred to Oklahoma City and in 1966 became a partner in charge of the tax department. Houghton is a CPA (Gold Medal Winner) and a member of the American Institute of CPAs, the Tax Committee of the IPAA, the Oklahoma Society of CPAs, past chairman of the Oklahoma Society's Federal and State Taxation Committee, and a former member of the Advisory Council of the Tax Institute of America. He received a BS in Business Administration from the University of Kansas and passed the Kansas bar examination in June 1954.

In computing net income there is a requirement that expenditures including "general and financial overhead" which may be attributable to mineral properties and to other activities shall be properly apportioned between the activities and further between the mineral properties. It is apparent that for purposes of the income limitation on the windfall tax, it will be advantageous to adopt and support methods of apportionment which minimize allocations to other activities.

For integrated producers who are not entitled to percentage depletion, there is no apparent disincentive to this approach. However for taxpayers entitled to percentage depletion, the additional amount of expense allocated to the mineral properties may have the effect of reducing percentage depletion, which cannot exceed 50% of the taxable income from the property.

Since the net income determination is on a property by property basis the interplay of percentage depletion and the windfall profit tax requires detailed computations.

Obviously, to the extent that decreasing net income reduces the windfall profit tax with no effect on depletion, or where it reduces depletion with no effect on the windfall profit tax, the overhead decision is obvious.

Where there are some properties with each of these situations as well as properties where there is a simultaneous effect on both depletion and the windfall profit tax, the complexity of the interplay of net income on the two items may be overwhelming.

The apportionment decision may be moot since the taxpayer will likely be required to continue apportionment methods previously adopted.

Computation factors. Due to the confusion and wide disparity in interpretations of such items as base price, valid certifications, etc., the producer's first responsibility should be to ascertain the factors used by the first purchaser in computing the tax and reviewing the tax impact of alternate interpretations.

Conclusion. Since the outcome of legislative and judicial efforts to ameliorate the windfall profit tax may be of doubtful benefit, producers should carefully review the problems and opportunities presented in the existing law.

While the complexity of this review is aggravated by the interplay of the tax with percentage depletion and the confining nature of the producer's existing practices, the possible savings resulting from timely educated decisions may be significant. END

Part III

Determination of the Tax

Generally, the removal price is the price at which a barrel of crude oil is sold on the premises from which it was produced. There are exceptions to this general rule for oil removed from the premises before being sold, for sales to related persons, where conversion or manufacture begins before leaving the premises, and for oil consumed on the property.

If the oil is removed from the premises before being sold, a constructive sales price is used. This constructive sales price is generally equivalent to the market or field price of similar grade or quality sold in the area. To determine the constructive sales price, the taxpayer uses the same rules as those for determining gross income from the property for percentage depletion. For sales to related persons (as defined in Sections 103a, b, and c), the sales price cannot be less than the constructive sales price.

If the conversion or manufacturing process begins on the premises, the oil is considered sold at the constructive sales price on the day conversion or manufacture begins. Any oil used on the premises in reinjection or for powering production equipment is not considered sold. However, oil used to power processing or manufacturing equipment is considered sold.

The base price for a barrel of crude oil depends upon the tier in which it is classified. These base prices are adjusted for differences in quality and location. Generally, the base price for Tier I oil is the DOE upper tier ceiling price for May 1979 minus 21¢. For tiers II and III, the base prices are the highest posted price for each barrel of uncontrolled oil of the same grade and quality from the same or a nearby field on December 31, 1979, multiplied by the fraction \$15.20/\$35.00 for Tier II oil and \$16.55/\$35.00 for Tier III oil.

The adjusted base price is adjusted for post-1979 inflation. This adjustment is made by multiplying the base price by the GNP implicit price deflator for the second calendar quarter preceding the quarter for which the adjustment is being calculated divided by the GNP implicit price deflator for the quarter ended June 30, 1979 (which is 163.79):

$$\text{base price} \times \frac{\begin{array}{c}\text{GNP implicit price deflator}\\ \text{for second quarter preceding}\\ \text{the quarter for which}\\ \text{calculation is being made}\end{array}}{163.79}$$

The adjustment for Tier III oil is identical except that the numerator is multiplied by $(1.005)^n$, where n is the number of calendar quarters, including the last quarter of 1979 preceding the quarter for which the calculation is being made. The adjustments to base prices of all tiers is done quarterly, and the IRS generally publishes the inflation adjustment factor a few weeks before the quarter for which the adjustment applies.

NEW DEVELOPMENTS IN

Taxation of oil & gas

EDITED BY BILLY M. MANN, CPA

The Crude Oil Windfall Profit Tax of 1980: How it will affect oil companies

by **FREDRIC J. ATTERMEIER**

The Crude Oil Windfall Profit Tax, enacted after intense consideration in Congress, is an excise tax on domestically produced crude oil which contains many unusual features and will be the focal point for oil company taxation for years ahead. Mr. Attermeier analyzes the tremendous impact of this new law on the operations of oil companies.

THE Crude Oil "Windfall" Profit Tax Act (WPT) of 1980 (P.L. 96-223) was signed into law on 4/2/80 to be retroactively effective to 3/1/80.

Despite its title the WPT is not a "profit" tax. Although it includes a net income limitation, the WPT is in fact an excise tax which has the object of taxing part of the revenues resulting from the phased decontrol of domestic crude oil prices.

Background of "Windfall" Profit Tax

The WPT is an unusual piece of legislation in that it has grafted the complexity of Department of Energy (DOE) price controls onto a piecemeal combination of the excise tax, income tax and administrative provisions of the Code. A rudimentary familiarity with DOE price regulations and the President's program of phased decontrol is essential to an understanding of the Windfall Profit Tax.

Domestic crude oil prices have been controlled by one or another government agency since the Nixon Administration wage-price freeze of 1971. Price controls on other phases of the economy have expired, however, the petroleum industry is still constrained by price controls.

By January 1979 the DOE regulated most domestic crude oil production in three categories:

1. Lower tier oil is derived from properties which first began production before 1973. The price of this oil has been controlled at a level which approximates its 1974 price (10 CFR Section 212.73), plus certain inflation adjustments and currently sells for approximately $6.50 per barrel.

2. Upper tier oil is that oil from properties which first began production after 1972 plus production on a lower tier property above a certain volume. In order to provide incentives for exploration the price of this oil was allowed to increase to a price measured by the September 1975 uncontrolled level (10 CFR Section 212.74) of approximately $13, with adjustments.

3. Stripper oil is produced from properties whose average daily flow is ten barrels per day or less, per well. Stripper production is not price controlled, and in early 1979 it sold for the then world price of approximately $16 per barrel. It currently sells for more than twice that amount.

The distinctions among these three tiers are made only for pricing purposes. "Lower" and "upper" refer to the prices received, not the depth of the geological formations from which the oil is obtained, and in many cases the oil itself is chemically identical. In fact a considerable amount of lower tier oil is superior in refining properties and could demand a higher free market price than much of the upper tier oil, which sells for more than twice as much, while some of the market-priced stripper is inferior to the controlled oil which sells for one-sixth to one-third as much.

Decontrol of crude oil prices. In April 1979 the President exercised his executive authority to deregulate the price of all domestic crude oil in phases. The intent was to encourage conservation and increased exploration by raising domestic prices to world levels while easing the dislocations which might be involved if all domestic crude oil production were deregulated at once on 9/30/81, the expiration date of the price control legislation.

The DOE price control regulations are extraordinarily complex, and their phase-out will be accomplished with regulations nearly as complex. The control of oil at lower tier prices is accomplished by the maintenance of a base production control level (BPCL) for each DOE controlled property (10 CFR Section 212.72). The BPCL represents the volume of oil produced from a property during a certain period. Although the computation details are beyond the scope of this article, the BPCLs most commonly used at this time represent the monthly average production from a property during the six months ended March 1979.

Any production above the BPCL can be sold under DOE regulations at the upper tier price (10 CFR Section 212.72). To effect the deregulation of lower tier oil the BPCL was lowered 1.5% per month during 1979. The decontrol began with June 1979 production using an immediate 9% (1.5% × 6) retroactive reduction in the lower tier BPCL (10 CFR Section 212.76(a)(3)(i)). Through 12/31/79 the BPCL had been reduced by 18% (1.5% × 12) and stood at 82% of the March 1979 level. Oil produced from properties on which production began after 1978 is free of price controls (10 CFR Section 212.79). The intent of this provision is to encourage drilling for new reservoirs of oil and gas.

In January 1980 the second phase of crude oil decontrol began. It consists of two parts:

1. The BPCL reduction increased from 1.5% to 3% per month (10 CFR Section 212.76(a)(3)(ii)). The combination of the 18% BPCL reduction in 1979 and the 63% (3% × 21) to be reduced in the 21 months between January 1980 and the expiration of price controls in September 1981 will result in an 81% reduction in the March 1979 BPCL. The remaining 19% will be released on 10/1/81.

2. The upper tier of price controls began to phase out. Each month beginning with January 1980, 4.6% of the oil controlled at upper tier prices is completely decontrolled and can sell at market price.[1] During the 21 months be-

Article reprinted courtesy of *Journal of Taxation*, May 1980, pp. 258–264

tween January 1980 and September 1981 this process will release 96.6% (4.6% × 21) of the upper tier controlled oil to market prices. The remaining 3.4% will go to market price on 10/1/81. Of course, at the expiration of price controls the 19% of lower tier oil released to upper tier through the expiration of price controls will pass immediately to market price, since the upper tier of price controls will expire simultaneously.

Decontrol Under WPT

OPEC prices were approximately $16 per barrel at the time of the President's decontrol announcement, which included a proposal for an excise tax to capture a portion of the increased income producers would derive from this decontrol. The legislation which finally emerged from Congress is analogous to that which the President proposed in 1979. The tax divides domestic crude oil production into three tiers, which should not be confused with the DOE pricing tiers.

The computation of the tax is essentially the same in each tier. Starting with the removal price of the oil (usually the same as its sales price) a deduction is allowed for a base price adjusted for inflation and for the difference in state severance taxes imposed on the oil above what they would have been had the oil sold at its controlled price. The excess, if any, of the removal price over the sum of the adjusted base price and severance tax adjustment is called a "windfall" profit by the statute. The "windfall" on each barrel is limited to 90% of the net income attributable to that barrel.

Depending upon the tier into which the production falls and the status of the producer as independent or non-independent, the tax computed is a simple application of a rate to the computed "windfall" profit.

Under Section 4987(b) the rates are:

	Integrated Producers	*Independent Producers*
Tier 1	70%	50%
Tier 2	60%	30%
Tier 3	30%	30%

For example if one barrel of stripper oil (Tier 2) were removed and sold for $40.00 at a time when its adjusted base price was $15.60 in a state with a severance tax of 5%, the WPT would be computed as follows:

Removal (sales) price			**$40.00**
Reduced by:			
Adjusted base price		**$15.60**	
Severance tax adjustment:			
Severance tax actually imposed $40.00 × 5%	**$2.00**		
Severance tax which would have been imposed had the barrel been sold at its adjusted base price $15.60 × 5%	**(.78)**	**1.22**	
Total Adjustments			**(16.82)**
"Windfall" Profit			**23.18**
Tax Rate			**60%**
WPT on this barrel			**$13.91**

The computation as generalized for any tier can be represented graphically as in the box on p. 262.

The distance between the two curves measures the "windfall" profit at any point (the larger bracketed amount). The WPT is part of this profit, as depicted by the smaller bracketed amount.

The WPT is levied in addition to all other taxes currently placed on the oil. For instance all of the increased revenue would be subjected to Federal and state income taxation as well as state and local severance and *ad valorem* taxes. The WPT is deductible under Section 164(a)(5) for Federal income tax purposes, as any other excise tax would be.

Exempt crude oil

Generally all crude oil produced in the U.S. is subject to the WPT. Four specific exemptions have been included in the statute:[2]

1. *Qualified governmental or charitable interest:* The production now owned or later acquired by state governments, political subdivisions of state governments and agencies of these units if the net income from the production is dedicated to public purposes (Section 4994(a)). Net income to a governmental unit is defined as the gross income from production less any production costs and severance taxes borne by the gross income (Section 4994(a)(2)). A similar exemption is granted to medical and educational charities if the interest was owned on 1/21/80 (Section 4994(b)). Churches and synagogues are not exempt unless the interest was held continuously since 1/21/80 for the benefit of a medical or educational charity (Section 4994(b)(1)(A)(ii)). Most other charitable organizations, including private foundations, will be liable for the WPT. No interest acquired by a charitable organization after 1/21/80 is exempt.[3]

2. *Exempt Indian Oil:* Production owned by an Indian tribe or one of its members or by an Indian tribal organization (Section 4994(d)). As with the charitable-organization exemption this production must have been held by the qualified person on 1/21/80. Production acquired thereafter will be taxable.

3. *Exempt Alaskan Oil:* Oil from reservoirs (other than the Saddlerochit production taxed in Tier 1) which are either north of the Arctic Circle or north of the Alaska-Aleutian mountain range and at least 75 miles from the nearest point of the Trans-Alaska Pipeline System (TAPS) (Section 4994(e)).

4. *Exempt front-end oil:* Certain production which is released from the lower tier of price controls to provide funds to finance enhanced tertiary recovery projects where independent producers own at least 50% of the operating interests (Section 4994(c)).

All exemptions from the WPT are to be strictly construed, and no statute providing for general tax exemptions will be effective to exempt production from the WPT. Any general exemption statutes passed in the future will not relieve a producer of WPT liability unless specific reference is made to a WPT exemption (Section 4996(g)). All other domestic crude oil is subject to the WPT. The taxable oil is divided into three tiers. Although the placement of a particular type of oil in a tier is dependent on its treatment for DOE price control purposes, the WPT tiers are quite different from the DOE price control tiers.

Tier 1. The WPT definition of Tier 1 oil is not very revealing in that it simply includes all non-exempt oil not in Tier 2 or Tier 3 (Section 4991(c)). Most Tier 1 oil will be that which is or was controlled by the DOE as lower or upper tier oil. In addition Tier 1 includes:

1. *Incentive or front-end tertiary oil:* Oil released from lower tier pricing by the DOE to provide funding for tertiary recovery projects and produced on projects controlled by integrated pro-

---

[*Fredric J. Attermeier, CPA, of the Texas Bar, is with the Tax Department of Texaco Inc. in Houston, Texas. He is a member of the ABA Natural Resources Subcommittee of the Section of Taxation.* *The author gratefully acknowledges the substantial contributions of Carl R. Peterson, CPA of the Tax Department of Texaco Inc., White Plains, New York, and G. George Varady, independent tax consultant, Houston, Texas.*]

ducers[4] (any additional production resulting from successful tertiary projects is taxed at the lower Tier 3 rates).

2. *Alaskan North Slope Oil:* Production from the Saddlerochit reservoir in Prudhoe Bay, Alaska. Should the TAPS tariff on this oil be reduced below $6.26 per barrel as a result of litigation in progress, the base price for this oil will increase by the amount of the reduction (Section 4996(d)(2)), leaving the producer in the same net position as he would have been in had the tariff not decreased.

3. *A catch-all provision:* Subjects any oil not taxed elsewhere to the Tier 1 tax. An example of the "oil" which would be taxed under this provision would be natural gas condensate which is classified by the DOE as crude oil but is not technically lower or upper tier.

The base price for production in Tier 1 is determined separately for each property. This price is the upper tier ceiling price as of May 1979 less 21 cents and will be adjusted quarterly for inflation (Section 4989(c)). The property-by-property determination of base price means that each producer will be required to figure his base price for that grade and location in May 1979. Although each producer's base price is likely to be different the overall average should be about $12.80 per barrel before inflation.

Although every barrel of oil produced on a domestic property is subject to the WPT, in many cases where the oil is controlled at lower tier prices no tax will result from the computation. For example, if oil is sold from a property at a time when the respective sales prices for lower tier, upper tier and uncontrolled oil are $7, $14, and $40 respectively, with a $13.50 adjusted base price in a state with a 5% severance tax, the determination of the "windfall" profit would be made separately for each classification of oil as follows:

DOE Tier	Removal Price /BBL	Adjusted Base Price /BBL	Severance Tax Adjustment	Tentative "Windfall" Profit/BBL
Lower	$ 7.00	($13.50)	None	None
Upper	14.00	(13.50)	($ .03)	$ .47
Uncontrolled	40.00	(13.50)	(1.33)	25.17

Because the tax is levied on each barrel (Section 4987(a)) and fraction of a barrel (Section 4987(c)), the excess of the adjusted base price over the removal price on lower tier oil does not reduce the "windfall" profit on upper tier or uncontrolled oil. The computation illustrated above is the first step of the WPT calculation. The "windfall" profit might be reduced by a net income limitation before the tax rate is applied.

Tier 1 has two tax rates. The general rate is 70%, but certain non-integrated producers will receive an "independent producer" 50% rate on a portion of their Tier 1 production.

Tier 2. Included in Tier 2 of the tax is production from properties classified by the DOE as stripper well properties and from the National Petroleum Reserve, a group of oil leases owned by the U.S. Government (Section 4991(d)). Calculation of the tax is similar to the calculation in Tier 1 except that the base price is the amount for which oil of the same grade and location would have sold in December 1979 if the average price of uncontrolled oil in the U.S. had been $15.20, adjusted for inflation (Section 4989(d)(1)(B)(i)). The IRS will issue regulations on how this base price should be calculated. The tax rate is generally 60% in Tier 2, but independent producers will be entitled to a 30% rate on part of their Tier 2 production.

Following decontrol of crude oil prices in September 1981 producers will find it advisable to continue surveillance of properties for stripper classification. For WPT purposes the June 1979 energy regulations under which stripper oil is defined (Section 4991(d)(1)(A)) are treated as continuing in effect after price controls expire (Section 4996(b)(8)(D)), so this reclassification can be made. The sales price of the oil would be the same regardless of the classification after decontrol, but the stripper classification will provide much better after-tax realization. Assuming a $40.00 removal price and a 5% severance tax with respective Tier 1 and Tier 2 adjusted base prices of $13.00 and $15.50 the WPT difference per barrel at the integrated producer rates would be:

	Removal Price	Adjusted Base Price	Severance Tax Adjustment	"Windfall" Profit	Rate	WPT
Tier 1 rates	$40.00	$13.00	$1.35	$25.65	70%	$17.96
Tier 2 rates	40.00	15.50	1.23	23.27	60%	13.96
Difference in per-barrel realization						$4.00

If the production qualified for the lower independent producer rates the difference would be $5.85 per barrel.

Tier 3. Tier 3 includes three classifications of oil whose production Congress believed would be responsive to higher net wellhead prices:

1. *Newly discovered oil:* Production from Outer Continental Shelf leases for which the lease was entered into on or after 1/1/79 plus onshore properties from which there was no production in 1978 (Section 4991(e)(2), 10 CFR Section 212.79).

2. *Heavy oil:* Crude oil which is so dense and viscous that its recovery by normal pumping means is almost impossible. For this reason expensive techniques must be applied, generally including heating the oil underground in order to reduce its viscosity so that it can be pumped to the surface. Because the recovery methods involved in obtaining this oil are very expensive and because a number of domestic reservoirs contain huge quantities of this oil, its price was decontrolled by the President in the hope that greater production would occur. To avoid defeating the purpose of this decontrol with the WPT the crude was placed in Tier 3 in order to provide a higher after-tax realization to the producer (Section 4991(e)(1)(B)).

Heavy oil was decontrolled in two stages by the President. The first step released oil technically defined as American Petroleum Institute (API) 16° and lower. The API gravity measurement is a method of comparing the density or specific gravity of oil with the specific gravity of water. The significance of the measurement is that as the API gravity declines the oil becomes more viscous and difficult to produce. In December 1979 the President announced decontrol of somewhat lighter oil, that 20° API or less. The WPT legislation retained the 16° definition (Section 4991(e)(3)), hence production with weighted average gravity greater than 16° API but less than or equal to 20° API is considered heavy oil for purposes of price decontrol but Tier 1 for purposes of the WPT.

After the expiration of price controls in September 1981 producers will be well advised to monitor gravity for oil from all properties. If the gravity of this oil moves to 16° API or less it should be reclassified as heavy since the definition of production in Tiers 1 and 2 specifically excludes any oil which could be classified in Tier 3.[5]

3. *Incremental tertiary oil:* That oil produced from a property in excess of a base level which was produced prior to the commencement of a tertiary recovery project (Sections 4991(e)(1)(C) and 4993). Tertiary recovery projects use the more exotic and expensive methods of extracting oil from a formation

following the reduction of the natural pressurization of the field (primary recovery) and the standard enhanced recovery operations such as water flooding (secondary recovery).

This production should be distinguished from the front-end tertiary incentive oil taxed in Tier 1 for projects controlled by integrated producers and exempt for those controlled by independents. Front-end incentive oil is that released from lower tier prices on one property to provide additional funds with which to engage in a tertiary project, usually on a different property. If a tertiary project is successful, the increased production above a base is called incremental tertiary oil and it is taxed in Tier 3.

Oil in Tier 3 will have a base price equal to the amount for which oil of that grade and location would have sold had the average price of domestic uncontrolled crude in December 1979 been $16.55 per barrel (Section 4989(d)(1)(B)(ii)). The details for computing this base price will be covered in IRS regulations, and the base price will be adjusted at a rate slightly greater than inflation. The WPT rate is 30% for all producers.

Imposition of the tax

The WPT is imposed on each producer of taxable crude oil removed from the premises of a domestic lease (Section 4986) after 2/29/80 (Section 4996(b)(7)). It is the removal of the oil from the premises, not its sale, which triggers the WPT. This rule applies the tax at the earliest point at which reliable data are available. If oil removed from the premises of a domestic lease before 3/1/80 is paid for after 2/29/80, no WPT will be due.

The statute defines the producer as any person with an economic interest in taxable crude oil (Section 4996(a)(1)(A)), hence royalty and working interest owners will both be subject to the WPT. To avoid the filing of the many returns which would result if every person with an economic interest in crude oil filed quarterly WPT returns, the statute provides that the first purchaser will calculate the WPT and withhold it from the payment to the producer (Section 4995(a)(1)(A)). This provision would supersede any agreement which requires the first purchaser to remit gross proceeds to his vendor.[6]

When the tax is withheld the producer is not required to file a return (Section 4995(a)(5)) since in most cases the tax will have been withheld at the proper rate, and filing a return would be pointless since no refund would be available. If the producer takes advantage of this simplification the statute treats him as having filed a WPT return on the day his income tax return would be due without extension for purposes of calculating the period of limitations for credit or refund (Section 6511(h)(1)). He is also treated as having paid the WPT on the last day of February in the year after the calendar year during which oil is removed from the premises (Section 4995(a)(4)). These provisions protect a producer from a perpetual tolling of the statute of limitations because he filed no return.

Special withholding provisions

Despite the fact that a producer anticipates taking advantage of the net income limitation the WPT is to be withheld at the full rate (Section 4995(a)(2)(B)). The final legislation gives the Treasury the power to institute a system of reduced or exempt withholding in the case of producers who are entitled to an exemption or a reduction of rate because of the 1,000 barrel per day independent producer special rate.[7] Until Regulations are adopted, however, all withholding must be effected at the maximum rate for each tier. Producers with exemptions or reduced withholding rates will file WPT returns and claim their refunds from the IRS until the Regulations are adopted.

Removal price

The removal price of oil for purposes of the WPT will generally be the price for which it is sold (Section 4988(c)(1)). In certain cases, related parties (as defined in Section 103(b)(6)(C)) purchase oil from one another, and the law provides that the removal price on such sales will not be less than the constructive sales price for determining gross income under Section 613 (Section 4988(c)(2)).

This same removal price would apply if oil were removed from the premises before sale (Section 4988(c)(3)) or if refining processes were begun before removal from the premises (Section 4988(c)(4)). A general provision allows the Treasury to adjust the removal price to fair market value.[8]

Adjusted base price

The base price for each tier will be adjusted quarterly to take into account inflation occuring after the base price determination (Section 4989). Since base prices over the entire period of the WPT's application will use 1979 prices as a starting point in all three tiers, Congress felt that it would be proper to provide an inflation adjustment so that the difference being taxed would better reflect the increase in oil prices in excess of general inflation.

While the mechanics of the adjustment is complex it allows for inflation between mid-1979 and the second quarter preceding the computation. Tier 3 oil includes a small additional adjustment. The product of the base price and inflation adjustment provides an addition to the base price to yield the adjusted base price.

Initial Tier 2 and 3 base prices

Because Tier 2 and 3 base prices are to be calculated using a reference price to be provided by IRS Regulations which is to reflect differences for grade and location and because of the requirement that withholding begin with payments for oil removed in March 1980, the statute provides a method by which first purchasers can calculate the base price for Tiers 2 and 3 without awaiting the promulgation of Regulations. Both the Tier 2 and 3 base prices are eventually to be determined as if the average price of uncontrolled domestic crude in December 1979 had been a certain

[1] This oil is called "market level new crude" (10 CFR Section 212.72) although the word "new" is not strictly correct. The oil sells at new oil (uncontrolled) prices, but is not production from new properties.

[2] Section 4991(a). Sections 4996(b)(3) and (4) provide that "domestic" includes the U.S. as defined in Section 638 and possessions of the United States.

[3] H. Rep't No. 96-817, 96th Cong., 2d Sess. 108 (1980).

[4] Section 4994(c). Although this oil is subject to the WPT a refund is available to an integrated producer whose expenses of producing the oil exceed his revenue.

[5] Section 4991(c)(2) (Tier 1) and Section 4991(d)(2) (Tier 2).

[6] Section 4995(a)(1)(B). H. Rep't No. 96-817, *supra* note 3 at 112.

[7] Sections 4995(a)(2)(A)(i) and 6050C(a)(3).

[8] Section 4996(f). S. Rep't No. 96-394, 96th Cong., 1st Sess. 65, 67.

[9] H. Rep't No. 96-817, *supra* note 3 at 96.

[10] H. Rep't No. 96-817, *supra* note 3 at 104.

[11] H. Rep't No. 96-817, *supra* note 3 at 105.

[12] H. Rep't No. 96-817, *supra* note 3 at 106.

[13] H. Rep't No. 96-817, *supra* note 3 at 106.

[14] Sections 6076(a) and 4996(b)(7).

[15] Section 4995(b)(1). H. Rep't No. 96-817, *supra* note 3 at 112.

amount. Tiers 2 and 3 will use a substitute base price which will be in effect until final Regulations can be adopted. The formula under Section 4989(d)(2) by which this base price will be calculated is:

$$\text{Highest posted 12/31/79 price for same grade and location of uncontrolled crude} \times \frac{\$15.20 \text{ (Tier 2) or } \$16.55 \text{ (Tier 3)}}{\$35}$$

If no posting was made for the particular oil on 12/31/79, for the grade and location involved, a comparison is made to the nearest domestic field (Section 4989(d)(2)(A)(ii)). The House Conference Report indicates that no retroactive adjustments after 1/14/80 will be allowed to the December 31 price and that a posted price to qualify for base price determination must be "published in writing by a purchaser of a substantial volume of crude oil in the field."[9] A minimum base price is also established to cover areas where December 1979 postings were unusually low. This minimum base price is the price which would have applied to the oil in May 1979 had it been subject to upper tier ceiling prices plus $1 in Tier 2 or $2 in Tier 3 (Section 4989(d)(3)).

Severance tax adjustment

Before application of the WPT rates the difference between the removal price and the adjusted base price is reduced by a severance tax adjustment (STA) (Section 4996(c)). The intent of the STA is to reflect the realities of reduced effective wellhead prices to producers when the sales price of their production increases in a jurisdiction which imposes percent-of-value severance taxes. The STA is the amount by which the severance tax actually imposed on a barrel of taxable crude exceeds that which would have been imposed had the barrel been sold at its adjusted base price. Per-barrel taxes will not provide STA relief since the severance tax imposed at the removal price would be identical to that imposed at the adjusted base price leaving a difference of zero. The STA has three limitations.

1. The maximum rate at which the STA can be calculated is 15% (Section 4996(c)(3)(A)). Presumably this maximum rate is cumulative of all the taxes imposed by a state. For example, if a state imposed two 10% severance taxes on the same barrel, the STA would be based on the 15% limit rather than a 20% rate.
2. The severance tax must apply equally to all portions of the removal price if the tax was passed or increased after 3/31/79 (Section 4996(c)(3)(B)). Hence the Congress has effectively disallowed a STA for any state WPTs which might later be imposed.
3. Severance taxes imposed by Indian tribes and taxes of any description imposed by sub-units of state governments will not qualify for the STA.[10]

Severance taxes for WPT purposes are those taxes levied on the removal of crude oil which use the value of the oil as their basis (Section 4996(c)(2)). The House Report makes it clear that any tax satisfying this definition will qualify regardless of the title of the state statute under which it is levied. Likewise a tax based on reserves in the ground or net proceeds will not qualify for the STA.[11]

Graphic Computation of WPT for any Tier

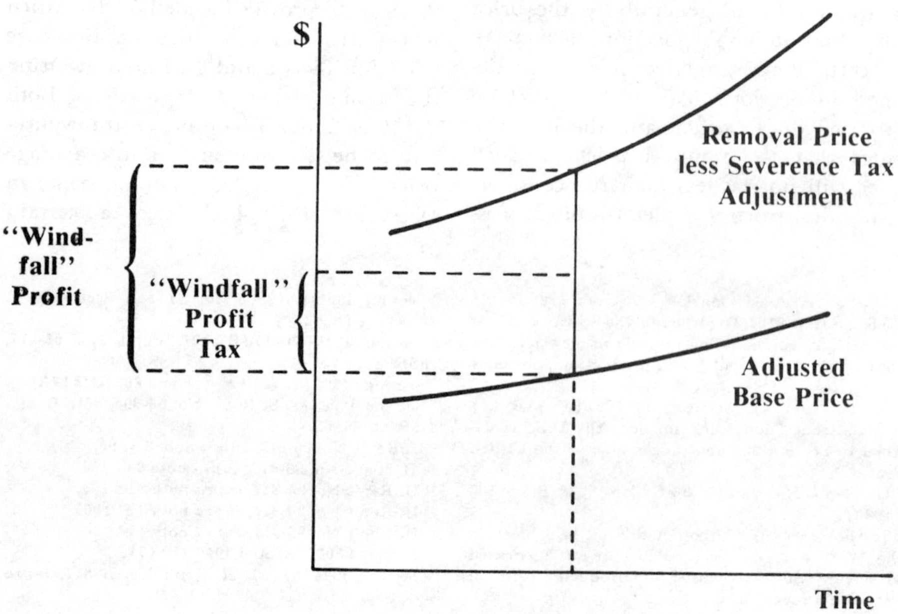

Net income limitation

The amount of "windfall" profit taken into account for purposes of computing the tax is limited to 90% of the net income attributable to each barrel (Section 4988(b)). The net income limitation (NIL) is a limitation on the amount of "windfall" profit carried to the WPT computation, not a limit on the tax imposed. When a property becomes marginally economic the reduction in the WPT as a result of the lower "windfall" profit used in calculating the tax will allow the property to continue to operate in situations where it could not if there were no NIL.

For the NIL the definition of "property" is that of Section 613(a) (Section 4988(b)(3)(A)) rather than the DOE property definition which controls the pricing of crude oil, and taxable income from the property is determined on the basis of the producer's taxable year. Four deductions are not allowed in computing the "net income" for NIL purposes (Section 4988(b)(3)(B)):

1. Depletion (percentage or cost)
2. The WPT itself
3. Intangible drilling and development costs, except those incurred on non-productive wells, called "Section 263(c) costs" by the statute
4. The cost of chemicals injected into the ground to increase the tertiary oil recovery rates if the taxpayer elects to capitalize the costs for WPT purposes. Section 193, added to the income tax provisions by the WPT, allows these expenses to be deducted for income tax purposes.

To compensate for the disallowance of these deductions the net income from the property is reduced by cost depletion computed in a special way (Section 4988(b)(3)(C)).

In addition to those types of costs which would ordinarily be capitalized by a taxpayer for income tax purposes in the calculation of cost depletion the statute allows the IDCs (Section 263(c) costs) and the cost of tertiary injectants expensed to be capitalized in the basis of the property.[12] Cost depletion is then deducted from the property's income as if the taxpayer had used cost depletion for all taxable periods.

In the case of cash basis taxpayers who have fully expensed IDCs through the years and to a lesser extent for accrual basis taxpayers whose detailed IDC records are not good, the maximum reduction of net income from the property will be dependent upon reconstructing all IDCs and tertiary injectants ever expensed on the property as well as lease acquisition costs, screening costs and other capitalizable expenses.

The capitalization of IDCs and tertiary injectants and their subsequent depletion could work to a producer's advantage; if they were expensed in the year of drilling for NIL purposes, the net income would usually be negative. This would provide no real NIL advantage past the year of drilling or injection as there is no carryover of losses for NIL purposes.

The recomputed net income from the property attributable to crude oil is divided by the number of barrels of crude produced during the taxable year (Section 4988(b)(2)). The lesser of 90% of the net income per barrel or the "windfall" profit calculated for the barrel from the removal price and adjustments is the amount taxed for that barrel.

When both oil and gas are produced on the same property an allocation of joint production expenses must be made between the oil and gas. In the absence of evidence to the contrary the allocation of these expenses will be made on the basis of the gross income from each product. The NIL must be computed separately for each property for each barrel if the producer wants to derive the maximum benefit from the NIL.

There is a possibility that many separate computations will be necessary each year since lower tier, upper tier, free-market price and heavy oil between 16° and 20° API gravity could be included in Tier 1 from the same property. Since removal price is likely to vary several times each month and since the tax is assessed separately on each barrel, the total number of separate NIL computations could be very large.

Lease acquisition costs are capitalized for purposes of computing NIL cost depletion, so depletion could be increased and the WPT reduced through transfers of proven properties at prices in excess of the transferor's acquisition costs. For this reason cost depletion for NIL purposes is limited to the amount which would have been calculated by the transferor when a proven property is transferred after 1978 (Section 4988 (b)(4)(A)). "Proven property" has the same meaning for WPT purposes as it does for percentage depletion (Section 4988(b)(4)(B)).

Independent producers

Certain independent producers are granted reduced WPT rates on the first 1,000 barrels of average daily production of taxable crude oil in Tiers 1 and 2. An independent producer for WPT purposes is a non-integrated producer who is not denied percentage depletion by either Section 613A(d)(2) (larger retailers) or Section 613A(d)(4) (larger refiners) (Section 4992(b)(1)).

To qualify for reduced rates, production must be derived from a working interest in existence on 1/1/80 (Section 4992(d)(2)(A)). Therefore royalty owners will not receive a Section 4992 benefit. The statute rules out most conversions of ineligible royalty interests to working interests which would be eligible for the lower rates by providing that to be valid the royalty must have been subject to the right to convert on or before 2/20/80 (Section 4992(d) (2)(B)).

If an exempt producer's Tier 1 and 2 oil exceeds a daily average of 1,000 barrels, the limit will be allocated between Tier 1 and Tier 2 in the same proportion that these quantities make up the producer's Tier 1 and Tier 2 total production (Section 4992(c)(2)). For example, suppose an independent producer has average daily production of:

	Barrels	%
Tier 1	960	60
Tier 2	640	40
	1,600	100

Then 62.5% (1,000/1,600) of this producer's oil from Tiers 1 and 2 will be entitled to lower rates. The 62.5% will be allocated proportionately to the production from Tiers 1 and 2. Therefore 600 barrels of Tier 1 and 400 barrels of Tier 2 oil will receive the lower rates, and the remaining barrels will be taxed at the higher rates:

	Total Barrels of Production	Portion with Reduced Rates	Barrels Taxed at Reduced Rates	Remaining Barrels Taxed at Regular Rates
Tier 1	960	62.5%	600	360
Tier 2	640	62.5%	400	240
	1600		1000	600

Within each tier the production is allocated to the reduced rates starting with the highest removal price (Section 4992(c)(2)(B)). In Tier 1 the 960 barrels produced in the example above would receive reduced rates for the 600 barrels with the highest removal prices, a decided advantage since these would be the barrels with the highest "windfall" profit and the highest WPT. No oil would have to be allocated under the reduced rate computation to Tier 3 or to exempt oil (Section 4992(d)(1) (C)), the production on which independents do not enjoy a WPT tax rate advantage.

To avoid the proliferation of 1000 barrel amounts the WPT will require the allocation of the 1000 barrel amount among persons who are members of the same related group. Persons for whom the allocation is required are controlled groups of corporations and other business entities and family members to include spouses and minor children (Section 4992(e)).

If properties are transferred after 1/1/80, the lower rates are generally denied unless the transferee is himself qualified and can demonstrate that his transferor was qualified at all times since that date for independent producer rates. The transferor cannot have had production in excess of 1000 barrels at any time since January 1, 1980 or all of his properties will be tainted on transfer from that point (Section 4992(d)(3)).

Partnerships

The WPT calculation is treated as a flow through item for members of a partnership (Section 4996(a)(1)(B)). In the common situation in which the statute will treat the partner rather than his partnership as the producer of the oil, the partnership will not deduct the WPT it pays. The Conference Report indicates that the payment of WPT by the partnership is treated as a distribution of money to the partner.[13] The WPT can only be calculated at the partner level because the partners could be subject to different tax rates and have different NIL computations. For example, an oil and gas partnership could have as members an integrated oil company, a non-integrated oil company and an exempt charitable organization.

The partner-level WPT computation will increase the compliance burden on partnerships which engage in oil and gas activities since the WPT information will have to be circulated to partners so that they can prepare their own WPT returns.

In situations where at least one partner might be benefited by the calculation of the NIL the partnership will supply enough information to the partners to allow them to compute the net income from each property for WPT purposes. This, of course, will not be the same as the net income for the 65% of net income limitation for percentage depletion purposes because of the differences in cost depletion allowable under the WPT and income tax limitations.

Administrative provisions

Returns for the WPT are to be filed on a calendar quarter basis although the first return will cover only March 1980.[14] The due date for returns if required is the last day of the second month following the close of the calendar quarter. The Treasury is empowered to promulgate and adopt Regulations with respect to the reporting required, but certain information is required to permit the producer to compute his WPT and file a return should he be entitled to an exemption, reduced rates or relief under the NIL provision. Reporting to producers by first purchasers will therefore have to include the following information by WPT tier:

1. The month and year in which the oil was removed from the premises
2. The number of barrels removed and classification within the tier
3. The removal price of the oil
4. The adjusted base price of each barrel
5. The amount of WPT withheld from the first purchaser's payment to the producer.

Amounts withheld by first purchasers will be deposited twice a month if the first purchaser is an integrated company.[15] The Treasury is empowered to establish Regulations under which the WPT will be deposited. Non-integrated refiners who purchase under delayed payment contracts may make deposits of WPT as late as two months after the month in which the oil was purchased (Section 4995(b)(2)(A)(ii)). Other independent first purchasers not in the refining business will have 45 days after the month in which the oil was purchased to make tax deposits (Section 4995(b)(2)(A)(i)).

The WPT contains a provision by which the operator and first purchaser of the property may make a joint election that the operator is the party who must make the deposits and provide information to the producers of the oil (Section 4995(a)(7)). This election would simplify the details of reporting to producers when the operator of a property is the person primarily responsible for disbursing the proceeds of sales to interest owners. If this election is made and results in a shift of the reporting burden from an integrated purchaser to an independent producer, the stricter depositary requirements for integrated producers will apply to WPT withholding on the property (Section 4995(a)(7)(A)(ii)).

Included in the statute are both civil and criminal penalties for failure to supply required information (Section 7241). The IRS cannot begin deficiency procedures against a producer nor can a suit for refund be filed before the last day of February following the calendar year in which the oil is removed (Section 4995(a)(8)). Because DOE reclassifications after the close of a taxable period could change the amount of the tax due, the WPT contains a provision extending the statute of limitations for one year following the effective date of reclassification (Section 6501(q)(2)). ☆

IRS toughens stance on special IDC allocations

In Ltr. Rul. 8008054 the IRS disallowed a partnership's special allocation of all intangible drilling costs (IDC) to the limited partners, as lacking "substantial economic effect." In so doing, it repudiated the liberal stance it had adopted in *Rev. Rul.* 68-139, 1968-1 CB 311.

Partnership P was formed by Corporation M which contributed leases for oil and gas development valued at arm's length. Various limited partners contributed cash. M also was obligated to contribute cash for equipment and to pay drilling and development expenses in excess of those paid by the limited partner's contributions.

Under the payout arrangements, M would receive twice its contributions in return plus interest and the limited partners would receive their contributions in return plus interest.

In the first year of operation, expenditures for the development of the leases included IDC costs deductible under Section 263 and other expenses which had to be capitalized. The partnership agreement allocated all of the IDC to the limited partners (to the extent of their contributions).

The Service disallowed the special allocation under pre-TRA 76 Section 704(b)(2) as made for tax avoidance purposes and lacking in substantial economic effect. (Since the substantial economic effect standard is applicable currently, the ruling and the pre-76 Regulation should still apply.)

The Service stated that the allocation of deductible expenditures to the limited partners to the extent of their contributions did not affect, and was not necessitated by, the exploration activities. Thus, there was no business reason for the allocation.

Further, since the payout obligations were fixed, if M were to have paid more IDC and fewer equipment costs (but in the same aggregate amount) it would receive the same payout. Thus, a different allocation would not have affected dollars received by M or the partners.

Additionally, both the expenditures giving rise to IDC and the capitalizable costs were incurred during drilling. Thus, an allocation according to deductibility does not reflect the fact that they arose from the same source.

The overall effect of the arrangement was to allow the limited partners deductions in the amount of their contributions. Accordingly, in light of the factors enumerated in Reg. 1.704-1(b)(2), the allocation fails.

In *Rev. Rul.* 68-139, a partner donated leases for a 26/32 partnership share and two partners donated cash for 3/32 shares each. There, without analysis, the Service ruled that an allocation of IDC to the two cash partners met the substantial economic effect test. The IRS also noted that such an allocation, to be valid, had to be made in accordance with *Orrisch*, 55 TC 395 (1970), *aff'd* by CA-9 Reg. 1.704-1(b)(2).

The Service has now clearly stepped back from this stance. It noted that the Ruling "does not sanction unrestricted allocation of IDC among partners and, on its facts, requires such deductions to be allocated to at least any contributors of cash."

Accordingly, here, the limited partners were charged with a share of the partnerships' nondeductible expenditures based on the partnership's percentage of cash used for such purposes.

It would appear that the Service has adopted a new, tougher stance on IDC allocations. Until clearer indications emerge, greater care must be taken with special allocations. ☆

NEW DEVELOPMENTS IN

Taxation of oil & gas

EDITED BY BILLY M. MANN, CPA

Problems under the windfall profit tax Prop. Regs: advising "first purchasers"

by MICHAEL I. SANDERS *and* RICHARD P. SILLS

Although the Proposed Regulations implementing the windfall profit tax go a long way toward filling in the gaps left by Congress, ambiguities remain. The authors analyze the Regs and point out difficulties with the standards imposed for certifications, tier classification, base price and other factors used in calculating the tax.

On April 2, 1980, President Carter signed the Crude Oil Windfall Profit Tax Act of 1980 (P.L. 96-223) into law as part of his program to decontrol domestic crude oil prices.[1] Two days later, the Treasury issued a comprehensive set of Proposed Regulations under the Act (TD 7690); and on April 25, Treasury issued additional Proposed Regulations relating principally to "integrated oil company" certifications and deposits (TD 7694).

The Act was effective retroactively; it imposes a "windfall profit tax" upon producers of crude oil removed from the premises of a domestic lease after February 29, 1980.[2] In view of this retroactivity and the significant revenue impact of the Act, Treasury acted under extraordinary time constraints in drafting Regulations so promptly. Its task was more difficult than usual because of the complexity of the Act, and the adaptation of tax law principles to highly-specialized subject matter that has generally been in the domain of a different agency, the Department of Energy (DOE). It is, therefore, not surprising that some aspects of the Proposed Regulations need further refinement to provide standards by which practitioners may advise their clients on how to comply, and to provide taxpayers with workable day-to-day guidance.

Although the windfall profit tax is imposed upon the producer, the first purchaser has the primary administrative responsibilities: it must calculate the tax, deduct and withhold the tax from the purchase price, deposit the tax, and file quarterly and yearly returns with the Service. The first purchaser, therefore, will have the ongoing responsibility for administering the tax and trying to interpret its own responsibilities in connection with the tax. In addition to the time-consuming administrative obligations, the first purchaser may become liable for the tax as a consequence of failure to withhold or underwithholding.

Whether the first purchaser withholds tax, and how much it withholds, will generally depend on information furnished by other parties, such as the producer or operator. Typically, the party required to furnish the information is the seller of the oil, from whom the tax is being withheld, and with whom the purchaser has a continuing business relationship. In light of these factors, a number of issues arise in the implementation of the withholding rules, such as:

1. To what extent may a purchaser rely on information in the certifications furnished to it, without being required to cross-check or conduct independent verification? The statute and Regulations provide that the purchaser may use the information in the certification unless it has "reason to believe" that it contains information which is not correct, but that standard is not clarified.

2. What should the purchaser do if the certification is not furnished on time, or is obviously incorrect, but the purchaser has access to the relevant information from a different source? May the purchaser make a good-faith estimate of the correct amount to withhold, or must it, as the Regulations suggest, withhold an amount which will clearly be excessive (perhaps a multiple of the tax due)?

3. When IRS determines that a purchaser has failed to withhold a sufficient amount of tax, will the purchaser invariably be liable for the deficiency if the producer fails to pay it? While the language of the Proposed Regulations suggests absolute liability in this situation, some form of "good faith" or "reasonable cause" test would seem more appropriate, as discussed below.

Another significant issue is the extent of the administrative responsibility imposed on the purchaser under the Proposed Regulations. For example, the purchaser must make retroactive adjustments in withholding even when the initial under- or over-withholding was caused through no fault of its own, such as when the producer fails to provide a certification on time.

This article analyzes and discusses the more significant provisions of the Proposed Regulations, with particular emphasis on their effect on the first purchasers[3] of domestic crude oil.

Computation of tax

The windfall profit tax, an excise tax, is computed by multiplying the applicable tax rate by the "windfall profit" on a barrel of crude oil (Section 4987, Prop. Reg. 150.4987-1). The "windfall profit" is the removal price (usually the actual selling price) of the barrel minus the sum of the "base price" (adjusted for inflation) and the "severance tax adjustment" (Section 4988, Prop. Reg. 150.4988-1). The taxable windfall profit with regard to any barrel of crude oil is limited, however, to 90% of the "net income attributable to such barrel."

Rate of tax. The tax rates, generally, are 70% for tier one oil, 60% for tier two oil, and 30% for tier three oil (Section 4987, Prop. Reg. 150.4987-1). However, producers who qualify as "independent producers" are taxed at reduced rates—50% on tier one oil and 30% on tier two oil—for 1,000 barrels per day of their combined qualifying production of tier one and two oil (Sections 4987, 4992, Prop. Regs. 150.4987-1, 150.4992-1). Moreover, certain kinds of producers and certain types of oil are exempt from tax entirely.[4]

Tier system. All nonexempt crude oil produced in the U.S. is classified in one

Article reprinted courtesy of *Journal of Taxation*, August 1980, pp. 92–96 of three tiers. The general tax structure is the same for each tier, except that each has a different rate of tax (see above), and each has a different base price, that is, the amount above which the selling price is subject to tax.

Tier one oil is all nonexempt oil which is not tier two and three oil (Section 4991, Prop. Reg. 150.4991-1), and is generally controlled lower- or upper-tier oil under DOE regulations.

Tier two oil consists of oil produced from stripper well properties[5] and from a National Petroleum Reserve in which the U.S. has an economic interest (Section 4991, Prop. Reg. 150.4991-1).

Tier three oil includes heavy oil, newly-discovered oil, and incremental tertiary oil[6] (Section 4991 (e), Prop. Reg. 150.4991-1(b)). There appears to be an ambiguity as to whether oil is "newly discovered" if derived from a property which did not produce oil in commercial quantities in 1978, but which, nevertheless, had some production during that year. Section 4991(e)(2) and Prop. Reg. 150.4991-1(b) provide that "newly discovered oil" has the same meaning for this purpose as under the June 1979 energy regulations. Those regulations (10 CFR Section 212.79(b)) define newly-discovered oil as oil sold after 5/31/79 and produced from either an outer continental shelf area where the lease was entered into on or after 1/1/79 or an on-shore property from which there was no production in 1978. However, the legislative history of the Act indicates that newly-discovered oil should include production from an on-shore property which did not produce oil in commercial quantities in 1978, *e.g.,* when the 1978 production was incident to the drilling of exploratory or test wells.[7]

Since the more liberal interpretation of "newly discovered oil" supplies an incentive to drill for new oil, Treasury may wish to interpret Section 4991(e)(2) to provide that if the 1978 oil production from a property was not in commercial quantities, subsequent production will be treated as tier three newly-discovered oil. This could be done by amending Prop. Reg. 150.4991-1(b) accordingly, and defining therein what constitutes production in "commercial quantities."

Independent producer oil. An independent producer is a nonintegrated oil company which in any taxable quarter has gross retail sales of $1,250,000 or less, or refinery runs of 50,000 or fewer barrels per day (Sections 4992(b), 613A(d)(2) and (4); Prop. Reg. 150.4992-1(b)). The special tax rates discussed above apply, in effect, to only the first 1,000 barrels per day of an independent producer's tier one and two production attributable to a working interest, which was in existence on 1/1/80 or was derived from a qualifying overriding royalty in existence on that date and subject to a binding contract before 2/21/80 to convert to an operating interest[8] (Section 4992(d), Prop. Reg. 150.4992-1 (d)). Thus, for example, assume an independent producer produces 1,500 barrels of tier one working interest oil and 1,000 of tier two working interest oil per day throughout a calendar quarter. A total of 1,000 barrels per day are subject to the special reduced rate, and the remaining 1,500 barrels are taxed without regard to independent producer status. Further, the 1,000 barrels per day eligible for the reduced tax rate are allocated between tiers one and two in proportion to production for the quarter, *i.e.,* 600 barrels per day of tier one, and 400 barrels per day of tier two.

Base price. Since the taxable "windfall profit" is limited to the excess of the selling price over the base price, the definition of "base price" is crucial to the computation of the tax. If all other factors are equal, then the higher the base price, the lower the tax.

In the case of tier one oil, the base price is the ceiling price which would have applied to the oil under the March 1979 energy regulations if it had been produced and sold in May 1979 as upper tier oil, reduced by 21¢ (Section 4989, Prop. Reg. 150.4989-1(b)).

In the case of tiers two and three oil, Prop. Reg. 150.4989-1(c)(2) establishes an interim rule for determining the base price for oil removed before October 1980. Under this rule, the base price is the product of (1) the highest posted price for 12/31/79[9] for uncontrolled crude oil of the same grade, quality, and field (or, if not available for the particular field, then for the nearest field for which it is available), multiplied by (2) the fraction $15.20/35.00 for tier two oil, or the fraction $16.55/35.00 for tier three oil.[10]

A posted price for 12/31/79 may be used only if it was posted on or before 1/14/80 and was published in writing by a purchaser of a substantial volume of crude oil in the field. In this regard, Treasury may not have considered the difficulty that the purchaser or operator may encounter in determining the volume of oil purchased by the party posting the price. Usually, this would be confidential business information which a purchaser is not likely to disclose to a competitor.

In addition, the Proposed Regulations fail to define three crucial terms: "substantial volume of crude oil," "field" and "published in writing." Even when the parameters of a field are defined by industry custom, it may be unclear what is a "substantial volume" of a field's production. Is "substantial" to be measured in absolute terms, or relative to the field's production? (In other words, may a given quantity of oil be viewed as "substantial" for one field but not for another?)

The Proposed Regulations also provide no guidance for determining whether a price is "published in writing." For example, does a letter to a selected group of regular business contacts qualify, or does the Regulation require something more "public"? How many producers or operators must re-

[1] For a detailed explanation of the Act and the President's decontrol program, see Attermeier, *The Crude Oil Windfall Profit Tax of 1980: How it will affect oil companies,* 52 JTAX 258 (May, 1980).

[2] A producer is the holder of an economic interest with respect to the crude oil in place in the ground (Prop. Reg. 150.4996-1(b)).

[3] For convenience, these will generally be referred to simply as "purchasers."

[4] Oil produced by state governments, by medical and educational charities and by Indian tribes is exempt from the windfall profit tax. Certain Alaskan oil and front-end tertiary oil (where independent producers own at least 50% of the operating interests) are also exempt. See Section 4994.

[5] A stripper well property is one in which the average daily production is ten barrels or less for any consecutive 12-month period after 1972.

[6] "Heavy oil" is all crude oil produced from a property if during the last month prior to 7/1/79 for which the property had production, or during the tax quarter, crude oil produced and sold from the property had a specific gravity of 16 degrees API or less, corrected to 60 degrees Fahrenheit (Section 4991, Prop. Reg. 150.4991-1). "Incremental tertiary oil" is the monthly oil production from a property in excess of the monthly base level which represents the property's production prior to the commencement of a "qualified tertiary recovery project" (Section 4993, Prop. Reg. 150.4993-1). The monthly base level is the average monthly production from the property for the six-month period ended 3/31/79 reduced by 1% for each post-1978 month up to the project's beginning date and by 2.5% for each month after that (Section 4993(b), Prop. Reg. 150.4993-1(a)(2)).

[7] Conference Report, H. Rep't No. 96-817, 96th Cong., 2d Sess. (1980), p. 98.

[8] The working interest and the overriding royalty interest must be in existence as such an interest on 1/1/80. Since royalty owners do not have operating interests, they do not qualify for the lower tax rate.

ceive notice of the posting for it to be considered "published"? These are questions which obviously need to be resolved in the Regulations.

Moreover, a "posted" price is merely a price at which an offer has been made to purchase oil; sometimes, no oil from that field is actually sold at that price. The Proposed Regulations appear to permit the use of a posted price in determining the base price regardless of whether or not oil from that field actually has been sold at the posted price.

Prop. Reg. 150.4989-1(d) provides that the average grade or quality of the production from a property in May or December 1979 shall be used for purposes of computing a base price. It provides that the base price, once determined, is not to be adjusted for later changes in grade or quality. However, the regulations make no provisions for variations in gravity, even though it is common practice in the industry to post prices only for oil of 40 degrees API gravity, and to discount the price for oil of a lower gravity.

This absence of guidance as to critical issues leaves the parties who must prepare certifications and the purchasers who must rely on them uncertain as to how to proceed. Considering the magnitude of potential tax dollars involved, such parties need to be concerned about making "judgment calls" which a revenue agent may determine to be incorrect upon subsequent audit. The risk of doing so is greater here than in the typical case: ordinarily, the taxpayer's own tax liability is involved, so that if he takes a position which IRS determines to be wrong, he must simply pay back the amount he incorrectly "saved" by making the wrong decision. Here, by contrast, the purchaser is computing and paying over another party's tax liability, so if it withholds and pays over an amount which is later determined to be insufficient, the purchaser, in effect, may be held liable to IRS for an "underpayment" which did not "save" that purchaser one penny.

With regard to "judgment calls" required of the purchaser, one typical problem may occur when inconsistent base price certifications are received from different producers in the same field. For example, suppose a purchaser buys crude oil of the same grade, quality and field from two producers. Relying on different postings, one producer certifies that the highest 12/31/79 posted price for such oil is $38, while another certifies $41.

If the purchaser becomes aware of the conflict,[10a] an untenable business dilemma results: using the $41 base price will result in a lower tax on the producer. But, if the purchaser uses that price, it may risk being held liable by IRS if that decision is later determined to be incorrect, notwithstanding that it acted in good faith. On the other hand, if the purchaser uses the $38 price, it may lose a substantial portion of its business, as producers which certify higher base prices are likely to sell to competing purchasers which accept those prices for purposes of the tax. Still worse, if the conflict is viewed as providing a "reason to believe" that one or both certifications are incorrect, then (as will be discussed in Part II of this article) the Regulations may be interpreted to require the tax to be computed using a base price of $11.01 (as adjusted for inflation), which may yield a tax which substantially exceeds the correct figure.

Only clear guidance from Treasury will solve this dilemma. Assuming that the basic types of oil and the fields can be reliably identified and described according to industry usage, it may be feasible for Treasury to eliminate this problem by publishing tables which establish—for purposes of the "base price" computation—the 12/31/79 price of each type of oil in each field. Under this approach, any conflict would be resolved definitively by Treasury, rather than having various producers and purchasers reach their own separate (and perhaps different) conclusions.

If it is not practical for Treasury to promulgate such a table, the Proposed Regulations should establish clear standards for determining what is a price "published in writing," what constitutes a "field" and how much oil is a "substantial volume" therein, and whether the posting of a price is sufficient to justify its use for this purpose without any showing that oil was purchased at that price. Furthermore, a party which makes a good-faith determination based on a reasonable interpretation of those standards should be protected from the risk of being "second-guessed" by IRS on audit.

In addition, Treasury should address (either in the Regulations or by a Ruling or other announcement) the issue of whether the applicable base price should be adjusted for variations in gravity.

Finally, to promote uniformity in the computation of the applicable base price, which requires multiplying the 12/31/79 price by the fraction in Prop. Reg. 150.4989-1(c)(2), Treasury may wish to prescribe the number of decimal places to which the fractions $15.20/35.00 (.43428571428) and $16.55/35.00 (.47285714285) may be rounded off. The number of places used can make a significant difference in the amount of the tax due. For example, assume a 12/31/79 highest posted price of $37 per barrel, current selling price of $39 per barrel, and inflation adjustments of 0.195 for tier two and .0246 for tier three. Assuming also that the independent producer rate is not applicable, the computations to two places (Line 1) and to seven places (Line 2) are as follows:

	Tier Two		Tier Three	
	Base Price	Tax Due	Base Price	Tax Due
(1)	16.22	13.66	17.82	6.35
(2)	16.38	13.57	17.93	6.32

Adjusted base price. Under the Act, the base price is periodically "adjusted" for inflation by adding to it the product of the base price and the "inflation adjustment" for the calendar quarter in which the crude oil is removed. Pursuant to the statutory formula, the inflation adjustments for oil removed during March 1980 are .0195 for tiers one and two oil and .0246 for tier three oil (Prop. Reg. 150.4989-1(a)). For oil removed in the second quarter of 1980, the inflation adjustments are .0422 for tiers one and two oil and .0527 for tier three oil and for the third quarter, 1980, .0649 for tiers one and two and .081 for tier three (Notices 80-3, 80-6, IRB 1980-17,23 and IRB 1980-24,21).[11]

Severance tax adjustment. As noted above, the "severance tax adjustment" is another key component in the calculation of the taxable "windfall profit." Severance taxes are imposed by various states on the extraction of oil, and the purpose of the adjustment is to exclude from the taxable windfall profit the amount of the severance tax imposed on the windfall profit portion (the excess of the selling price over the ad-

[*Michael I. Sanders and Richard P. Sills are partners in the Washington, D.C., law firm of Ginsburg, Feldman, Weil and Bress. Mr. Sanders, a former Chairman and presently Special Advisor of the Exempt Organizations Committee of the ABA Tax Section, has appeared on several occasions in* The Journal.]

justed base price) of the price of a barrel of oil. The adjustment, when available, thus reduces the amount of the "windfall profit."

The amount of the adjustment is the amount by which the state severance tax actually imposed upon a barrel of oil exceeds the state severance tax which would have been imposed if the barrel had been sold at its adjusted base price (Section 4996, Prop. Reg. 150.4996-2). However, to qualify for the adjustment, a severance tax must be levied by a state as a percenatge of the gross value of the crude oil removed, up to a maximum rate of 15%. A tax levied as a fixed fee per barrel on the value of reserves, or on the basis of net proceeds from production, is not treated as a severance tax for this purpose.

State taxes on crude oil vary considerably from state to state, not only in amount but in the manner in which they are imposed. Some taxes clearly will qualify for the severance tax adjustment under the above-described test, and others clearly will not; but in some unclear or "borderline" cases, a purchaser may have difficulty determining whether a state-imposed tax qualifies for the severance tax adjustment. Some state taxing authorities have reached no conclusion as to whether that state's tax qualifies as a severance tax for purposes of the Act. Ultimately, rulings and litigation will resolve on a piecemeal basis the issue of which taxes qualify and which do not. IRS could eliminate this initial confusion among purchasers if it would publish an all-inclusive list of those state taxes which it recognizes as "severance taxes" qualifying for the adjustment under the Act. In view of the limited number and easily identifiable nature of the state taxes in question, the compilation and publication of such a list appears to be feasible.

Net income limitation. Under the Act, the taxable windfall profit on a barrel of oil may not exceed 90% of the net income attributable to the barrel (Section 4988(b)(1)). However, the Act also requires the purchaser to withhold the tax in full without regard to this limitation (Section 4995(a)(2)(B)). This may result in substantial overwithholding when the limitation is applicable.

Under the Proposed Regulations, when the net income limitation is applicable, the producer may recover the overwithheld amount by filing a claim for refund with the Service after the last day of February following the close of the calendar year, but not until it has filed its income tax return for the year (Prop. Reg. 150.6402-1(b) and (c)). In view of the statute, the Regulations cannot provide for any withholding adjustment to take the limitation into account; but they could authorize a more prompt refund procedure, such as by allowing refund claims to be filed immediately following the end of the year. (Section 4995(a)(8) provides that no court proceeding for a refund may be brought before the last day of February after the close of the calendar year in which the oil is removed, but does not so restrict an administrative proceeding for a refund.)

Withholding requirements

Although the Act established the windfall profit tax withholding concept, it gave Treasury considerable discretion to create by Regulation the procedures for implementation. In general, the purchaser must compute the tax on the basis of information contained in certifications furnished to it by the operators and producers from which it buys the oil.

Operator certifications. Prop. Regs. 150.4995-1(b)(1) and 150.6050C(1)(c) require the purchaser to compute the amount to be withheld on the basis of information contained in a certification, which must be provided to the purchaser by the operator (or the producer if there is no operator) no later than the 15th day of the month following the calendar month in which the oil was removed. For example, the certification relating to oil removed in July must be furnished by August 15. The Proposed Regulation requires that the certification be signed under penalties of perjury and contain the following information which affects determination of the liability:

1. The tier of the oil, and if it is tier three oil, whether the oil is newly-discovered oil, heavy oil, or incremental tertiary oil.
2. The total amount, and the amounts by tier and category, of oil purchases.
3. The adjusted base price for each tier of oil.
4. The state severance tax adjustment, if any, for each tier of oil.
5. The property from which the oil was removed.[12]

Producer certifications. The producer must also provide a separate certification to either the operator[13] or the purchaser if its oil is exempt (in which case there is no withholding), or if it qualifies as an independent producer entitled to withholding at lower rates (Prop. Reg. 150.4995-2). However, that section requires an independent producer's certificate to certify that "the *entire* amount of the producer's oil expected to be sold to the purchaser" is subject to the reduced rates (emphasis added). This "all-or-nothing" approach is not required by the statute.

Under the Proposed Regulation, if an independent producer's production exceeds 1,000 barrels per day, and is all sold to a single purchaser, that purchaser would appear to be prohibited from reducing its withholding to take into account the lower rates applicable to that producer's first 1,000 barrels per day. And, under Prop. Reg. 150.6402-1 (c), the independent producer may not claim a refund of the over-withheld money from the IRS until March 1 of the following year.

A similar problem occurs when an independent producer sells to a single

[9] The average grade and quality of the oil produced from the property in December 1979 is used in determining the base price.

[10] The interim tier two and three base price must at least equal the sum of (1) The ceiling price which would have applied to such oil under the March 1979 energy regulations if it had been produced and sold in May 1979 as upper tier oil, and (2) $1 in the case of tier two oil, or $2 in the case of tier three oil.

[10a] The circumstances under which a first purchaser may rely on certifications is another important concern and is discussed in the second part of this article which will appear in the subsequent issue.

[11] The inflation adjustment for tier three oil is greater than the tier one and two adjustment due to a 2% annual "kicker" intended to encourage production.

[12] The certification should also include the following information, if applicable: (1) whether the oil is exempt Alaskan or front-end oil (the other information is not required if the oil is exempt); and (2) the TAPS (Trans-Alaska Pipeline System) adjustment, if any, and the average removal price for the month, in the case of oil from the Sadlerochit Reservoir.

[13] The operator is the person who holds an operating mineral interest in the property and bears more of the responsibility for the management and operation of crude oil production from the property than any other holder of such an interest (Prop. Reg. 150.4996-1(c)).

[14] Also, the purchaser does not have to withhold the tax if the oil is removed from the premises before sale or refined on the premises (Prop. Reg. 150.4995-1(a)).

[15] During an interim period (until 30 days after the publication of final Regulations) the purchaser may withhold or not, at its option, on the production of integrated oil companies (Prop. Reg. 150.4995-1(a)(3)). However, once the purchaser receives an integrated oil company's certificate, it may no longer withhold.

purchaser some oil which qualifies as "independent producer oil" and other oil which does not. For example, assume the producer sells to a purchaser 500 barrels per day of "independent producer oil" and 25 barrels per day of oil derived from a royalty interest owned by that producer which does not qualify as a "working interest" under Prop. Reg. 150.4992-1(d)(2). Since the 25 barrels are not "independent producer oil" (as defined), Prop. Reg. 150.4995-2(c) would appear to prohibit the purchaser from using the lower withholding rates with regard to the producer's 500 barrels per day which clearly qualify as "independent producer oil."

This overwithholding required by the Proposed Regulations seems inconsistent with the Congressional intent to provide tax relief to independent producers; it may be particularly harmful to an independent producer who is dependent upon oil revenues for his livelihood. Moreover, it provides independent producers with an economic incentive to split their production among two or more purchasers in order to receive the reduced withholding rate. (For example, an independent producer which produces and sells 2,500 barrels per day to a single purchaser will now be encouraged to sell 1,000 barrels per day of that production to a different purchaser in order to receive a substantially higher payment net of withholding tax.) This may disrupt existing business relationships between purchasers and producers.

An obvious way to alleviate this problem would be to require the purchaser to withhold at different rates (*i.e.*, part at the independent producer rate, part at the regular rate) on its payments for oil from a single producer. Treasury may have considered and rejected this approach on the ground that it would be excessively difficult for purchasers to administer, which is indeed the case. However, a useful compromise solution would be to amend Prop. Reg. 150.4995-2 to permit an independent producer to certify eligibility for the reduced rate on a property-by-property basis. Thus, the producer would have to certify only that all of its production expected to be sold to that purchaser from a particular property qualifies for the reduced rate. This would mitigate the effect of the overwithholding on an independent producer which sells oil from more than one producing property, or which sells some oil that does not qualify under the rules as "independent producer oil."

This compromise seems workable in practice since purchasers' computer systems are typically set up on a property-by-property basis. It would not ordinarily be difficult for a purchaser to withhold at the independent producer rate on its purchases from one property, and to withhold at the regular rate on its purchases from the same producer at a different property. Although this approach may not make the withholding process totally precise, in many cases (*i.e.*, when the producer sells oil from more than one property) the withholding would be more accurate than under Treasury's current proposal.

Another method would be to permit independent producers to file quarterly claims for refund, like integrated oil companies (Prop. Reg. 150.6402-1(b)); or, at the least, for IRS to pay interest on the refund received in the subsequent year. Although legislation may be required for the latter changes, it would be consistent with IRS' recognition of the substantial time value of the use of money.

Finally, the Regulations do not explicitly state how frequently the exempt or independent producer must certify its status, but they do require a producer to revoke a certification which has ceased to be accurate by notifying the purchaser of this fact (Prop. Reg. 150.4995-2(d)). This suggests that an exempt or independent producer need submit only a single certification to the purchaser, and that the purchaser may rely on such certification each time it makes a purchase from that producer, until and unless the producer notifies the purchaser of a revocation. Treasury should clarify this point.

Integrated oil company certifications. Integrated oil companies generally are required to deposit their own tax liabilities twice a month, and are not subject to withholding by purchasers (Section 4995(b)(1)). An oil company is "integrated" if it both produces oil and is either a "retailer" of oil, natural gas, or a product derived therefrom, or a "refiner" of crude oil, as defined in paragraphs (2) and (4) respectively of Section 613A(d), but not an "independent refiner," as defined (Section 4995(b)(3), Prop. Reg. 150.4996-1(g)). Under these definitions, a company is "integrated" if, for example, it produces oil and also sells gasoline through retail outlets operated by that company or a "related person," and it derives more than $1,250,000 in total gross receipts from its retail gasoline sales during the taxable period.

Prop. Reg. 150.4995-1(a)(3), as amended in the April 25 notice, provides that the purchaser is not required to deduct and withhold tax from a producer which "is an integrated oil company . . . that has furnished a certificate to the purchaser pursuant to paragraph (c)(2) of §150.4995-2. . . ."[14] Such certificate is required to state that the producer is an integrated oil company, that it will deposit its own windfall profit tax liability, and therefore no withholding should be made.

If the integrated oil company is also the operator of the property, the certification is mandatory, and must be furnished to the first purchaser by the due date of the first operator's certification. Where the integrated oil company is not the operator it may, at its option, furnish a certification; if it does, it may do so to either the operator or the purchaser.[15]

The Proposed Regulation is silent as to whether a purchaser may rely on a producer's certificate of its integrated status, or whether it is required to verify such status, in order to be relieved of the withholding requirement. One could assume reasonably that Treasury did not intend to require the purchaser to make an independent determination of the producer's "integrated" status. Indeed, that determination would often be impossible for the purchaser to make without a detailed examination of books, records and financial statements. A producer may not appear to be an integrated oil company (*i.e.*, because it is not one of the well-known retailers), but it may have retail outlets at a distant location with sufficient sales to permit it to qualify as "integrated" under the above definition.

If Treasury did not intend to require the purchaser to verify the status of a certifying producer, the above-cited language of Prop. Reg. 150.4995-1(a)(3) should be modified to require only that the producer furnish the requisite certificate of its "integrated" status, so the purchaser may rely on such certificate.

The second part of this article, which will appear in the September issue of THE JOURNAL, will discuss the effect of the Proposed Regulations on the extent of the first purchaser's liability for the tax and the substantial administrative requirements and record-keeping burdens imposed on the purchasers. ☆

NEW DEVELOPMENTS IN

Taxation of oil & gas

EDITED BY BILLY M. MANN, CPA

Proposed Regs. expand first purchasers' duties beyond Windfall Profit Tax Act

by **MICHAEL I. SANDERS** *and* **RICHARD P. SILLS**

Although given broad latitude by Congress to prescribe Regulations under the Windfall Profit Tax, the Treasury seems to have shifted too many burdens of collecting and administering the tax to first purchasers. The authors examine the new rules and suggest ways in which both the Treasury's and purchasers' concerns could be met.

A PRIOR ARTICLE discussed the computation of the windfall profit tax and the withholding requirements imposed on first purchasers under the Proposed Regulations issued by the Treasury two days after President Carter signed the Act into law.[1] Here, we consider the extent of the first purchaser's liability and the record-keeping requirements imposed by the Regulations.

Extent of liability

Section 4995 provides that, "[e]xcept to the extent provided in [the Treasury] regulations," the purchaser shall withhold the tax in the amount prescribed by the statute, and "shall be liable for the payment of the tax required to be withheld." Thus, Treasury has ample authority to define and to limit the circumstances in which the purchaser becomes liable for the tax. However, the Proposed Regulations may be interpreted to impose liability on the purchaser under a variety of circumstances, which seems particularly unwarranted in cases where the purchaser has received no economic benefit whatsoever as a result of the withholding error. In a sense, the Proposed Regulations may be construed to require the purchaser to act at its peril when fulfilling its statutorily-imposed role as a withholding and collection agent for the Treasury.

There are many circumstances in which a conscientious purchaser, acting in good faith, cannot readily ascertain the correct amount of tax it is responsible for withholding. This may occur, for example, when there is uncertainty as to the correct amount of the base price (*e.g.*, where producers submit conflicting certifications), or as to the classification of a producer (*e.g.*, whether it is an independent producer or an exempt producer).

Three closely-related questions arising under the Proposed Regulations are:

1. To what extent may a purchaser rely on information in a certification furnished by the operator or producer?

2. When a certification is lacking or appears incorrect or incomplete, may a purchaser make a good-faith determination as to the relevant information?

3. Under what circumstances may a purchaser be relieved of liability for tax which is "required to be withheld," but which in fact is not withheld?

Reliance on certifications. Section 4995 (a)(2) provides that the purchaser shall determine the amount to be withheld on the basis of the certification furnished to it, unless the purchaser "has reason to believe that any information contained in such certification is not correct"; otherwise, the purchaser shall determine such amount "under regulations prescribed by the Secretary." Following this language, Prop. Reg. 150.4995-1(b)(1) provides that a purchaser may compute the amount of tax to be withheld on the basis of information in the operator's certification, "if the purchaser has no reason to believe that any information contained in that certification that affects the computation of the windfall profit tax is not correct."

On the other hand, if the purchaser "has reason to believe" that any such information is not correct, or if no certification is provided, and assuming the purchaser pays either the upper-tier ceiling price or an uncontrolled price for the oil, then Prop. Reg. 150.4995-1(b) (2) apparently requires it to deduct and withhold from the purchase price an amount equal to 70% of the excess of the removal price over $11.01 (as adjusted for inflation) plus the amount of the severance tax adjustment (if known).

As an example of the distortion this may create, assume that the oil in question is tier two oil removed in March 1980, so that the inflation adjustment is .0195; and that the selling price is $40. The producer has certified that the highest posted price on 12/31/79 was $39, but the purchaser "has reason to believe" that the correct amount of such highest posted price was $37. Under these circumstances (and assuming no severance tax adjustment), the per-barrel tax computed on the basis of the producer's certification would be $13.64. Using the figures that the purchaser believes correct, the tax would be $14.17. However, Prop. Reg. 150.4995-1(b)(2) appears to prohibit the purchaser from making this type of good-faith recomputation of the tax. It seems to require, instead, the use of the $11.01 figure, as adjusted, which would yield a tax of $20.15—over 40% more than the amount the purchaser believes to be correct. Besides depriving the producer of the use of a substantial sum of money, computing the tax in this manner virtually assures that the producer will ask the purchaser to make a retroactive adjustment, with the resulting burden and cost.

Despite the serious consequences of the purchaser having "reason to believe" that a certification is incorrect, Prop. Reg. 150.4995-1(b)(1) does not provide any guidance as to when a purchaser may have such "reason." Suppose, for example, a purchaser receives certifications from hundreds or thousands of producers with regard to the highest posted 12/31/79 price of sundry types of oil in various different fields. Out of all those certifications, it is likely that there will be some inconsistencies. In view of the expeditious processing required, it is practically impossible to compare and cross-check all of these certifications. Under the Proposed Regulation, it is not clear whether IRS would

Article reprinted courtesy of *Journal of Taxation*, September 1980, pp. 138–141

treat such an inconsistency between certificates as a "reason to believe" that certain ones are incorrect. If IRS did treat such an inconsistency as such a "reason to believe," it would, in effect, shift the burden for the accuracy of the certified information from the producer/operator, where it is placed by the statute, to the purchaser.

The legislative history[2] suggests that Congress intended to permit the purchaser to rely on a certificate except in an "abuse" case, such as where the purchaser knowingly participated in a material misrepresentation which rendered the certificate incorrect. It is important for Treasury to have an effective remedy in the abuse situation, but purchasers must also be able to process certificates quickly and compute the tax based on certified information, without the requirement of cross-checking or verification. Considering both sides' principal concerns, the Regulations should construe the statute in favor of allowing purchasers to process a certification and rely on it, unless either the certification is obviously erroneous on its face (*i.e.*, it contains internally inconsistent information), or the purchaser participates knowingly and willfully in an act of misrepresentation with regard to the information in the certification. The purchaser should not have to compare an apparently regular certification with others, and Treasury should make this clear, either by Regulation or through other guidance.

Absent or incorrect certifications. Regardless of the first purchaser's diligent efforts to encourage operators to furnish timely and correct certifications, it is inevitable that many will not. Some operators may simply lack sophistication in this regard; others may not have access to skilled legal or accounting guidance relating to this tax.

As discussed above, a literal reading of Prop. Reg. 150.4995-1(b) (2) suggests that the first purchaser has no choice but to use the $11.01 base price (as adjusted for inflation) in computing the withholding tax from those operators who fail to certify, or who furnish obviously incorrect certifications. Use of this figure will clearly distort the amount of tax withholding, as shown by the example above, as well as effectively preventing the first purchaser from buying oil in a competitive market. In particular, this distortion will result in significant overwithholding from a class which includes the least-affluent independent operators who often do not possess sophisticated business skills. Typically, these may be the same operators who are most dependent on their oil revenues for their livelihoods.

To impose a withholding rate which substantially exceeds the taxes owed is contrary to the general purpose of a withholding system, which is to provide a means for timely collection of the amount of tax likely to be due. While overwithholding in this circumstance may appear to be sanctioned by the legislative history,[3] it is not required by Section 4995(a)(2)(A) (ii).

Moreover, as noted above, the Proposed Regulation imposes a serious burden on the first purchaser. In effect, the Regulations say that the purchaser must first withhold an amount which it knows to be grossly excessive, and subsequently sustain a significant expense and administrative burden to correct the prior overwithholding, after the operator becomes aware of the situation and demands a prompt retroactive adjustment. IRS may be inundated with explanatory statements attached to Forms 720 reflecting these adjustments.

Treasury may be able to avoid many of these problems if the Regulations were to permit an election by the first purchaser to use its good-faith reasonable judgment to estimate the correct price, and withhold based on that estimate. A first purchaser making such election would be required to retain the information on which the estimate was based, and to furnish this information to IRS at the time of an audit.

Liability of the purchaser. With regard to the extent of the purchaser's liability, the Senate Finance Committee expressed a rather liberal view, stating that the purchaser "ordinarily would not be responsible for any tax deficiency attributable to the operator's misrepresentation of the oil purchased." Rather, the purchaser would be liable if it withholds the tax but fails to pay it over to the Government, or if it becomes a party to any misrepresentation of the oil purchased. In addition, the first purchaser "could be liable, depending upon the circumstances, for negligence in satisfying its obligations."[4]

By contrast, Prop. Reg. 150.4995-1 (e) provides in effect that a purchaser is absolutely liable for tax which is required to be withheld, whether or not it is actually withheld by the purchaser, unless the tax is paid by some other party, or is ultimately determined not to be due (*e.g.*, if the net income limitation applies).

Liability would appear to be warranted if the purchaser has derived an economic benefit by withholding the tax and failing to pay it over, or if it has acted in willful disregard of the statute and Regulations. But, in many cases where too little tax is withheld, the purchaser will have derived no economic benefit whatsoever. Under all the circumstances—lack of economic benefit, the fact that Congress imposed the tax on another party, and the inevitable errors that will be made because of the novelty and complexity of this tax—a standard of absolute liability may frequently be unfair. Moreover, it shifts the imposition of the tax from the producer to the purchaser. While the Proposed Regulation gives the purchaser a right of reimbursement against the producer, this remedy may be of no practical value if the producer becomes insolvent or cannot be located.

A more appropriate treatment might be to provide that in cases where tax is "required to be withheld" but in fact is not withheld, the purchaser is not liable for such tax if the failure to withhold or the underwithholding is due to reasonable cause and is not due to willful disregard of the Regulations.

This type of "good faith" test is consistent with Congress' intent. Moreover, such a modification would appear to be permitted under Section 4995 (a)(1) (B), which does not explicitly require liability for tax which is not actually withheld. In addition, it would be consistent with numerous other provisions of the Code, under which liability is conditioned upon the "knowing" or "willful" nature of the violation, and liability may be negated by showing that an inadvertent violation was "due to reasonable cause" or was the result of an action taken in good faith.[5] Moreover, such a modification would distinguish between situations in which the purchaser realizes an economic benefit by withholding the tax and failing to pay

---

[*Michael I. Sanders and Richard P. Sills are partners in the Washington, D. C., law firm of Ginsburg, Feldman, Weil and Bress. Mr. Sanders, a former Chairman and presently Special Advisor of the Exempt Organizations Committee of the ABA Tax Section, has appeared often in* THE JOURNAL.]

it over, and situations in which the purchaser inadvertently does not withhold or withholds too little.

Administrative requirements

The Proposed Regulations impose substantial administrative responsibilities and record-keeping requirements upon purchasers. In view of the very substantial costs of compliance, Treasury may wish to consider whether these requirements can be reduced without compromising Treasury's concerns for orderly administration of the tax and accumulation of relevant data. Several of the most significant administrative requirements are discussed below.

Withholding adjustments. Section 4995 (a)(3)(A) provides that "withholding errors made by a purchaser" must be corrected by that purchaser "[t]o the extent provided in regulations prescribed by the Secretary," by making appropriate adjustments in the amounts withheld from subsequent payments to the same producer for crude oil removed during the same calendar year. Thus, Congress gave Treasury considerable discretion to provide the extent and nature of the adjustments which a purchaser must make to correct its own errors.

However, the Proposed Regulations appear to require the purchaser to make adjustments in a wider variety of circumstances, including situations where another party has made an error or has failed to furnish required information. Prop. Reg. 150.4995-1(c) states that if the purchaser ascertains[6] that the amount of tax withheld from any payment for crude oil was more or less than the amount of tax prescribed under the Act (without regard to the net income limitation), the purchaser must correct the discrepancy by adjusting the amounts to be withheld from subsequent payments to the same seller for oil removed during the same calendar year, without regard to whether the subsequent payments relate to oil from the same property.

As noted, the purchaser's obligation to make such withholding adjustments under the Proposed Regulations is not limited to situations involving errors actually made by the purchaser, such as an incorrect calculation. Rather, such obligation extends to discrepancies arising for such reasons as failure to withhold during March 1980 (prior to enactment of the Act), the producer's failure to submit a timely or correct certification, or the producer's submission of a retroactive certification as to independent producer status, exempt status or base price.

When a purchaser does not receive a timely exempt or independent producer certification—which will probably occur often, particularly when small producers are involved—it is required to withhold tax without regard to any exemption or reduced rate. Then, when the producer becomes aware of the additional withholding caused by his failure to file timely, he is likely to file a retroactive certification and demand that the purchaser make a prompt retroactive adjustment.

By requiring purchasers to make retroactive adjustments in such circumstances, the Proposed Regulation adds significantly to the purchaser's responsibilities. This added responsibility will often be costly, in terms of both increased personnel hours and additional cost of computerized data processing equipment.

The final Regulations should not require a purchaser to make a retroactive adjustment when an exempt or independent producer files a late or incorrect certification. Such requirement in the Proposed Regulations effectively "penalizes" the purchaser (in terms of administrative costs) for the producer's noncompliance, and reduces the economic incentive for the producer to file correct and timely certifications.

The producer or operator could remedy any withholding discrepancies directly with the IRS, by filing an annual return reflecting any overpayment or underpayment, and effectively "netting out" the amounts. This approach would be analogous to the established practice in the income tax withholding system, and would avoid multiple adjustments throughout the year.

Depositary requirements. Purchasers are required by Prop. Reg. 150.4995-3(c) to deposit the withheld windfall profit tax with an authorized Federal tax depositary within 45 days after the close of the month during which the oil was removed.[7] In the case of independent refiners who purchase oil pursuant to contracts under which no payment is made before the 46th day after the end of the month in which the oil is removed, deposits may be made before the first day of the third month following the month of removal, under Prop. Reg. 150.4995-3(b). Under Prop. Reg. 150.4995-3(a), integrated oil companies must deposit twice a month the tax they withhold as purchasers and the tax on their own production (unless the purchaser is required to withhold the tax).[8] These deposits are due on the ninth day following the semi-monthly period in which the oil was removed.

Returns and statements. Section 4997(a) provides that each taxpayer, producer, purchaser and operator "shall keep such records, make such returns, and furnish such information . . . with respect to such oil as the Secretary may by regulations prescribe." Thus, Treasury has wide discretion as to the requirements for keeping records and filing returns.

Prop. Reg. 150.4997-1(a)(1) requires first purchasers, depositing producers, and integrated oil companies to file quarterly Form 6047, the windfall profit tax schedule, and Form 720, the Federal excise tax return. They must file these forms with the Service Center serving their geographical area by the last day of the second month following the end of the quarter (Prop. Reg. 150.6076-1).

Prop. Reg. 150.4995-1(c) requires that every return[9] on which an overpayment or underpayment is adjusted must include "a statement explaining the adjustment, designating the return period to which the adjustment relates, and setting forth such other information as may be required by the instructions to the return." This rule appears to require the purchaser to give "individual-

[1] Sanders and Sills, *Problems under the windfall profit tax Prop. Regs.: advising "first purchasers,"* 53 JTAX 92 (August, 1980).
[2] S. Rep't No. 96-394, 96th Cong., 1st Sess. 63 (1979).
[3] Conference Report, H. Rep't No. 96-817, 96th Cong., 2nd Sess. 112 (1980).
[4] S. Rep't No. 96-394, *supra* note 2.
[5] See, *e.g.*, Sections 4221(c), 4941(a)(1) and (2), 4942(a)(2), 4944(a)(2), 4945(a)(2), 4951(a)(2), 4952(a)(2), and 4974(c).
[6] An error is "ascertained" when the first purchaser has sufficient information to be able to determine the amount of tax imposed by the statute (Prop. Reg. 150.4995-1(c)).
[7] If a producer's oil is not subject to withholding, he must deposit the tax within 45 days after the close of the removal month.
[8] The semi-monthly periods consist of the first 15 days of the month and the remainder of the month. The Regulations set out "safe harbor" rules for making estimated deposits of the tax on an integrated oil company's own production.
[9] Other than when an adjustment is completely made within the same taxable period in which the problem occurred.
[10] Two copies must be filed with IRS if Form 6248 contains information on withholding adjustments.
[11] If the refund is based upon the net income limitation, the claim for refund cannot be filed until the producer's income tax return for the year is filed (Prop. Reg. 150.6402-1).

ized" attention to thousands of adjustments which must be reported on returns. This would slow down considerably the computerized processing of withholding data, and is not needed to rectify the withholding error. If such explanations are necessary, a system of "checkmarked boxes" would probably be less burdensome than the furnishing of a narrative statement.

The purchaser is required to furnish each producer, operator or partnership from which it purchases oil with a monthly statement showing the total windfall profit tax withheld (or that none was withheld because an exemption certificate was supplied) for oil removed during that month (Prop. Reg. 150.4997-2(b)). The monthly statement must be submitted by the end of the first month following the month in which the oil was removed.

The purchaser is also required to furnish each producer, operator, or partnership from which it purchases oil with an annual information statement on Form 6248 (Prop. Reg. 150.4997-2(c)). One copy of each Form 6248 furnished to a seller of oil must be filed with the Service.[10] Form 6248 must be submitted to the seller by January 31, and to the IRS by the end of February, of the year following the year in which the windfall profit tax was withheld.

Prop. Reg. 150.4997-2(c) provides that where the purchaser did not withhold tax from a person who furnished an exemption certificate, the purchaser must include in the Form 6248 information regarding the tax consequences that "would have occurred" if the exemption certificate had not been received. This requirement that the purchaser compute a "hypothetical" tax liability is not suggested by either the statute or the legislative history. When this task is added to the amount of other information required in Form 6248, and taking into consideration the number of these forms to be completed, it seems unduly burdensome and of doubtful relevance to any actual tax liability.

The Regulations require producers who owe tax at the end of the year to file an annual return by the last day of the first February following the close of the calendar year (Prop. Regs. 150.4997-1(a)(2) and 150.6076-1). Under Prop. Reg. 150.6402-1(c), producers who have overpaid their tax liability through overwithholding may not file a claim for refund for the overpayment until after the same date.[11] For production not subject to withholding, integrated oil companies may file claims for refund quarterly or may claim credits for overpayments on their quarterly returns (Prop. Reg. 150.6402-1(b)). A producer may claim an overpayment as a credit on his income tax return for the year (Prop. Reg. 150.6402-1(c)).

Joint election for withholding by operator. Section 4995 (a)(7) provides that the operator and the first purchaser may make a joint election to have the operator withhold and deposit the tax, although the election may be limited by Treasury to situations where substituting the operator for the purchaser is "administratively more practicable." Prop. Reg. 150.4995-4(a) provides that substitution of the operator is administratively more practicable only where the operator is otherwise required to make deposits as a purchaser of oil produced from a different oil reservoir.

This limitation restricts too severely the flexibility contemplated by Section 4995 (a)(7). For example, substitution would appear to be advantageous where the operator, rather than the first purchaser, holds the basic "division order"—the statement identifying the exact nature of the ownership interests in the property. In that situation, the first purchaser pays the operator for the oil, and the operator distributes the money among the ownership interests. If the operator is willing to assume the responsibilities imposed on the "purchaser" under the Act, and is in a better position (due to possession of the division order) to discharge those responsibilities than the purchaser, it appears reasonable to permit, rather than to prohibit, substitution.

Conclusion

Treasury has accomplished promptly the massive and difficult task of providing temporary guidance under a novel and complicated law. As Treasury undoubtedly recognizes, there is a residue of problems which may be substantially cured by further refinement of the Proposed Regulations.

It would be helpful if the final Regulations provided more explicit guidance to the purchaser and its counsel, to facilitate uniform compliance with the Act in the best interest of Treasury and taxpayers. Pending the publication of final Regulations, such guidance could be furnished in the form of TIRs or other announcements.

Further, the Proposed Regulations may be interpreted to subject the purchaser to liability for the tax under a variety of circumstances in which the purchaser's error is inadvertent (and may be due to ambiguities in the rules), and in which the purchaser derives no economic benefit whatsoever from the error. Liability in such cases is generally unwarranted, and seems inconsistent with Congress' intent. The Proposed Regulations should be modified to avoid imposing liability when the purchaser has acted in good faith.

Moreover, Treasury should carefully reconsider both the necessity of frequent and detailed adjustments and the Government's need for information not essential to the computation of tax liability and balance these against the additional cost to the industry of preparing and furnishing that information and the increased cost to the Government of processing and storing those items. ☆

The Crude Oil Windfall Profit Tax Act of 1980 and the Proposed Regulations

By J. DENNY MOFFETT *

The author discusses the provisions of the recently enacted Crude Oil Windfall Profit Tax Act of 1980 with a view to enlightening the tax practitioner as to the impact it will have on its clients.

J. Denny Moffett is a member of Conner, Winters, Ballaine, Barry & McGowen, Tulsa, Oklahoma.

Article reprinted courtesy of *Taxes — the Tax Magazine*, June 1980, pp. 417–423

Introduction

On March 7, 1980, the committee of conference composed of representatives of the United States House of Representatives and the United States Senate concluded work on the Crude Oil Windfall Profit Tax Act of 1980 ("the Act") and in its report agreed to recommend to their respective bodies the passage of the Act enumerated H. R. 3919.[1] Despite limited protestations to the contrary, the Act became law as agreed to by the conference committee when President Carter signed the legislation on April 2, 1980. The Act, however, is generally retroactive to March 1, 1980. Coinciding with the signing of the Act, the Treasury Department issued temporary regulations, which will also serve as a basis for proposed rulemaking.[2]

The Act, its genesis and its effect will undoubtedly continue to be much discussed and, in particular, criticized. It is, at best, the result of a consummate demonstration of political compromise in a system described by Theodore Parker

* This article is an expansion of an article that previously appeared in the *Oklahoma Bar Journal*.

[1] Crude Oil Windfall Profit Tax Act of 1980, Conference Report, H. R. Rep. No. 96-817, 96th Cong., 2nd Sess. (1980) (hereinafter cited as Report). Unless otherwise noted, all references are to the Act and the Joint Explanatory Statement contained in the Conference Report. Once signed by the President, the Legislation became Public Law 96-223.

[2] Treas. Reg. Sec. 150.0 et seq., T. D. 7690.

as "the science of exigencies." Analysis of the political, economic and social effects of the Act will be reserved for those learned in such matters. The purpose of this article is to acquaint the practitioner with the scope of the Act, its provisions and its complexity so that an understanding will be reached with respect to its impact on your clients.

The Act has provisions that affect everyone from low-income families to multinational corporations. The seven major parts of the Act are as follows: part 1 imposes the windfall profit tax on domestically produced crude oil; part 2 expands current residential energy tax credits; part 3 provides incentives for business to conserve energy and utilize alternative energy sources; part 4 provides an energy subsidy to low-income families; part 5 provides guidelines for the distribution of windfall profit revenue; part 6 is a bundle of essentially unrelated although significant income tax changes including repeal of the carryover basis rules; and part 7 restricts the authority of the President to control oil importation. Notwithstanding that all of these parts of the Act are noteworthy aspects of this country's overall plan to reduce the consumption of energy, the most controversial section and the section that will have the most direct impact on the oil and gas industry is part 1—the imposition of the windfall profit tax on domestically produced crude oil.

Broad Effect of Tax

Every individual, family, partnership, trust or corporation that receives income from production of oil will be affected as will every operator of oil and gas properties and every refiner. While integrated oil companies and royalty owners will absorb the greatest portion of the tax impact, independent producers (and their investors) are also to be taxed substantially. The technical and administrative burdens will be distributed among the producers, whether integrated or independent, the operator, and the refiner or other first purchaser. In addition to criminal penalties, the Act provides strict civil penalties that can be imposed whether or not the violation is flagrant. Tax deficiencies and any applicable penalties will be assessed against a producer for any misrepresentation about oil sold and the first purchaser is subject to civil and criminal penalties for failing to withhold and/or make deposits unless such failure was caused by a misrepresentation of the producer.

Imposition of Tax

The windfall profit tax is an excise, or severance, tax on domestically produced crude oil; specifically on the excess of the selling price over the base price. The tax is officially denoted as being "temporary" in the sense that it will "phase out" beginning not later than January 3, 1991.[3] The Act states that the tax will phase out either over a 33-month period beginning in January, 1988 or one month after the federal government has collected an aggregate of $227.3 billion from the tax, but in any event on January 1, 1991.

The tax is paid by the producer and collected by the first purchaser based on certifications by the operator. All crude oil that is taxable is classified in one of three tiers. The essential elements of the computation of the tax are identical for each tier. Any state severance taxes and the base price reduce the selling price to provide the windfall profit. The windfall profit is then reduced by the net income adjustment, if applicable, multiplied by the applicable tax rate to provide the windfall profit tax. The tier distinctions are based upon the classification of crude oil, which affects the tax rate and the base price. In addition, certain categories of producers are eligible for reduced rates on all or part of their production or are entirely exempt from the tax.

Generally, the Act imposes the tax on all producers of domestic crude oil. Producers include all owners of "economic interests"[4] with respect to the crude oil. Specific exemptions exist for federal, state and local governments provided the proceeds are used for a public purpose; medical and educational charities if the properties were owned by the charity on January 21, 1980; churches if the proceeds are dedicated to the use of a charitable medical or educational institution and the church owned the property prior to January 22, 1980; production from properties owned on January 21, 1980 by an Indian tribe or Indian tribal organization where the proceeds are paid to the U. S. Treasury to the credit of tribal or native trust funds; and crude oil produced before 1992 by any corporation organized under the Alaska Native Claims Settlement Act.

[3] The legislative history, oddly, makes no reference to any other tax passed by this Congress or any other legislative body, which automatically is "phased out."

[4] See Treas. Reg. Sec. 1.611-(b)(1). In *Burton-Sutton Oil Co. v. Commissioner*, the Supreme Court defined an economic interest as the possibility of profit "dependent solely upon the extraction and sale of the oil" from a person's rights to production, 46-1 USTC ¶ 9243, 328 U. S. 25, 34.

Crude Oil Taxed

Once it is determined that a producer is not exempt, the calculation of the tax requires the classification of the crude oil into one of three tiers, which determines the base price, the windfall profit and the respective rates of tax on the windfall profits. The only production exempt from the tax based upon classification and, hence, not included in any of the tiers, is (a) production from north of the Arctic Circle other than from the Sadlerochit reservoir, (b) Alaskan oil south of the Arctic Circle but north of the Alaska-Aleutian mountain range if it is produced from a well located at least 75 miles from the nearest point on the Alaska Pipeline,[5] and (c) prior to October 1, 1981, oil that is deregulated by the Department of Energy ("DOE") as "front-end tertiary oil" except that which could have been decontrolled by DOE under other provisions or oil decontrolled to finance prepaid expenses. All other oil is classified as either tier one, two or three oil.

Tax Calculation

For all three tiers of oil, the windfall profit is determined by subtracting from the actual selling price the base price and the severance tax adjustment. The severance tax adjustment, applicable to all three tiers, permits the deduction of the amount of state severance taxes on the windfall profit from the selling price of the oil for purposes of computing the windfall profit. The deduction equals the difference between the severance tax that would have been imposed if the oil had been sold at the base price and the actual severance tax paid. Any increases in a state severance tax after March 31, 1979, are deductible only if the tax applies equally to the entire price of the oil. A limitation of 15% is placed on the severance tax adjustment available. It is noted that any tax imposed by a state on the removal of crude oil as a percentage of the gross value qualifies for this purpose.[6]

Tier One Oil

Tier one oil is defined as all taxable oil except that oil specifically included in tier two or tier three—such tiers being stripper well oil, oil from a National Petroleum Reserve in which the U. S. has an economic interest, certain heavy oil, incremental tertiary recovery oil, and newly discovered oil. Generally, tier one includes all oil that would have been tier one or tier two oil if the pre-June 1979 price controls were still effective (oil discovered prior to 1979 and production from the Sadlerochit reservoir). The base price for tier one oil is the May 1979 upper tier ceiling price for the property less 21 cents. Although the national average price for such oil was $13.02 per barrel,[7] each producer must determine his own base price taking into account differences in grade, location and quality of the oil. The rate of tax for oil in tier one is 70% of the windfall profit.

Tier Two Oil

Tier two oil is defined as stripper well oil (oil from property that produces an average daily rate of production of 10 barrels or less) [8] and National Petroleum Reserve oil. The base price for tier two utilizes the average posted price for uncontrolled oil as of September, 1979, or $15.20, with adjustments to be made for grade, location and quality. Detailed regulations for calculating the precise base price for particular properties will be forthcoming from the Treasury.[9] Prior to the implementation of permanent regulations, an interim method is provided.[10] Windfall profits for tier two oil are taxed at the rate of 60%.

Tier Three Oil

Tier three oil includes certain heavy oil, incremental tertiary oil, or newly discovered oil. Heavy oil is defined as oil that has a weighted average gravity of 16.0 degrees API or less for

[5] The Report explains that this exemption "reflects the concern of the conferees that taxation of this production would discourage exploration and development of reservoirs in areas of extreme climatic conditions." Report at 103.

[6] This might include taxes variously denoted as gross production, severance, excise and conservation taxes, depending upon the jurisdiction.

[7] For Sadlerochit reservoir oil, the base price is adjusted upward to reflect decreases in the Alaska Pipeline tariff below $6.26.

[8] At the time of certification as a stripper well the rate must be 10 barrels per day or less. Subsequent increases in production do not remove the stripper well designation.

[9] "The Treasury regulations prescribing the permanent method of determining tier two base prices must estimate the price at which oil from a particular property would have sold in December 1979 if all domestic oil had been uncontrolled and the average price for domestic crude oil, other than North Slope Alaskan oil, had been $15.20. Thus, if oil from a particular property typically sells for 80 percent of the price of oil of national average grade, quality and location, based on market price differentials prevailing in December 1979, its tier two base price should generally be 80 percent of $15.20, or $12.16." Report at 96.

[10] Treas. Reg. Sec. 150.4989-1(c)(2).

the last month of production prior to July, 1979 or that has such a specific gravity or less for the taxable period.

Incremental tertiary oil is the production in excess of a decline curve[11] on a property on which a qualified[12] tertiary project is undertaken. Generally, only production from a tertiary project undertaken after May 31, 1979 will qualify, provided, however, certain significantly expanded projects or DOE-certified projects commencing prior to May 31, 1979 may qualify. Producers may self-certify their tertiary projects or a competent governmental body may certify them in advance as meeting certain criteria: use of a qualified tertiary recovery method, implementation in accordance with sound engineering principles "which can reasonably be expected to result in more than an insignificant increase in the amount"[13] of oil ultimately recovered, and compliance with regulations to be promulgated by the Treasury. The Act permits production to qualify only so long as the tertiary process affects that production and the project is in effect. This determination will be generally on a case-by-case basis.

Newly discovered oil, the remaining category of tier three oil, includes production from a property that did not produce oil in commercial quantities during the calendar year 1978 and is sold after May, 1979. For purposes of the Act, the definition of property as defined in the Department of Energy regulations is adopted. Generally, a specific property will be equivalent to the lease of which it is a part. The Treasury is accorded the privilege of making technical amendments to this definition.

It is noted that oil produced from a property transferred after 1978 will not qualify for stripper, heavy, or newly discovered oil if such oil would not have received the same classification had the property not been transferred.

The base price for tier three oil is $16.55, adjusted for grade, quality and location. In particular, the base price for tier three oil is to be determined using the same formula as utilized for tier two oil.[14] The tax rate on tier three oil is 30% of the windfall profit.

Inflation Adjustment

The above discussed base prices and rates of taxation for the three tiers are subject to several additional adjustments. In computing the windfall profit for each of the three tiers, the base price of every barrel of oil is adjusted for inflation occurring after the second quarter of 1979 on a cumulative basis using the Gross National Product deflator as the measure of the rate of inflation. However, the adjustments are lagged by two quarters. Thus, the adjustments for the first quarter of 1981 will be based on the inflation rate for the third quarter of 1980. In addition, tier three oil, and only tier three oil, has an additional inflation adjustment "kicker" of 2% per year pursuant to which the base price is adjusted upward by ½% quarterly.

Special Rates for Independent Producers

Of extreme importance to many in the oil business are the special tax rates applicable to independent producers. Independent producers are generally defined as a working interest owner who is neither a retailer within the meaning of Code Section 613A(d)(2) nor a refiner within the meaning of Section 613A(d)(4).[15]

Independent producers, following the philosophy adopted in the percentage depletion laws, are permitted to apply special rates of taxation to their windfall profit on the first 1,000 barrels a day of tier one and tier two oil. Generally, royalty owners and owners of certain transferred properties are not eligible for the reduced rates. The special tax rates are 50% (rather than 70%) for tier one oil and 30% (rather than 60%) for tier two oil. To the extent an independent producer's qualifying production exceeds 1,000 barrels a day, the reduced rates must be applied ratably as between the tier one and tier two oil. The special rates are then applied within each tier to the oil with the highest selling price.

Certain related parties must allocate the 1,000 barrel limitation between them. The definition of related parties is generally the same as for depletion purposes[16] with the important exception that a producer and a controlled corporation must share the 1,000 barrel limit.[17] Where

[11] Report at 101.

[12] Qualified tertiary methods include: miscible fluid displacement, steam drive injection, microemulsion, in situ combustion, polymer augmented water flooding, cyclic steam injection, alkaline flooding, carbonated water flooding, and immiscible carbon dioxide displacement specifically excluding water flooding and immiscible natural gas injection.

[13] Report at 13.

[14] Report, supra note 8, at 96.

[15] Congress has wisely, in this instance and numerous others, adopted language or definitions that parallel provisions of existing law.

[16] See IRC Sec. 613A(c)(8).

[17] The "control" test applies if the taxpayer owns at least 80% of the voting stock and 80% of every other class of stock.

the taxpayer is a member of more than one related group, he is required to make his allocation by reference to the group that results in the smallest daily barrel allocation to that taxpayer. With respect to partnerships, the computations regarding allocations are made at the partner level and no special allocations are permitted as between joint venturers.

The special independent producer's rates are not available for production from properties transferred after 1979 if the transferor was a royalty owner, an integrated oil company or a producer whose production at any time between 1979 and the date of transfer was in excess of 1,000 barrels a day.[18] Properties transferred from trusts or partnerships are deemed to be owned by the beneficiaries or partners proportionately in determining eligibility of the transferee for the reduced rate. Finally, related parties who must allocate the 1,000 barrel limit may transfer properties so long as the parties continue to be related.

The only overriding royalty interests to which the special rates apply are those that convert to a working interest pursuant to a binding agreement in effect on February 20, 1980, but the rate is not applicable until the time of conversion.

Net Income Limitation

The final adjustment to be made to the calculations discussed in this article is the net income limitation. The Act provides that regardless of the tax owed by a producer under the above calculations, no producer will be required to pay a windfall profit tax in excess of 90% of the net income from a property. For purposes of this determination, the producer may capitalize qualified tertiary injectant costs. Net income is defined as taxable income from the property, with adjustments for depletion and intangible drilling and development costs, i. e., cost depletion must be utilized and the intangibles must be capitalized. The windfall profit tax does not, for this purpose, reduce the net income, but, in computing the 50% of net income limitation, the tax probably will be required to be deducted.

Summary of Calculations

The following chart demonstrates the calculations required to compute the windfall profit tax.

CALCULATION OF WINDFALL PROFIT TAX

I. Computation of Windfall Profit:

Selling Price
Less — Severance Tax Adjustment
Less — Base Price
- a. Tier One Oil = 12.81 (average) plus inflation adjustment
- b. Tier Two Oil = 15.80 (average) plus inflation adjustment
- c. Tier Three Oil = 16.55 (average) plus inflation adjustment plus 2% annual kicker

Equals — Windfall Profit

II. Computation of Tax on Windfall Profit:

Windfall Profit
Less — Net Income Adjustment
Times — Tax Rate
- a. Tier One Oil = 70% General Rate; 50% Independent Producer Rate
- b. Tier Two Oil = 60% General Rate; 30% Independent Producer Rate
- c. Tier Three Oil = 30% All Producers

Equals — Windfall Profit Tax

Interaction with other Sections

The effect of the windfall profit tax on other sections of the tax laws is not clear at this early stage. However, the windfall profit tax is a deduction from gross income and in computing percentage depletion the gross income is not reduced by the windfall profit.

Administration of the Tax

Administratively, the Act will be supervised by the Internal Revenue Service, and a myriad of

[18] Significant distinctions between this rule and the transfer rules for percentage depletion purposes are apparent. Transfers between individuals and controlled

(Continued on following page.)

regulations will be promulgated. The Treasury has been granted broad authority to implement the administrative provisions of the Act through regulations. The Tax Court, Court of Claims and U. S. District Courts will have jurisdiction over windfall profit cases.

The responsibilities for certification, withholding, depositing, and reporting under the Act will be spread among the producer, operator and first purchaser. Generally, the operator must certify all necessary information upon which to compute the tax to the first purchaser. It will be the first purchaser's responsibility to withhold and deposit the tax and file quarterly returns summarizing all purchases for the quarter. Where the withholding does not satisfy a producer's windfall profit tax obligation for the year, such producer is required to file an annual return and remit additional tax due. Indeed, if the first purchaser receives no certification information or has reason to believe the information is incorrect, then the amount must be withheld based upon regulations to be prescribed, which may require the maximum withholding possible to encourage certification. Such return is due on the last day of the second month after the last quarter. The IRS has already issued its Form 6047 for reporting purposes (Appendix A). In addition, a worksheet for windfall profit tax calculation has been adopted (Appendix B). Tax deposits are to be made semimonthly by integrated oil companies; independent refiners must make deposits 45 days after the month of purchase unless they are a party to a delayed payment contract, in which case the deposit must be made within 60 days after the last day of the month of purchase. Refunds or credits resulting from overwithholding may not be obtained until after year-end.

Without doubt, the above article is only a sketch of the windfall profit law. Complex issues remain to be solved by the regulators, the Treasury, the House and Senate committees in future fine tuning and, of course, lawyers, accountants and the courts. ●

(Footnote 18 continued.)
corporations are permitted and so long as independent producers with less than 1,000 barrels per day transfer properties to another in the like category, the special rates continue to apply.

APPENDIX A

Form **6047** (April 1980) Department of the Treasury Internal Revenue Service

Windfall Profit Tax

▶ See Separate Instructions.
▶ Attach to Form 720.

Use Only for Taxable Period Ending March 31, 1980

Name | Employer identification number

A Type of person filing Form 6047 (Check all applicable boxes) ☐ First purchaser ☐ Electing operator ☐ Producer

B Deposit Rules ☐ 45 day deposit rules ☐ 60 day deposit rules ☐ Semi-monthly deposit rules

C Number of barrels of incremental tertiary oil (as defined in Department of Energy regulations) purchased during the taxable period ▶ ....

D Number of Known Producers ▶ .... Other Entities (see instructions) ▶

E Number of barrels of exempt oil	Tier one	Tier two	Tier three
(1) Qualified governmental interests			
(2) Qualified charitable interests			
(3) Exempt Indian oil			
(4) Exempt Alaskan oil			
(5) Exempt front-end oil			

F Number of barrels of lower tier oil (as defined in Department of Energy regulations) purchased during the taxable period ▶

Windfall Profit Tax Liability	Number of barrels of oil (a)	Aggregate removal value (b)	Aggregate adjusted base value (c)	Aggregate state severance tax adjustment (d)	Tax (e)
1 Tier one, other than Sadlerochit oil:					
A "Controlled" oil					
(1) Subject to 70% tax rate					
(2) Subject to 50% tax rate					
B "Uncontrolled" oil					
(1) Subject to 70% tax rate					
(2) Subject to 50% tax rate					
2 Tier one, Sadlerochit oil:					
A "Controlled" oil taxed at 70%					
B "Uncontrolled" oil taxed at 70%					
3 Tier two oil taxed at 60%					
4 Tier two oil taxed at 30%					
5 Tier three, newly discovered oil					
6 Tier three, incremental tertiary oil					
7 Tier three, heavy oil					
8 Total (add lines 1 through 7, column (e), also enter amount on page one, Form 720)					

Schedule of Deposits Under Semi-monthly Deposit Rules

	Period	Amount of liability	Date of deposit	Amount of deposit
First Month	1st–15th day			
	16th–last day			
	Total for month			
Second Month	1st–15th day			
	16th–last day			
	Total for month			
Third Month	1st–15th day			
	16th–last day			
	Total for month			
Final Deposit Made For Taxable Period				
Total Deposits (enter as part of line 4(e), Form 720)				

Schedule of Deposits Under 45 Day and 60 Day Deposit Rules

Month	45 day		
	Amount of liability	Date of deposit	Amount of deposit
1			
2			
3			
	60 day		
	Amount of liability	Date of deposit	Amount of deposit
1			
2			
3			

Form **6047** (Ap

APPENDIX B

Worksheet for Windfall Profit Tax for All Oil Other than Sadlerochit Oil

1. Number of barrels of oil	
2. Removal Price	
3. Base Price	
4. Inflation Adjustment	
5. Multiply line 3 by line 4	
6. Adjusted Base Price (add line 3 and line 5)	
7. Severance Tax Adjustment	
8. Add line 6 and line 7	
9. Windfall Profit (subtract line 8 from line 2)	
10. Rate of Tax (see instructions)	
11. Multiply line 9 by line 10	
12. Windfall Profit Tax (multiply line 1 by line 11)	

Worksheet for Windfall Profit Tax for Sadlerochit Oil

1. Number of Barrels of Oil		
2. Removal Price (average monthly price)		
3. Base Price		
4. Inflation Adjustment		
5. Multiply line 3 by line 4		
6. Add line 3 and line 5		
7. TAPS Adjustment:		
(a)	6.26	
(b) TAPS tariff for preceding quarter		
(c) Subtract 7(b) from 7(a). (If less than zero, enter zero.)		
8. Add line 6 and line 7(c)		
9. Severance Tax Adjustment		
10. Add line 8 and line 9		
11. Windfall Profit (subtract line 10 from line 2)		
12. Rate of Tax (enter 70%)		
13. Multiply line 11 by line 12		
14. Windfall Profit Tax (multiply line 1 by line 13)		

Vesting Proposals Will Not Affect Some Determination Letters

If adopted as published, the regulations proposed in April on vesting provisions of qualified retirement plans will not affect some plans that previously obtained favorable determination letters based on vesting that is less rapid than the schedule set forth in the regulations. The schedule in the proposed regulations mandates vesting of 40% after four years of service plus an additional five percent for each of the next two years plus an additional 10% for each ensuing year with full vesting after 11 years. Reliance on such a letter would be justified provided that "the plan did not receive a determination letter which makes no finding as to whether the vesting schedule is discriminatory."

Otherwise, a plan with less rapid vesting than the schedule contained in the proposals will probably have to request a new determination letter even though the prior letter was issued pursuant to Rev. Procs. 75-49 and 76-11. It is "anticipated" that the new regulation would replace the tests contained in those releases.—News Release, CCH STANDARD FEDERAL TAX REPORTS, ¶ 6566.

COMPARATIVE ANALYSIS OF TAX-EXEMPT STATUS FOR FEDERAL INCOME AND WINDFALL PROFIT TAXATION

Prof Craig E. Reese
Robert L. Black, CPA*

Congress may have inadvertently levied a tax on many religious and charitable organizations, which are generally exempt from federal, state, and local taxes, when it enacted the Crude Oil Windfall Profit Tax Act of 1980.[1] For the past quarter century, these organizations have been given economic interests in crude oil producing property because such donations are a useful income tax planning device.[2] Other such organizations may have been given land upon which crude oil was subsequently discovered in commercial quantities. Thus, a tax-exempt group's share of the revenue from crude oil production could be subject to the Windfall Profit Tax (hereinafter WPT) unless the revenue from the crude oil produced therefrom is dedicated to specified educational and/or medical purposes.[3]

Needless to say, nonqualifying religious and charitable institutions are puzzled by the imposition of the WPT on their share of the revenue from crude oil production simply because they do not satisfy the rather restrictive

---

* Drs. Craig E. Reese and Robert L. Black are Assistant Professors of Tax Accounting at the University of Texas, Austin, Texas.

1 Act of Apr. 2, 1980, Pub. L. No. 96-223.

2 For a more detailed explanation of the federal income tax advantages of making charitable contributions of oil and gas producing property, see "Making Charitable Contributions of Oil and Gas Interests," in 1980 *P-H Oil & Gas/Natural Resources*, Para. 4025.

3 I.R.C. § 4994(b).

Article reprinted courtesy of *Oil & Gas Quarterly*, March 1981, pp. 459-496

requirements established for exemption from the WPT. Ironically, their tax-exempt status for federal income tax purposes precludes their taking advantage of the Section 164(a)(5) income tax deduction for WPT paid or accrued, except where the tax-exempt group has a working interest in an oil producing property. In addition, the Section 6429 $1,000 income tax credit for WPT paid or accrued in 1980[4] is unavailable to tax-exempt groups.[5]

Several legislative proposals to either exempt a small amount of a royalty owner's daily production from the WPT or to exempt an eleemosynary or a religious organization's royalty interest from the WPT were introduced late in 1980. We anticipate that several such exemptions from the WPT will be proposed during the first session of the ninety-seventh Congress, beginning in January 1981. Thus, help may be on the way; however, during the interim, religious and charitable organizations and their advisors should become familiar with the requirements for exemption from the WPT for both practical (compliance and planning) and political reasons. In the short term, they must pay the correct amount of WPT, and they should arrange their affairs so that this is only the minimum amount due. Moreover, a well-informed *cadre* of representatives for religious and charitable organizations should improve the chances for enactment of tax relief for those tax-exempt groups incurring the WPT under the current federal tax law.

---

4 *The Omnibus Reconciliation Act of 1980,* Pub. L. No. 96-499, December 5, 1980.

5 The credit is only applicable to individuals (with allocation within a family), estates, and qualified family farm corporations. Although some tax exempt organizations pay tax on their unrelated business income (UBI), § 512(b)(2) of the 1954 Code excludes royalties from UBI. Thus, where a tax-exempt group with royalty income pays tax on its UBI, it would be unable to deduct WPT or to credit $1,000 WPT against its federal income tax. However, § 509 private foundations subject to the § 4940 excise tax on investment income would be able to deduct WPT from royalty income in arriving at net investment income.

The following comparative analysis of tax-exempt status begins with the rationale for the federal income tax exemption of nonprofit organizations. Then the more limited tax-exempt status for windfall profit taxation is analyzed as part of a general explanation of "exempt" oil. A tabular summary of the tax-exempt status of various groups is also provided as a basis for our analysis of the policy options for imposing the WPT on tax exempt groups. Finally, there is an evaluation of the prospects for reforming the tax exemption from windfall profit taxation.

Tax-Exempt Organizations Under the Federal Tax Statutes

As already noted, it is a curious feature of the WPT that many organizations exempt from federal income taxes (among others) are subject to the WPT. Beyond the obvious loss of additional revenue to carry on their exempt-function activities, most of these organizations are now for the first time subject to a tax on a portion of their passive income.[6] As will be explained subsequently, this is a quantum leap, without theoretical basis, from the tax-exempt status they have traditionally enjoyed.

The Tax-Exempt Tradition

An exemption from taxation for nonprofit organizations can be traced back as far as the British Statute of Charitable Uses of 1601 and early state constitutional exemptions.[7] Congress initially avoided statutory tax exemptions, at least directly, by *specifically stating* those

6 This discussion generally will not consider the quasi-exempt status of private foundations as defined in I.R.C. § 509. However, their role in defrocking the tax exempt status of some eleemosynary organizations—whether justified entirely, in part, or not at all—will be noted later.

7 Boris I. Bittker & George K. Rahdert, "The Exemption of Nonprofit Organizations from the Federal Income Tax," 85 *Yale L. J.* 301 (1976).

entities subject to the customs and excise taxes enacted. This method of exemption by statutory omission continued when the first income tax, in the Act of 1861,[8] also excluded nonprofit organizations.

In the latter half of the 19th Century, Congress struggled over whether income taxes were direct taxes forbidden by the Constitution. Following the landmark decision in *Springer v. United States,*[9] in which the Supreme Court held income taxes to be a constitutionally permissible indirect tax, Congress enacted the Tariff of 1894.[10] This Act imposed a flat 2 percent corporate rate on all organizations *not specifically exempted.* No longer did the method of exemption by statutory omission prevail. This new all-inclusive method of taxation required specific exemptions to avoid the tax. Therefore, Congress prescribed Section 32 within the Act to exempt

> ... corporations, companies or associations organized and conducted solely for charitable, religious, or educational purposes.[11]

Other references were made to application of the tax to "corporations, companies, or associations *doing business for profit* [emphasis added]."[12]

This Act was short-lived, however. In another landmark case, *Pollock v. Farmers' Loan & Trust Co.,*[13] the Supreme Court revoked the license granted in *Springer* by turning about-face and holding the new income tax to be an unconstitutional direct tax.

8 Act of Aug. 5, 1861, ch. 119, §§ 49–51, 12 Stat. 292, 309–10.

9 102 U.S. 602 (1880).

10 Act of Aug. 27, 1894, ch. 349, § 32, 28 Stat. 556.

11 *Id.*

12 *Id.*

13 157 U.S. 429 (1895).

Circumventing the principle of an income tax as a direct tax, which *Pollock* established, Congress enacted the Corporation Excise Tax Act of 1909.[14] By construing the tax as an excise rather than an income tax, its constitutionality was upheld.[15] But more importantly for this discussion, it is within this Act that the seeds of the statutory language creating the present Section 501 exexempt status were found. More specifically, the Act exempted "any corporation or associations organized and operated exclusively for religious, charitable, or educational purposes."[16] Although the list of exempt organizations has expanded over the years, every Revenue Act since the Corporation Excise Tax Act of 1909 has contained similar provisions.[17]

Types of Nonprofit Organizations

There are presently twenty-four types of organizations which are enumerated in Section 501 and are exempted from taxation under Section 501(a). Bittker and Rahdert categorize the most important nonprofit organizations among them as either "public service" or "mutual benefit" organizations. Under each category, the following classification of types of organizations is suggested:[18]

Public Service	Mutual Benefit
1. Charitable	1. Social clubs
2. Educational	2. Consumer cooperatives and similar organizations
3. Scientific	3. Labor unions
4. Social Welfare	4. Trade associations
5. Churches and other religious organizations	
6. Political parties	

14 Act of 1909, Pub. L. No. 61-6, ch. 6, § 38, 36 Stat. 11, 112–17.

15 Flint v. Stone Tracy Co., 220 U.S. 107 (1911).

16 Corporation Excise Tax Act, *supra* N. 14.

17 For citations to specific Acts, see James J. McGovern, "The Exemption Provisions of Subpart F," 29 *Tax Law.* 523, 529 n. 32 (1976).

18 Bittker & Rahdert, *supra* N. 7, at 305–6.

Except for political parties, it can be argued that public service (generally Section 501(c)(3) type) organizations exist as nonprofit entities for eleemosynary purposes. In contrast, mutual benefit organizations, although deserving of nonprofit status, are generally not of a philanthropic nature because they usually exist for the benefit of their members. An important tax distinction between these categories is that donors to public service organizations usually receive an income tax deduction under Section 170 (for types (1) to (5) above) or a limited tax credit under Section 41 (for political contributions). No charitable deduction is permitted for contributions to mutual benefit organizations, although some taxpayers are permitted tax deductions under Section 162 for dues payments and other assessments to some mutual benefit organizations (*e.g.,* labor unions or trade associations).

It is a subset of the public service type of organization that the drafters of the WPT chose to exempt. It is an expanded subset of public service organizations, however, that we believe—and shall argue subsequently—deserve exemption from the tax. We do not believe the mutual benefit type of organizations, whose tax privileges have been traditionally limited by Congress, are necessarily entitled to a WPT exemption.[19] The largest portion of WPT-affected organizations are public service organizations with endowments supporting their exempt function. It is therefore rather inconsequential to either a mutual benefit organization's receipts or to the federal government's revenue whether an organization is also exempt from the WPT. Hence, because these organizations may have less theoretical support for additional exemptions and because of the insignificant amounts of

---

19 We realize that this position may, in part, be contradictory given some basis for a general exemption of all nonprofit organizations from the WPT. Nevertheless, in a spirit of compromise and with a sense of political reality, we hope only to justify expansion of the current exemptions by demonstrating a substantial theoretical basis for exempting most public service organizations.

tax involved, any proposal for their exemption will not be considered further.

Justification for Exempt Status

It is beyond the scope of this paper to attempt a thorough justification of exemption from the federal income tax. Others have attempted this task and succeeded quite adequately.[20] Nevertheless, a brief review of the principal arguments advanced by them follows.

Bittker and Rahdert, having culled the legislative history of continuing exemptions, suggest that Congress has relied on the following four rationales at different times: (1) the concept of "income" and the objectives of nonprofit organizations do not mesh; (2) when compared to individual and corporate taxes, small amounts of revenue are involved; (3) informal operations that are often staffed by volunteers would find recordkeeping burdensome; and (4) these groups are motivated by a benevolent spirit.[21] Commenting on their first rationale, Bittker and Rahdert note how conceptually difficult the measurement of "income" for a public service organization is:

> From its inception, the federal income tax has been imposed not on gross receipts or gross income, but on an adjusted net amount—roughly speaking, gross income less business expenses. As a guide in computing "net" or "taxable" income, an extensive body of legal and accounting principles derived from business and financial practice has been developed. But these principles rest on the premise that the organization seeks to maximize its profit, and hence are not a satisfactory way of measuring the success of organizations that reject this basic premise.[22]

---

20 See, for instance, Lawrence M. Stone, "Federal Tax Support of Charities and Other Exempt Organizations: The Need for a National Policy," 20 *U. So. Cal. Tax Inst.* 27-78 (1968); Bittker & Rahdert, *supra* N. 7; and McGovern, *supra* N. 17.

21 See Bittker & Rahdert, *supra* N. 7, at 304.

22 *Id.* at 307.

In another review of exempt status, James McGovern attributes the exemption provisions to three basic factors—heritage, morality, and special interest legislation. Heritage refers to the century-old tradition of exempting from taxation the activities of philanthropic organizations. Morality is the idea that it would be improper to tax (and only generate meager revenues from) a group formed for nonprofit purposes to benefit charitable recipients or its members. Special interest legislation is based on the belief that some exemption provisions were established after intense lobbying by special interest groups.[23]

The concept of "morality" also encompasses the promotion of growth in eleemosynary organizations for the benefit of society as a whole. Moreover, it implies that when such organizations furnish these goods and services, the government is relieved of providing them.[24]

Taxation of Nonprofit Organizations

Although in general nonprofit organizations should be exempt from taxation, certain types of activities and organizations fall outside of the rationale for exemption. In taxing some organizations and activities, the government has exercised its prerogative to apply a tax in those circumstances when exemption is inappropriate. Ultimately, government must retain its supervisory power to tax or exempt wealth. When exemption has been limited by Congress, one or more of the following maxims were usually being violated:[25]

1. Since exemption constitutes a diversion of federal revenues, the government should ensure that intended public purposes are met.

---

23 See McGovern, *supra* N. 17, at 325–27.

24 Stone, *supra* N. 20, at 45, claims that "morality" is the principal justification for exempting charitable organizations.

25 For a discussion of these items, see Stone, *supra* N. 20, at 62.

2. The federal tax base should not be unduly eroded.
3. Concentrations of economic power should not be vested in such organizations so as to create unfair competition with private enterprise or go beyond market control.

Unrelated business income tax. Concern over the encroachment of tax-exempt organizations on private business—the third item above—prompted Congress to address this issue head-on in the Revenue Act of 1950.[26] By amendment of the 1939 Code, Sections 421 through 424 subjected business operations unrelated to an organization's exempt purpose to corporate tax rates.[27] A specific incident which fueled the Congressional fires involved the acquisition of a large macaroni company by a feeder corporation organized to benefit the law school at New York University. It was claimed that this was unfair competition. In effect, these entities were tax-subsidized insofar as they could sell their products for less or they might use their untaxed earnings to expand more rapidly. On the surface, the taxation of unrelated business income made sense. Moreover, it discouraged a drift away from passive investments, which traditionally had been the mainstay of philanthropic endowments.

Debt-financed acquisitions. The 1950 legislation also had included as "unrelated business income" certain passive income on business leases of debt-financed property. This inclusion was expanded in the Tax Reform Act of 1969[28] to embrace virtually any acquisition by a tax-exempt organization of property (*e.g.,* tangible personal property, real property, and corporate stock) with debt

26 Act of 1950, Pub. L. No. 81-814, 64 Stat. 906.

27 I.R.C. (1954) §§ 511–513, as amended, contain the current provisions.

28 I.R.C. § 514; Act of Dec. 30, 1969, Pub. L. No. 91-172, § 121(d)(1). The Tax Reform Act of 1976, Pub. L. No. 94-455, Oct. 4, 1976, and the Revenue Act of 1978, Pub. L. No. 95-345, Nov. 6, 1978, further modified the major revision of 1969.

financing. The rationale supporting this taxable situation was that exempt organizations should not be permitted to "trade on their exemption," *i.e.,* acquire property with borrowed funds and then use tax-free income to retire the debt. The 1969 amendment of Section 514 was prompted by the situation in *Commissioner v. Brown,*[29] where the Supreme Court upheld capital gains treatment to the former shareholders of a closely held corporation that was sold to a charity for a small downpayment and amortization of the debt-financed balance from tax-free future earnings.

Taxation of property with "acquisition indebtedness" supposedly discourages increased competition for financing, which a continuing exemption might provoke, and counters situations analagous to *Brown.* However, under many circumstances there is no justifiable rationale to preclude exempt organizations from using debt financing. Since the exempt organization receives no tax deduction for the interest paid and because the income (*e.g.,* rent) from the project is tax-free, the whole project is a wash taxwise. This is unlike the denial of deduction by Section 265(2) for interest on debt used to finance tax-free state and local bonds.[30]

Private foundations. Self-dealing abuses by insiders and unwarranted privileges prompted Congress to include in the Tax Reform Act of 1969 a series of excise taxes on private foundation investments. These taxes, ranging from 2 to 15 percent of either investment income or its value, are imposed by Sections 4940 to 4945. Applicable tax bases include a foundation's net investment income, undistributed income, excess business holdings,

---

29 380 U.S. 563 (1965).

30 For an expanded discussion of the different theories and their appropriateness for this provision, see Bittker & Rahdert, *supra* N. 7, at 321-24.

investments jeopardizing charitable purpose,[31] and expenditures for lobbying and electioneering and certain grants.

The taxation of private foundations represented a major shift in policy, not so much because these entities were singled out for differential treatment, which was theoretically justifiable, but because the *manner* of taxing exempt organizations was radically altered. Taxes on unrelated business income (starting in 1951) and all debt-financed property (beginning in 1970) were specifically aimed at maintaining nonprofit organizations that were tax-free only so long as their financial dealings were appropriate for the activities of their exempt function. However, once they had the appearance—whether in fact intended or not—of "trading on their exemption," such income was tainted and subject to the income tax. In contrast, private foundations have been subject since 1969 to *excise* taxes on all their income, which is predominately *passive.* Moreover, under some circumstances, not only income but also certain types of private foundation *investment values* are used as a tax base. The preceding emphasized terms highlight these differences—excise taxes on passive income and investment values—between private foundations and regular tax-exempt organizations.

In the next section, we suggest how this trend has now been extended through the WPT to apply an *excise* tax on the *passive* oil and gas incomes of many formerly exempt (*i.e.,* Section 501(c)(3)) organizations. We believe this extension violates basic doctrines, set out earlier, that

---

31 The jeopardy investments category is particularly irritating to the oil industry. Treas. Reg. § 53.4944-1(a)(2) states that "investments in working interests in oil and gas wells" are generally considered to be speculative investments, although not *per se* a violation of § 4944. The statute establishes a tax of 5% of the amount invested and applies to both the foundation and its manager. If not paid within a "correction period," the tax escalates to 25%.

justify exemption of philanthropic organizations in the first place. Moreover, we feel that if this single tentacle of taxation is permitted to grasp a passive income source (such as a royalty interest in crude oil) that was formerly entirely free of federal taxes, then it may not be too long before other types of passive income received by tax-exempt organizations could be drawn into its clutches. The appropriateness of this new spectre of taxation needs to be addressed while it is still in its infancy.

Windfall Profit Taxation

In respect to taxable domestic crude oil production, the WPT is intended to transfer a significant proportion—30 to 70 percent—of the marginal revenue from the oil sold at decontrolled prices. The "windfall profit" is the difference between the crude oil base price—lower tier, upper tier, and "free market" or uncontrolled—and the higher prices at which *domestic* crude oil has been and will be selling as a result of the gradual decontrol of crude oil prices that began on June 1, 1979. The Department of Energy (DOE) crude oil base price is "indexed," *i.e.*, adjusted for inflation, and increased by the incremental amount of any state severance, *i.e.*, the severance tax on the difference between the base price adjusted for inflation and the sales (or removal) price of the crude oil produced. However, certain crude oil produced in the United States is not subject to windfall profit taxation; consequently, the producer thereof does not incur a WPT on production.

There are essentially four categories of crude oil—Exempt oil, and taxable oil in Tiers One, Two, and Three.[32] The following summary is a comparative analysis of the DOE price control and windfall profit tax classification systems for *taxable* domestic crude oil:

---

32 I.R.C. § 4991.

DOE Price Control Category	Windfall Profit Tax Category
Lower tier or old oil	Tier One
Upper tier or new oil	Tier One
Market-priced oil	Tier One
Alaskan North Slope oil	Tier One
Marginal oil	Tier One
Stripper oil	Tier Two
Naval (National) Petroleum Reserve oil	Tier Two
Newly discovered (post-1978) oil	Tier Three
Heavy oil	Tier Three
Incremental tertiary oil	Tier Three

Nontaxable domestic crude oil is exempt either because it is a type which is specifically excluded or because the producer is exempt from the WPT. There are three types of domestic crude oil production that are not taxable. Specifically, certain Alaskan oil, certain Indian oil, and "front-end" (or tertiary incentive) oil are excluded from windfall profit taxation. In addition, crude oil production is exempt from windfall profit taxation where the production is from a "qualified" governmental interest or a "qualified" charitable (medical or educational) interest, *i.e.,* because the producer is tax exempt.

Nontaxable Types of Crude Oil Production

In general, the first purchaser of any domestic crude oil withholds WPT from payments to producers because the former is liable for the tax.[33] First purchasers of "exempt oil," however, do not have to withhold WPT from payments to producers thereof.[34] "Exempt oil" implicitly includes foreign crude oil insofar as the WPT is only applicable to domestice crude oil,[35] which is defined as crude oil produced from an oil well located in the United

33 Treas. Reg. § 150.4995-1(a).

34 Treas. Reg. § 150.4995-1(b)(3).

35 I.R.C. § 4991(a).

States or in a United States possession (as defined in Section 638).[36] As explained above, "exempt oil" explicitly encompasses crude oil from both a qualified governmental interest and a qualified charitable interest, as well as exempt Indian oil, except Alaskan oil, and exempt "front-end" (or tertiary incentive) oil.

There are several circumstances under which domestic crude oil production would be classified as "exempt Indian oil." In general, domestic crude oil is excluded from taxation where the producer, as of January 21, 1980, is an Indian tribal organization, and where the mineral interests from which the oil is produced are either held in trust by the United States for the tribe, member, or organization, or held by the tribe, member, or organization subject to a restriction on alienation imposed by the United States because the interest is held by an Indian tribe, an individual member of an Indian tribe, or an Indian tribal organization.

Exempt Indian oil also includes domestic crude oil that is (a) produced by a native corporation organized under the Alaskan Native Claims Settlement Act (as in effect on January 21, 1980), (b) produced from mineral interests held by such native corporation insofar as the interests were received under the aforementioned Act, and (c) removed from the premises by 1992. Finally, exempt Indian oil encompasses domestic crude oil production, the proceeds from the sale of which are deposited in the U.S. Treasury to the credit of tribal or native trust funds pursuant to a provision of law in effect on January 21, 1980.[37]

For domestic crude oil production to qualify as "exempt Alaskan oil," it must be produced from a reservoir from which oil is being produced in commercial quantities

---

36 I.R.C. § 4996(b).

37 I.R.C. § 4994(d).

through a well located north of the Arctic Circle or from a well located on the northerly side of the divide of the Alaskan-Aleutian Range and at least seventy-five miles from the nearest point on the Trans-Alaska Pipeline System. Notwithstanding the above definition, exempt Alaskan oil does not include production from the Sadlerochit reservoir on the Alaskan North Slope (ANS),[38] which was technically classified as "upper tier" oil although it had been selling at below-ceiling market (uncontrolled) prices to accommodate high transportation costs,[39] *i.e.,* the Trans-Alaska Pipeline System (TAPS) tariff. Thus, ANS oil actually sold at world market prices in 1978 and 1979 when TAPS tariff was included.

By far the most complex exclusion provisions are those applicable to "exempt front-end tertiary oil," which is defined as any domestic crude oil that is removed from the premises before October 1, 1981, and that is treated as "front-end oil" by reason of a "front-end tertiary project" on one or more properties each of which is a "qualified project." The latter term means any oil property if, on January 1, 1980, 50 percent or more of the operating mineral interest in such property is held by persons who were "independent producers" per Section 613A (as amended for WPT purposes by Section 4992(b)) for the last quarter of 1979.

"Front-end oil" is defined as any domestic crude which was not subject to a first-sale ceiling price under DOE regulations solely by reason of the front-end tertiary provisions of such regulations. Similarly, "front-end tertiary project" means any project which qualifies under the front-end tertiary provisions of the DOE regulations. Finally, "front-end tertiary provisions" are the provisions

38 I.R.C. § 4994(e).

39 Jamie Replogle, "DOE Update: The Decontrol Strategy," *Petroleum Independent* 60–62 (August 1979).

of Section 212.78 of the DOE regulations, which exempt crude oil from ceiling price limitations to provide financing for tertiary projects (as such provisions took effect on October 1, 1979), and any amendments of such regulations to the extent such amending is for purposes of coordinating DOE and Treasury regulations.[40] The "front-end tertiary (incentive) crude oil" provisions can succinctly be described in the context of the decontrol of crude oil prices as "lower" and/or "upper" tier oil which may be sold at "free market" or uncontrolled prices so that the additional revenues can be used to finance tertiary recovery projects.[41]

In respect to any front-end tertiary project that is not on qualified property, *i.e.,* where more than half of the operating mineral interest is held by an integrated oil company producer, the excess of the "allowed expenses" of the taxpayer related to such project over the "tertiary incentive revenue" will be treated as a payment of windfall profit tax made on September 30, 1981. However, the amount of payment or credit for windfall profit taxes cannot exceed the aggregate tax imposed by Section 4986 in respect to the front-end oil of that producer removed after February 1980, and before October 1981. For purposes of this refund (or credit) for the tertiary projects of integrated producers, "tertiary incentive revenue" has the meaning given such term by the front-end tertiary provisions of the DOE regulations.

In some cases, a taxpayer may be liable for taxes on production from a tertiary project encompassing both qualified and nonqualified property. In such cases, the taxpayer must treat the front-end oil related thereto as attributable first to tertiary projects of independents, *i.e.,* from qualified property.

---

40 I.R.C. § 4994(c).

41 44 Fed. Reg. 18,677, March 29, 1979, as amended.

For purposes of the exclusion and credit (refund) for front-end tertiary oil, including the application of the DOE front-end tertiary provisions, there are limitations on the deduction of "prepaid expenses." In general, the "allowed expenses" are determined under front-end tertiary provisions, *i.e.,* DOE regulations, but such expenses cannot include any amount attributable to periods after September 30, 1981. Moreover, any other expenditures should be treated as attributable to periods before October 1, 1981, only to the extent that, as provided in Chapter 1 (income tax), deductions for such expenditures (including depreciation of related capital expenditures) are properly allocable to periods before October 1, 1981. Finally, an action should be treated as taken before October 1, 1981, or any other date if it would have been taken before such date but for an Act of God, a severe mechanical breakdown, or an injunction.[42]

Tax-Exempt Entities

As indicated above, the crude oil production of a state or local governmental entity is generally exempt from windfall profit taxation. Moreover, the production of certain charitable, medical, and educational organizations is not subject to windfall profit taxation. Such tax-exempt status is intended to exclude from taxation the economic interests of virtually all state and local governments, certain charitable groups, and most medical and educational organizations.

A "qualified governmental interest" means an economic interest (royalty or working interest) in crude oil if (a) such interest is held by a state or political subdivision (county, city, school district, etc.) thereof (or by an agency or instrumentality of a state or political subdivision thereof); and (b) under the applicable state or local law, all of the net income received pursuant to such interest is

42 I.R.C. § 4994(c).

dedicated to a public purpose. In respect to a qualified governmental interest, "net income" means gross income reduced by production costs and severance taxes of general application to the extent that they are allocable to the governmental interest. In addition, any net income which, under applicable state or local law is placed in a permanent fund, the earnings from which are dedicated to public purposes, meets the requirement that net income be dedicated to a public purpose.[43]

The phrase "dedicated to a public purpose" is not defined anywhere in Chapter 45, nor can a definition thereof be found in the Congressional Committee Reports published along with the Crude Oil Windfall Profit Tax Act of 1980. Furthermore, Treasury Regulation Section 150.4994-1 simply refers to the Code for various definitions of exempt oil. Nevertheless, the aforementioned phrase, if narrowly construed by the IRS, might preclude WPT exemption for the royalty income of a state employees' retirement fund, or for the operating income of a state-owned corporation that produces crude oil primarily for public use but also sells its surplus production and uses the profits therefrom to expand or maintain operations.

A "qualified governmental interest" does not include crude oil production from land owned by the federal government or from a United States possession. Thus, where the federal government has an economic interest in crude oil production, including production from the National (Naval) Petroleum Reserves and royalties from the lease of federal land, the first purchaser or operator must withhold WPT from payments made for production owned by the federal government.[44] Apparently, a

---

43 I.R.C. § 4994(a).

44 U.S. Congress, Conference Committee, *Conference Report (No. 96-817) On the Crude Oil Windfall Profit Tax Act of 1980*, 96th Cong., 2d Sess., March 7, 1980, p. 107.

state's share of federal royalties is also subject to the WPT.[45]

A "qualified charitable interest" is defined as an economic interest in crude oil if such interest is held by a Section 170(c)(2) institution organized and operated exclusively for religious, charitable, scientific, or educational purposes. Moreover, the interest must be held either by an educational or medical organization or charitable group established to support public higher education as provided in Section 170(b)(1)(A), or by a religious group for the benefit of an educational or medical organization. Finally, the oil property must have been held by the qualified "public charity" on January 21, 1980, and at all times thereafter before the last day of the taxable period. Thus, an interest is treated as held by or for the benefit of a qualified public charity only if all the proceeds from such interest were dedicated on January 21, 1980, and at all times thereafter before the last day of the taxable period to that qualified public charity.[46]

The "qualified charitable interest" exemption is very limited in scope insofar as a qualified charitable organization must simultaneously meet certain requirements from both Section 170(b)(1)(A) and Section 170(c)(2). Section 170(b)(1)(A) provides the general 50-percent rule for limitations on the charitable contribution deduction of individuals. Similarly, Section 170(c)(2) is part of the Section 170(c) definition of charitable contributions. Thus, a charitable group which has a Section 501(a) exemption from income taxes for Section 501(c)(3) activities and meets the Section 4994(b) specified requirements of Section 170(c)(2) would not be tax exempt if it also did not meet the Section 4994(b) specified requirements of Section 170(b)(1)(A)(i) through (iv).

---

45 S. 2768, *Congressional Record,* May 28, 1980, pp. 55886–55887.

46 I.R.C. § 4994(b).

The specified requirements of Section 170(b)(1)(A) limit a qualified charitable interest to an economic interest either (a) held by an educational institution, an organization providing medical care, education and/or research, or a Section 501(a) organization established to support public higher education, or (b) held by a church or a convention (or association) of churches for the benefit of an educational institution or medical organization established to provide hospital or medical care, education, or research. In addition, Section 170(c)(2) provides for a WPT charitable exemption only where an organization is a corporation, trust or community chest, or a foundation that meets the following four tests. First, the organization must be created or organized in the United States or in any possession thereof, or under the law of the United States, any state, the District of Columbia, or any possession of the United States. Second, as noted above, it must also be organized and operated exclusively for religious, charitable, scientific, or educational purposes. Third, no part of the net earnings of the corporation, trust, community chest, or foundation may inure to the benefit of any private shareholder or individual associated with the organization. Finally, the organization may not be disqualified for tax exemption under Section 501(c)(3) by reason of attempting to influence legislation, and it may not participate or intervene (including the publishing or distributing of statements) in any political campaign on behalf of any candidate for public office.

An educational organization is described as an institution that maintains a regular faculty and curriculum and normally has a regularly enrolled body of students. The term includes institutions such as primary, secondary, preparatory or high schools, and colleges and universities.[47] Such institutions may be either privately or governmentally supported.

47 Treas. Reg. § 1.170A-9(b).

A hospital qualifies as a medical organization or facility where its principal purpose or function is the providing of medical or hospital care, medical education, or medical research. A rehabilitation institution, out-patient clinic, or community mental health or drug treatment center may qualify as a "hospital" provided that the aforementioned principal-purpose test is met. The term "hospital" does not include convalescent homes or homes for children or the aged, nor does the term include those institutions whose primary function is to train handicapped individuals for a vocation.[48]

In respect to organizations created and operated for the benefit of certain state and/or locally supported colleges and universities, such organizations must first meet the support test. The support test is satisfied if the organization receiving the contribution normally receives a substantial part of its support from either the general public or federal, state or local government, or from a combination thereof. In addition to meeting the support test, an organization must be created and operated exclusively to hold, receive, invest and administer property and to make expenditures to or for the benefit of a college or university which meets the support test.[49]

In respect to a church or convention (or association) of churches, qualification for the WPT exemption is limited to those religious groups holding an economic interest in crude oil for the benefit of an educational organization, an organization which supports federal, state, and locally and publicly supported educational institutions, or hospitals and medical research organizations. An interest is treated as held for the benefit of these organizations only if all the net proceeds from the production of oil are

48 Treas. Reg. § 1.170A-9(c).

49 I.R.C. § 170(b)(1)(A)(iv).

dedicated to the support of a medical facility or educational institution.[50]

The following tabular summary is a comparative analysis of the tax exempt entity for both federal income tax and WPT purposes. The limited scope of the WPT exemption is vividly exposed when it is compared to the exemption from federal income taxation.[51]

Rationalizing the Exemption for Qualified Charitable Interests

In this section, the theoretical basis for a complete exemption from WPT for all charitable, educational, religious, scientific, etc. (*i.e.,* Internal Revenue Code Section 501(c)(3), or hereinafter CERS) organizations holding economic interests in oil properties is examined. Furthermore, some of the political constraints in the legislative process during enactment of the WPT that conceivably led to the present limited exemptions are discussed.

Organizations and Tax Revenues Involved

There are more than 825,000 organizations that have received an "exempt status" for federal income tax purposes.[52] It has been estimated that about one-third (or approximately 275,000) of these are CERS organizations.[53] Yet this estimate is probably too low. For example, member churches of a religious organization often rely on the Section 501(c)(3) exemption granted the national organization. There is therefore a significant under-

50 Conference Committee, *supra* N. 44, at 108.

51 The tabular summary is adapted from the *Exempt Organization Handbook,* which is part of the *Internal Revenue Manual.* See I.R.M. 7751, Exhibit 200-1.

52 *The Wall Street Journal,* Dec. 15, 1980, at 42, col. 1.

53 Boris I. Bittker & Lawrence M. Stone, *Federal Income Taxation* 222 (5th ed. 1980).

Tax-Exempt Status: Comparative Analysis of Income and Windfall Profit Taxation

Code Section	*Description of Organization*	*General Nature of Activities*	*Exempt From Income Tax*	*Exempt From WPT*	*Contributions Deductible*
115(1)	State and local government	Government services	Yes	Yes[1]	Yes
115(2)	U.S. Possessions	Government services	Yes	No	Yes
501(c)(1)	Corporations Organized Under Act of Congress (including Federal Credit Unions)	Instrumentalities of the United States	Yes	No	Yes
501(c)(2)	Title Holding Corporation for Exempt Organization	Holding title to property for an exempt organization	Yes[2]	No	No[3]
501(c)(3)	Religious, Educational and Charitable Organizations	Activities of nature implied by description of class of organization	Yes[2]	Yes[4]	Yes
501(c)(4)	Civic Leagues, Social Welfare Organizations, and Local Associations of Employees	(a)Promotion of community welfare, and (b) Charitable, educational, or recreational activities	Yes	No	No[3]
501(c)(5)	Labor, Agricultural and Horticultural Organizations	Educational or instructive, the purpose being to improve conditions of work, and to improve products and efficiency.	Yes[2]	No	No[3]
501(c)(6)	Business Leagues, Chambers of Commerce, Real Estate Boards, Etc.	Improvement of business conditions of one or more lines of business	Yes[2]	No	No[3]

Tax-Exempt Status: Comparative Analysis of Income and Windfall Profit Taxation (Continued, Part 2)

Code Section	*Description of Organization*	*General Nature of Activities*	*Exempt From Income Tax*	*Exempt From WPT*	*Contributions Deductible*
501(c)(7)	Social and Recreation Clubs	Pleasure, recreation, and social activities	Yes[2]	No	No[3]
501(c)(8)	Fraternal Beneficiary Societies and Associations	Lodge providing for payment of life, sickness, accident, or other benefits to members	Yes	No	Yes[5]
501(c)(9)	Voluntary Employees' Beneficiary Associations	Providing for payment of life, sickness, accident or other benefits to members	Yes[2]	No	No[3]
501(c)(10)	Voluntary Employees Beneficiary Associations (including federal employees)	Providing for payment of life, sickness, accident and other benefits to members	Yes[2]	No	No[3]
501(c)(11)	Teachers' Retirement Fund Associations	Teachers' associations for payment of retirement benefits	Yes[2]	No	No[3]
501(c)(12)	Benevolent Life Insurance Associations, Mutual or Cooperative Telephone Companies, Etc.	Activities of a mutually beneficial nature similar to those implied by the description of class of organization	Yes[2]	No	No[3]
501(c)(13)	Cemetery Companies	Burials and incidental activities	Yes[2]	No	Yes
501(c)(14)	State Chartered Credit Unions and Mutual Reserve Funds	Loans to members. Exemption as to building and loan associations and cooperative banks repealed by Revenue Act of 1951, affecting all years after 1951.	Yes[7]	No	No[3]

Tax-Exempt Status: Comparative Analysis of Income and Windfall Profit Taxation (Continued, Part 3)

Code Section	*Description of Organization*	*General Nature of Activities*	*Exempt From Income Tax*	*Exempt From WPT*	*Contributions Deductible*
501(c)(15)	Mutual Insurance Companies or Associations	Providing insurance to members substantially at cost	Yes[2]	No	No[3]
501(c)(16)	Cooperative Organizations to Finance Crop Operations	Financing crop operations in conjunction with activities of a marketing or purchasing association	Yes[2]	No	No[3]
501(c)(17)	Supplemental Unemployment Benefit Trusts	Provides for payment of supplemental unemployment compensation benefits	Yes[2]	No	No[3]
501(c)(18)	Employee Pension Funds	Provides retirement benefits for employees who are the sole contributors thereto	Yes	No	No[3]
501(c)(19)	War Veterans' Organizations	Activities of a mutually beneficial nature	Yes[2]	No	Yes
501(c)(20)	Group Legal Services, Trusts or Organizations	Provides group legal services to members of a qualified group legal services plan	Yes	No	No[3,8]
501(c)(21)	Black Lung Disability Trust Funds	Satisfy liability for disability compensation under Black Lung Acts	Yes	No	No[3,8]
501(d)	Religious and Apostolic Associations	Related business activities Communal religious community	Yes[2]	No	No
501(e)	Cooperative Hospital Service Organizations	Performs cooperative services for hospitals	Yes	No	Yes

Tax-Exempt Status: Comparative Analysis of Income and Windfall Profit Taxation (Continued, Part 4)

Code Section	*Description of Organization*	*General Nature of Activities*	*Exempt From Income Tax*	*Exempt From WPT*	*Contributions Deductible*
501(f)	Cooperative Service Organizations Operating Educational Organizations	Performs collective investment services for educational organizations	Yes	No	Yes
521(a)	Farmers' Cooperative Associations	Cooperative marketing and purchasing for agricultural producers	Yes	No	No
527	Political Organizations	Influencing public elections, including selection, nomination election and appointment of any individual to political or public office	Yes[2]	No	No[9]
528	Homeowners Associations	Providing condominium or real estate management services for the mutual benefit of its members.	Yes[2]	No	No

[1] Although the crude oil revenue of state and local government (and political subdivisions thereof) is generally exempt from the WPT, there are situations where state and local government may be subject to the WPT, *e.g.,* where state and local government receive a share of federal royalties from an economic interest.

[2] Subject to unrelated business income (UBI) tax as provided in §§ 511–514.

[3] Rev. Rul. 54-243, 1954-1 C.B. 92 provides for the establishment of a charitable fund by an organization exempt under § 501 (other than § 501(c)(3)), contributions to which would be deductible.

[4] For a detailed analysis of which § 501(c)(3) organizations are exempt, see text above.

[5] Yes, if used for § 501(c)(3) purposes.

[6] Contributions to perpetual care fund are deductible.

[7] But mutual reserve funds are subject to UBI tax.

[8] Contributions by employers to qualified group legal plans and to qualified black lung trust funds are deductible business expenses.

[9] § 41 provides a limited tax credit for political contributions.

statement of the number of CERS organizations with a single religious affiliation.

Certainly not all or even a large proportion of CERS organizations have economic interests in crude oil property. The subset of the CERS group representing qualified charitable interests exempt from the WPT under Section 4991(b)(1) is known to the IRS, though, because such organizations are required to file an exemption certificate.[54] An expansion of the WPT exemption to all CERS organizations should substantially increase the number of organizations filing an exemption certificate.

The revenue impact of extending exemptions to all CERS organizations, however, is more important than knowing the absolute number of eligible organizations. Estimating this impact is particularly difficult because CERS organizations do not report income from an economic interest in crude oil and because decontrol and the OPEC cartel are causing oil prices to escalate. In our judgment, when the WPT has been in effect for about one year (by the spring of 1981), the results of exempting qualified charitable interests will suggest a significant miscalculation of expected revenue losses. While expanding the scope of the WPT exemption to all CERS organizations may be theoretically justifiable, the accompanying loss of revenue *could* be a limiting factor in any such extension. In other words, the need to find a balancing source of revenue may loom as an obstacle to any revision of the WPT exemption. On the other hand, the amounts of foregone revenue—as originally estimated or subsequently realized—are probably inconsequential when compared to either total federal tax revenue or WPT revenue.

---

54 The IRS requires that a completed Exemption Certificate (Part I) of Form 6458, Certification and Election Form, be filed. Announcement 80-106, 1980-33 I.R.B. 22; Prop. Treas. Reg. § 150.4995-2(b).

Published reports of expected revenue losses from the present educational and medical exemption are limited. The House bill contained no such provision, and therefore no estimates of the revenue impact were made in passing H.R. 3919.[55] When the exemption was provided for in the Senate bill, its revenue effect was estimated at $199 million or about $20 million per year over the ten-year expected life of the WPT.[56] In addition to correcting a technical error in the statute, the Conference Committee changed the holding date for eligibility from October 24, 1979, to January 21, 1980;[57] but changes were rather inconsequential modifications for revenue estimation purposes.

As suggested, the revenue losses associated with the current WPT exemption for qualified charitable interests are probably underestimated. Although liberalizing eligibility for exemption most likely would increase the number of new WPT-exempt organizations, there would have to be a many fold increase in the estimated $20 million annual revenue loss before these amounts would be significant to the federal budget. They are hardly relevant presently.

The Tradition of Exemption From Taxation

As noted previously, there is a tradition of exempting nonprofit organizations from federal income taxes. Similar provisions exist for numerous other taxes imposed by the federal government and at state and local levels.

State and local taxes. It is an established principle of state and local taxation that nonprofit (especially CERS) organizations are exempt from most types of taxation.

---

55 H.R. 3919, 96th Cong., 1st Sess. (1979).

56 Staff of the Joint Committee on Taxation, 96th Cong., 1st Sess., *Conference Comparison on H.R. 3919* 48 (Comm. Print 1979).

57 Conference Committee, *supra* N. 44.

Perhaps the classic example is the exemption from state and local *ad valorem* taxes—*e.g.,* church real property—for some or all CERS organizations. Exemptions from income and franchise taxes are also fairly uniform across the states. Many states, *e.g.,* New York and Texas, exempt CERS organizations from state and local sales taxes, too.

Other federal taxes. Congress has not limited the CERS organization tax exemption to the federal income tax. Section 3121(b)(8) excludes employees of CERS organizations from FICA (social security) taxes unless an employee has elected to be covered. Similarly, Section 3306(c)(8) exempts CERS organizations from paying federal unemployment taxes (FUTA) on their employees.[58] Another federal tax privilege is the special rules for CERS employee-deferred annuities under Section 403(b). Both FICA and FUTA taxes are excise taxes, as are the WPT and the repealed excess profits taxes, which are discussed in the next section.

Excess profits taxation. Congress has deemed the "excess" profits produced during wartime as a suitable basis for imposing a temporary tax. Such a tax has been considered appropriate at these times because demand is heightened when wage and material costs have often been controlled. Excess profits tax acts were passed during each of the world wars and the Korean conflict.[59] These acts exempted CERS organizations from the excess profits excise tax.[60]

58 §§ 3309 and 3304(a)(6), however, do not grant the states the same prerogative of exempting CERS organization employees from state unemployment insurance coverage.

59 The Revenue Act of 1918, Pub. L. No. 65-254, Feb. 24, 1919; The Second Revenue Act of 1940, Pub. L. No. 76-801, Oct. 8, 1940; Excess Profits Tax of 1950, Pub. L. No. 81-814, Sept. 23, 1950.

60 The World War II and Korean excess profits acts were passed under the 1939 Internal Revenue Code, wherein reference was made to § 101 (the predecessor to § 501 in the 1954 Code) organizations being exempt from the tax.

Perhaps just as interesting for the present analysis was the fact that certain "war measures" in the World War II excess profits tax legislation also exempted income from strategic minerals and certain natural resources (including natural gas) resulting from greater than normal output.[61] These exemptions were intended to stimulate wartime output.[62] It is interesting to note that the present "war" against dwindling energy resources might be considered by some as a situation analagous to those existing during previous times. This assertion, however, questions the validity of the WPT, an inquiry beyond the scope of this article.

Some interesting characteristics of the WPT come to light when it is compared side by side with an excess profits tax. Although the WPT is not technically an excess profits tax, it was "sold" to Congress and the general public as a tax on the excess profits presumably created by higher oil revenues. On the other hand, while the WPT is technically an excise tax (as were prior excess profits taxes), the manner in which it is statutorily constructed and implemented does not conform to excise tax definitions. It is not a traditional excise tax becaue it is not a tax on the *privilege of selling or using* crude oil, but is instead a tax on *removing* crude oil.[63]

In summary, then, substantial precedent exists for exempting CERS organizations from virtually all forms of taxation. The decision to apply the WPT to many of these organizations violates the tradition established in

61 Int. Rev. Code of 1939, §§ 731, 734, 735, 450, and 453.

62 A thorough examination of the history, including the circumstances surrounding passage, of excess profits taxation is contained in Randolph E. Paul's classic work, *Taxation in the United States* (1954).

63 Frank Burke, Jr., "The Windfall Profits Tax—The Power of Taxation or the Taking of Property?" 22 *Am. Oil & Gas Rep.* 12 (March 1980). This article also contains a brief discussion of many constitutional issues raised by the WPT.

prior tax acts. In the past, only when Congress felt that these organizations unjustifiably benefited from their exemption were taxes instituted. For instance, the unrelated business income tax established in 1950 and the debt-financed property and private foundation rules of 1969 can be rationalized because they are designed to block organizations from unfairly trading on their exemption.

It seems unlikely that CERS organizations with economic interests in oil would be unjustly enriched by a complete exemption. Admittedly, the CERS organizations in oil-producing states probably benefit more than those in nonproducing states. Yet, if the oil income is being used by CERS organizations for their philanthropic purpose, a condition required to maintain their exempt status, why should it matter what the source is?

As explained above, all of the justifications for exempting organizations from the federal income tax have been applied in the past to other taxes. Moreover, such justifications are just as relevant today for exempting all CERS organizations from the WPT. Simply stated, a complete exemption from the WPT is theoretically defensible and its implementation would be rather inconsequential for federal revenues. We fail, therefore, to see how anything but a complete exemption for these organizations can be rationalized.

Nevertheless, the exigencies of the political forum in which these decisions are made may have dictated the present situation. Thus, in the next section, the manner in which the WPT was passed by Congress is considered. This analysis provides some insight into how the restricted number of exemptions from the WPT for eleemosynary organizations prevailed.

The Legislative History of the Exemption from Windfall Profit Taxation

When Chairman Al Ullman (D-Oregon) of the House Ways and Means Committee introduced H.R. 3919 on May 3, 1979, he was fulfilling President Carter's promise of April 15, 1979, to impose a windfall profit tax on domestic crude oil production. The WPT was deemed necessary to reduce the "windfall" profits of oil producers. The "windfall" would allegedly result from the gradual decontrol of crude oil prices, which was also announced on April 5, 1979, during President Carter's television address to the nation. In the original bill, taxable crude oil was defined as all domestic crude oil other than qualified Alaskan oil, *i.e.,* oil produced from a well north of the Arctic Circle. Hence, neither state and local governments, nor CERS organizations were envisioned as tax-exempt entities for WPT purposes. Also, Indian oil and "front-end" tertiary incentive oil were not excluded from the WPT. In summary, the original WPT bill would have ignored the traditional principle of tax exemption for government and CERS organizations.[64]

Less than a week after H.R. 3919 was introduced in the House, the Committee on Ways and Means began hearings on the proposal to tax windfall profits and use the proceeds to establish an energy trust fund.[65] Needless to say, the Carter Administration, the oil industry (including independent producers), and consumer and environmental groups were well-represented during the hearings; however, no representatives from state and local government or CERS organizations testified on behalf of traditional tax-exempt groups. It is not surprising that

64 *The Crude Oil Windfall Profit Tax Bill of 1979,* H.R. 3919, 96th Cong., 1st Sess., May 3, 1979.

65 U.S. House of Representatives, Committee on Ways and Means, *Hearings on Proposed Windfall Profits Tax and Creation of Energy Trust Fund,* 96th Cong., 1st Sess., May 9–11 and 16–18, 1979.

the WPT bill passed by the House on June 28, 1979, did not include an exemption for CERS organizations. In contrast, under the bill as passed, state and local governments and their instrumentalities would have been exempt from the WPT to the extent that the net proceeds of their economic interests were dedicated to public education or a permanent fund for public education. There still were no provisions for exempting Indian oil or "front-end" tertiary incentive oil. In fact, except for education-dedicated governmental interests, the House bill was almost identical to the Carter Administration's bill proposed by Chairman Ullman.[66]

The Senate and the Committee on Finance deliberated from early July to mid-December 1979, before passing a substitute version of H.R. 3919. Not only did the Senate significantly amend the House version of the WPT bill, but it also added tax incentives to encourage residential energy conservation, tax incentives for businesses to encourage energy conservation and production of alternative energy sources, financial aid to low-income persons, a tax credit based on increases in residential heating costs, provisions for establishing three trust funds for transportation, low-income energy assistance and taxpayers, and a provision repealing "carryover basis" for inherited property.[67]

More specifically, the Senate expanded the exemption from the WPT to include as follows: (1) state and local government or any agency or instrumentality thereof if all of the net proceeds of their economic interest were dedicated to *any* public purpose; (2) charitable educational institutions, charitable medical facilities and churches (or conventions thereof) to the extent that they

66 *The Crude Oil Windfall Profit Tax Bill of 1979,* H.R. 3919, 96th Cong., 1st Sess., June 28, 1979.

67 U.S. Senate, Committee on Finance, *Report (No. 96-394) on the Crude Oil Windfall Profit Tax Act,* 96th Cong., 1st Sess., Nov. 1, 1979.

have dedicated proceeds to charitable educational or medical institutions if their economic interest was owned on or before October 24, 1979, or received as a bequest after that date; (3) oil production from Tribal Trust Lands, of restricted Indian lands, paid into native or tribal trust funds and by Alaskan Regional Native Corporations; (4) certain front-end tertiary incentive crude oil; and (5) federal oil production and royalties from production on federal lands.

The first two exemptions were included in the bill reported by the Senate Finance Committee. The exemption for Indian oil was a floor amendment proposed by Senator Mike Gravel (D-Alaska) and adopted by a voice vote. In addition, a floor amendment sponsored by Senators Randolph (D-W. Virginia) and Percy (R-Illinois) and passed by a voice vote provided an exemption for oil deregulated after September 30, 1980, to finance tertiary projects using carbon dioxide or tertiary surfactants. Furthermore, Senator Russell Long (D-Louisiana) sponsored an amendment, adopted by a voice vote, which provided for exemption of federal production and royalties. Finally, a floor amendment sponsored by Senator Lloyd Bentson (D-Texas) and adopted by a vote of fifty-three to forty-two would have exempted independent producers and royalty owners from the WPT on the first 1,000 barrels per day of otherwise taxable oil production beginning October 1, 1980.[68] The latter amendment would have exempted virtually all CERS organizations, as well as most other tax-exempt groups with an economic interest in oil production owning one or more royalty interests with total daily production of 1,000 barrels or less per day.

As noted above, the House hearings on the WPT bill were dominated by testimony from the Administration and the oil industry, along with a few representatives for

68 Staff of the Joint Committee on Taxation, *supra* N. 56, at 1-9.

consumers and the environment. The addition of a special rule to exempt state or locally owned oil producing property from WPT (where net proceeds were dedicated to public education) during deliberations by the House Ways and Means Committee was made possible by the presence of representatives from oil producing states on the Committee and through lobbying by state officials, such as Texas Land Commissioner Bob Armstrong, from oil producing states.[69]

Similarly, the Senate hearings on the WPT were dominated by testimony from the Administration and the oil industry, especially the major oil companies and the independent producers.[70] However, the Senate Finance Committee was not influenced much by the oil industry's public testimony or lobbying efforts; consequently, a series of floor amendments during the Senate debate on the Finance Committee's version of the WPT bill effected the few concessions made to the oil industry. Conversely, the Senate Finance Committee expanded the House exemption for state and local government and added a limited exemption for charitable educational institutions and medical facilities and for religious groups to the extent they support educational institutions and medical facilities.[71]

Several of the exemptions were amended and two were deleted when the Conference Committee settled the differences between the House and Senate versions of the WPT bill. The exemption of 1,000 barrels or less per day of the otherwise taxable oil production of independent producers and royalty owners was successfully amended to provide only for a reduced rate of taxation for the 1,000

69 Washington Bureau, "House Panel OKs State Exemption in Windfall Tax," *The Dallas Morning News,* June 21, 1979, p. 48A.

70 U.S. Senate, Committee on Finance, *Hearings on Windfall Profit Tax and Creation of Energy Trust Fund,* 96th Cong., 1st Sess., July 10, 1979.

71 Staff of the Joint Committee on Taxation, *supra* N. 56.

barrels per day of independent producer oil; royalty owners were not exempt. Furthermore, the exemption of oil production from National (Naval) Petroleum Reserves and federal royalties was dropped. Thus, the federal government is paying the WPT too, *i.e.,* revenues from federal oil production and royalties are being switched from one type of account classification to another. The Senate tax exemption for medical and educational charities was expanded somewhat (as previously explained); the closing date was deferred slightly from October 24, 1979, to January 21, 1980; bequests after the closing date were deleted from the exemption. In respect to the exemption for Indian oil, the conference agreement limited it to production from mineral interests held by, or on behalf of, Indian tribes or individual Indians, and held on the January 21, 1980, closing date. Similarly, exempt Alaskan oil was technically limited to oil produced from wells north of the Arctic Circle excepting that from the Sadlerochit Reservoir of the Alaskan North Slope. Finally, the front-end tertiary incentive oil exemption was limited to projects prior to an October 1, 1981 closing or cut-off date, and the rules for qualifying were made much more complex.[72]

In summary, the development of the WPT exemption is inconsistent with the tax-exempt tradition of the federal tax system. Rather than beginning with a broad exemption for government, CERS organizations, and other organizations generally exempt from federal income taxation, and then limiting its scope to minimize abuses (*e.g.,* unrelated business income is taxable), the Carter Administration's original proposal provided for only one limited exemption—Alaskan oil produced from a well north of the Arctic Circle. Thoughtful members of House Ways and Means, in conjunction with lobbying by state officials from oil producing states, provided the basis for initially adding certain state and local govern-

72 Conference Committee, *supra* N. 44, at 93-95, 107-110.

ment oil production and royalties to the exemption list. Finally, an even more thoughtful Senate and its Finance Committee provided the impetus for expanding the WPT exemption to virtually all state and local government oil production and royalties, as well as to charitable educational institutions, charitable medical facilities, religiously supported educational institutions and medical facilities, and charitable organizations established to support state or local public education.

One could attribute the Carter Administration's omission of a WPT exemption for state and local government as well as for CERS organizations to lack of knowledge of the ownership of crude oil producing property in the oil producing states. Nevertheless, once the problem was made known to the Administration, traditional federal tax policy would seem to dictate the addition of a broad exemption for governmental and CERS entities. In testimony before the Senate Finance Committee, the Administration not only opposed the House exemption for state or local government crude oil production dedicated to public education, but it also recommended further limitations on its exemption for Alaskan oil.[73] Moreover, there would seem to be constitutional questions implicit in taxing state and local revenue from royalties or other economic interests in oil producing property, *i.e.*, the principle of intergovernmental immunity from taxation.

Constitutional questions also seem evident when one considers the imposition of a WPT on religious organizations, because the current law only exempts religious organizations to the extent that they dedicate their net oil production revenues to charitable educational institutions and charitable medical facilities. Insofar as the issue of sovereignity over Indian lands is still unclear pending resolution of several conflicting federal court decisions, the introduction of a tax exemption for Indian oil is a prudent, although perhaps temporary, policy decision.

73 *BNA Daily Tax Report* (#133), July 10, 1979, p. J-15.

Prospects for Reforming the Exemption From Windfall Profit Taxation

The Republican platform called for a strategy that boosts the domestic supply of energy. President Reagan not only campaigned on his party's platform but he also embellished it with several specific proposals for increasing domestic production and reducing oil imports. For example, he advocated the decontrol of wellhead prices of oil and natural gas. Moreover, he advocated the repeal of the WPT as it applies to newly discovered oil, stripper oil, tertiary recovery oil, heavy crude oil, and small volume royalty owners. Furthermore, he supports the inclusion of a "plow-back" provision and the acceleration of the phase-out of the WPT.[74] To the best of our knowledge, President Reagan has not publicly advocated liberalizing the WPT exemption for CERS organizations.

Probably the best hope for exempting CERS organizations from the WPT lies with the proposed exemption for small volume royalty owners. After the WPT was enacted on April 2, 1980, several bills to exempt various amounts of a royalty owner's daily oil production were introduced in the Congress. Since the Senate is controlled by Republicans and the Democratic majority in the House has been reduced significantly, a Reagan Administration proposal to exempt a small amount of a royalty owner's daily production may be enacted.

Although not the theoretically preferred solution, the exemption of 1,000 barrels per day of a royalty owner's oil production would seem to have the effect of exempting virtually all CERS organizations from the WPT. Therefore, amending the WPT law to exempt small volume royalty owners from taxation should eliminate the possibility of taxing, among others, widows and orphans (in charity-operated institutions) by imposing the WPT on many CERS organizations.

---

74 "Candidates' Energy Views Summarized," *Crude Oil Pricing/Windfall Profit Tax Information Service,* October 1, 1980.

WPT tier 1 crude subject to built-in excess withholding

ROBERT E. STATHAM, Threshold Development Co., Ft. Worth
KEN L. KEENUM, Willis Energy Co., Ft. Worth

PHASED decontrol of crude oil pricing causes the most uniform application of the net income limitation in 1980 to be with respect to properties which began production before 1973.

In examining the applicability of the net income limitation to Tier 1 properties with pre-1973 production we have constructed a comprehensive case study to illustrate what we believe is a "built-in" excess withholding situation on production from such properties.

This situation is caused by a fundamental difference between the calculation of the tentative tax base — the windfall profit per barrel used for withholding purposes—and the net income limitation per barrel which limits the tax base and therefore the tax imposed. The tentative tax base is calculated by reference to the removal price of each barrel of taxable crude oil removed from the property. The net income limitation, however, is calculated with respect to

Fig. 1

Lower tier oil movement to upper tier and market levels

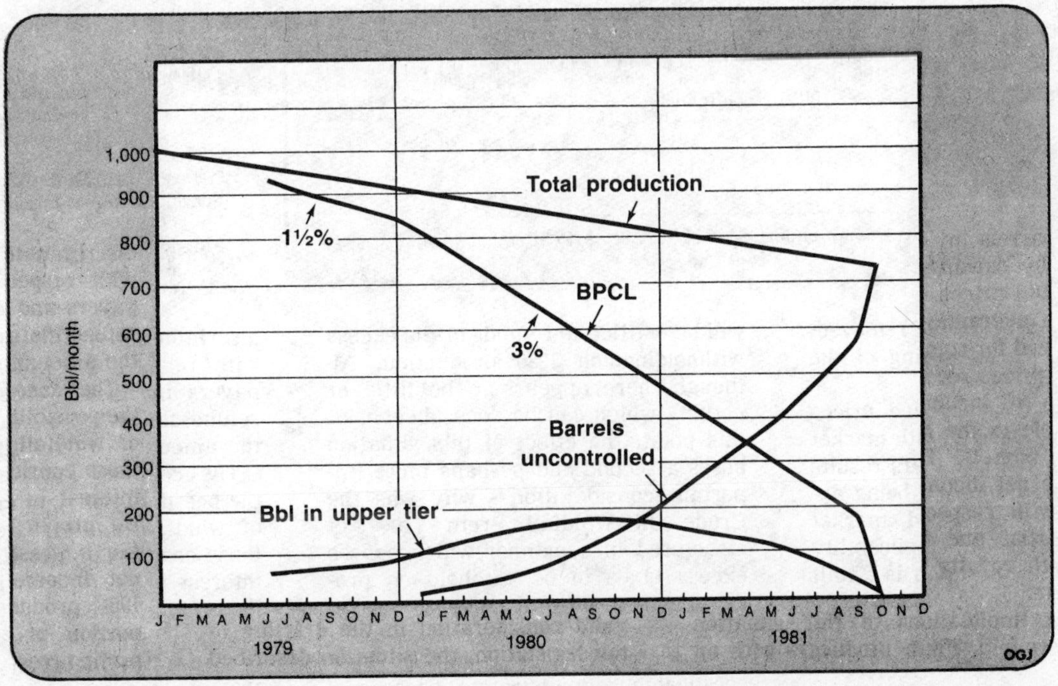

Article reprinted courtesy of *Oil & Gas Journal*, 20 October 1980, pp. 125–131

Table 1

Movement of lower tier oil to upper tier and market levels—BPCL*

	1 Total production	2 BPCL oil remaining lower tier	3 Oil moved to upper tier (1) − (2)	4 Multiplier	5 Oil moved to uncontrolled (3) × (4)	6 Oil remaining upper tier (3) − (5)
1979						
Jan	1,000					
Feb	992					
Mar	984					
Apr	976					
May	968					
Jun	960	910	50			50
Jul	952	895	57			57
Aug	944	880	64			64
Sep	936	865	71			71
Oct	928	850	78			78
Nov	920	835	85			85
Dec	912	820	92			92
	11,472					
1980						
Jan	904	790	114	.046	5	109
Feb	896	760	136	.092	13	123
Mar	889	730	159	.138	22	137
Apr	882	700	182	.184	33	149
May	875	670	205	.230	47	158
Jun	868	640	228	.276	63	165
Jul	861	610	251	.322	81	170
Aug	854	580	274	.368	101	173
Sep	847	550	297	.414	123	174
Oct	840	520	320	.460	147	173
Nov	833	490	343	.506	174	169
Dec	826	460	366	.552	202	164
	10,375					
1981						
Jan	819	430	389	.598	233	156
Feb	812	400	412	.644	265	147
Mar	805	370	435	.690	300	135
Apr	798	340	458	.736	337	121
May	791	310	481	.782	376	105
Jun	784	280	504	.828	417	87
Jul	777	250	527	.874	461	66
Aug	771	220	551	.920	507	44
Sep	765	190	575	.966	555	20
Oct	759	— — —	100% decontrolled	— — —	759	
Nov	753				753	
Dec	747				747	
	9,381					

*1,000 bbl/month as 6 month average ending Mar. 31, 1979, 10% nominal production decline (.8333% per month)

Table 2

Summary of production pricing*

	Lower tier bbl	Upper tier bbl	Market level bbl
1979			
Jan	1,000		
Feb.	992		
Mar.	984		
Apr	976		
May	968		
Jun	910	50	
Jul	895	57	
Aug	880	64	
Sep	865	71	
Oct	850	78	
Nov	835	85	
Dec	820	92	
	10,975	**497**	—
1980			
Jan.	790	109	5
Feb	760	123	13
Mar	730	137	22
Apr	700	149	33
May	670	158	47
Jun	640	165	63
Jul	610	170	81
Aug	580	173	101
Sep	550	174	123
Oct	520	173	147
Nov	490	169	174
Dec	460	164	202
	7,500	**1,864**	**1,011**
1981			
Jan	430	156	233
Feb	400	147	265
Mar	370	135	300
Apr	340	121	337
May	310	105	376
Jun	280	87	417
Jul	250	66	461
Aug	220	44	507
Sep	190	20	555
Oct	....	....	759
Nov	....	....	753
Dec	....	....	747
	2,710	**881**	**5,710**

*Movement of lower tier oil to upper tier and market levels BPCL—1,000 bbl/month as 6 month average ending Mar. 31, 1979 10% nominal production decline (.8333% per month)

all barrels of crude oil removed, thereby causing an averaging of the removal prices.

The averaging of controlled prices received for some barrels with market level prices received on others results in the net income limitation being applicable to the higher priced, market level barrels. Thus the applicability of the net income limitation is "built in" with respect to pre-1973 Tier 1 properties and is applicable for 1980 to both royalty and working interest owners.

The implications of this situation are two-fold. First, producers with an economic interest in such properties will be entitled to refunds of the excess withholding on 1980 production. Although there appears to be little or nothing which can be done about it at this point, the effect of this situation poses a second and perhaps more important consideration — why was the Crude Oil Windfall Profit Tax Act structured in a manner which causes excess taxes to be withheld on production from oil properties where the net income limitation is virtually certain to apply?

Although administrative ease is a valid consideration in the drafting of tax legislation, the situation described in this case study appears to approach discriminatory confiscation, especially with respect to unsophisticated taxpayers and those whose cost for filing refund claims will approach or exceed the amount of refund due them.

The case study data also reveals the possibility of significant reductions of windfall profits taxes in 1981 for those considering the disposition of an interest in pre-1973 Tier 1 properties. By proper timing of the disposition the interest owner may control the net income limitation applicable to 1981 production, thus eliminating a portion of his liability for windfall profit taxes.

There has been much discussion con-

Table 3

Windfall profit tax Tier 1 oil*

1980	Lower tier	Upper tier	Market level	Adjusted base price
Jan	6.34	13.74	38.00	
Feb	6.38	13.83	38.00	
Mar	6.42	13.93	38.00	13.03
Apr	6.46	14.03	38.00	13.32
May	6.51	14.13	38.00	13.32
Jun	6.56	14.24	38.00	13.32
Jul	6.61	14.35	38.00	13.61
Aug	6.66	14.46	38.00	13.61
Sep	6.71	14.57	38.00	13.61
Oct	6.76	14.68	38.00	13.90
Nov	6.81	14.79	38.00	13.90
Dec	6.86	14.90	38.00	13.90
1981				
Jan	6.91	15.01	40.00	14.20
Feb	6.96	15.12	40.00	14.20
Mar	7.01	15.23	40.00	14.20
Apr	7.06	15.34	40.00	14.50
May	7.11	15.45	40.00	14.50
Jun	7.16	15.56	40.00	14.50
Jul	7.21	15.67	40.00	14.80
Aug	7.26	15.78	40.00	14.80
Sep	7.31	15.89	40.00	14.80
Oct	N/A	N/A	40.00	15.10
Nov	N/A	N/A	40.00	15.10
Dec	N/A	N/A	40.00	15.10

*Assumed removal prices per bbl and adjusted base price

Table 4

Net revenue before windfall profit tax

	Gross revenue-WPT tier 1					
	Lower tier	**Upper tier**	**Market level**	**Total**	**Severence tax**	**Net before WPT**
1980						
Jan	5,009	1,498	190	6,697	308	6,389
Feb	4,849	1,701	494	7,044	324	6,720
Mar	4,687	1,908	836	7,431	342	7,089
Apr	4,522	2,090	1,254	7,866	362	7,504
May	4,362	2,233	1,786	8,381	386	7,995
Jun	4,198	2,350	2,394	8,942	411	8,531
Jul	4,032	2,440	3,078	9,550	439	9,111
Aug	3,863	2,502	3,838	10,203	469	9,734
Sep	3,691	2,535	4,674	10,900	501	10,399
Oct	3,515	2,540	5,586	11,641	535	11,106
Nov	3,337	2,500	6,612	12,449	573	11,876
Dec	3,156	2,444	7,676	13,276	611	12,665
	49,221	**26,741**	**38,418**	**114,380**	**5,261**	**109,119**
1981						
Jan	2,971	2,342	9,320	14,633	673	13,960
Feb	2,784	2,223	10,600	15,607	718	14,889
Mar	2,594	2,056	12,000	16,650	766	15,884
Apr	2,400	1,856	13,480	17,736	816	16,920
May	2,204	1,622	15,040	18,866	868	17,998
Jun	2,005	1,354	16,680	20,039	922	19,117
Jul	1,803	1,034	18,440	21,277	979	20,298
Aug	1,597	694	20,280	22,571	1,038	21,533
Sep	1,389	318	22,200	23,907	1,100	22,807
Oct	N/A	N/A	30,360	30,360	1,397	28,963
Nov	N/A	N/A	30,120	30,120	1,386	28,734
Dec	N/A	N/A	29,880	29,880	1,374	28,506
	19,747	**13,499**	**228,400**	**261,646**	**12,037**	**249,609**

cerning whether the Crude Oil Windfall Profit Tax Act is an integral part of our national effort to reduce dependence on foreign energy sources or a stumbling block to that goal enacted as the political price of decontrol.

Many articles also have discussed the background of decontrol and provided an overview of the act.

Accordingly, the topics discussed here are limited to those having a direct relationship to the taxation of Tier 1 properties with pre-1973 crude oil production.

Crude oil price decontrol. The maximum selling price for domestic crude oil production from properties with commercial production in calendar year 1978 is controlled by reference to a tier system regulated by the Department of Energy. Lower tier oil ("old oil") is oil produced from properties which had production in 1972 and which does not exceed the adjusted Base Production Control Level (BPCL) for the property. A one time election was available to producers in 1979 to update BPCL to reflect average daily production for the six month period ended Mar. 31, 1979, the election to be effective June 1, 1979.

If the election was made, the updated BPCL was reduced by 9% effective June 1, 1979 and reduced 1½% per month for the remaining six months in 1979. If the election was not made BPCL continued to be based on average monthly production in 1975. In either case, BPCL is reduced by 3% each month beginning Jan. 1, 1980.

Upper tier oil is production in excess of the BPCL for a property but which is not uncontrolled oil, and includes production from a "marginal property." Uncontrolled oil includes production classified as "heavy oil," certain production from tertiary recovery projects, and "market level new crude oil."

Market level new crude oil is production released from upper tier pricing to uncontrolled status at an additive 4.6% per month rate, beginning Jan. 1, 1980. For example, production otherwise subject to upper tier pricing is released to market level at the following rates: 4.6% for January 1980 production, 9.2% for February 1980 production, 13.8% for March 1980 production. The amount of oil released to market level increases by 4.6% each month through September 1981.

Thus, for properties with pre-1973 crude oil production which are not "marginal properties" and do not involve tertiary recovery projects nor "heavy oil," there will be three different selling prices for 1980 production—the controlled prices established for lower tier and upper tier oil and the uncontrolled price received for "market level new" oil.

Windfall profit tax provisions. A tier system is also used for purposes of the C.O.W.P.T.A. Tier 1 oil is defined by the act as oil other than Tier 2 or Tier 3 oil. In general, Tier 1 oil includes DOE lower tier, upper tier, and market level new oil.

The tentative tax base (for withholding purposes) is equal to the removal price less the adjusted base price and the severance tax adjustment.

The removal price is generally the selling price of the oil, whether established by DOE regulation or by the market for crude. The base price for Tier 1 oil is the May 1979 DOE upper tier ceiling price for the property, less 21¢, and is adjusted quarterly for inflation.

The severance tax adjustment is generally removal price minus adj. base price times severance tax rate. Thus, the following formula depicts the calculation of the tentative windfall profit on a particular barrel of crude oil in most cases:

(Selling price − Adj. Base Price) × (100% − Severance Tax Rate)

The windfall profit calculated in this manner is used for withholding pur-

Table 5

1980 WPT withholding—⅛ royalty owners

	Removal price per bbl	Adjusted base price	Severance Tax adjustment	Windfall profit per bbl	Tax rate, %	WPT WH per bbl	⅛ share production bbl	Windfall profit tax withheld — Upper tier	Market level	Total by month
Mar—UT	13.93	13.03	.04	.86	70	.60	17.13	10.28		
ML	38.00	13.03	1.15	23.82	70	16.67	2.75		45.84	56.12
Apr—UT	14.03	13.32	.03	.68	70	.48	18.63	8.94		
ML	38.00	13.32	1.14	23.54	70	16.48	4.13		68.06	77.00
May—UT	14.13	13.32	0.4	.77	70	.54	19.75	19.67		
ML	38.00	13.32	1.14	23.54	70	16.48	5.88		96.90	107.57
Jun—UT	14.24	13.32	.04	.88	70	.62	20.36	12.62		
ML	38.00	13.32	1.14	23.54	70	16.48	7.88		129.86	142.48
July—UT	14.35	13.61	.03	.71	70	.50	21.25	10.63		
ML	38.00	13.61	1.12	23.27	70	16.29	10.13		165.02	175.65
Aug—UT	14.46	13.61	.04	.81	70	.57	21.63	12.33		
ML	38.00	13.61	1.12	23.27	70	16.29	12.63		205.74	218.07
Sep—UT	14.57	13.61	.04	.92	70	.64	21.75	13.92		
ML	38.00	13.61	1.12	23.27	70	16.29	15.38		250.54	264.46
Oct—UT	14.68	13.90	.04	.74	70	.52	21.63	11.25		
ML	38.00	13.90	1.11	22.99	70	16.09	18.38		295.73	306.98
Nov—UT	14.79	13.90	.04	.85	70	.60	21.13	12.68		
ML	38.00	13.90	1.11	22.99	70	16.09	21.75		349.96	362.64
Dec—UT	14.96	13.90	.05	.95	70	.67	20.50	13.74		
ML	38.00	13.90	1.11	22.99	70	16.09	25.25		406.27	420.01
						UT	204.03			
						ML	124.16	**117.06**	**2,013.92**	**2,130.98**
						Taxable	328.19			

poses but is not the tax base. The tax base is, with respect to each barrel of taxable crude oil produced, the lesser of the tentative windfall profit calculated above or 90% of the net income per barrel of crude oil produced from the property for the calendar year.

Thus, the net income limitation on the tax base may cause excess withholding of tax.

The temporary regulations specifically provide that, in determining the amount of windfall profit tax to be deducted and withheld by purchasers, the net income limitation shall not be taken into account.

If an operator has been substituted for the purchaser, with respect to a property, apparently the operator would not be liable for withholding tax on its own interest in production from the property but rather would be required to deposit the tax imposed on its interest (Temporary Regulation Section 150.4995(f)). This point has not been clarified but apparently an operator who has been substituted for a purchaser could take the net income limitation into account in calculating the deposit requirement with respect to its own interest in the property.

Case study—assumptions and calculations. To illustrate the excess withholding on pre-1973 Tier 1 properties, we have used the following fact situation:

- The property in question was acquired subject to a ⅛ royalty by an independent oil company in 1971. Drilling was successfully completed in 1972 and resulted in commercial production of crude oil (only) from one well completed at a depth of 4,500 ft.
- The property is located in West Texas; the crude oil produced is West Texas sour.
- Production from the property does not qualify as "heavy oil," nor does the property qualify as a "marginal property" since average daily production from the well exceeded 25 b/d during 1978.
- Average daily production from the well for the six-month period ending Mar. 31, 1979 was approximately 33 bbl. The election to revise BPCL was made and resulted in a revised BPCL of 1,000 bbl per month; thus BPCL was reduced by 9% (90 bbl) to 910 bbl for June 1979, was reduced 1½% (15 bbl) each month for the remainder of 1979, and reduced by 3% (30 bbl) each month beginning in January 1980.
- Total production from the well is assumed to be declining at a 10% nominal rate (.8333% per month).
- The assumed removal prices for lower tier and upper tier oil are those posted by Amoco Production Co. for West Texas sour, gravity of 40° API, for January through August 1980, and are projected for September 1980 through December 1981. Market level prices have been assumed to be $38 for 1980 and $40 for 1981.
- The adjusted base price used is actual for the first three quarters of 1980, and is projected for the fourth quarter of 1980 and for 1981. (The May 1979 upper tier ceiling price posted by Amoco for West Texas sour, gravity of 40° API, was $12.99; the Tier 1 inflation adjustment factors for the first three quarters of 1980 are 1.0195, 1.0422, and 1.0649, respectively.)

Decontrol of prices applicable to production. Table 1 illustrates the calculation of price decontrol applicable to the property. Note that oil released from lower tier to upper tier classifi-

Table 6

1980 WPT withholding—⅞ working interest owners

	Removal price per bbl	Adjusted base price	Severance Tax adjustment	Windfall profit per bbl	Tax rate, %	WPT WH per bbl	⅞ share production bbl	Windfall profit tax withheld: Upper tier	Market level	Total by month
Mar—UT	13.93	13.03	.04	.86	50	.43	119.87	51.54		
ML	38.00	13.03	1.15	23.82	50	11.91	19.25		229.27	280.81
Apr—UT	14.03	13.32	.03	.68	50	.34	130.37	44.33		
ML	38.00	13.32	1.14	23.54	50	11.77	28.87		339.80	384.13
May—UT	14.13	13.32	.04	.77	50	.39	138.25	53.92		
ML	38.00	13.32	1.14	23.54	50	11.77	41.12		483.98	537.90
Jun—UT	14.24	13.32	.04	.88	50	.44	144.37	63.52		
ML	38.00	13.32	1.14	23.54	50	11.77	55.12		648.76	712.28
July—UT	14.35	13.61	.03	.71	50	.36	148.75	53.55		
ML	38.00	13.61	1.12	23.27	50	11.64	70.87		824.93	878.48
Aug—UT	14.46	13.61	.04	.81	50	.41	151.37	62.06		
ML	38.00	13.61	1.12	23.27	50	11.64	88.37		1,028.63	1,090.69
Sep—UT	14.57	13.61	.04	.92	50	.46	152.25	70.04		
ML	38.00	13.61	1.12	23.27	50	11.64	107.62		1,252.70	1,322.74
Oct—UT	14.68	13.90	.04	.74	50	.37	151.37	56.01		
ML	38.00	13.90	1.11	22.99	50	11.50	128.62		1,479.13	1,535.14
Nov—UT	14.79	13.90	.04	.85	50	.43	147.87	63.58		
ML	38.00	13.90	1.11	22.99	50	11.50	152.25		1,750.88	1,814.46
Dec—UT	14.96	13.90	.05	.95	50	.48	143.50	68.88		
ML	38.00	13.90	1.11	22.99	50	11.50	176.76		2,032.74	2,101.62
						UT	1,427.97			
						ML	**868.84**	**587.43**	**10,070.82**	**10,568.25**
						Taxable	**2,296.81**			

Table 7

Net checks to owners, 1980

	⅛ royalty owners: Net before WPT	WPT withheld	Net to owner	⅞ working int. owners: Net before WPT	WPT withheld	Net to owner
1980						
Jan.	783	N/A	783	5,477	N/A	5,477
Feb.	826	N/A	826	5,781	N/A	5,781
Mar.	874	56	818	6,120	281	5,839
Apr.	929	77	852	6,500	384	6,116
May	992	108	884	6,942	538	6,404
June	1,061	142	919	7,424	712	6,712
July	1,135	176	959	7,946	878	7,068
Aug.	1,215	218	997	8,505	1,091	7,414
Sept.	1,300	264	1,036	9,101	1,323	7,778
Oct.	1,391	307	1,084	9,733	1,535	8,198
Nov.	1,488	363	1,125	10,419	1,814	8,605
Dec.	1,588	420	1,168	11,119	2,102	9,017
	13,582	**2,131**	**11,451**	**95,067**	**10,658**	**84,409**

cation for a particular month is included in the calculation of oil released from upper tier to uncontrolled (market level new) classification for the same month.

Table 2 summarizes the portion of total production each month for which lower tier, upper tier, and market level prices will be received by the interest owners.

Fig. 1 shows total production, BPCL and the decontrol of pricing applicable to total production.

Removal prices/adjusted base price. Table 3 lists the assumed removal prices and adjusted base prices for 1980 and 1981.

Net after severance taxes but before withholding. Table 4 calculates gross revenue attributable to lower tier, upper tier, and market level new oil by multiplying the applicable monthly production in each classification (Table 2) by the assumed removal prices (Table 3).

Gross revenue from the property is reduced by Texas severance taxes equal to 4.6%.

Windfall profit tax withheld. Table 5 calculates the windfall profit tax withheld from royalty owners for each production month in 1980 applicable to upper tier and market level new production.

There is of course, no windfall profit tax on lower tier production since the controlled price for such production is never in excess of the adjusted base price.

Table 6 makes the same calculation for the working interest owners, who are assumed to have been certified as "independent producers" with respect to the property's entire production, thus the 50% tax rate is applicable.

Net check to interest owners. Table 7 summarizes the net revenue after windfall profit tax withholding distributable to the interest owners for 1980 production.

Net income limitation—1980. Table 8 calculates the net income limitation per bbl for 1980 and the "built in" excess withholding on 1980 production attributable to withholding on market level new production. The net income per bbl calculated does not take into

Table 8

Effect of net income limitation, 1980

	Royalty owners	Working int. owners
Net revenue (before WPT withholding)	13,582	95,067
Divided by total bbls produced	1,296.88	9,078.12
Net income per bbl*	10.47	10.47
Multiplied by 90%	.90	.90
Net income limitation per bbl*	9.42	9.42
Taxable (post Feb. 1979) market level new production in bbl	124.16	868.84
Multiplied by net income limitation per bbl*	9.42	9.42
Total windfall profit applicable to taxable market level new production	1,169.59	8,184.47
Multiplied by tax rate	.70	.50
WPT or market level new production	818.71	4,092.24
Less: WPT withheld on market level new production	2,013.92	10,070.82
Excess withholding on 1980 production	1,194.87	5,978.58
WPT withheld on market level new production, %	59	59
Total WPT withheld, %	56	56
Net check to owners, %	10	7

*Deductions available in computing the net income per bbl for windfall profits tax purposes (other than severance taxes), i.e., production expenses, "as if" depletion, depreciation, and allocable overhead have not been considerd.

Table 9

Tentative windfall profit

	1st Q	2nd Q	3rd Q	4th Q
Removal price	40.00	40.00	40.00	40.00
Less: Adjusted base price	(14.20)	(14.50)	(14.80)	(15.10)
	25.80	25.50	25.20	24.90
Multiplied by (100% − 4.6%)	.954	.954	.954	.954
Tentative windfall profit per bbl	**24.61**	**24.33**	**24.04**	**23.75**

Table 10

Planning opportunities for 1981

Date disposition	1 Year-to-date net revenue	2 Year-to-date production	3 Net income per bbl, (1) ÷ (2)	4 90% N. I. limitation, (3) × .9
1-31-81	13,960	819	17.05	15.35
2-28-81	28,849	1,631	17.69	15.92
3-31-81	44,733	2,436	18.36	16.52
4-30-81	61,653	3,234	19.06	17.15
5-31-81	79,651	4,025	19.79	17.81
6-30-81	98,768	4,809	20.54	18.49
7-31-81	119,066	5,586	21.32	19.19
8-31-81	140,599	6,357	22.12	19.91
9-30-81	163,406	7,122	22.94	20.65
10-31-81	192,369	7,881	24.41	21.97
11-30-81	221,103	8,634	25.61	23.05
12-31-81	249,609	9,381	26.61	23.95

Date disposition	5 Average tentative windfall profit per market level bbl	6 Excess windfall profit per market level bbl (4) − (5)	7 Taxable market level bbl year-to-date	8 Total windfall profit eliminated (6) × (7)
1-31-81	24.61	9.26	233	2,158
2-28-81	24.61	8.69	498	4,328
3-31-81	24.61	8.09	798	6,456
4-30-81	24.53	7.38	1,135	8,376
5-31-81	24.48	6.67	1,511	10,078
6-30-81	24.45	5.96	1,928	11,491
7-31-81	24.37	5.18	2,389	12,375
8-31-81	24.31	4.40	2,896	12,742
9-30-81	24.27	3.62	3,451	12,492
10-31-81	23.94	1.97	4,210	8,294
11-30-81	23.71	.66	4,963	3,276
12-31-81	23.54	(.41)	5,710	

account "as if" depletion or allocable overhead which may be deducted by either royalty owners or working interest owners, nor deductions for lease operating expenses and depreciation which would apply to working interest owners only.

Thus, the net income limitation calculated is not affected by deductions which would vary on different properties but rather is based on factors which can be reasonably projected prior to the accumulation of all the applicable data. The "built in" excess withholding calculated is therefore a "floor" amount; the actual excess withholding may be substantially greater, especially for working interest owners.

Conclusions. The key to the excess withholding situation on pre-1973 Tier 1 properties is the decline in crude oil production versus the BPCL decline for such properties. So long as production declines less rapidly than 3% a month, windfall profit taxes on 1980 production are certain to be overwithheld.

Given the control of production in Texas for conservation purposes, it appears that almost all pre-1973 Tier 1 properties in Texas will be subject to the net income limitation in 1980. In some states, where maximum production is allowed, the production decline could conceivably approach or exceed 3% a month; in such cases the impact of the net income limitation may be significantly reduced.

The case study data for 1981 production reveals an attractive planning opportunity. Based on the case study data, the net income limitation (ignoring all deductions except severance taxes) for 1981 will be $23.95 per bbl, calculated as follows:

Total net revenue		$249,609
Divided by total bbl produced		9,381
Net income per bbl		26.61
Multiplied by 90%	×	.90
Net income limitation per bbl	$	23.95

The tentative windfall profit per bbl (for withholding purposes) of market level new oil for each quarter for 1981 would be calculated as in Table 9.

Using this data (and the assumed market prices/adjusted base prices for 1981 inherent therein) the net income limitation may be only marginally applicable, and there would be no significant "built in" excess withholding as was the case in 1980, so long as the property is held by the interest owners for the entire calendar year.

If an interest owner disposes of his interest during 1981, however, the "built in" excess withholding caused by the structure of the C.O.W.P.T.A. for 1980 production may be created by the interest owner for 1981 production simply by disposing of the interest at the optimum point.

Using the case study data, Table 10 depicts the net income limitation for the property as if a taxpayer's interest in the property is disposed of during 1981, and indicates that the optimum point for disposal of an interest in the property during 1981 is about Aug. 31, 1981. At that point, approximately 18% of the year to date windfall profit tax applicable to an owners interest can be eliminated by disposal of the interest.

Many of the amounts used in the case study are hypothetical, such as the price at which uncontrolled oil is sold. Accordingly, the impact of the net income limitation with respect to production from pre-1973 Tier 1 properties shown in the case study is only an estimate for what we believe to be a typical situation. However, we conclude that the net income limitation will have widespread application to production from such properties.

Those who own interests in such properties may determine the effect of the net income limitation with respect to their particular property interests by using data available to them in an analysis similar to that depicted in Tables 1 through 9.

The case study data indicates that the withholding rate with respect to the "tentative windfall profit" on market level new crude oil production in 1980 should have been approximately 30% rather than 70%, or 50% as in the case of independent producers.

To the extent this situation causes the overpayment of windfall profit taxes for which refund claims are never filed or increases taxpayers' costs of compliance, the C.O.W.P.T.A. will have served to overtax producers by its very structure. It is unfortunate that those most likely to be overtaxed are those who can least afford it, the owners of relatively small royalty and working interests.

The planning opportunities illustrated by the case study with respect to 1981 production should be considered by those contemplating dispositions of pre-1973 Tier 1 properties. This technique may be especially valuable in related party transfers during 1981.

END

Calculators quickly find Tier I revenue, volume, WPT

Frank W. Lewis
Resource Analysis
& Management Group
Oklahoma City, Okla.

Dipak K. Sinha
The Oklahoma Department of Energy
Oklahoma City, Okla.

The Crude Oil Windfall Profit Tax Act of 1980 is a complex piece of legislation causing independent producers and royalty owners difficulty in calculating Tier I production revenues, volumes and windfall profit taxes.

New terminology, complex decline rates and the ending of phased decontrol have left producers and royalty owners without a rapid and accurate method of projecting taxes and revenues. Programmable calculators can provide this information quickly and easily to any level of management.

A Texas Instruments TI-59 programmable calculator, using the accompanying program listing, provides a method for calculating revenues, volumes, and taxes for any month of production under any category of Tier I production.

The program determines whether the production is "new", old, or marginal and calculates the appropriate revenues, volumes, and taxes for each of the three pricing categories: lower, upper, and market level crude oil. Although the program computes only one month at a time, monthly series may be entered in sequence.

As with any computer program, results are only as accurate as the input data. Therefore, accuracy must be maintained in determining all of the data inputs.

Special care must be maintained in determining the Base Production Control Level (BPCL) and the pricing structures as they are paramount in the calculation of the monthly 3% decline of the Adjusted Base Production Control Level and in computation of Windfall Profit Taxes. To aid in understanding, a brief explanation of the terms listed in the sample input shown in Table 1 follows.

Table 1

Sample input and output

INPUT

STO		Old production	Marginal production	"New" production	Tier 1 production after decontrol
01	Base price	13.38	13.38	13.38	13.38
04	Original BPCL	1,400.00	0	0	0
05	Lower selling price	6.66	6.46	6.89	0
06	Upper selling price	15.06	14.63	15.55	0
07	Market level selling price	36.00	36.00	37.00	38.00
08	Volume	1,300.00	800.00	1,000.00	500.00
09	WPT rate	.50	.50	.50	.50
10	Severance tax	.07	.07	.07	.07
11	Old cumulative deficiency	+100.00	0	0	0
12	Inflation adjustment	1.0649	1.0422	1.0924	1.1187
13	T value	6	2	10	12
14	Marginal production	0	1	0	0
15	"New" production	0	0	1	0
16	Decontrolled production	0	0	0	1

OUTPUT

RCL					
02	90% limit? y/n 1/0	1	1	0	0
17	Lower volume	812.00	0	0	0
18	Upper volume	308.42	652.80	448.00	0
22	Market level volume	179.58	147.20	552.00	500.00
11	New cumulative deficiency	+588.00	0	0	0
21	Adjusted BPCL	812.00	0	0	0
25	Gross value lower	5,407.92	0	0	0
26	Gross value upper	4,644.74	9,550.46	6,966.40	0
27	Gross value market level	6,645.02	5,299.20	20,424.00	19,000.00
34	Total gross value	16,517.69	14,849.66	27,390.40	19,000.00
28	State severance tax lower	378.55	0	0	0
29	State severance tax upper	325.13	668.53	487.65	0
30	State severance tax market level	452.55	370.94	1,429.68	1,330.00
35	Total state severance tax	1,156.24	1,039.48	1,917.33	1,330.00
23	WPT upper	116.16	209.45	193.74	0
24	WPT market level	1,816.27	1,509.96	5,744.50	5,354.48
36	Total WPT	1,932.43	1,719.41	5,938.24	5,354.48
31	Net received lower	5,029.37	0	0	0
32	Net received upper	4,203.45	8,672.48	6,285.01	0
33	Net received market level	4,196.20	3,418.29	13,249.82	12,315.53
19	Total net received	13,429.02	12,090.77	19,534.84	12,315.53

Before decontrol

Tier I. The Tier I base price is the May 1979 selling price in $/bbl for "Upper Tier" production from the property, less 21 cents. Prices must be appropriately adjusted for gravity and sulphur content if the production warrants.

Base Production Control Level (BPCL). The BPCL is the base from which the program computes the monthly adjusted BPCL. According to Federal Regulations, if a producer so elected, the BPCL is the monthly average production for a 6-months interval, October 1, 1978 thru March 31, 1979.

Under certain circumstances, if no certification was made, the BPCL is the lower of the average monthly production during 1972 or 1975 reduced by 75%. In either case, the adjusted BPCL declines from 82% of the original BPCL at the rate of 3% per month beginning January 1, 1980. In the event that you are interested in only the net revenue share of total production, adjust the original BPCL by the same ratio.

If uncertainity exists as to the BPCL volume, exercise caution in its selection and consult your attorney or tax

Article reprinted courtesy of *Oil & Gas Journal*, 16 March 1981, pp. 80–84

Program listing, Tier I Windfall Profit Tax

000	00	0	067	08	08	134	08	08	201	18	18	268	43	RCL	334	42	STO	400	24	24
001	42	STO	068	42	STO	135	75	-	202	61	GTO	269	12	12	335	31	31	401	55	÷
002	02	02	069	18	18	136	43	RCL	203	14	D	270	95	=	336	43	RCL	402	43	RCL
003	42	STO	070	00	0	137	18	18	204	76	LBL	271	42	STO	337	26	26	403	22	22
004	21	21	071	42	STO	138	95	=	205	13	C	272	19	19	338	75	-	404	55	÷
005	01	1	072	17	17	139	42	STO	206	00	0	273	58	FIX	339	43	RCL	405	43	RCL
006	32	X≷T	073	61	GTO	140	17	17	207	42	STO	274	02	02	340	29	29	406	09	09
007	43	RCL	074	16	A'	141	61	GTO	208	17	17	275	52	EE	341	75	-	407	95	=
008	16	16	075	76	LBL	142	16	A'	209	42	STO	276	22	INV	342	43	RCL	408	42	STO
009	67	EQ	076	11	A	143	76	LBL	210	18	18	277	52	EE	343	23	23	409	40	40
010	13	C	077	43	RCL	144	18	C'	211	43	RCL	278	42	STO	344	95	=	410	53	(
011	43	RCL	078	04	04	145	43	RCL	212	08	08	279	19	19	345	42	STO	411	43	RCL
012	15	15	079	65	X	146	21	21	213	42	STO	280	22	INV	346	32	32	412	34	34
013	32	X≷T	080	53	(	147	42	STO	214	22	22	281	58	FIX	347	43	RCL	413	75	-
014	01	1	081	93	.	148	17	17	215	76	LBL	282	53	(	348	27	27	414	43	RCL
015	67	EQ	082	07	7	149	43	RCL	216	14	D	283	43	RCL	349	75	-	415	35	35
016	12	B	083	06	6	150	08	08	217	43	RCL	284	06	06	350	43	RCL	416	54	)
017	43	RCL	084	75	-	151	75	-	218	17	17	285	75	-	351	30	30	417	65	X
018	14	14	085	93	.	152	43	RCL	219	65	X	286	43	RCL	352	75	-	418	93	.
019	32	X≷T	086	00	0	153	17	17	220	43	RCL	287	19	19	353	43	RCL	419	09	9
020	00	0	087	03	3	154	95	=	221	05	05	288	54	)	354	24	24	420	55	÷
021	67	EQ	088	65	X	155	42	STO	222	95	=	289	65	X	355	95	=	421	43	RCL
022	11	A	089	43	RCL	156	18	18	223	42	STO	290	53	(	356	42	STO	422	08	08
023	43	RCL	090	13	13	157	61	GTO	224	25	25	291	01	1	357	33	33	423	95	=
024	13	13	091	54	)	158	16	A'	225	43	RCL	292	75	-	358	43	RCL	424	42	STO
025	32	X≷T	092	95	=	159	76	LBL	226	18	18	293	43	RCL	359	25	25	425	39	39
026	01	1	093	42	STO	160	17	B'	227	65	X	294	10	10	360	85	+	426	32	X≷T
027	22	INV	094	21	21	161	43	RCL	228	43	RCL	295	54	)	361	43	RCL	427	43	RCL
028	67	EQ	095	43	RCL	162	08	08	229	06	06	296	65	X	362	26	26	428	40	40
029	12	B	096	11	11	163	42	STO	230	95	=	297	43	RCL	363	85	+	429	22	INV
030	43	RCL	097	85	+	164	17	17	231	42	STO	298	18	18	364	43	RCL	430	77	GE
031	04	04	098	43	RCL	165	00	0	232	26	26	299	65	X	365	27	27	431	19	D'
032	65	X	099	08	08	166	42	STO	233	43	RCL	300	43	RCL	366	95	=	432	25	CLR
033	93	.	100	75	-	167	18	18	234	22	22	301	09	09	367	42	STO	433	69	OP
034	02	2	101	43	RCL	168	76	LBL	235	65	X	302	95	=	368	34	34	434	00	00
035	95	=	102	21	21	169	16	A'	236	43	RCL	303	42	STO	369	43	RCL	435	01	1
036	42	STO	103	95	=	170	53	(	237	07	07	304	23	23	370	28	28	436	02	2
037	17	17	104	42	STO	171	93	.	238	95	=	305	53	(	371	85	+	437	00	0
038	43	RCL	105	11	11	172	09	9	239	42	STO	306	43	RCL	372	43	RCL	438	01	1
039	08	08	106	32	X≷T	173	00	0	240	27	27	307	07	07	373	29	29	439	00	0
040	75	-	107	00	0	174	08	8	241	43	RCL	308	75	-	374	85	+	440	00	0
041	43	RCL	108	77	GE	175	75	-	242	25	25	309	43	RCL	375	43	RCL	441	06	6
042	17	17	109	17	B'	176	93	.	243	65	X	310	19	19	376	30	30	442	01	1
043	95	=	110	43	RCL	177	00	0	244	43	RCL	311	54	)	377	95	=	443	00	0
044	42	STO	111	08	08	178	04	4	245	10	10	312	65	X	378	42	STO	444	00	0
045	18	18	112	75	-	179	06	6	246	95	=	313	53	(	379	35	35	445	69	OP
046	43	RCL	113	43	RCL	180	65	X	247	42	STO	314	01	1	380	43	RCL	446	01	01
047	17	17	114	21	21	181	43	RCL	248	28	28	315	75	-	381	23	23	447	02	2
048	32	X≷T	115	95	=	182	13	13	249	43	RCL	316	43	RCL	382	85	+	448	07	7
049	43	RCL	116	42	STO	183	54	)	250	26	26	317	10	10	383	43	RCL	449	02	2
050	08	08	117	19	19	184	65	X	251	65	X	318	54	)	384	24	24	450	04	4
051	77	GE	118	32	X≷T	185	43	RCL	252	43	RCL	319	65	X	385	95	=	451	03	3
052	15	E	119	00	0	186	18	18	253	10	10	320	43	RCL	386	42	STO	452	00	0
053	43	RCL	120	77	GE	187	95	=	254	95	=	321	22	22	387	36	36	453	02	2
054	08	08	121	17	B'	188	42	STO	255	42	STO	322	65	X	388	43	RCL	454	04	4
055	42	STO	122	43	RCL	189	19	19	256	29	29	323	43	RCL	389	31	31	455	03	3
056	17	17	123	19	19	190	43	RCL	257	43	RCL	324	09	09	390	85	+	456	07	7
057	00	0	124	32	X≷T	191	18	18	258	27	27	325	95	=	391	43	RCL	457	69	OP
058	42	STO	125	43	RCL	192	75	-	259	65	X	326	42	STO	392	32	32	458	02	02
059	18	18	126	11	11	193	43	RCL	260	43	RCL	327	24	24	393	85	+	459	69	OP
060	76	LBL	127	77	GE	194	19	19	261	10	10	328	43	RCL	394	43	RCL	460	05	05
061	15	E	128	18	C'	195	95	=	262	95	=	329	25	25	395	33	33	461	01	1
062	61	GTO	129	43	RCL	196	42	STO	263	42	STO	330	75	-	396	95	=	462	42	STO
063	16	A'	130	11	11	197	22	22	264	30	30	331	43	RCL	397	42	STO	463	02	02
064	76	LBL	131	42	STO	198	43	RCL	265	43	RCL	332	28	28	398	19	19	464	76	LBL
065	12	B	132	18	18	199	19	19	266	01	01	333	95	=	399	43	RCL	465	19	D'
066	43	RCL	133	43	RCL	200	42	STO	267	65	X									

OGJ

Table 2

Tier I windfall profit tax rates

Category	Tax Rate
Independent producer	0.5
Major producer or royalty owner	0.7

Table 3

Monthly T values and inflation adjustments

Month of production		T value	Inflation Adjustments
March	1980	1	1.0195
April	1980	2	1.0422
May	1980	3	1.0422
June	1980	4	1.0422
July	1980	5	1.0649
August	1980	6	1.0649
September	1980	7	1.0649
October	1980	8	1.0924
November	1980	9	1.0924
December	1980	10	1.0924
January	1981	11	1.1187
February	1981	12	1.1187
March	1981	13	1.1187
April	1981	14	
May	1981	15	
June	1981	16	
July	1981	17	
August	1981	18	
September	1981	19	
October	1981	20	
November	1981	21	
December	1981	22	

consultant for a fuller understanding of this or any other term.

Lower Tier selling price. The Lower Tier selling prices should be available from the monthly production statement. Use the price in $/bbl that corresponds to the month of production you entered as current volume.

The Lower Tier price should be appropriately adjusted to reflect the physical characteristics of the production.

Upper Tier selling price. The Upper Tier selling prices should be available from your monthly production statement. Use the price for the month of production corresponding to the current volume.

Enter the price in $/bbl adjusted for sulphur and gravity.

Market level crude oil price. The market level crude oil price is the deregulated selling price and should be available from your production statements.

Use the price in $/bbl for the month of production. If any of the current selling prices or base prices are adjusted for sulphur or gravity, all prices must be similarly adjusted.

Current volume. Current volume is the volume of monthly production in barrels for the property. All prices and volumes of production should be for the same month, except the original BPCL.

Windfall profit tax. Choose the appropriate tax rate from Table 2. The selection of the tax rate depends solely on whether you are an independent producer or in the category of royalty owner or major producer. Enter the tax rate as a decimal equivalent rather than a percentage. An independent producer, for purposes of this article, produces less than 1,000 b/d.

State severance tax. Each producing state has a tax on the production of oil. Only taxes based on the value of production are eligible for the severance tax adjustment. Input the appropriate severance tax rate for the property as a decimal equivalent. In the event the severance tax rate does not change for a subsequent monthly computation, it need not be re-entered.

Original data storage positions are not altered during program computations. Successive months of production from the same property may be run with minimal data re-entry.

Cumulative deficiency. If monthly production exceeds the adjusted BPCL, any decreases in future production below the adjusted BPCL will have to be subtracted from Upper Tier production when monthly production returns to levels above the adjusted BPCL. Cumulative deficiency calculations began June 1, 1979 and must be carried forward for each month as applicable for your production.

The program internally adjusts production and the adjusted BPCL to compute the cumulative deficiency for each month. It need not be reentered for successive monthly applications. Marginal, "new", or any Tier I production after decontrol requires no cumulative deficiency or BPCL input.

Inflation adjustments. The inflation adjustments for each calendar quarter can be found in the Federal Register. Current and historical monthly inflation adjustments are found in Table 3. The product of the monthly inflation adjustment and the Tier I base price is the adjusted base price which is computed and rounded to the nearest cent.

T values. To facilitate programming, an arbitrary method of assigning numerical values to production months was selected for Windfall Profit Tax computations. These T values are used as coefficients to reflect the passage of time. Table 3 also provides appropriate T values.

Marginal production. If your average daily production in 1978 is less than is shown on the following table, your production qualifies as marginal production. Marginal production for March 1980, up to 20% of the 1978 BPCL, is allocated to Lower Tier, the remainder to Upper Tier. The BPCL for March 1980 is 31 times the average daily production of 1978.

After March all marginal production is allocated to Upper Tier and the BPCL is no longer needed. Enter a "1" if your production is marginal, "0" if it is not.

Average completion depth, ft	Average production in 1978, b/d
2000 - 3999	20
4000 - 5999	25
6000 - 7999	30
8000 - 9999	35
Each additional 2,000-ft interval	5 additional bbl

"New production". In general, "new" production is production from a property whose first production is on or after January 1, 1973 and which produced crude oil in 1978. All "new" production is allocated to upper tier production. Enter a "1" if your production is "new", "0" if not.

As a general rule, production from marginal, old and "new" properties are mutually exclusive. The production pattern from a single property should not fluctuate from one category to another in successive months.

90% income limitations. The Crude Oil Windfall Profit Tax Act of 1980 provides that taxable windfall profits for any barrel of production shall not be greater than 90% of the net income for an average barrel of production from that property. Statham and Keenum (OGJ, Oct. 20, 1980, p. 125) stated that in old oil Tier I properties where "production declines less rapidly than 3% a month, windfall profit taxes are certain to be over withheld." More recent analysis points out that even in the case of royalty owners, whose Tier I production declines at less than 3% and whose only deductions, with few exceptions, from gross income are state severance taxes, the 90% limit will allow refunds.

Furthermore, the refunds due working interest owners will be larger as they are allowed more deductions in the computation of their 90% income limitation. Some of the deductions working interest owners may claim in the net income calculation are severance taxes, lease operating expenses, work over costs, allocated expenses, and certain elements of cost depletion, depreciation, and amortization.

The program calculates the 90% limitation based on severance taxes only on a monthly basis. Based on internal program calculations, storage in RCL 02 of "1" infers that excess withholding probably occurs, "0" the opposite. If the PC-100 printer is used, the program will print the message "90% Limit", when the 90% limitation is violated.

The program calculations are not intended as an absolute indication of excessive withholding of windfall profit taxes. The Internal Revenue Service has defined the period of computation for the 90% limitation to be the period of 10 months, March through December 1980 for calendar tax periods. All revenues and applicable expense during this period are to be aggregated to find the average net income per barrel for that period.

That number is computed in all the 90% income limitations along with the Windfall Profit Tax of market level crude oil. You may file for over-withholding of Windfall Profit Taxes only once a year.

It appears that only market level crude oil, when coupled with lower or upper production, will be priced high enough to easily violate the 90% standard. As a general rule, the Upper Tier prices are too low to allow them to qualify for the 90% limitation. However, decontrol will make it more difficult for royalty owners and working interest owners to qualify.

After decontrol

The ending of phased decontrol by President Reagan does not affect Windfall Profit Taxes or the 90% income limitation for the months between March 1, 1980 through January 28, 1981. However, the program, beginning January 28, 1981 and thereafter, automatically adjusts Tier I production for full decontrol.

Data entry is no longer required after January 28, 1981 for the cumulative deficiency, BPCL, Lower Tier and Upper Tier prices. Enter "0" in the applicable storage positions. Only the T value, base price, current volume, inflation adjustment, severance tax rate and Windfall Profit Tax rate must be entered. A "1" in data position STO 16 indicates that production is on or after January 28, 1981 and is decontrolled. A "0" refers to production prior to January 28, 1981. In order to aid in program verification, four examples of input and output data are provided in Table 1.

Conclusion. The Windfall Profit Tax remains a complex and enerous tax. The authors' purpose was to develop for small producers and royalty owners a rapid and simple method of computing and verifying their Tier I revenues and tax liabilities.

The use of the TI-59 programmable calculator provides a quick and reliable method computing the revenues, production volumes, and Windfall Profit Taxes for any month of production.

Programmable calculators can also be used in the computation of Windfall Profit Taxes for Tier II and Tier III. The most complex calculations involve Tier I, but Tier II and Tier III could easily be programmed. ▪

The authors...

Frank W. Lewis

Dipak K. Sinha

Frank W. Lewis is an associate with the Resource Analysis & Management Group, concentrating on analysis of energy matters. He received a masters degree in economics from the University of Oklahoma and is a member of several professional organizations.

Dipak K. Sinha is an energy analyst with the Oklahom Department of Energy, specializing in oil and gas resources. He holds a masters degree in mechanical engineering from the University of Oklahoma and is an associate member of ASME.

Part IV

Severance Tax Adjustment

For purposes of the WPT, a severance tax is defined as a tax on the removal of oil from the ground levied on the gross value of the oil.

The severance tax adjustment is an addition to the base price used in the calculation of windfall profit. The adjustment addition is limited to the amount of severance tax levied on the windfall profit element of the price of a barrel of oil, up to a maximum of 15 percent. To prevent states from enacting or raising severance taxes at the expense of the U.S. Treasury, any post-March 31, 1979, severance tax increases or impositions can be taken into account only if the tax applies to the entire sales price of a barrel of oil (not just the windfall profit element). In the absence of this rule, by raising or imposing severance taxes on only the windfall profit element, a state could collect a large portion of the windfall profit to which the federal tax normally would apply. Moreover, insofar as the severance tax is a deduction (from the windfall profit to which the WPT rates will apply) and not a credit, the total tax burden on the producer would increase.

SEVERANCE TAX ADJUSTMENT UNDER THE WINDFALL PROFIT TAX

Hak K. Dickenson, Esq.*

Once a producer has determined that he has severed taxable crude oil within the meaning of the Crude Oil Windfall Profit Tax Act of 1980,[1] he must then compute the applicable windfall profit tax (WPT) on a per barrel basis. In calculating the WPT applicable to the barrel, one of several items the producer must take into account is the severance tax adjustment. Succinctly stated, the severance tax adjustment is that part of the removal price of a barrel of crude oil which Congress has exempted from the WPT. The purpose of this exemption is to avoid hardship a producer must suffer as a result of the combined effect of having to pay the WPT, the severence tax, and state, local, and federal income taxes.[2] Thus, although the severance tax adjustment is a deduction in computing the WPT, it is a form of a tax credit in the sense that to the extent of the state severance tax paid, no federal severance tax is imposed. More precisely, the deduction [Section 4996(c)(1) amount][3] is the difference between the actual severance tax imposed with respect to a barrel of oil and the tax which would have been imposed had the oil been sold at its adjusted base price.

For example, assume that a barrel of crude oil properly classified as tier 1 is severed by a producer who is an integrated oil company. Further assume the adjusted

---

* H. K. Dickenson is a tax attorney for the Marathon Oil Company, Findlay, Ohio.

1 Pub. L. No. 96-223 (1980).

2 Senate Finance Committee Report, No. 96-394, p. 55.

3 I.R.C. § 4996(c)(1) (hereinafter cited as the Code).

Article reprinted courtesy of *Oil & Gas Tax Quarterly*, December 1980, pp. 257–283

base price of the barrel is $13.00; the sales price of the the barrel is $30.00; and the state imposes a severance tax at the rate of 10 percent which applies to the gross value of crude oil produced. The severance tax adjustment and the WPT is computed as follows:

Severance tax adjustment		Windfall profit tax	
$30.00	Gross value	$30.00	Removal price
(13.00)	Adjusted base price	(13.00)	Adjusted base price
		(1.70)	Severance tax adjustment [§ 4996(c)(1) amount]
$17.00	Portion of gross value entitled to severance tax adjustment	$15.30	Taxable windfall
× 10%	Tax rate	× 70%	Tax rate for tier 1
$ 1.70	§ 4996(c)(1) amount	$10.71	WPT

WHAT CONSTITUTES A SEVERANCE TAX?

Neither the House Bill[4] nor the Senate amendment[5] provided for a definition of the term "severance tax." Consequently, prior to the Conferees' version the producers, following the WPT bill, foresaw many potential definitional problems connected with the severance tax adjustment. For instance, if a severance tax imposed by a state is levied on the basis of a fixed fee per barrel, would such tax qualify as a "severance tax"? The difficulty here is carving-out the severance tax attributable to the windfall portion of the removal price when the amount of that tax would be the same whether levied on the basis of the adjusted base price or on the removal price of a barrel of oil. Another question typically raised was whether the

4 H.R. 3919, The Crude Oil Windfall Profit Tax Act of 1979.

5 *Id.*

local laws would apply in determining the nature of the severance tax.[6]

The Conferees resolved these questions as well as others by specifically defining the term "severance tax."[7] Section 4996(c)(2)[8] essentially provides four requirements which must be met before a charge (fee) qualifies as a severance tax. The requirement that the charge constitutes a "tax" is perhaps the most easily overlooked of the four. Not all levies or assessments imposed by a government authority are taxes.[9] Thus, a payment for some special priviledge granted or services rendered by a government does not normally constitute a tax. For instance, in I.T. 3511[10] the IRS distinguished taxes from other charges:

> A tax is an enforced contribution, exacted pursuant to legislative authority in the exercise of the taxing power [as opposed to the regulatory power], and imposed and collected for the purpose of raising revenue to be used for public or governmental purposes, and *not as a payment for some special privilege granted or services rendered.* Taxes are, therefore, distinguishable from various other charges imposed for particular purposes under particular powers or functions of government. (Emphasis added)

---

6 Prior to the Conferee's definition of a severance tax it appeared that the local laws would determine whether a tax would be characterized as a severance tax. Typically, under the local laws a tax would be analyzed in terms of the true nature of the tax, *i.e.,* is the true nature of the tax a property, excise, or an income tax? See, Miller v. Buck Creek Co., 269 P. 43 (1928).

7 Conference Committee Report, No. 96-817, p. 105, specifically provides that adjustment for a severance tax based on a fixed fee per barrel would not be allowed an adjustment because the amount of that tax would be the same whether levied on the basis of adjusted base price or on the removal price of a barrel of oil.

8 I.R.C. § 4996(c)(2).

9 See generally, 71 Am. Jur. 2d St. Tax. § 10; Treas. Reg. § 1.164-4.

10 I.T. 3511, C.B. 1941-2, 90.

In the ruling, because dog licenses and automobile title and registration charges were primarily imposed for regulatory purposes, they were not taxes. Similarly, a payment for a special privilege to explore, develop, and extract oil and gas from a foreign government-owned petroleum company was held to be a royalty rather than a tax.[11] However, the Revenue Service has ruled that charges imposed by a municipality for essential services such as fire and police protection are a tax.[12] The rationale for the ruling appears to be that where the charges collected are commingled with the general revenue funds of the city, rather than specifically earmarked for a special purpose, the charges are in substance a tax.

For the purposes of the WPT adjustment the issue of whether a particular charge exacted may constitute a severance tax under the Code will arise in the area of conservation charges or fees. For instance, Wyoming imposes an oil and gas conservation charge as follows:

> There is hereby levied and assessed on the value at the well of all oil and gas produced, severed and sold or transported from the premises in Wyoming where produced a charge not to exceed two-fifths of one (1) mill on the dollar .... All moneys so collected shall be remitted to the state treasurer for deposit in an account within the earmarked revenue fund and shall be used exclusively to pay the costs and expenses incurred in connection with the administration and enforcement of this act (chapter 94, Session Laws of Wyoming, 1951).[13]

Similiar statutory language can also be found in other states which impose oil and gas conservation fees and

---

11 Rev. Rul. 76-215, 1976-1 C.B. 194.

12 Rev. Rul. 61-182, 1961-2 C.B. 42.

13 Wyo. Stat. § 30-5-116(b).

charges. In a strict sense these charges fail to meet the characteristics of a tax inasmuch as such charges are not only imposed for regulatory purposes but are also specifically earmarked for certain purposes.[14] On the other hand, a persuasive argument can be made that because the principal purpose of the severance tax adjustment is to ameliorate the effect of multiple tax burden imposed by the state and federal governments, these statutes should be construed in favor of the taxpayers to permit a severance tax adjustment for such charges.

Assuming that a payment constitutes a tax, the second test to be applied is whether the tax is "imposed by a state." The Senate Finance Committee reported that the severance taxes imposed by the Indian tribes under the jurisdiction of the Secretary of the Interior would be treated in the same manner as a state-imposed severance tax.[15] However, this position was abandoned since the final legislation is couched in terms of "taxes imposed by a state." Such language also disqualifies from the severance tax adjustment those severance taxes imposed by the political subdivisions of a state, such as a municipality, county, or transit authority. In most cases there should not be too much problem in distinguishing which governmental authority is imposing the severance tax. However, difficulty may be encountered in certain situations.

An example of such difficulty would be New Mexico Oil and Gas Ad Valorem Production Tax[16] Assuming that the tax otherwise qualifies as a severance tax within the meaning of the Code, there is uncertainty as to whether this tax can be classified as being imposed by the state. The pertinent statute provides that the State Depart-

---

14 *E.g.,* Arkansas, Colorado, Mississippi, Oklahoma, and Utah.

15 Senate Finance Committee Report, p. 105.

16 N.M. Stat. Ann. § 7-32-1.

ment of Revenue and Taxation has the authority and the duty to administer the tax, including supervision over the property valuation and collection of the delinquent taxes. On the other hand, but for a small portion of the revenue, all of the revenue goes to the county in which the oil and gas property is located.[17] Query: Is the New Mexico Ad Valorem Production Tax imposed by the state or a political subdivision? The IRS should resolve the uncertainty as soon as possible by giving guidance on the issue.

The third and fourth requirements for determining whether a particular charge constitutes a severance tax within the meaning of the Code deal with the nature of the tax.[18] Prior to the Conferees' version of the WPT, many producers following the legislation considered looking to the particular local law to determine the nature of the tax. In such cases, however, particularly where a state has a severance tax statute "in lieu" of a property tax, a controversy often arose as to whether the true nature of such tax constituted a property tax or an excise tax. A prime example of this type of a controversy involves Oklahoma Gross Production Tax. For years the taxpayers were uncertain as to the nature of the tax until the state supreme court held such tax to be an excise rather than property tax in the case of *Apache Gas Product Corp.* v. *Oklahoma Tax Commission.*[19]

The Conferees resolved these potential problems by expressly providing for a federal standard based on two requirements. These requirements are: 1) the tax must be "imposed with respect to the extraction of oil," and 2) the tax must be determined on the basis of "gross value" of extracted oil. Thus, any state tax which meets these re-

17 N.M. Stat. Ann. § 72-30-7.

18 I.R.C. § 4996(c)(1)(A) and (B).

19 509 P.2d 109 (1973).

quirements is classified as a severance tax regardless of its official name or title.[20]

For many states, the determination as to whether a particular tax is "imposed with respect to extraction of oil" is not difficult. Typically, a state tax statute may provide that the tax is a privilege or license tax "to be predicated upon the quantity of [natural resources] severed."[21] Thus, any tax imposed with respect to incidents or basis other than the extraction of oil (such as a tax based on the ownership of property) does not qualify as a severance tax. For the same reason, a tax levied based on the value of reserves is not a severance tax.[22]

With respect to the requirement that a tax must be determined on the basis of "gross value" of extracted oil, again, for most states such a requirement is not difficult to satisfy. The term "gross value" generally means the same as the sales price, market value, or market price. Therefore, a tax levied on the basis of a value (such as net proceeds from production) which is less than the gross value is not a severance tax. In this regard, it should be that a tax such as the Louisiana severance tax should not be considered to be levied on the basis of net proceeds. The Louisiana tax on oil and condensate is calculated on the basis of 12-1/2 percent of value.[23] Such value is the higher of the gross receipts received from the first purchaser (less certain transportation charges) or the posted field price. It appears that the deduction for transportation charges, which is an allowance for delivering crude oil from the wellhead to the point of sale, should not defeat

---

20 Conference Committee Report, p. 105.

21 Ark. Stat. Ann. § 84-2102.

22 Conference Committee Report, p. 105.

23 La. Rev. Stat. § 633(7)(a) and 8(a).

the gross value test since the purpose of the net back was to merely establish the gross value at the wellhead.

In summary, in determining whether a particular charge qualifies for the severance tax adjustment, all four of the aforementioned requirements must be met. Otherwise, a particular charge fails to qualify for the severance tax adjustment. It should also be noted that a severance tax may not be taken into account to the extent the total rate of severance tax imposed by a state exceeds 15 percent.[24] With respect to any change in the state laws after March 31, 1979, increases in the rate of severance tax are taken into account only if the increase applies to the entire removal price of the barrel.[25]

EVALUATION OF VARIOUS STATE SEVERANCE TAXES

In the preceding section of this article, statutory requirements for the severance tax adjustments have been discussed. Set forth below is an analysis of various states' taxes based on the application of the statutory requirements. It is necessary to emphasize at the outset that the conclusions made herein are the opinion of the writer. Consequently, the conclusions may not necessarily reflect the position of the IRS or some taxpayers.

Alaska

OIL AND GAS PRODUCTION TAX[26]

This tax is levied on all oil produced within the state. The tax is equal to either the percentage-of-value amount or the cents-per-barrel amount, whichever is greater, multiplied by the economic limit factor. The cents-per-

24 I.R.C. § 4996(c)(3)(A).

25 I.R.C. § 4996(c)(3)(B).

26 Alaska Stat. § 43.55.011 *et seq.*

barrel amount equals \$.60 per barrel on old crude oil and \$.80 per barrel for all other taxable crude oil.[27] The percentage-of-value equals 12.25 percent of the gross value of taxable oil at the point of production.[28] The gross value at the point of production equals the actual sales price at arm's length less transportation costs from the point of production to the sales delivery point.[29] In certain situations, instead of the sales price the prevailing value must be used in determining the gross value at the point of production.[30]

Because this tax is measured on the basis of the greater of either the cents-per-barrel or the percentage-of-value, there is a question as to whether such tax could be considered a severance tax under the Code. However, so long as a producer's tax liability is calculated on the basis of the percentage-of-value basis, the gross value test under the Code appears to have been satisfied. This type of analysis would be consistent with Congress' intent to deny a deduction only in cases where the amount of severance tax is the same regardless of whether such tax is levied on the adjusted base price or removal price, *i.e.,* because the severance tax attributable to the "windfall" portion can be ascertained, there is no reason why the severance tax adjustment should be denied.

OIL AND GAS REGULATION AND CONSERVATION TAX[31]

This tax is levied upon the producer of oil, measured on the basis of 1/8 of one cent on each barrel of oil. Being as

---

27 Alaska Stat. § 43.55.011(c).

28 Alaska Stat. § 43.55.11(b).

29 Reg. § 15 AAC 05.701(b).

30 Reg. § 15 AAC 05.701(c).

31 Alaska Stat. § 43.57.010.

such, the fixed rate would fail one of the tests. Thus, this tax is not deductible for WPT purposes.

Arkansas

SEVERANCE TAX[32]

This is a privilege or license tax "to be predicated upon the quantity [of natural resources] severed." The tax rates on the severance of the natural resources depend on the type of minerals.[33] In the case of oil, the tax is on 5 percent of market value of such oil determined at the time and point of severance. However, an exception on the tax rate is carved-out for oil produced from a stripper well.[34] Because all the requirements of the Code are met, this severance tax is deductible in computing the WPT.

ADDITIONAL SEVERANCE TAX[35]

Beginning on February 28, 1977, in addition to the severance tax (Ark.Stat.Ann. § 84-2102), an additional tax of five mills (5/10 of one cent) per barrel of oil produced within the state is imposed. Most of the money collected from such additional tax is earmarked for "State Arts and Humanities Oil Museum Fund." Because this additional tax is based on a fixed rate per barrel, the requirements of the Code are not met and it is not deductible in computing the WPT.

CONSERVATION CHARGE[36]

The Oil and Gas Commission is authorized to assess against each barrel of oil produced a "charge" not to

---

32 Ark. Stat. Ann. § 84-2101 *et seq.*

33 Ark. Stat. Ann. § 84-2102.

34 Ark. Stat. Ann. § 84-2102(e).

35 Ark. Stat. Ann. § 84-2102.1.

36 Ark. Stat. Ann. § 53-106.

exceed 10 mills on each barrel. All monies so collected are required to be used to pay the expenses and costs in connection with administration of oil and gas conservation law. This "charge" does not appear to qualify as a tax. Consequently, such charge may not be deductible as a severance tax in computing the WPT.

Colorado

SEVERANCE TAX[37]

This is an annual tax upon the gross income of crude oil severed within the state. Excepted from the tax is oil produced from any well which produces on the average 10 barrels or less a day.[38] The tax for crude oil equals gross income times the following rates:

under $25,000	2%
$25,000 and under $100,000	3%
$100,000 and under $300,000	4%
$300,000 and over	5%

"Gross income" means the market value at the wellhead determined by actual sales price, or the value of the severer's income as computed for Colorado and federal income tax depletion purposes, whichever is higher.[39] Because this state tax is imposed with respect to the extraction of oil and measured by "gross income," all requirements of the Code are met and the tax is deductible as a severance tax in computing the WPT. Additionally, it should be noted that the royalty payment withholding and property tax paid on oil are credited in computing the severance tax liability.

---

37 Colo. Rev. Stat. § 39-29-105.

38 Colo. Rev. Stat. § 39-29-105.

39 Colo. Rev. Stat. § 39-29-102.

CONSERVATION TAX[40]

A charge not to exceed one mill on the dollar is imposed for severing oil and gas. Funds raised from this "charge" are specifically earmarked as "oil and gas conservation fund." No such funds are to be commingled with the general fund. Because this charge does not appear to qualify as a tax, a doubt exists as to whether the charge is deductible as a severance tax under the WPT.

WITHHOLDING OF ROYALTY PAYMENTS[41]

Every producer is obligated to withhold from every royalty payment made to any person having an interest in any oil produced an amount equal to 3 percent of such royalty payment. Such tax paid is creditable against the severance tax imposed by Section 39-29-105.[42] Because the withholding of royalty payment would wash out the severance tax effect, only the severance tax should be taken as a severance tax deduction for the purpose of computing WPT.

Indiana

PETROLEUM SEVERANCE TAX[43]

This tax is imposed at the rate of 1 percent of the value of crude oil and other hydrocarbons severed.[44] "Value" means the price paid for such crude oil and other hydrocarbons or their fair market value at the time of severance if gathered for consumption by the severing party.[45] Be-

---

40 Colo. Rev. Stat. § 34-60-122.

41 Colo. Rev. Stat. § 39-29-111.

42 Colo. Rev. Stat. § 39-29-105.

43 Ind. Code § 6-8-1-1 *et seq.*

44 Ind. Code § 6-8-1-8.

45 Ind. Code § 6-8-1-4.

cause all the requirements under the Code are met, this severance tax is deductible in computing the WPT.

Kansas

Unlike the taxes imposed by most states on the production of oil, Kansas' tax on production of oil is not directly imposed by statute. Rather, the enabling laws allow the Kansas Department of Health and Environment (Department)[46] and the State Corporation Commission (Commission)[47] powers to levy fees and costs which are commonly designated as an oil production tax and a conservation tax, respectively. Under the Commission Rule 28-40-9, an assessment designated as an "oil field waste disposal" fee imposed is equal to $.002 per barrel of oil produced and removed from the lease. Under the Department's Rule 82-2-116, a charge levied is equal to $.003 per barrel of oil marked and used. Under the Department's Rule 82-2-700, there is also assessed a charge of $.0002 per barrel for plugging abandoned oil or gas wells.

On these three charges or fees, there is considerable question as to whether they would constitute "taxes." Assuming *arguendo* that these charges are taxes, all such charges would still disqualify as a severance tax for the reason that such charges are based on a fixed fee per barrel.

Kentucky

OIL PRODUCTION TAX[48]

Every producer of crude petroleum oil is obligated to pay a tax equal to 4½ percent of the market value of

---

46 Kan. Stat. §§ 65-171.d–65-171.f.

47 Kan. Stat. §§ 55-601–55-611.

48 Ky. Rev. Stat. § 137.120 *et seq.*

all crude petroleum produced by him within the state. A "producer" includes any person owning an interest in crude oil produced within the state.[49] The market value is to be determined by the Department of Revenue.[50] Generally, market value at the place of production is the actual sales price.[51] Because all the requirements of the Code are met, this oil production tax is deductible in computing the WPT.

Louisiana

Under the authority of the Louisiana Constitution,[52] a tax is imposed upon "all natural resources severed from the soil or water," including oil and condensate.[53] The tax is paid by owners at the time of the severance.[54] Generally, the making of the reports and payment of the taxes shall be by those actually engaged in the operation of severing.[55]

The tax is at the rate of 12-1/2 percent of value.[56] Such value is generally the higher of the gross receipts received from the first purchaser less certain transportation charges, or the posted field price. The tax rate on oil produced from a well incapable of producing more than 25 barrels of oil per day and that also produces 50 percent saltwater per day is 6-1/4 percent.[57] A stripper well (a

---

49 Ky. Rev. Stat. § 137.120.

50 Ky. Rev. Stat. § 137.160(2).

51 *E.g.,* Cumberland Pipeline Co. v. Commonwealth, 15 S.W.2d 280 (1929).

52 La. Const. art. X, § 21.

53 La. Rev. Stat. § 47:631 *et seq.*

54 La. Rev. Stat. § 47:632.

55 La. Rev. Stat. § 47:635.

56 La. Rev. Stat. §§ 633(7)(a) and (8)(a).

57 La. Rev. Stat. § 633(7)(b).

well incapable of producing more than 10 barrels a day) is taxed at the rate of 3-1/8 percent.[58] Because all the requirements under the Code are met, this tax is deductible.

Michigan

SEVERANCE TAX[59]

Under the authority of the Michigan Constitution,[60] the legislature may provide for alternative means of taxation of certain real and personal property "in lieu" of general ad valorem taxation. Pursuant to that legislative authority, a severance tax is imposed on each producer engaged in the business of severing oil or gas from the soil. A producer is defined to include not only a person who owns oil but also those who are entitled to take oil in kind or a share of the monetary proceeds from the sale of oil as of the time of its production or severance.[61]

The tax rate on any crude oil, other than crude oil derived from stripper well property and marginal properties, is 6.6 percent of the gross cash market value of the total production of oil for the taxable period. Stripper well property and marginal properties are taxed at the rate of 4 percent and they are defined by the Emergency Petroleum Allocation Act of 1973[62] and the Federal Department of Energy regulations,[63] respectively. Because all the Code requrements are met, this severance tax qualifies for the WPT adjustment.

---

58 La. Rev. Stat. § 633(7)(c).

59 Mich. Comp. Laws Ann. § 205.301 *et seq.*

60 Mich. Const. art. IX, § 3.

61 Mich. Comp. Laws Ann. § 205.312.

62 15 U.S.C. § 757 (1973).

63 10 C.F.R. §§ 212.72-212.77 (1979).

OIL PRIVILEGE FEE[64]

Michigan also imposes an oil privilege fee not in excess of 1 percent based on the gross cash market value of oil and gas produced within the state.[65] Currently, this fee is 2/10 of 1 percent of the market value of each barrel of crude oil produced within the state. This "fee," as originally written, was designated as a "severance tax" but it is now redesignated as a "fee for monitoring, surveillance, enforcement and administration of act...." The proceeds of the funds are to be credited to the general fund.[66] The fees are to be collected by the Revenue Division of the Department of Treasury in the same manner and at the same time as the severance tax.[67] While the tax is designated as a "fee," because the fee is actually levied for revenue raising rather than regulatory purposes, and because the revenue is not specifically earmarked as the tax was under the Wyoming statute, this fee should be regarded as an additional severance tax.[68] Hence, this fee should be deductible as a severance tax in computing the WPT.

Mississippi

SEVERANCE TAX[69]

A monthly privilege tax is imposed on every person engaging in the business of producing or severing oil within the state.[70] The amount of such tax is measured by

---

64 Mich. Comp. Laws Ann. § 319.22.

65 Mich. Comp. Laws Ann. § 319.22.

66 Mich. Comp. Laws Ann. § 319.22(3).

67 See Mich. Comp. Laws Ann. § 205.301 *et seq.*

68 See "Editorial Comment," Mich. St. Tax Rep. (CCH) Para. 45-102.

69 Miss. Code Ann. § 27-25-501 *et seq.*

70 Miss. Code Ann. § 27-25-503.

6 cents per barrel or 6 percent of the value thereof at the point of production, whichever is greater. "Value" means sales price or market value at the mouth of the well.[71] In the cases of transactions in which the value of oil is not determined at arm's length, the Tax Commission determines such value. As in the case of Alaska severance tax, even though this tax is determined on the "greater of" basis, if the tax is actually paid on the value basis, the gross value test under the Code should be met. Therefore, this severance tax meets all the requirements of the Code and is deductible in computing the WPT.

OIL MAINTENANCE CHARGE[72]

For conservation purposes, a charge not to exceed eight mills is levied on each barrel of oil produced in the state. Because this charge is imposed for regulatory purposes, coupled with the fact that the funds raised from the charge are specially earmarked, such charges appear not to meet the requirements as a tax under the Code. Thus, this conservation charge does not appear to qualify for a severance tax adjustment in computing the WPT.

Montana

OIL AND GAS SEVERANCE TAX[73]

This tax is imposed on every person engaged in the business of producing crude oil or carrying on the business of owning, controlling, or managing any well from which crude oil is extracted. There are two tax rates: 2.1 percent of the first $6,000 of the total gross value of crude oil produced, and 2.65 percent of the total gross

---

71 Miss. Code Ann. § 27-25-501(d).

72 Miss. Code Ann. § 53-1-71 *et seq.*

73 Mont. Rev. Codes Ann. § 15-36-101 *et seq.*

value of that portion of production in excess of the first $6,000 of gross value. Because all the requirements of the Code are met, this severance tax is deductible for WPT purposes.

OIL & GAS CONSERVATION[74]

This tax is designated as a "privilege and license tax" and it is imposed for defraying the expenses incurred in the operation of the Board of Oil and Gas Conservation.[75] The tax is paid by the operators and producers of oil and gas, and the tax rate is not to exceed 2/10 of 1 percent of the market value of each barrel of crude oil produced. The Board, pursuant to certain guidelines, fixes the rate "from time to time."[76] All money collected under the oil and gas conservation provisions are specially earmarked for use by the Board and for no other purpose.[77] Because of the foregoing features of the charge there is some question as to whether this "tax" may be deductible as a severance tax.

RESOURCES INDEMNITY TRUST TAX[78]

This is an annual tax paid by the persons engaged in the business of mining, extracting, or producing a mineral;[79] "mineral" includes oil.[80] This tax is a flat fee of $25 plus the additional amount. The additional amount is calculated on the basis of the gross value of product

---

74 Mont. Rev. Codes Ann. § 82-11-010 *et seq.*

75 Mont. Rev. Codes Ann. § 82-11-131.

76 Mont. Rev. Codes Ann. § 82-11-131(2).

77 Mont. Rev. Codes Ann. § 82-11-135.

78 Mont. Rev. Codes Ann. § 15-38-101 *et seq.*

79 Mont. Rev. Codes Ann. § 15-38-104.

80 Mont. Rev. Codes Ann. § 15-38-103(3).

produced during the calendar year immediately preceding the calendar year for which the additional amount is calculated. The tax rate on the additional amount is 1/2 of 1 percent of the amount of gross value of mineral extracted in excess of $5,000. But for the flat fee, this tax appears to qualify for the severance tax adjustment.

Nebraska

OIL AND GAS SEVERANCE TAX[81]

Under the severance tax provisions, the tax is imposed for severing oil and gas. Such tax is to be paid by the person engaged in the severing of such oil and gas.[82] The tax is paid at the rate of 2 percent of the value of oil and gas immediately after the severance of such oil and gas.[83] Because all the requirements of the Code are met, this tax qualifies for the severance tax adjustment.

OIL AND GAS CONSERVATION CHARGE[84]

A charge not to exceed 4 mills on the dollar is levied and assessed at the well of all oil and gas produced within the state.[85] Currently, the Conservation Commission has fixed the rate of 1 mill on the dollar effective July 1, 1980. Much like the Wyoming conservation charge, the funds raised are specifically earmarked for furthering the purposes of encouraging and promoting the development, production and utilization of natural resources of oil and gas in such a manner as to prevent waste. The charge, therefore, is specifically imposed for regulatory purposes

---

81 Neb. Rev. Stat. § 57-701 *et seq.*

82 Neb. Rev. Stat. § 57-702.

83 Neb. Rev. Stat. § 57-703.

84 Neb. Rev. Stat. § 57-901 *et seq.*

85 Neb. Rev. Stat. § 57-919.

and not for revenue raising purposes. Accordingly, the Nebraska conservation charge does not appear to qualify for a severance tax adjustment.

New Mexico

OIL AND GAS SEVERANCE TAX[86]

This tax is imposed on all products that are severed and sold. "Products" includes oil, natural gas, or liquid hydrocarbon.[87] The tax is measured by volume of the products severed, and sold products. Previously, the tax rate was 45 cents on each barrel of oil or other hydrocarbon plus the surtax. However, under legislation (S.B. 119) passed and signed by the Governor on February 29, 1980 (effective March 1, 1980), the tax rate is changed to 3-3/4 percent of taxable value of crude oil or other hydrocarbons severed. "Taxable value" generally means the actual cash value received for such oil or other hydrocarbons less royalties paid to the United States, state of New Mexico and Indians. In the event that the cash value is received in a non-arm's length transaction, the oil and gas accounting division, which administers this tax, may determine the value of such oil or gas.

Because this new tax applies with respect to the entire removal price of a barrel of oil, the tax qualifies for the severance tax adjustment.

OIL AND GAS CONSERVATION TAX[88]

This tax is levied on all products which are severed and sold.[89] "Product" includes oil and hydrocarbons.[90] The

86 N.M. Stat. Ann. § 7-29-1 *et seq.*

87 N.M. Stat. Ann. § 7-29-2.E.

88 N.M. Stat. Ann. § 7-30-1 *et seq.*

89 N.M. Stat. Ann. § 7-30-4.

90 N.M. Stat. Ann. § 7-30-2.E.

measure of tax is 19/100 of 1 percent of the taxable value of sold products.[91] The definition of taxable value is identical to the one in the severance tax provisions. All provisions of Article 30 of N.M.S.A., which cover the oil and gas conservation tax both in form and in substance, are couched in terms that relate more to a tax rather than a regulatory measure. Therefore, the New Mexico oil and conservation tax should be deductible for the purposes of the WPT.

OIL AND GAS EMERGENCY TAX[92]

This tax is a privilege tax on the business of every person severing products within the state.[93] "Products" includes oil and other hydrocarbons.[94] The tax is 2.55 percent of the taxable value of such oil or other hydrocarbons severed. The definition of "taxable value" is identical to its defintion for severance tax and conservation tax purposes. However, the incidences of the taxes are different. In the cases of the severance tax and the conservation tax, "severance and sale" triggers the tax. While revenue for school districts is traditionally raised by property taxes, this privilege tax should qualify for the severance tax adjustment.

OIL AND GAS AD VALOREM PRODUCTION TAX[95]

It is very difficult to determine whether this tax is entitled to the severance tax adjustment under the WPT. As discussed previously, the question is whether the tax is imposed by the state or the local governments.[96]

---

91 N.M. Stat. Ann. § 7-30-4.

92 N.M. Stat. Ann. § 7-31-1 *et seq.*

93 N.M. Stat. Ann. § 7-31-4.

94 N.M. Stat. Ann. § 7-31-2.E.

95 N.M. Stat. Ann. § 7-32-1 *et seq.*

96 See previous discussions on this tax at "What Constitutes a Severance Tax?"

North Dakota

OIL AND GAS PRODUCTION TAX[97]

This tax is imposed upon all oil and gas produced within the state. The tax rate is at 5 percent of the gross value of such oil at the well.[98] The production tax is in lieu of all ad valorem taxes imposed by the state or any other unit of the government.[99] "Gross value" is the actual cash price received in a transaction.[100] However, if oil or gas is sold under circumstances in which the sale price does not reflect the cash value, then the Tax Commissioner may require the taxes to be paid on the basis of the prevailing price then being paid at the time of production in the same field for oil of a like kind, character and quality of oil.[101] Because all the requirements under the Code are met, the North Dakota oil and gas production tax is deductible in computing the WPT.

Oklahoma

GROSS PRODUCTION TAX[102]

This tax is equal to 7 percent of the "gross value" of the production of minerals, oil and gas.[103] The gross value is the actual cash value of the oil and gas at the time and place of production.[104] However, in case oil and gas is sold

---

97 N.D. Cent. Code § 57-51-01 *et seq.*

98 N.D. Cent. Code § 57-51-02.

99 N.D. Cent. Code § 57-51-03.

100 N.D. Cent. Code § 57-51-05.2

101 N.D. Cent. Code § 57-51-05.4

102 Okla. Stat. Ann. tit. 68, § 1001 *et seq.*

103 Okla. Stat. Ann. tit. 68, § 1001(b).

104 Okla. Stat. Ann. tit. 68, § 1010(b)(5).

under circumstances where the sales price does not represent the cash value, the Tax Commission has the authority to determine the tax on the basis of the prevailing price in effect at the time of production in the same field for oil and gas of like kind, quality, and character.[105] This tax should be subject to the severance tax adjustment.

PETROLEUM EXCISE TAX[106]

The statute imposes an excise tax equal to .085 of 1 percent of the gross value on each barrel of petroleum produced within the state. The incidence of the tax is identical to the Gross Production Tax and the "gross value" is determined in the same manner as it is under the Gross Production Tax. Much like the Wyoming conservation charge, the funds generated from the Petroleum Excise Tax are specifically earmarked for "conservation fund." However, unlike the Wyoming conservation charge, the Oklahoma Petroleum Excise Tax was passed under the authority of the state's taxing rather than regulatory powers. Hence, this charge appears to constitute a tax and qualifies for the severance tax adjustment.

Texas

OIL PRODUCTION TAX[107]

An occupation tax on oil produced within the state is imposed at the rate of 4.6 cents per barrel. However, when the price of oil exceeds one dollar per barrel, the tax rate is 4.6 percent of the market value of such oil.[108] The tax is collected by the purchaser who is required to withhold

---

105 Okla. Stat. Ann. tit. 68, § 1001(f).

106 Okla. Stat. Ann. tit. 68, § 1101 *et seq.*

107 Tex. Rev. Civ. Stat. tit. 122A, art. 4.01.

108 Tex. Rev. Civ. Stat. tit. 122A, art. 4.02.

the amount of such tax from payments due to the producer.[109] This tax meets all the requirements of the Code and the payment of it is entitled to the severance tax adjustment.

Utah

MINING OCCUPATION TAX[110]

Every person owning an interest in oil or other hydrocarbon substances produced from a well is obligated to pay an occupation tax equal to 2 percent of the value at the well.[111] "Value thereof at the well" is the value established under a bona fide contract. If no bona fide contract exists, then the Tax Commission has the power to determine the reasonable fair cash value of the substance at the well.[112] An annual exemption in the amount of $50,000 is allowed per "well" from the payment of this occupation tax. This exemption is prorated among the interest owners. Because this Utah tax meets all requirements of the Code, such tax is deductible as a severance tax in computing the WPT.

CONSERVATION CHARGE[113]

For purposes of paying the administrative expenses, the oil and gas conservation laws impose on the market value at the well of all oil and gas produced, a charge not to exceed two mills on the dollar. Because this "charge" does not appear to constitute a tax, such charge probably is not entitled to be included in the severance tax adjustment.

---

109 Tex. Rev. Civ. Stat. tit. 122A, art. 4.03.

110 Utah Code Ann. § 59-5-66 *et seq.*

111 Utah Code Ann. § 59-5-67.

112 Utah Code Ann. § 59-5-67(d).

113 Utah Code Ann. § 40-6-14.

West Virginia

BUSINESS AND OCCUPATION TAX[114]

A tax is imposed for the privilege of engaging in the business of severing or extracting any natural resource products. An amount equal to 4.34 percent of the "value of the articles produced as shown by the gross proceeds derived from the sale thereof by the producer is taxed." "Gross proceeds of sales" means the value actually received from a sale without regard to any deduction on account of the cost of property or expense of any kind.[115] Because this West Virginia tax meets the requirements of the Code, the tax is deductible as severance tax in computing the WPT.

Wyoming

PRODUCTION TAX[116]

An excise tax equal to 2 percent of the value of gross product extracted is imposed on the privilege of severing or extracting different types of minerals and natural resources (including petroleum) within the state.[117] In addition to this tax, an excise tax equal to 2 percent of the value of the gross product extracted is levied upon the privilege of severing or extracting "any valuable deposit" in the state except stripper production. Since "any valuable deposit" does include oil, the total excise tax imposed on production of oil is 4 percent of the value of gross product extracted. The value of the gross product extracted is ordinarily the fair cash market value of product sold at the mine.

---

114 W. Va. Code art. 13, ch. 11, § 2-(a).

115 W. Va. Code art. 13, ch. 11, § 1.

116 Wyo. Stat. § 39-6-301 *et seq.*

117 Wyo. Stat. § 39-6-302.

Although this state tax qualifies as a severance tax under the Code, there are some mechanical problems in computing the deductible amount since severance tax is paid currently on an annual basis, but is measured by the previous year's production. Because this severance tax is measured by the production for the year preceding the year in which the severance tax is computed and paid, there will be a difference between the current year's production, base price and the market value of oil from which the WPT is computed.

It should be pointed out that for the state of Wyoming, these problems will be limited to the tax year 1980. Beginning tax year 1981, Wyoming severance tax will be paid on the basis of the current year's production.[118]

PROPERTY TAX[119]

A second tax on oil is actually imposed by the Wyoming Constitution.[120] The Constitution provides for the assessment of mines producing specified minerals, including "mineral oil or other valuable deposits," on the basis of the gross product produced during the preceding year. This tax is in addition to the ad valorem taxes on surface improvements. The land from which minerals are being produced is, however, not taxed. The value of the gross product for the preceding year is the fair market value of the product at the mine; such valuation procedure being ostensibly identical to that applicable in respect of the severance tax (§ 39-6-302, Wyo. Stat.). However, this gross production tax is imposed by the local governments and, therefore, is not part of the WPT adjustment.

---

118 S. 10, 45th Leg. (1980); Wyo. Stat. 339-6-304.

119 Wyo. Stat. § 39-2-202.

120 Wyo. Const. art. XV, § 3.

OIL AND GAS CONSERVATION CHARGE[121]

This charge was discussed previously.[122] It appears that because the charge does not constitute a tax, the tax is not deductible for purpose of the severance tax adjustment.

CONCLUSION

The severance or production taxes imposed by a large number of states clearly qualify for the severance tax adjustment under the WPT. However, with respect to the severance taxes imposed by states such as Colorado, New Mexico and Wyoming, there exists considerable controversy among the producers as to whether such taxes qualify for purposes of the severance tax adjustment. Even those cases where the particular tax is deemed deductible by the general consensus, disagreements still exist over how the tax is to be calculated for the purposes of the WPT withholding. An additional area of controversy is whether the "conservation fees or charges" imposed by the various states constitute a tax. The traditional piecemeal approach to obtaining revenue rulings for each state in determining whether such state's tax qualifies as a severance tax may be inappropriate. Time is of the essence. The producers should be provided with as much guidance as soon as possible by the IRS to assure uniformity in treatment of the taxes in order to minimize the withholding errors between the operators and the first purchasers. In the absence of clear direction by the IRS with respect to the severance taxes, a state of confusion and uncertainty will prevail among the taxpayers, much in the same way as the area of the foreign tax credit.

---

121 Wyo. Stat. § 30-5-116.

122 See *supra* n. 13 and the corresponding discussion at "What Constitutes A Severance Tax?"

Part V

Net Income Limitation

The windfall profit on a barrel of crude oil is limited to 90 percent of the net income attributable to the barrel. The net income attributable to a barrel of crude oil is determined by dividing the taxable income from the property attributable to taxable crude oil by the number of barrels of taxable crude oil produced from the property.

Taxable income from the property is determined the same way as for percentage depletion purposes except:

1) There is no deduction for
   (a) percentage or regular cost depletion
   (b) intangible drilling and development costs on productive wells
   (c) windfall profit tax
   (d) qualified tertiary injectant expenses; the taxpayer has the option to capitalize or deduct qualified tertiary injectant expenses for purposes of the net income limitation computation
2) A deduction for input or as-if cost depletion is allowed. This cost depletion deduction is determined "as if" the taxpayer had always used cost depletion for all periods he owned the property and had capitalized all intangibles on productive wells and capitalized qualified tertiary injectant expenses.

If a transfer of the property to another taxpayer would result in an increased input or as-if cost depletion deduction, the transferee must take into account only the allowable cost incurred by the transferor and the post-transfer costs incurred by the transferee in computing his input or as-if depletable basis.

Because of the difficulties experienced by operators and first purchasers in computing the net income limitation, the final reporting of WPT information on Form 6248 has been delayed three times by the IRS. Now November 30, 1981, is the reporting deadline for the 1980 tax year as of the latest delay issued on August 28, 1981.

NET INCOME LIMITATION UNDER THE WINDFALL PROFIT TAX

David E. Wulf, CPA*

Earlier this year a cloud known as the Crude Oil Windfall Profit Tax Act of 1980 descended upon the entire oil industry. It enveloped practically all producers, including major companies and independents as well as royalty owners. A few special producers such as those governmental, charitable, and Indian tribal interests which were qualified, were exempt from the tax. Except for some relief which was granted to independent producers through certain reduced rates of tax, things looked dark. As taxpayers groped their way through the fog of the temporary regulations, a silver lining appeared. In a rare moment, Congress had included a provision which was based on economic reality. That provision was the net income limitation (NIL) contained in Internal Revenue Code Section 4988(b)(1), which states, "The windfall profit on any barrel of crude oil shall not exceed 90 percent of the net income attributable to such barrel."

Legislative History

The net income limitation concept remained basically the same through all three versions of the "windfall profit" tax bill. The House of Representatives version of the H.R. 3919 bill provided for a new Section 4989(b)(1) which stated that the windfall profit on any barrel of crude oil should not exceed the net income attributable to such barrel. The Senate amendment was the same as the House Bill, except that the limitation of 100 percent of

---

* David E. Wulf is the Tax Systems Coordinator at Cities Service Company, Tulsa, Okla.

Article reprinted courtesy of *Oil & Gas Tax Quarterly*, December 1980, pp. 217–235

net income was changed to the present 90 percent. The Joint Conference Committee version followed the Senate amendment and provided new rules relating to the election to capitalize qualified tertiary injectant expenses. The Joint Conference Committee also made some minor technical corrections relating to the transfer of proven properties and treatment of production payments, which resulted in the NIL provisions contained in the current law being almost verbatim of the original House Bill.

In discussing the NIL provisions, the House Ways and Means Committee report No. 96-304 does little more than paraphrase the law. The Senate Finance Committee report No. 96-394 virtually repeats the discussion contained in the House report while making certain additions to the NIL provisions. These additions relate to the treatment of production payments and to allocation of costs on properties producing both oil and gas. The Joint Conference Committee report contains only two sentences of discussion about the NIL provisions, both of which are primarily concerned with the election to capitalize qualified tertiary injectants.

Net Income Limitation Provisions Based on Economic Principles

The rationale behind the NIL provisions is based on sound economic principles. As a result of price controls and consumer demand, the price of a barrel of oil has little relation to the cost of producing such barrel. The misnamed "windfall profit" tax is not a tax on profits, but is instead a tax based on the selling price of the barrel of oil being taxed. In discussing the need for a "windfall profit" tax, the House committee report (page seven) states that the "windfall profit" tax will tax away a fair portion of the additional revenues from decontrol while allowing producers to receive very high prices for those types of oil whose production can be expected to increase in response to a price incentive. The report continues:

> The committee's windfall profit tax is carefully designed to impose relatively high tax rates where production cannot be expected to respond very much to further increases in price and relatively low tax rates on oil whose production is likely to be responsive to price.

The Senate committee report (page 2) states:

> In designing the tax, the committee attempted to reduce or eliminate the tax burden on those types of oil the production of which is likely to be relatively sensitive to changes in tax rates or prices. It tried to maintain a higher tax burden on types of oil whose production is likely to be less sensitive to price changes.

The House committee report in its summary (page 2) and the Senate committee report in its overview (page 29) state that in order to prevent the tax from burdening high-cost properties, thereby making continued operation of such properties uneconomical, the "windfall profit" subject to tax would be limited to some percentage of the net income from the property. If the windfall tax were to make a property uneconomical to operate, a disincentive to produce would be created and the producers would no doubt shut-in the well. The creation of such disincentive to produce and the resulting decrease in production clearly would be contrary to the intent of Congress stated in the above-quoted discussions of the House and Senate committees. The net income limitation represents recognition by Congress of some of the economics involved in the operation of an oil property.

Congress appears to have recognized also that even though a single property may produce barrels of oil which are sold at different prices due to Department of Energy price controls *(i.e.,* lower tier, upper tier, and world market prices), the economic cost of producing such barrels is the same for each barrel. In order to properly evaluate the economic profitability of such a property, net income from the property must be determined by comparing the total gross income from the property with the total costs incurred on such property. The resulting economic net income from the property would apply equally to each barrel produced from the property, so that in order to determine the true economic net income of any barrel from the property, the net income from the property would simply be divided by the number of barrels produced from such property. Congress has recognized this basic economic concept by providing in Section 4988(b)(2) that the net income attributable to a barrel shall be determined by simply dividing the taxable income from the property (attributable to oil) for the entire taxable year by the number of barrels of taxable oil produced from the property during the taxable year.

Congress has also attempted to minimize taxpayer and IRS confusion and disagreement by providing in Section 4988(b)(3) that, in general, the taxable income from the property shall be determined under Section 613(a), the general rule for percentage depletion. Percentage depletion has been limited to 50 percent of "taxable income from the property" since 1926. The methodology for determining taxable income from the property provided by Treasury Regulations Section 1.613-5 is supported and clarified by an old and significant body of case law and rulings and is probably defined as well as any tax law ever could be. Most producers have been dealing with the concept of "taxable income from the property" for many years and have systems in place to provide the data necessary to determine taxable income from the property. Several substantial differences do exist between the determination of taxable income from the property under Sections 613(a) and 4988(b)(3), but these should not be an insurmountable problem for most taxpayers.

Mechanics of the Net Income Limitation Calculation

The NIL calculation is made separately by each producer based on his own income and expenses, independent of the income and expenses of any other producers who have an interest in the property. Each producer will utilize his percentage of revenues and direct operating expenses from the property along with his own calculations of depletion and overhead to determine his own taxable income on his share of the barrels of production from the property.

The starting point for the NIL calculation is the producer's gross income from the property. Gross income from the property as referred to in Section 613(a) is defined by Treasury Regulations Section 1.613-3 as "the amount for which the taxpayer sells the oil or gas in the immediate vicinity of the well." This definition is also supported and clarified by an established body of case law and rulings and should be easily determined by most taxpayers. The tax term "gross income from the property" if often confused by nontax production related personnel with the industry concept of gross revenue on the lease or 8/8 of the lease revenues. Nontax personnel involved in the evaluation of a property should be aware that the term refers to the company's share of the lease revenues based on the company's interest in the property (7/8, etc.), the amount often referred to as "company net revenue."

In the case of a property where there is a production payment, Section 4988(b)(5) provides that gross income from the property includes the value of that portion of the oil produced which is applied in discharge of the production payment. This amount of gross income must be taken into account in computing the taxable income limit of both the producer who created the payment and the producer who owns the payment. Neither the House Bill nor the House committee report (page 38) specified whether the creator or owner of the payment was required to include the payment in gross income. The Senate amendment contained exactly the same provision as the House Bill. The Senate committee report (page 60), however, specified that both the creator and the owner must include the payment in gross income. The Joint Conference Committee resolved the uncertainty by including the wording contained in the present law which specifies both creator and owner.

The taxable income from the property is computed under Treasury Regulations Section 1.613-5 and is defined as gross income from the property less all allowable deductions. These deductible items include operating expenses such as pumping and switching labor, car expense, radio rentals, wiping rags, small hand tools, treating chemicals (not injectants), oil filters, cleaning fluids, fuel, water, electricity, communications, compressor rentals, surface rentals, salt water disposal expense, etc. Also included are maintenance expenses such as maintenance labor (roustabout, gangpusher, truck driver, mechanic, etc.), maintenance transportation, well pulling, swabbing, replacement material, dirt work, tank cleaning, equipment repairs, welding, oil roads, paint and painting, weed and snow removal, chemical weed control, paraffin cutting, thawing lines, etc. Also included are workover maintenance expenses such as acidizing, fracturing, cleaning out, scaling casing, etc. Other direct expenses include ad valorem taxes and production taxes. Another direct expense is the cost of "qualified tertiary injectant expenses" (as defined in new Section 193) which the taxpayer has not elected to capitalize. For net income limitation purposes, under Section 4988(b)(3)(E) a producer may elect to capitalize and recover through cost depletion qualified tertiary injectant expenses regardless of his treatment of such expenses for income tax purposes. This election is made on a property by property basis and can be revoked only with the consent of the IRS. The time and manner for making the election will be prescribed in future regulations.

Treasury Regulation Section 1.613-5 continues that in addition to operating expenses, the producer is required to deduct certain selling expenses, administrative and financial overhead (including interest expense), depreciation, taxes and losses. Expenditures such as these, which may be attributable both to oil and gas properties and to other activities (refining, retail marketing, chemicals, minerals, etc.), must be properly apportioned to the oil and gas properties and to such other activities. Furthermore, where a producer has more than one property, deductions which are not directly attributable to a specific property (such as regional production office expenses) must be properly apportioned among all the producer's properties.

Under Treasury Regulations Section 1.613-5(c)(2), intangible drilling and development costs, which were expensed, would also be deducted in arriving at taxable income from the property. However, for purposes of the net income limitation calculation of taxable income from the property, Section 4988(b)(3)(D) states in a confusing manner (through the use of a double negative) that only intangible drilling costs on nonproductive wells (dry holes) may be deducted. All other intangible drilling costs which are expensed for income tax purposes (Section 263(c) costs) are required by Section 4988(b)(3)(C) to be capitalized and recovered through a special cost depletion deduction used for net income limitation purposes only.

The calculation of the special cost depletion deduction is the most significant difference between the determination of taxable income from the property for income tax purposes and taxable income from the property for net income limitation purposes. All intangible drilling costs on productive wells, which were expensed in prior years, must be capitalized, and cost depletion must be recomputed on the sum of these capitalized intangible drilling costs and leasehold costs as if cost depletion had been deducted in all prior years (even if percentage depletion had been deducted for income tax purposes in a prior year). The result of this "as if" computation will be the recomputed 1980 opening balance of depletable basis. The annual calculation of "as if" cost depletion for net income limitation purposes for 1980 and later years will be based on this recomputed opening balance of depletable basis and any current year additions of leasehold costs, intangible drilling costs of productive wells, or qualified tertiary injectant expenses capitalized under the election allowed by Section 4988(b)(3)(E). The "as if" cost depletion is computed on a unit of production basis in the same manner that regular cost depletion is computed.

Where a property produces both oil (or condensate) and gas, taxable income from the property must be allocated among the various products. The Senate committee report (pages 58 and 59) states that "costs on properties producing both oil and gas are allocated under the rule generally applicable for percentage depletion purposes. (See Sec. 613A(c)(7)(C).)" Both Section 613 and the regulations thereunder appear to be silent as to any general rule of allocation. The discussion in Treasury Regulations Section 1.613-5 on alloction of expenses between a mineral property and other activities or between various mineral properties appears to give the taxpayer substantial latitude, provided the method used is "proper." The specific facts and circumstances of the taxpayer would determine the propriety of any particular method of apportionment used under Treasury Regulations Section 1.613-5.

Section 613A(c)(7)(C), as referred to in the Senate committee report, states that if both oil and gas are produced from the property during the taxable year, then the taxable income from the property used in applying the 50 percent limitation for percentage depletion contained in Section 613(a) must be allocated between the oil production and the gas production on the basis of the gross income of each product, but only for purposes of Sections 613A(c)(7)(A) and (B). Sections 613A(c)(7)(A) and (B) deal with the computations required in connection with oil or gas production in excess of the depletable oil quantity or depletable gas quantity. Proposed Treasury Regulations Section 1.613A-3(d)(3) simply reiterates Section 613A(c)(7)(C) and expands the distinction between oil and gas to further differentiate between regulated natural gas, natural gas sold under a fixed contract, and all other natural gas. Thus, while Section 613A(c)(7)(C) provides a general rule that requires the use of gross income as the method of apportionment, the rule only applies to one specific situation.

The language contained in the Senate committee report leads the reader to assume that a general rule requiring apportionment based on gross income exists for purposes of Section 613(a) and Treasury Regulations Section 1.613-5 when, in fact, such a rule exists only for purposes of the calculation required by Sections 613A(c)(7)(A) and (B). Perhaps the Senate committee understood this and intended that, for purposes of the net income limitation, the gross income method of apportionment be used in the determination of taxable income from the property attributable to oil. However, such an intention is not readily apparent from the language contained in either the Senate committee report or the act itself. While this question may be resolved by a ruling or regulations at some later date, for now it appears that the facts and circumstances methodology allowed by Treasury Regulations

Section 1.613-5 may be used for purposes of the net income limitation to allocate and apportion deductions from gross income in determining taxable income from the property attributable to oil.

A further apportionment of taxable income from the property attributable to oil must be made to determine the amount of taxable income attributable to "taxable crude oil." Taxable crude oil is defined in Section 4991(a) as all domestic crude oil that is not exempt from "windfall profit" tax. Inasmuch as "taxable" and "exempt" barrels are artificial distinctions made by law, it would appear that the only appropriate method of apportionment would be barrels of taxable crude oil produced compared to total barrels of production. The result of such an apportionment would be taxable income from the property attributable to taxable crude oil which, when divided by the number of barrels of taxable crude oil from such property, produces the net income attributable to a barrel as defined in Section 4988(b)(2). It should be noted that the same net income attributable to a barrel could be determined by dividing taxable income from the property attributable to all oil by the total number of barrels produced from such property, based on the assumption that on any specific property, the net income attributable to a "taxable" barrel should be the same as the net income attributable to an "exempt" barrel.

Ninety percent of the net income attributable to a barrel is the net income limitation for each barrel produced from that property. The net income limitation for that property is compared to the "windfall profit" (not the "windfall profit" tax) on each barrel from the property. Where the "windfall profit" exceeds the net income limitation on any barrel on a property, the taxpayer is eligible for a refund equal to such excess times the "windfall profit" tax rate applicable to such barrel.

The question has been raised as to whether or not production prior to the March 1, 1980, effective date of the "windfall profit" tax should be considered in the determination of the net income attributable to a barrel. For example, in the case of a calendar year taxpayer, is net income attributable to a barrel determined on the basis of income, expense, and production for a ten-month period rather than the twelve-month period? The inclusion of the phrase "the taxable income from the property for the taxable year" in Section 4988(b)(2)(A) appears to leave no doubt that Congress intended that net income attributable to a barrel be based on the twelve-month period (assuming the taxpayer's taxable year contains twelve months). Section 4988(b)(3) discusses the determination of "taxable income from the property," not "taxable income from the property attributable to taxable crude oil." Section 4988(b)(3)(C), in discussing the deduction for "as if" cost depletion, states that the cost depletion deduction is that which would have been "allowable for the taxable year with respect to the property," not that which would have been allowable for some other period. Congress is aware that most taxpayers have accounting systems designed to maintain tax accounting records and to report on an annual (taxable year) basis. To require the reporting of taxable income on some period other than a taxable year would most likely require the taxpayer to use estimates or prorations. Use of estimates and prorations to determine tax liability certainly does not achieve the accuracy and fairness Congress desires in the administration of our tax laws. Few, if any, taxpayers have an accounting system designed to compute "as if" cost depletion on a monthly basis.

Having determined the "taxable income from the property for the taxable year," Section 4988(b)(2)(A) requires the taxpayer to determine the portion of such taxable income attributable "to taxable crude oil." Taxable crude oil is defined in Section 4991 to be all domestic crude oil which is not one of five specific types of oil exempt from "windfall profit" tax. Nowhere does Section 4991 or Temporary Treasury Regulations Section 150.4991-1(a) state any time period in which oil must be produced to qualify as "taxable crude oil." Thus, any barrel of oil produced during a taxpayer's taxable year and prior to March 1, 1980, which is not one of the five specific types listed in Section 4991(b) is by definition a barrel of "taxable crude oil" even though no tax is collected on such barrel.

It would appear that Congress, through the use of the long-established concept of taxable income determined under Section 613(a) and the standard accounting period of a taxable year, intended to minimize any increase in the taxpayer's accounting burden. The result of this intention to minimize the taxpayer's accounting burden and the desire to reflect the basic economics of operating an oil property as discussed earlier, is that each barrel of oil produced from a specific property in any taxable year should have the same amount of taxable income attributable to it, regardless of whether such barrel is "taxable" or "exempt" and regardless of the day within the taxable year such barrel was produced.

Information Exchange and Refund Rules

Section 4997(a) provides that each taxpayer liable for "windfall profit" tax shall keep such records, make such returns, and furnish such information to both the Internal Revenue Service and to other persons having an interest in the oil as prescribed by regulations. Temporary Treasury Regulations Section 150.4997-2(c)(1) requires that each calendar year the purchaser shall furnish to each producer from whom purchases were made during such year, a statement containing the quantity, removal price, severance tax adjustment, TAPS adjustment, adjusted base price, and "windfall profit" tax liability (computed without regard to the net income limitation) for oil in each tier that was removed during that calendar year. Temporary Treasury Regulations Section 150.4997-2(c)(4) requires this statement to be furnished on Form 6248 which will be published later this year. The statement (Form 6248) must be furnished on or before March 31 following the calendar year to which the statement applies per Temporary Treasury Regulations Section 150.4997-2(c)(5). This statement will provide the producer with the information necessary for him to calculate the "windfall profit" on each of his barrels of production in order to make his net income limitation comparison and determine any overpayment of tax.

A producer who has overpaid his "windfall profit" tax due to the application of the net income limitation is eligible for a refund of the overpayment. The temporary regulations which prescribe rules relating to this refund are divided into two sections. Temporary Treasury Regulations Section 150.6402-1(c) deals with overpayment of amounts deducted and withheld from the producers; Temporary Treasury Regulations Section 150.6402-1(b)(2) deals not with an overpayment which is attributable to amounts deducted and withheld, but which instead relates to amounts the producer has deposited himself on tax liability on his own production. In both situations, the producer may file a claim for refund for the overpayment or he may claim a credit against his income tax liability. However, the silver lining is slightly tarnished inasmuch as the producer may not file a claim for credit or refund until such time as he files his income tax return for the taxable year which includes December 31 of the calendar year in which the barrels of oil giving rise to the refund were produced. This restriction should not inconvenience calendar year taxpayers, but will result in a hardship for fiscal year taxpayers. A taxpayer whose fiscal year ends September 30, 1980, will not be able to obtain credit or refund of an overpayment of "windfall profit" tax attributable to net income limitation for that year until he files his income tax return for fiscal year ending September 30, 1981, which for all practical purposes will be some three to nine months after September 1981!

Furthermore, under Temporary Treasury Regulations Section 150.6402-1(c), a claim for credit or refund of an overpayment attributable to amounts deducted and withheld may not be filed prior to March 1 following the calendar year in which the oil was produced. This requirement comes about because under Section 4995(a)(4) the producer is treated as having paid any amounts withheld from him on the last day of February following the calendar year in which the oil was produced. Thus a calendar year taxpayer would be deemed to have paid amounts withheld on his 1980 production on February 28, 1981, and could file for a refund attributable to amounts withheld anytime after that date (but still not before he files his income tax return).

The requirement that a claim for refund of overpayment of "windfall profit" tax attributable to net income limitation may not be filed until the producer files his income tax return has caused taxpayers to consider other methods of recovery. Two of the methods considered were the "quickie refund" of an overpayment of estimated income tax, and the reduction of quarterly payments of estimated income tax.

The Senate version of the bill contained a provision to add Section 6429, which would have allowed expedited refunds of overpayments attributable to the net income limitation. This provision was dropped by the Conference Committee along with a provision which would have allowed the IRS to prescribe regulations pertaining to the offset of estimated income tax payments with excess "windfall profit" taxes.

Section 6154, which requires installment payments of estimated income tax, defines estimated income tax to be the excess of an estimate of the regular corporate income tax imposed by Section 11 (or the alternative tax imposed by Section 1201, if applicable) over the estimated credits against tax provided by "part IV of subchapter A of chapter 1," which is Sections 31 through 53. These credits include the foreign tax credit, possession tax credit, investment tax credit, lube oil credit, WIN credit, and new jobs credit. Section 6655, which provides a penalty for underpayment of estimated tax and provides exceptions to the penalty, defines income tax in the same manner. (Sections 6015 and 6654, which relate to estimated income tax of an individual, contain a substantially similar definition.) Section 6425, which provides for a quick refund of an overpayment of estimated income tax by a corporation, also defines income tax liability in the same manner.

Presently, part IV of subchapter A of chapter 1 contains no provision which allows a credit against income tax liability for any overpayment of "windfall profit" tax, attributable to net income limitation or otherwise, nor does the IRS have authority to prescribe regulations to modify the definitions contained in Sections 6154, 6655, and 6425 (or 6015 and 6654) to allow such a credit. Thus, until such time as Congress amends these sections or part IV, taxpayers may not reduce their payments of estimated income tax by an overpayment of "windfall profit" tax, and corporate taxpayers may not consider an overpayment in determining the amount of quick refund under Section 6425.

One possible method of earlier recovery is a reduction of the amounts of "windfall profit" tax required to be deposited by integrated oil companies. This method is based on an interpretation of Sections 4995 and 4986 and Temporary Treasury Regulations Section 150.4995-1(a).

The first purchaser of domestic crude oil is required by Section 4995(a)(1)(A) to withhold "windfall profit" tax from the amounts payable to the producer of such oil. Temporary Treasury Regulations Section 150.4995-1(a) provides that the first purchaser is not required to withhold on those purchases where the producer is an integrated oil company. Section 4995(b)(1) provides that an integrated oil company shall make deposits twice a month of:

(A) those amounts the company has withheld as a first purchaser under Section 4995(a)(1)(A), and

(B) the company's liability for the "windfall profit" tax imposed by Section 4986 with respect to oil for which withholding is not required.

This is reiterated in Temporary Treasury Regulations Section 150.4995-3(a)(1).

In the case of an integrated oil company, the "oil for which withholding is not required" would be the integrated oil company's own production under Temporary Treasury Regulations Section 150.4995-1(a). The "tax imposed by Sec. 4986" is the "windfall profit" excise tax imposed on the "windfall profit" from taxable crude oil. Section 4988(b)(1) limits the "windfall profit" on any barrel to 90 percent of the net income attributable to such barrel. A literal reading of Sections 4986 and 4988 leads to the conclusion that the "tax imposed by Sec. 4986" is the producer's ultimate liability: the "windfall profit" tax liability after application of the net income limitation. Thus, the argument may be made that in determining the amount of tax required to be deposited by an integrated oil company on its own production, the integrated oil company may consider the effect of the net income limitation and reduce the amount which would have otherwise been deposited.

At an informal meeting between representatives of the oil industry and the IRS, a member of the IRS delegation stated that it was his opinion that the intention of the Joint Conference Committee was to allow an integrated oil company to consider the net income limitation in determining the amount to be deposited on such company's own production where there was no withholding. The IRS representative felt this matter would be clarified by regulations at a later date. Until such time as this issue is clarified by an IRS pronouncement, the taxpayer has one more difficult decision to make as to which interpretation he will follow.

Opportunities for Tax Planning

Planning opportunities in the area of the net income limitation do not appear to be as great as some taxpayers have been led to believe. Although the effect of the net income limitation should certainly be considered in determining the timing of both additional development drilling expenditures and a large amount of unusual or infrequent maintenance expenditures, the effect on the net income limitation that results from the timing of these expenditures appears to be a minor consideration in view of the other criteria (loss of production, maximization of revenues, availability of equipment and personnel, weather and season, etc.) which affect a decision as to the timing of such expenditures. The requirement to capitalize intangible drilling costs on productive wells and recover such costs through the "as if" cost depletion calculation means that the effect on net income limitation will be based on the ratio of production to reserves, which for most successful wells will only result in additional cost depletion of less than several dollars a barrel.

As a general rule on properties having upper tier production, producers will probably derive a greater net income limitation benefit where maintenance expenditures are incurred in 1980 rather than in 1981. On any such property, the 3 percent monthly BPCL decline and the 4.6 percent monthly volumetric release will cause a significantly greater proportion of the barrels produced to be sold at world market price in 1981 than in 1980, thereby resulting in a much higher net income per barrel on that property in 1981 than in 1980 (assuming relatively constant production and operating expenses). For these properties, producers are almost certain to obtain some net income limitation benefit in 1980, and thus any additional amounts of maintenance expenditures would increase the amount of net income limitation benefit they receive. (If production were to increase in 1981 due to a workover in 1980, there would be an even greater proportion of barrels sold at world market price, and correspondingly, and even greater net income per barrel.)

In the case of stripper and newly discovered properties, producers will obtain a net income limitation benefit only where the lifting costs are substantial in relation to revenues. For these properties, any unusual maintenance expenditures will, as a general rule, produce a larger amount of net income limitation benefit if incurred in 1980 rather than in 1981, assuming that after the maintenance, production increases. The fewer barrels of production the expense relates to, the greater the impact on net income limitation on a per barrel basis *(i.e.,* greater expense per barrel results in a smaller net income limitation per barrel). If there is no increase in production after the maintenance, the expenditure will produce the same net income limitation effect regardless of the year incurred. As a general rule, an unusual maintenance expenditure should not be delayed and should preferably be incurred in a single calendar year, rather than split between years, to have the greatest change of providing an increased net income limitation benefit.

There will, of course, be exceptions to these general rules. Although the effect on the net income limitation appears to be a minor factor in the determination of the timing of expenditures, the producer must base his decision on the end result of the interaction of several factors which include changes in reserve estimates, production, prices, and operating costs, in addition to "windfall profit" tax and net income limitation. The end result of the interaction of these factors upon which the producer would base his decision will be after tax income and cash flow to the producer, not simply the amount of reduction of "windfall profit" tax. For years producers have been considering changes in reserve estimates, production, prices, and operating costs in their decisions as to additional drilling and maintenance expenditures. Now as a result of the "windfall profit" tax and net income limitation, producers have two more factors to consider in an already complex and difficult decision.

[Editor note: Regulations were issued after type-setting that have clarified the information exchange and refund rules. The amendments published on November 5, 1980 clarify that producers may take the net income limitation into account in depositing their own tax under Temporary Reg. Sec. 150.4995-3(a) or (f) when the first purchaser is not required to withhold (discussed on pages 232 and 233). These amendments also amended Temporary Reg. Sec. 150.6402-1 to permit refund claims to be filed any time after February 28 without having to wait until the Federal Income Tax Return was filed (discussed on pages 229 and 230). Fiscal year producers are allowed to file two claims for refund or credit each calendar year, thereby eliminating the hardship discussed on pages 229 and 230.]

Part VI

Treatment of Royalty Owners (Nonoperating Interests)

With the exception of the special rates applicable to independent producer oil discussed previously, the tax rates on the windfall profit on crude oil production are:

Tier I: 70%
Tier II: 60%
Tier III: 30%

The lower independent producer rates apply to qualified production, one of the criteria for which is attributable of a working or operating interest. Royalties are nonoperating interests and therefore do not constitute qualified production eligible for the lower rates.

The net income limitation is rarely if ever of use to the royalty or other nonoperating interest owner. This is because, by its very nature, the nonoperating interests owner does not incur costs deductible in determining net income from the property. However, a cost for which the royalty or nonoperating interest owner is frequently liable and pays is the state severance tax levied on the removal of the oil. This cost is of some tax benefit because it lowers the windfall profit to which the tax rate is applied.

For 1980, there was a one-time $1,000 credit for royalty owners for windfall profit taxes paid. As a result of the Economic Recovery Act of 1981, this credit will be raised to $2,500 for 1981, and there will be an exemption of 2 barrels per day in 1982–1984 and 3 barrels per day for 1985 and years thereafter. Certain members of families, etc., will be required to share this credit much the same as they must now share the independent producer amount. Also, there are special transfer rules applicable to prevent spreading the production among taxpayers and increasing credits available with respect to the same production. The credit is available to individuals, estates, and family farm corporations. Generally, the credit is not available with respect to windfall profit taxes paid on production from any property transferred after a specific date. There is an exception for transfers between those who must share the credit.

The WPT is a deductible excise tax for federal tax purposes. Since it is a deduction from adjusted gross income (an above-the-line deduction), it is available even though an individual may not itemize deductions. For an explanation of the change in the treatment of royalty owners' WPT effected by the Economic Recovery Act, see the postscript chapter at the end of the text.

TAXATION OF NET PROFITS INTERESTS UNDER THE WINDFALL PROFIT TAX

Frank M. Burke, Jr., CPA
Steven F. Meyer, CPA*

On April 2, 1980, the windfall profit tax ("WPT") on domestic crude oil became law with the enactment of the Crude Oil Windfall Profit Tax Act of 1980 ("Act"). The WPT, designated by the Act as an excise tax, was proposed and ultimately supported on the premise that domestic crude oil producers would realize "windfall profits" from future OPEC price increases coupled with the Administration's phase-out of crude oil price controls, which were scheduled to expire in October 1981.**

The objective of this article is not to contest the rationale for the WPT nor to argue as to its validity. Previous articles have served this purpose well.[1] Rather, the

---

* Frank M. Burke, Jr., CPA and Steven F. Meyer, CPA are partner and manager, respectively, in Peat, Marwick, Mitchell & Co., Dallas, Texas.

** The authors would like to thank their associates, C. W. Russell, Dallas, Texas, and Vance K. Maultsby, Jr., Washington, D. C. for their helpful comments on the original draft of this article.

1 See Burke, "The Windfall Profit Tax—The Power of Taxation or the Taking of Property?" *The American Oil & Gas Reporter,* Vol. 22, No. 12, pp. 12-13 (March 1980); see also Chapman, "Government Windfall From Windfall Profits," *Fortune,* Vol. 101, p. 60 (March 24, 1980).

Article reprinted courtesy of *Oil & Gas Tax Quarterly*, December 1980, pp. 195-216

intent of the authors is to point out the complications created by applying the WPT to crude oil attributable to net profits interests and to offer viable alternatives to resolve the problems created by taxing holders of such interests.

Net Profits Interest Defined

A net profits interest is an interest in minerals in place that is defined as a share of gross production from a property, measured by net profits from the operation of the property.[2] A net profits interest is created out of a working interest and has a similar duration. In many respects, a net profits interest is considered a type of royalty and as such, may be described as a net royalty. Determination as to whether a net profits interest is actually a royalty is to a large extent controlled by the circumstances under which it is created. Where the net profits interest reflects a part of the price, rent or consideration which a lessee pays to a lessor as remuneration for use of a mineral producing property, it has been held that such an interest represents a royalty interest.[3]

Unlike the overriding or fee royalty, income accruing to the net profits interest is reduced by specified development and operating costs as stipulated by the net profits agreement. The net profits interest generally bears expenses only to the extent of its share of the income. The holder thereof is not required to pay out, advance, or

---

2 Williams and Meyers, *Manual of Oil and Gas Terms* (4th ed. 1976), p. 362.

3 See Louisiana Land & Exploration Co. v. Donnelly, 394 F. 2d 273 (5th Cir. 1968) where the court of appeals held that a royalty based on 8-1/3 percent of net profits was a royalty under Louisiana state law and was accorded the same treatment as a royalty for purposes of determining the liability for and deduction of state severence taxes withheld in favor of such interest. See also Kirby Petroleum Co. v. Commissioner, 326 U.S. 599 (1946) where the payment for the priviledge of extraction made to the lessor by the lessee was based on "net income." As determined under the lease, such payment of "net income" was held to be rent or royalty paid by the lessee for the privilege of extraction.

become liable for such costs as is the working interest owner. If there is no net profit from the operation of the property, the net profit owner receives nothing. If there is a net loss from operations, he receives nothing but is not liable for any share of the loss. In most cases, until any accumulated net losses are offset by future net profits from operation of the property, the owner of the net profits interest will receive no income. Since the net profits interest is not directly liable for operating costs, the net profits interest is regarded as a nonoperating interest in the minerals in place similar to an overriding royalty interest or production payment.[4]

Generally, a net profits interest is defined in the net profits agreement as a stated percentage of the operator's net profit from the operation of the property. The instrument creating the interest clearly defines such terms as "gross income from the property," "operating expenses," "depreciation," and other items, and should describe in some detail the accounting procedures to be followed by the operator of the property. Although the net profits account may or may not be charged with development and equipment costs and credited with the proceeds of equipment sales, a net profits interest does not have a depreciable interest in the equipment. If the interest is credited with the proceeds of sale of equipment, the net profits interest should never receive more than the gross income attributable to its share of production. The net profits interest may be created by a separate assignment, or it may be retained by the lessor upon the assignment of the working interest. In any case, it represents an agreement between the parties defining their respective interests in production.

---

4 Treas. Reg. § 1.614-2(b) in defining the term "operating mineral interest" under § 614(a) of the Code specifically indicates that such term does not include royalty interests or similar interests such as production payments or net profits interests.

Although a net profits interest is defined as an interest in minerals in place, the determination of a net profits interest as an economic interest has not always been clear. Several cases have held that certain net profits interest payments do not qualify as "economic interests," and hence, production attributable thereto is not considered subject to depletion.[5] In such instances, the courts have held that a net profits interest was merely a contractual consideration for the assignment of property based on a net profit from its operation and was not an interest in gross production. However, commencing with the landmark case of *Kirby Petroleum Co. v. Commissioner,*[6] the courts have consistently viewed the net profits interest as being a right to gross production measured by net income and as such, representing an interest in production. In the *Kirby* case it was ascertained that "the 'net profit' payments . . . flow directly from the taxpayers' economic interest in the oil and partake of the quality of rent..." The position that a net profits interest represents an economic interest was further supported by the Supreme Court's decision in *Burton-Sutton Oil Co. v. Commissioner.*[7] It is now well established that a net profits interest constitutes an economic interest for Federal income tax purposes.

Overview of the WPT

The WPT is a deductible[8] excise tax imposed on the windfall profit (as defined) from taxable crude oil re-

---

5 In O'Donnell v. Helvering, 303 U.S. 370 (1938) and again in Elbe Oil Land Dev. Co. v. Helvering, 303 U.S. 372 (1938) the Supreme Court held that the amounts received from production in accordance with the net profits agreement were not subject to depletion.

6 Note 3, *supra.*

7 328 U.S. 25 (1946).

8 I.R.C. § 164(a)(5), as amended by Pub. L. No. 96-223.

moved from the premises after February 29, 1980. The tax applies only to production from wells in the United States or in a possession of the United States.

For purposes of the WPT, crude oil is generally defined as a mixture of hydrocarbons that exists as liquids in underground reservoirs and remains liquid at atmospheric pressure after passing through surface separating facilities. The term also includes condensate recovered in associated or nonassociated production by mechanical separators located at any point at or before the inlet side of a gas processing plant, and natural gas liquid treated as crude oil under the June 1979 energy regulations. The term, however, does not include synthetic petroleum, such as oil production from shale or tar sands.[9]

The structure of the WPT is such that taxable crude oil is classified in one of three tax tiers. The first tier, or tier 1 oil, includes all taxable domestic crude oil produced by taxable persons and removed from the premises of production with the exception of: (1) oil from stripper well properties, (2) oil in which the U.S. has an economic interest and which is produced from a National Petroleum Reserve, (3) newly discovered oil, (4) certain heavy oil, and (5) incremental tertiary oil. The second tier, tier 2 oil, consists of (1) oil produced from stripper well properties and (2) oil produced on a National Petroleum Reserve, while tier 3 oil includes newly discovered oil, certain heavy oil, and incremental tertiary oil.

Generally, for each tier the tax base (or "windfall profit") is the difference between the removal (or selling) price of the oil and the adjusted base price, minus an adjustment for state severance tax on the windfall profit. However, in no case may the windfall profit on a barrel of crude oil exceed 90 percent of the net income attributable to such barrel.[10]

---

9 H.R. Rep. No. 96-817, 96th Cong., 2d Sess. 114 (1980).

10 I.R.C. § 4988.

Each of the three tiers is subject to a specific windfall profit tax rate and a different base price. The general windfall profit tax rates are 70 percent for tier 1 oil, 60 percent for tier 2 oil and 30 percent for tier 3 oil. An exception to these rates applies to qualifying independent producers who, with respect to limited quantities of oil, are taxed 50 percent on tier 1 oil and 30 percent on tier 2 oil.[11]

To qualify for the special rates provided independent producer oil, production must be tier 1 or tier 2 oil attributable to the independent producers' *working interests*, which were in existence as such interests on January 1, 1980, or which are attributable to qualified overriding royalty interests.[12] Royalty and similar nonoperating interests (whether payable in kind or otherwise) are ineligible for the reduced rates.[13]

The WPT is imposed on the producer of the taxable crude oil by virtue of the producer's ownership of the economic interest in such oil. Actual payment of the tax may be made (1) directly by the producer in the case of oil converted on or removed from the premises prior to sale, or (2) indirectly through withholding and depositary requirements imposed on first purchasers of the taxable crude oil.[14]

The Act and the regulations issued thereunder define the term "producer" to mean the holder of the economic interest with respect to the crude oil.[15] In the case of a partnership, the tax is imposed directly on the partners'

---

11 I.R.C. § 4987.

12 I.R.C. § 4992(d).

13 H.R. Rep. No. 96-817, 96th Cong., 2d Sess. 109 (1980).

14 Temp. Treas. Reg. § 150.4995-1.

15 I.R.C. § 4996(a)(1)(A); Temp. Treas. Reg. § 150.4996-1(b).

proportionate shares of the partnership's production. Generally, each partner's share of crude oil is determined on the basis of the partner's proportionate share of the partnership income.[16]

The Act provides specifically that no persons are exempt from the windfall profit tax unless an exemption for them is provided explicitly in the Act or future legislation.[17] Generally, exemptions from the tax are provided crude oil attributable to economic interests held by a state or political subdivision, or by an agency or instrumentality of a state or political subdivision (including an educational institution), where all the net income received is dedicated to a public purpose.[18] Furthermore, crude oil attributable to interests held by medical and educational charities, as well as Indian and certain Alaskan oil production, is exempt from the WPT, provided that such economic interests were held before January 22, 1980.[19] Finally, crude oil designated as "tertiary incentive crude oil" under the energy regulations, which is from a project that is at least 50 percent owned by independent oil producers,[20] and Alaskan crude oil produced from designated geographical locations are generally exempt from the tax.[21]

Net Profits Interests—Treatment For Depletion Purposes

Although the concept of "economic interest" is fundamental to the determination of which persons bear the liability for the payment of the WPT, the term "economic

16 I.R.C. § 4996(a)(1)(B).

17 I.R.C. § 4996(g).

18 I.R.C. § 4994(a).

19 I.R.C. §§ 4994(b) and (d).

20 I.R.C. § 4994(c).

21 I.R.C. § 4994(e).

interest" is not defined in the Act. One of the few references to the term "economic interest" appears in the Senate Report language discussing the treatment of production payments. In this regard, it states that "the windfall profit tax will be imposed, as is true for all taxable oil, on the owner of the economic interest as determined under Federal income tax provisions."[22]

For federal income tax purposes, the determination of whether a property interest qualifies as an economic interest is critical to the allowance of a deduction for depletion. It is generally accepted that it is the owner of a capital investment or economic interest in the oil in place who is entitled to the deduction for depletion.[23] In this regard the regulations contain the following statement:

> Annual depletion deductions are allowed only to the owner of an economic interest in minerals . . . . An economic interest is possessed in every case in which the taxpayer has acquired by investment any interest in minerals in place . . . and secures, by any form of legal relationship, income derived from the extraction of the mineral . . . to which he must look for a return of his capital.[24]

Since the holder of a net profits interest is presently entitled to an allowance for depletion as an owner of the economic interest in crude oil, and by such ownership is also liable for the WPT, a review of the treatment of holders of net profits interests for depletion purposes may provide some insight as to how such interests should be taxed under the WPT.

---

22 S. Rep. No. 96-394, 96th Cong., 1st Sess. 62 (1979).

23 Burton-Sutton Oil Co., Inc. v. Commissioner, note 7, *supra*. See also Anderson v. Helvering, 310 U.S. 404, 407 (1940); Kirby Petroleum Co. v. Commissioner, note 3, *supra*.

24 Treas. Reg. § 1.611-1(b)(1).

GROSS INCOME FROM THE PROPERTY

The owner of an economic interest is allowed a deduction for percentage depletion based on a specified percentage of the gross income from the property, excluding from such gross income an amount equal to any rents or royalties paid or incurred by the taxpayer in respect of the property.[25] Gross income from the property in the case of a net profits interest is generally considered to be the net payment from production.

Although a net profits interest is defined as a share of gross production measured by net profits from the operation of the property, the holder of such an interest retains only a "net profits" interest in the oil and gas in place.[26] Accordingly, the base upon which the holder of the net profits interest computes his deduction for depletion is the net profits amount and not a proportionate share of gross revenues, based on his net profits percentage. The holder of the economic interest may not "construct a theoretical gross income by recourse to the expenses of production operations."[27]

As an illustration, assume that a taxpayer has a 25 percent net profits arrangement, and during the taxable year the working interest, burdened by the net profits interest, produced oil and gas with gross income amounting to $40,000. Further assume expenses are $20,000, such that the taxpayer received $5,000 under the net profits arrangement (25 percent of $20,000, the net income from the property). Under these circumstances, the taxpayer's gross income from the property for depletion

---

25 I.R.C. § 613(a).

26 United States v. Thomas, 329 F.2d 119 (9th Cir. 1964), *cert. denied*, 379 U.S. 819 (1965), *rehearing denied*, 381 U.S. 921 (1966).

27 Helvering v. Mountain Producers Corp., 303 U.S. 376 (1938). See also Felix Oil Co. v. Commissioner, 144 F. 2d 276 (9th Cir. 1944).

purposes would be $5,000, instead of $10,000 (or 25 percent of $40,000).

It is important to note that although the courts and the Revenue Service have not allowed a net profits holder to "gross-up" income to reflect production expenses deducted in arriving at the net profits payment, severance taxes and in certain cases, ad valorem taxes, paid in behalf of the net profits owner by the working interest owner may be added back to the net profits amount to arrive at gross income from the property for depletion purposes.[28]

IMPACT ON DEPLETABLE OIL QUANTITY

The Tax Reduction Act of 1975 effectively repealed the allowance of percentage depletion with respect to all domestic and foreign oil and gas production as of January 1, 1975, with limited exceptions.[29] These exceptions include retention of percentage depletion on domestic "fixed contract gas," domestic "regulated gas," and certain domestic geothermal production, as well as for a per-day barrel exemption for oil and other gas production attributable to "independent producers and royalty owners."[30]

Percentage depletion is retained under the independent producer and royalty owner exemption with respect to so much of the average daily production of domestic oil

---

28 In Louisiana Land & Exploration Co. v. Donnelly, note 3, *supra*, the 5th Circuit held that a taxpayer who had a "net profits royalty" could gross-up income by the severance taxes applicable thereto, since payment of such taxes by the working interest owner represented payment of additional royalty to the taxpayer. See also Rev. Rul. 75-182, 1975-1 C.B. 176, which provides that ad valorem and gross production taxes paid to the state by an operator of a working interest in oil and gas properties are includable in the net profits interest owner's gross income from the property, subject to depletion and excludable from the operator's gross income from the property.

29 I.R.C. § 613A(a).

30 I.R.C. § 613A(c).

as does not exceed the depletable oil quantity.[31] The depletable oil quantity, reduced by the amount of the taxpayer's average daily secondary or tertiary production, was initially set at 2,000 barrels per day in 1975 and was reduced thereafter until the amount is 1,000 barrels per day for 1980 and later years.[32]

In computing a taxpayer's average daily production of domestic crude oil and natural gas, the taxpayer's aggregate production of domestic oil or natural gas during the taxable year is divided by the number of days in the taxable year.[33] To determine the taxpayer's aggregate production of domestic oil or natural gas, one must look to all interests in production held by such taxpayer during the taxable year. In the case where the taxpayer holds a partial interest (including any interest held in a partnership), the taxpayer's portion of that production will be determined by multiplying the total production from the property by the taxpayer's percentage participation in the revenues from such property.[34]

An obvious question is raised concerning the amount of production which a holder of a net profits interest must include in his aggregate production of domestic oil and natural gas with regard to such interest. The proposed regulations provide that with respect to a holder of a net profits interest in an oil and gas property, such taxpayer's production shall be deemed to be that portion of production which produced the same fraction of the property's gross income as the fractional interest of the taxpayer in the net profits from the property.[35] To illustrate and

---

31 I.R.C. § 613A(c)(1).

32 I.R.C. § 613A(c)(3).

33 I.R.C. § 613A(c)(2).

34 Prop. Treas. Reg. § 1.613A-7(f)(3).

35 *Ibid.*

compare this with the prior example: Assume that the $40,000 of gross income attributable to the working interest represents 1,000 barrels of oil and gas production. Applying the fractional interest of the taxpayer in the net profits from the property (25 percent) to the production which produced the property's entire gross income results in the holder of the net profits interest including 250 barrels (being 25 percent of 1,000 barrels) in his aggregate domestic oil and gas production. This result differs substantially from the barrels which would be included in the taxpayer's aggregate production if the holder of the net profits interest had included only the fraction of production which reflected his interest in the gross income for depletion purposes. In this case, the barrels of production attributable to his interest would be the ratio of gross income from the property attributed to the net profits interest ($5,000 from the prior example) over $40,000 (or 1/8) times the total production of 1,000 barrels, or 125 barrels.

While it may be argued that the proposed regulations should be revised to provide that the holder of a net profits interest is deemed to have an interest in the gross income from the property equal to the amount of net profits received, this thinking does not reflect the Revenue Service's current position. We shall see in alternative approaches to the computation of the WPT that the Revenue Service's position in this regard may, in fact, be extremely beneficial to the holder of the net profits interest insofar as determination of the interest holder's WPT liability is concerned.

Calculation of the Tax

Unless otherwise exempted, it is clear that the holder of a net profits interest, as an owner of the economic interest of oil in place, is subject to the WPT. Also, because a net profits interest is considered a nonoperating interest (in contrast to an operating mineral interest within the meaning of Section 614(d) of the Code), it is ineligible for the reduced rates accorded independent producer oil under the WPT. What is not clear is the manner in which the tax is computed, and how the administrative withholding and depositary requirements are applied.

The Act and the legislative history of the statute provide no guidance as to how the WPT should be computed in the case of a net profits interest. Furthermore, the Revenue Service has not taken a position regarding this issue through regulations, published rulings, or other administrative actions.

To be logical and consistent with what appears to be Congressional intent, any approach to calculation of the tax should incorporate the following concepts:

- The barrel production allocated to the net profits interest should include a ratable share of all categories of oil attributable to the working interest which is burdened by the net profits arrangement during the taxable period of concern;
- The holder of the net profits interest should be deemed to have a severance tax adjustment equal to the severance tax rate multiplied by the excess of the removal (or deemed removal) price over the adjusted base price.

In the absence of statutory or administrative guidelines for calculating the WPT, the net profits interest holder may take the position that his share of production (in barrels) is determined under the administrative authority of the Revenue Service as it applies to the allowance of deduction for percentage depletion. There are numerous instances within the Act and the temporary regulations thereunder that WPT terms are defined with reference to Section 613A of the Code.[36]

One approach to computing the WPT liability for a net profits interest owner is to follow the authority established by the proposed regulations under Section 613A of the Code. As previously illustrated, the amount of production (in barrels) attributed to the holder of the net profits interest is the gross production from the property multiplied by the fractional interest of the taxpayer in the net profits from the property. In a situation involving a 25 percent net profits arrangement, 25 percent of the production attributable to the working interest burdened by the net profits interest will be deemed attributable to the net profits interest. In instances where the net profits payment constitutes an economic interest, it is well established that gross income for depletion purposes is the net payment received from production. Combining these principles in the computation of the WPT, a logical presumption is that the price per barrel of oil in this case is the gross income for percentage depletion purposes divided by the production (in barrels) attributed to the net profits interest. This approach[37] may be illustrated by the following example:

Assume the following facts apply prior to determination of the net profits payment, where A is the working interest owner eligible for independent producer rates and B is the holder of the net profits interest:

---

36 For example, see I.R.C. §§ 4988(b)(4)(B), 4992(e)(3)(A), and Temp. Treas. Reg. § 150.4996-1(g).

37 The examples provided herein offer viable alternatives to computation of the WPT for holders of net profits interests and working interest owners in circumstances where net profits arrangements exist. These examples are not intended to include all possible alternatives, but provide a supportable position for determining the WPT liability associated with such property interests.

Net profits interest	25	percent
Total taxable barrels removed (working interest production)	1,000	barrels
Removal (or sales price)	$40	
Expenses incurred and includable in the determination of "net profits" without regard to severance taxes and WPT	$11,160	
Adjusted base price (tier 2 oil)	$16	
Severance tax rate	5	percent

<u>WPT Withheld by First Purchaser</u>

Removal price	$40.00
Adjusted base price	(16.00)
Severance tax adjustment ($40 − 16) × .05	(1.20)
Windfall profit per barrel	$22.80
Total windfall profit (1,000 bbls.)	$22,800
Rate (tier 2 oil, independent producer)	.30
WPT withheld from A	$6,840

<u>Income Attributable to the Net Profits Interest (NPI)</u>

Gross income	$40,000
Severance taxes (.05 × $40,000)	(2,000)
Expenses	(11,160)
WPT withheld	(6,840)
Net profits	$20,000
NPI percentage	.25
Income attributable to the NPI	$5,000

Production Attributable to the Net Profits Interest

1,000 bbls. × 25% = 250 bbls.

Net profits interest holder should be deemed to receive a ratable portion of all categories of oil removed during the taxable period.

WPT Liability of Net Profits Interest Holder

Deemed removal price ($5,000 ÷ 250)	$20.00
Adjusted base price	(16.00)
Severance tax adjustment ($20 − 16) × .05	(.20)
Windfall profit per barrel	$3.80
Total windfall profit (250 bbls.)	$950
Rate	.60
WPT liability of B	$570

WPT Liability of Working Interest Owner

Removal price	$40.00
Adjusted base price	(16.00)
Severance tax adjustment ($40 − 16) × .05	(1.20)
Windfall profit per barrel	$22.80
Total windfall profit (750 bbls.)	$17,100
Rate (tier 2 oil, independent producer)	.30
WPT liability of A	$5,130
Withheld by first purchaser with respect to A's interest[38]	(6,270)
Refundable to A	$(1,140)

38 The first purchaser withheld $6,840 of WPT with respect to the total amount of crude oil removed from the property; $570 reflects the amount of WPT withheld on behalf of the holder of the net profits interest and the remaining $6,270 is deemed paid by the working interest owner.

In the instant case, the amount of net profits from the property for the taxable period is 50 percent of the gross income ($20,000 divided by $40,000) attributable to the working interest prior to the net profits payment of 25 percent. Accordingly, the deemed removal price for the net profits interest owner in this illustration is $20 as compared to the $40 removal price for the working interest owner. Obviously, under this approach the ultimate windfall tax liability attributed to the net profits interest owner will be a function of the expenses incurred and includable in the determination of the net profits amount. In those instances where the gross income is not significantly reduced by allowable expenses, the net profits owner will have a significant WPT liability, not unlike the working interest owner. However, in situations where allowable expenses substantially reduce the net profits payment (and the deemed removal price), the deemed removal price will likely be below the adjusted base price, eliminating the entire WPT liability of the net profits interest owner. This appears reasonable since for most other interests, the owner would be able to avail himself of the 90 percent net income limitation to effectively eliminate his tax liability in similar circumstances.

Illustrated below is another approach to computation of the WPT for a net profits interest owner which may be appealing to the Treasury but which does not appear entirely consistent with the proposed regulations relating to percentage depletion. Rather than determining the production attributable to the net profits interest holder on the basis of applying the net profits interest percentage to total production, the holder of the net profits interest is deemed to have production (in barrels) from the property in the same ratio as his income received bears to the total gross income from the property. Assuming the same facts as in the prior example, this approach may be illustrated as follows:

WPT Withheld by Purchaser

WPT withheld from A (see prior example)	$ 6,840

Income Attributable to the Net Profits Interest (NPI)

Gross income	$40,000
Severance taxes (.05 × $40,000)	(2,000)
Expenses	(11,160)
WPT withheld	(6,840)
Net profits	$20,000
NPI percentage	.25
Income attributable to the NPI	$ 5,000

Production Attributable to the Net Profits Interest

$$\frac{\text{Gross income attributable to the NPI}}{\text{Total gross income attributable to working interest}} =$$

$$\frac{\$\ 5{,}000}{\$40{,}000} = 12.5\% \times 1{,}000 = 125 \text{ barrels}$$

WPT Liability of Net Profits Interest Holder

Removal price	$40.00
Adjusted base price	(16.00)
Severance tax adjustment ($40 − 16) × .05	(1.20)
Windfall profit per barrel	$22.80
Total windfall profit (125 bbls.)	$2,850
Rate	.60
WPT liability of B	$1,710

WPT Liability of Working Interest Owner	
Removal price	$40.00
Adjusted base price	(16.00)
Severance tax adjustment ($40 − 16) × .05	(1.20)
Windfall profit per barrel	$22.80
Total windfall profit (875 bbls.)	$19,950
Rate (tier 2 oil, independent producer)	.30
WPT liability of A	$ 5,985

Combined WPT Liability	
WPT liability of A	$ 5,985
WPT liability of B	1,710
Total WPT liability	$ 7,695
Withheld by first purchaser	(6,840)
Payable by B[39]	$ 855

It should be noted that the determination of income attributable to the net profits interest ($5,000) in each of the aforementioned examples included a deduction for WPT withheld and deposited by the first purchaser. This treatment is not atypical; most net profits agreements make provision for deduction of ad valorem taxes, state severance taxes, and other taxes, such as the WPT.

---

39 Since the net profits interest holder is not eligible for the reduced rates accorded independent producers, it appears obvious that any WPT payable in excess of that amount withheld by the first purchaser with respect to the combined interests of the working interest owner and the net profits interest owner should be the liability of the net profits interest owner.

However, following the line of reasoning established in *Louisiana Land & Exploration Co. v. Donnelly*[40] and Revenue Ruling 75-182,[41] it may be argued that the payment of the WPT by the working interest owner on behalf of the holder of the net profits interest (via withholding and deposit by the first purchaser) should be considered payment of additional rent or royalty to the net profits owner. The liability for the WPT follows the net profits interest holder as owner of the economic interest. Accordingly, the WPT withheld should be deemed paid directly by him and not deducted by the working interest owner prior to applying the net profits percentage to the amount of net profits from operation of the property. This situation may be compared to the case where oil is owned by a partnership. In such cases the WPT is imposed directly on the partners (as deemed producers). The tax is paid by the partnership, but is not treated by the partnership as a deduction of the partnership. Rather, any amount withheld from the partnership by a purchaser is treated as a distribution of money by the partnership to the partner.[42]

The administrative complications created by this arrangement in circumstances where a working interest is burdened by a net profits payment could be substantial. It would certainly require that a certification as to taxable status be furnished by the net profits interest holder to the working interest owner, not unlike the certification required of partners to a partnership.[43] It would appear that any effort to ascertain a reasonable estimate of the combined WPT liability of the net profits interest holder

---

40 Note 3, *supra.*

41 Note 3, *supra.*

42 H.R. Rep. No. 96-817, 96th Cong., 2d Sess. 106 (1980).

43 Temp. Treas. Reg. § 150.4995-2(e).

and the working interest owner prior to withholding by the first purchaser would be unworkable. Accordingly, the WPT would be withheld from the working interest based on certification procedures now prescribed.[44] In circumstances where this procedure results in overwithholding or underwithholding, the working interest should be eligible for withholding adjustments as provided for in the temporary regulations.[45] Any such adjustments, however, should only reflect the difference between the correct calculation of the combined WPT tax liability for the net profits interest holder and the working interest owner, determined without regard to application of the net income limitation.[46] The working interest owner will then, in effect, treat any amount withheld from the working interest by the purchaser partially as payment of the WPT with respect to the working interest, while the balance would represent a payment of WPT on behalf of the net profits interest owner with respect to such interest.

While this approach to satisfying the administrative requirements of withholding and depositing of the WPT appears complex, it is workable. Furthermore, in situations where the net profits interest constitutes an exempt interest, such as one held by a state or local government, this approach may be the only reasonable alternative to avoid imposing burdensome restrictions on WPT funds due exempt interests, as a result of erroneous withholdings by the first purchaser. To do otherwise would appear to be contrary to the intent of Congress when it created the various statutory exemptions under the Act.

---

44 See Temp. Treas. Reg. § 150.4995-2.

45 See Temp. Treas. Reg. § 150.4995-1(c).

46 I.R.C. § 4995(a)(2)(B).

Conclusion

From an administrative standpoint, the WPT is undoubtedly the most complex tax legislation ever enacted. The burdens imposed on producers, operators, and first purchasers in complying with the withholding, depositary, and filing requirements of the Act are overwhelming.

This article has dealt with only one facet of the WPT; namely, an analysis of the problems encountered in connection with imposing the tax on holders of net profits interests. In the absence of statutory guidelines, it is not at all clear what the Treasury's ultimate position will be with respect to taxing such interests. Until such time as definitive guidelines are provided by the Revenue Service in the form of regulations, published rulings, or other administrative actions, net profits interest holders will be required to carry on business without administrative sanction. In the meantime, the approaches analyzed herein should offer viable alternatives for calculating the tax and complying with the spirit of this new legislation.

IMPACT OF THE WINDFALL PROFIT TAX ON THE ROYALTY OWNER: WHAT YOU DON'T KNOW CAN HURT YOU!

Prof. Craig E. Reese*

When President Carter announced in early April 1979 his intention to decontrol domestic crude oil prices, he also proposed a "windfall profits" tax designed to redistribute the allegedly excessive profit that oil companies would earn as a result of the phasing out of price controls on U.S. oil production. Neither royalty owners, nor independent producers anticipated that they would incur the windfall profit tax (hereinafter WPT), inasmuch as they were not "big" oil companies, *i.e.,* integrated oil companies, and insofar as they had been treated more liberally by the Congress in 1975 when it repealed percentage depletion for all taxpayers except for royalty-owners and independent producers. Congressmen and Senators from the oil-producing states used their influence on the tax writing committees—House Ways and Means and Senate Finance—to effect amendments to the WPT legislation so that royalty-owners and independent producers would be exempt from the tax; however, the political power of the nonproducing states was too much to overcome, although independent producers received a lower tax rate on the same amount of daily production (1,000 barrels per day) for which they may take percentage depletion.

Royalty owners were literally "caught by surprise" in April and May of 1980 when they began receiving royalty checks that had been significantly reduced in amount to provide for WPT withholding. Many were "mad-as-hell"

* Dr. Craig E. Reese is an Assistant Professor of Tax Accounting at the University of Texas, Austin, Texas.

Article reprinted courtesy of *Oil & Gas Tax Quarterly,* December 1980, pp. 284–313

and they demanded Congressional action to correct the inequity they perceived. Royalty owners' associations were organized to pool resources and present a united front to the Congress. Moreover, Senators Bentsen, Boren, and Dole of Texas, Oklahoma, and Kansas, respectively, held public hearings in their states to allow royalty owners to explain how the WPT was inequitable.[1] Even Congressmen and Senators from nonoil producing states have received complaints about the WPT from constituents with royalty interests in property in oil-producing states.

Before Congress recessed for the November election campaign, some tax relief for the royalty owners seemed inevitable inasmuch as a one-time $1,000 WPT credit had been enacted as part of Congressional budget reconciliation.[2] Final enactment of the tax credit must await the deliberations of the "lame duck" Congress that returns to Washington after the November election. A more permanent solution to the obvious inequity of imposing the WPT on royalty owners and integrated oil companies at the same rate must await the first session of a new Congress in January 1981.

The following text includes an analysis of how various types of royalty owners are taxed for WPT purposes. In addition, there is an explanation of how a royalty owner claims a WPT credit (for taxes overwithheld by the first purchaser) and a WPT deduction on his (her or their) income tax return. Finally, there is an explanation of how the $1,000 WPT credit would affect the determination of income tax return tax liability or refund. However, a brief synopsis of the new law is provided first.

---

1 Brenton R. Schlender, "Windfall Tax on Little Oil," *Wall Street Journal,* July 7, 1980.

2 H.R. 7765, *The Omnibus Reconciliation Act of 1980,* pending December, 1980.

Concise Explanation of Windfall Profit Tax

In effect, the windfall profit excise tax recently enacted by the Congress and signed into law[3] by President Carter is not a tax on profits. The exaction is on a portion of the revenue derived from the production and sale of specified categories of domestic crude oil after February 28, 1980. Accordingly, to the extent that President Carter's announced schedule for decontrol of the prices for all categories of domestic crude oil results in increases in the revenue derived from the production and sale thereof, a portion—30 to 70 percent—of the marginal revenue for each category of crude oil will be taxed as a "windfall profit." Although the base price, which depends on the Department of Energy (DOE) controlled price, to be used for determining marginal revenue is "indexed" or adjusted for inflation, there is no provision for adjusting the "windfall profit" for any increases in the cost of production (except for a "net income limitation") or for the increased cost of exploration for, and development of, replacement crude oil reserves within the United States.

The Windfall Profit Tax Formula

As indicated above, the WPT is intended to transfer a significant proportion, 30 to 70 percent, of the difference between the crude oil base price—lower tier, upper tier and "free market" or uncontrolled—and the higher prices at which domestic crude oil has and will be selling as a result of the gradual decontrol that began on June 1, 1979. In general, no deduction for costs or expenses (except severance taxes) incurred in producing the crude oil are allowed, although the base price is "indexed," *i.e.,* adjusted for inflation. Thus, the base or "windfall profit" is the marginal revenue received upon the sale of domestic crude oil at decontrolled prices, but the amount of the

---

3 *The Crude Oil Windfall Profit Tax Act,* Pub. L. No. 96-223, April 2, 1980.

"windfall profit" tax base per barrel may never be greater than 90 percent of the "net income" per barrel. For purposes of determining this limitation, "net income" is rather restrictively defined. A general formula for determining the windfall profit tax is as follows:

Gross receipts from production and sale of crude oil

LESS

Gross receipts from foreign and selected domestic production and sale of crude oil

EQUALS

Gross taxable receipts from production and sale

LESS

Adjusted base price (base price per DOE controlled price adjusted) and incremental state severance tax

EQUALS

Windfall profit (limited to 90 percent of the "net income" from each category)

MULTIPLIED BY

Rate of tax (depends on category of oil)

EQUALS

Gross windfall profit tax

LESS

Overpayment and prepayment of taxes

EQUALS

Net windfall profit tax liability.

Taxable Crude Oil Production

The crude oil which is subject to taxation includes all domestically produced crude oil except oil from a "qualified" governmental interest, a "qualified" charitable or educational interest, exempt Indian oil, exempt Alaskan oil, and exempt "front-end" oil. There are essentially three categories of taxable crude oil defined in Section 4991. Tier Three oil includes "newly discovered oil," "heavy oil," and "incremental tertiary oil." Tier Two oil encompasses both "stripper oil" and oil from an economic interest in a National (Naval) Petroleum Reserve held by the federal government, but does not include Tier Three oil. Accordingly, Tier One oil encompasses all taxable crude oil excepting Tier Two and Tier Three oil.[4]

The following summary is a comparative analysis of the price control and windfall profit tax classification systems for domestic crude oil:

DOE Price Control Category	Windfall Profits Tax Category
Lower tier or old oil	Tier One
Upper tier or new oil	Tier One
Market-priced oil	Tier One
Alaskan North Slope oil	Tier One
Marginal oil	Tier One
Stripper oil	Tier Two
Naval (National) Petroleum Reserve oil	Tier Two
Newly discovered (post-1978) oil	Tier Three
Heavy oil	Tier Three
Incremental tertiary oil	Tier Three

The reduced rate of taxation for two types—Tier One and Tier Two—of independent producer oil has the effect

4 Treas. Reg. § 150.4991-1(b).

of creating two additional tax categories of oil. "Independent producer oil" is that portion of an independent producer's "qualified production" for a quarter that does not exceed the independent producer amount, *i.e.,* 1,000 barrels per day for the quarter. The "qualified production" of an independent producer is the number of barrels of taxable crude oil of which such person is the producer, which is produced during a quarter, which is Tier One or Tier Two oil, and which is attributable to the independent producer's working interest in an oil property.[5]

Computing the Windfall Profit

In general, the base for the windfall profit tax is the "removal price" of a barrel reduced by its "adjusted base price" and the state severance tax adjustment, but the windfall profit can never be greater than 90 percent of the net income attributable to such barrel. The "removal price" is the amount for which the barrel is sold, including any adjustments to the sales price made after sale. However, in the case of a sale between related persons as defined in Section 103(b)(6)(C), the removal price may not be less than the "constructive sales price" used for determining gross income from property under Section 613. The constructive sales price is also used where crude oil is either removed from premises before it is sold or deemed removed therefrom per Section 4988(c)(4). The removal price for oil removed during any calendar month from the Sadlerochit reservoir on the Alaskan North Slope is the average of the producer's removal prices for such month. Finally, an IRS district director may adjust the removal price in the case of any transaction to clearly reflect the fair market value of the oil removed.[6]

---

5 Treas. Reg. § 150.4992-2.

6 Treas. Reg. § 150.4998-1.

The "adjusted base price" is the base price for the barrel of crude oil plus an amount equal to such base price multiplied by the inflation adjustment for the calendar quarter in which the crude oil is removed from the premises, rounded to the nearest cent.[7] The inflation adjustment for any calendar quarter is the percentage by which the implicit price deflator for the gross national product for the second preceding calendar quarter exceeds such deflator for the calendar quarter ending June 30, 1979. There is an additional inflation adjustment for Tier Three oil. The first revision of the price deflator should be used in calculating the inflation adjustment.[8]

For March 1980 the inflation adjustment is 1.0195 in respect to Tier One and Tier Two oil; whereas, the adjustment for Tier Three oil is 1.0246. The IRS will publish future inflation adjustments periodically.[9] The adjustments for the balance of 1980[10] are as follows:

Quarter	Tier One	Tier Two	Tier Three
Second	1.0422	1.0422	1.0527
Third	1.0649	1.0649	1.0810
Fourth	1.0924	1.0924	1.1144

The base price for Tier One oil under Section 4989 is the ceiling price that would have applied to such oil under March 1979 DOE regulations if it had been produced and sold in May 1979 as "upper tier" oil reduced by 21 cents. For purposes of this determination, the grade and quality of the oil produced from the property in May 1979 is

---

7 Treas. Reg. § 150.4989-1(a).

8 I.R.C. § 4989(b).

9 Treas. Reg. § 150.4989-1(a).

10 Notices 80-3, 80-6 and 80-8 in IRB 1980-17 at 23, IRB 1980-24 at 21 and IRB 1980-37 at 17.

used.[11] Inasmuch as the May 1979 "upper tier" ceiling price averaged $13.02, the base price for Tier One oil is $12.81 per barrel,[12] adjusted for grade, quality, and location.

In general, the base prices for Tier Two oil and Tier Three oil are to be determined by the Secretary of the Treasury. The method prescribed by Treasury regulations is to be designed to yield, with respect to oil of any grade, quality, and field, a base price which approximates the price at which such oil would have sold in December 1979, if all domestic crude oil were uncontrolled and the average removal price for all domestic crude oil (other than Sadlerochit oil) were $15.20 per barrel for Tier Two oil and $16.55 per barrel for Tier Three oil. In addition, there is a special rule for determining base prices from March 1 through September 1980, inasmuch as Treasury regulations promulgated[13] September 29, 1980, established permanent rules for determining base prices in the future which were later deferred until mid-December.[14]

The interim rule provides that the base price is the product of the highest posted price for December 31, 1979, for uncontrolled crude oil of the same grade, quality and field multiplied by a fraction, the denominator of which is $35.00 and the numerator of which is $15.20 for Tier Two oil (or $16.55 for Tier Three oil). If there is no posted price, the highest posted price for such date for uncontrolled crude oil at the nearest domestic field for which prices for oil of the same grade and quality were posted for date, multiplied by 15.20/35.00 (or 16.50/35.00).

---

11 Treas. Reg. § 150.4989-1(b).

12 U.S. Congress, Conference Committee, *Conference Report (No. 96-817) On The Crude Oil Windfall Profit Tax Act of 1980,* 96th Congress, 2d Sess., March 7, 1980, p. 28.

13 T.D. 7721, IRB 1980-42 at 13.

14 Announcement 80-149, IRB 1980-45 at 31.

However, the interim base price may not be less than the sum of the ceiling price which would have applied to such oil under March 1979 DOE regulations if it had been produced and sold in May 1979 as "upper tier" oil, plus $1 in the case of Tier Two oil, or $2 in the case of Tier Three oil.[15] In summary, the base price for Tier Two oil is $15.20 adjusted for grade, quality, and location, while the base price for Tier Three oil is $16.55 adjusted for grade, quality, and location.

Once the base price is determined, it is not to be adjusted for later changes in grade or quality. Where the production from a property in May or December of 1979 varied in grade or quality during the month, the per barrel average grade and quality for the month is used to determine the base price. Finally, where there was no commercial production in May or December of 1979, the grade and quality of the oil produced in the first month of commerical production after May or December is used to determine the base price.[16]

There is also an adjustment to the adjusted base price of Alaskan North Slope oil from the Sadlerochit reservoir in the Prudhoe Bay oilfield. The adjusted base price of such oil is increased by any TAPS (Trans-Alaskan Pipeline System) adjustment, which is defined as the excess for any calendar quarter of $6.26 over the TAPS tariff (transportation cost) for the preceding calendar quarter. Thus, as the average per barrel amount for transporting crude oil through the TAPS decreases below $6.26, the adjusted base price for a barrel of such Alaskan North Slope oil is increased an equal amount.[17]

---

15 Treas. Reg. § 150.4989-1(c).

16 Treas. Reg. § 150.4989-1(d).

17 I.R.C. § 4996(d).

Severance Tax Adjustment

Finally, an amount approximately equal to the marginal increase in state severance taxes resulting from oil price decontrol should be added to the adjusted base price to determine the total deductions from the removal price in arriving at the windfall profit. Thus, one can deduct that portion of the state severance tax paid which is attributable to difference between the removal price and the adjusted base price, *i.e.*, incremental price or value.

For purposes of this adjustment for state excise taxes on the increase in crude oil prices, state severance tax is defined as any tax imposed by a state, but not including a political subdivision thereof, in respect to the extraction of crude oil that is determined on the basis of the gross value of the oil extracted. Neither an exaction levied on the value of crude oil reserves in the ground (property tax), nor an impost levied on the net proceeds from the production of crude oil (income tax) are considered state severance taxes. Moreover, a tax on the production of crude oil that is levied at a fixed amount per barrel is not a severance tax (but an excise tax on units of production).

There are two limitations on the severance tax deduction. One limits the deductible severance tax to 15 percent of the "incremental" price or value, *i.e.*, 15 percent (or less if lower tax rate) of the difference between removal and adjusted base prices. The other requires that any future increases in the severance tax must apply uniformly to all portions of the gross value of the oil.

In situations where the rate of a state severance tax exceeds 15 percent, the portion of the tax in excess of 15 percent on the "incremental" price or value of the crude oil can not be deducted in determining the windfall profit. In respect to increases in a state severance tax after March 31, 1979, there must be an equal increase in such taxes on all categories of oil. Thus, any amount of severance tax that exceeds the amount imposed under a state law in effect on March 31, 1979, is only deductible if such excess is attributable to an increase in the rate of tax (or imposition of a severance tax) that applies equally to all portions of gross value of each barrel of oil subject to such tax.[18]

Net Income Limitation

As indicated in the general formula and synopsis above, the tax base or "windfall profit" is the excess of the removal price of a barrel of crude oil over the sum of the base price of such a barrel adjusted for inflation *(i.e.*, the adjusted base price) and the amount of the state severance tax which exceeds the severance tax that would have been imposed if the barrel had been valued at the adjusted base price. However, the "windfall profit" on any barrel of oil can not exceed 90 percent of the "net income" attributable to that barrel—the "net income limitation" of Section 4988. Although the "net income limitation" is very important to taxpayers with an operating or working interest in domestic crude oil property, this limitation is generally beyond the scope of an explanation of the WPT for nonoperating interests insofar as the WPT liability of a royalty owner would rarely, if ever, be affected by the Section 4988 limitation; and therefore, any discussion thereof will be deferred.

Windfall Profit Tax Rate Structure

The determination of the taxable base for each category of domestic crude significantly complicates the calculation process. Delineating the type or category of crude oil produced is also a complicating factor because of the overlapping of price control and tax law taxonomies for classifying domestically produced crude oil. In contrast,

---

18 Treas. Reg. § 150.4996-2.

once the crude oil produced domestically has been properly classified, the determination of the appropriate tax rate has also been made, insofar as there is only one tax rate for each category of taxable crude oil. In essence, there are five different categories of oil and rates of taxation under Section 4987(b) which can be summarized as follows:

Category of Oil	Tax Rate
Regular Tier One	70%
Independent Producer Tier One	50%
Regular Tier Two	60%
Independent Producer Tier Two	30%
Tier Three	30%

In the case of a fractional barrel of taxable crude oil, Section 4987(b) and the Treasury regulations[19] provide that the tax imposed is the same fraction of the amount of tax imposed on the whole barrel.

Liability for the Windfall Profit Tax

Although the WPT is imposed on the crude oil producer,[20] which is defined as the holder of an economic working or royalty interest in oil property (as defined in DOE Regulation 212.72(a)),[21] the first purchaser of any domestic crude oil is liable for this Chapter 45 excise tax. Accordingly, the first purchaser of domestic crude oil must withhold an amount equal to the excise tax imposed thereon from his (her or their) payment to the producer of such crude oil.[22] Thus, the purchaser must file tax returns, keep records related thereto and furnish other

19 Treas. Reg. § 150.4987-1.

20 Treas. Reg. § 150.4986-1.

21 Treas. Reg. § 150.4996-1(b).

22 Treas. Reg. § 150.4995-1(a).

information to the Treasury as prescribed in their regulations. In addition, each partnership or fiduciary producing domestic crude oil, each operator of a well from which domestic crude oil is produced, and any other person liable for the Section 4986 excise must file such tax returns, maintain such records, and provide such other information as is required by the Treasury regulations.[23]

There are several important exceptions to the general rule that first purchasers are liable for, and must withhold the WPT imposed upon producers of domestic crude. For example, where the purchaser of domestic crude and the operator of the oil property from which the crude is produced jointly elect in respect to such property, the operator may be substituted for the purchaser for purposes of withholding and the payment of the excise tax on windfall profits.[24] For purposes of the WPT, an "operator" is generally defined as the person (or persons) primarily responsible for the management and operation of the production of crude oil from a property. However, persons (or person) holding operating mineral interests in a property may designate another person (or persons) as the "operator" of a crude oil producing property for purposes of the WPT.[25]

More importantly, in the case of domestic crude oil produced, processed, and sold (or used) by "integrated oil companies" (as defined in Section 613A(d)(2) and (4) for depletion purposes) there would be no purchaser and no withholding; and therefore, the integrated-oil-company producer is liable for the WPT on its own domestic production, as well as on any domestic crude oil it purchases from other producers.[26] Similarly, in the case of

---

23 Treas. Reg. § 150.4997-1.

24 Treas. Reg. § 150.4995-2(f).

25 Treas. Reg. § 150.4996-1(c).

26 Treas. Reg. § 150.4995-3(a).

domestic crude produced and either processed and sold (or used), or removed from the premises for processing and sale (or use) by a person who is not an "integrated oil company," there would also be no first purchaser and no withholding; and consequently, the producer is liable for the tax on both its own domestic production and the crude it purchases from other producers.[27]

Withholding and Depository Requirements

In general, the "purchaser" of domestic crude oil is required to deduct and withhold the WPT from amounts payable by that purchaser for the oil. The term "purchaser" includes only the first person purchasing domestic crude oil where "person" is defined in Section 7701(a)(1) to include an individual, a trust, estate, partnership, association, company, or corporation. There are three major exceptions to this general rule. If crude oil is "removed from the premises" before it is sold, then the producer is generally liable for paying (and thus depositing) the tax. Moreover, where the manufacture or conversion of crude oil into refined products begins before the oil is removed from the premises, then the producer is usually liable for paying the WPT. Similarly, if the producer of the oil is an "integrated oil company," there usually is neither a "first purchaser" not a withholding requirement; therefore, the integrated oil company must pay the WPT on its own behalf. Finally, an "integrated oil company" must pay the WPT in respect to many sales of its crude oil production to first purchasers.[28]

Every purchaser required to deduct and withhold the windfall profit tax is liable for the tax required to be withheld whether or not it is actually withheld by the

---

27 Treas. Reg. § 150.4995-3(f).

28 Treas. Reg. § 150.4995-1(a).

purchaser. However, in no event should the purchaser's liability for the tax required to be withheld exceed the producer's liability for the tax in respect to oil sold to that purchaser, and the purchaser's liability is abated to the extent that the producer's liability for the tax is paid (including payments by the producer or by the purchaser through adjustments in amounts later withheld). The producer from whom the correct amount was not withheld is liable to any purchaser for the amount of the producer's tax liability paid by the purchaser. The purchaser is relieved of liability to any other person for the amount of any tax withheld and paid to the Internal Revenue Service (IRS) or deposited with a duly designated depositary.[29]

Tax deposits must be made with a Federal Reserve bank or, at the depositor's election, with a financial institution authorized in accordance with Treasury Department Circular No. 1079. Each deposit must be accompanied by a federal tax deposit form for excise taxes (FTD Form 504) and the timeliness of the deposit is determined by the deposit received (or deemed received under Section 7502(e)) by a Federal Reserve Bank or by an authorized financial institution, whichever is earlier.[30]

If the amount of tax withheld from a producer for a calendar year is less than the total liability of the producer for the WPT in respect to oil removed during the calendar year and subject to withholding as prescribed by Regulation 150.4995-1, the producer must remit the difference with a timely return as required by Regulation 150.4997-1. Alternatively, the producer may deposit such difference on or before the last day for filing a tax return under Regulation 150.4997-1.[31]

---

29 Treas. Reg. § 150.4995-1(e).

30 Treas. Reg. § 150.4995-3(h).

31 Treas. Reg. § 150.4995-3(e).

Tax Accounting Requirements: Returns and Recordkeeping

In general, a person (purchaser or operator) required to withhold the WPT for any taxable period (calendar quarter) must file a tax return (Form 720, with Form 6047 attached thereto) not later than the last day of the second month following the close of a taxable period. The same filing requirement is applicable where oil production is not subject to withholding, as in the case of selected producers and integrated oil companies. Thus, the producers of crude oil in respect to which withholding is required are not required to file a windfall profit tax return in respect to such oil. However, an annual tax return (Form 6248) must be filed by each producer whose liability for WPT in respect to oil that was removed during the four taxable periods (calendar year) exceeds the amount of tax withheld in respect to that oil. Such annual returns must be filed not later than the last day of the first February following the close of the calendar year in which the oil giving rise to the underpayment was removed.[32]

In addition, each taxpayer liable for the WPT, each producer or purchaser of domestic crude oil, each operator of a property producing domestic crude oil and each partnership or other person (*e.g.*, estate or trust) either receiving information on behalf of, or providing information to, producers is subject to recordkeeping requirements. In general, such producers, purchasers, operators, partnerships, and other persons (*e.g.*, fiduciaries) must keep records of all documents, material, and information necessary for either determining the WPT or that affect his (her or its) administrative obligations under Chapter 45 or the regulations related thereto. This recordkeeping requirement includes material furnished to other persons, as well as information received from other persons.

32 Treas. Reg. §§ 150.4997-1(a) and 150.6076-1.

These records must be available at all times for inspection by authorized officers or employees of the IRS and must be retained as long as the contents thereof may be pertinent to the administration of the Internal Revenue Code.[33]

If a purchaser either is subject to the rules for withholding and depositing the WPT in respect to any crude oil purchase or would be subject thereto in the absence of an exemption certificate, such purchaser must furnish both monthly statements and an annual statement (on Form 6248) to each producer of the crude oil purchased. However, if payment for the oil purchased is made to the operator, rather than to the producer or to a partnership rather than the partners, the statements must be furnished to the operator or the partnership, respectively. Such purchaser must also file the annual information return with the IRS. Any person who receives a statement in respect to oil of which such person is not the producer must, within fifteen days of receipt of the statement, furnish to each producer or partnership of producers (and the IRS in the case of an annual statement) the information relating to that producer's or partnership's share of the oil purchased.

Each purchaser must furnish statements for each calendar month showing the total amount of WPT withheld by the purchaser from payments made to the producer, operator, or partnership in respect to oil removed during that month. Where the purchaser did not withhold tax from payments to that person because of the receipt of an exemption certificate, *i.e.,* where the producer or operator certifies to the purchaser that oil production is exempt, the monthly statement need only state the reason for the absence of withholding. Each monthly statement should be furnished before the first day of the

---

33 Treas. Reg. § 150.4997-1(b).

second month that begins after the close of the month to which the statement is applicable.

For each calendar year, the purchaser must furnish statements and must file information returns with the IRS. A separate statement must be furnished to and a separate information return must be filed for each producer, operator, or partnership to whom the purchaser made payments for oil purchased during the calendar year.

Each statement and information return should contain the following information in respect to oil for which that person received payment: (1) The quantity, removal price, severance tax adjustment, TAPS adjustment (if any), adjusted base price, and WPT liability (computed without regard to the net income limitation) for oil in each tier that was removed during that calendar year; (2) The total quantity of the taxable crude oil that was removed during that calendar year; (3) The total amount of the WPT liability, in respect to the oil, incurred during that year; and (4) The amount of WPT withheld by the purchaser in respect to the oil removed during each month of that year, and the total tax withheld in respect to oil removed during the year. For purposes of the preceding sentence, each category of Tier Three oil, independent producer oil withheld upon at a 50 percent rate, and independent producer oil withheld upon at a 30 percent rate should be treated as a separate tier. Where the purchaser did not withhold tax from payments to that person because of the receipt of an exemption certificate, the annual statement and information return should state that fact and should set forth the above information clearly identified as relevant to tax consequences that would have occurred had the exemption certificate not been received.

When the withholding adjustments mandated by Regulation 150.4995-1(c) are not completed during the calendar year, the purchaser must provide supplemental information in the annual statement and information return in respect to the person subject to the adjustment. The statement and information return should set forth the amount that has been either underwithheld or overwithheld, the amount actually adjusted, and the amount remaining unadjusted. Where the adjustment was due to underwithholding, the statement must also inform the recipient that the producer is liable for the amount of the WPT in excess of the amount of such tax withheld by the purchaser and that this information is being supplied to the IRS. Where the withholding adjustment was due to overwithholding, the statement should inform the recipient that the purchaser was unable to fully adjust the overpayment as required by Regulation 150.4995-1(c) and that the producer is eligible for a credit or refund which he (she or it) may claim on his (her or its) federal income tax return in accordance with the rules provided in Regulation 150.6402-1.

The annual statement and information return required for each person should also set forth as the amount deductible for federal income tax purposes the total amount of windfall profit tax withheld from payments made to each producer, operator, or partnership during the calendar year without regard to when the oil was removed. The annual statements required to be furnished on or before January 31 of the year immediately following the calendar year to which the statement is applicable, and the annual information returns required to be filed by a purchaser should be filed on or before the due date for the windfall profit tax return (Forms 720 and 6047) for the last taxable period of the calendar year, *i.e.,* February 29, 1980, or earlier.[34] For a more detailed explanation of the windfall profit tax based on the statute, Regulations

---

34 Treas. Reg. § 150.4997-2.

and Congressional Committee reports, see the June and September 1980 issues of the *Quarterly.*[35]

Having digested the above synopsis of the Chapter 45 excise tax (on domestic crude oil production) in which special emphasis has been placed on those provisions that are most pertinent to royalty owners, the reader should be prepared for the following commentary on the impact of the WPT on producers with a royalty interest in crude oil producing property. The analysis above and following relies on Congressional Committee reports, Treasury and DOE regulations, and those few Revenue Rulings (and announcements) which were available at the time of this writing (October 1980) in interpreting the statutory language of Chapter 45 (and related Internal Revenue Code sections) as it applies to royalty owners who are not explicitly exempt from the WPT.

Taxing the Royalty Owner

As noted above, the royalty owner generally incurs WPT on the same basis that the "integrated oil companies" do; whereas, only nontaxable persons with royalty interests, *i.e.,* "qualified" governmental, charitable, educational, and Indian interests, are exempt from the WPT. However, a person producing oil from his (her or its) own property and qualifying as an independent producer would pay WPT at lower rates on the first 1,000 barrels per day production if that person qualifies as an "independent producer." Conversely, royalty owners retain one advantage over the integrated oil companies insofar as they, along with independent producers, may

---

35 See Robert D. Shattuck, Jr., "The Crude Oil Windfall Profit Tax of 1980," *Oil and Gas Tax Quarterly,* June 1980, pp. 387-417; "Analysis of the Crude Oil Windfall Profit Tax: With an Emphasis on the Independent Producer," *Oil and Gas Tax Quarterly,* June 1980, pp. 418-449; and Craig E. Reese, "Temporary Windfall Profit Tax Regulations: Much Ado About Nothing?" *Oil and Gas Tax Quarterly,* September, 1980, pp. 1-65.

still deduct percentage depletion on the *full price* of the crude oil production, although the WPT must be taken into consideration in determining the 50 percent net income limitation on the depletion deduction.

In the following commentary on the imposition of the WPT, the term "royalty owners" is meant to encompass any owners of economic interests in oil properties who earn what is defined as royalties for income tax purposes, *i.e.,* landowner royalties, overriding royalties and net profits interests. As a frame of reference for further analysis, consider the case of a producer with a royalty interest. Ranch Peter O. Leum, our hypothetical taxpayer, owns 2,000 acres in South Texas upon which he "runs" several hundred head of cattle and raises sufficient feed-stuff for his own cattle in normal years. More importantly, ten wells have been drilled on Peter's property over the past quarter century. Wells drilled in 1955, 1963, 1966, 1969, and 1976 were abandoned as dry holes. Producing wells were drilled in 1957 (#2), 1971 (#7), 1973 (#8), and 1979 (#10). Furthermore, oil was discovered when a well was drilled in 1961, but the well was "shut-in" because the costs of production were greater than revenue at that time. With oil prices at over $30 per barrel in the market, Peter anticipates production from this "shut-in" well in the near future if the property can be classified as "newly discovered." In the case of all producing wells, Peter has a standard one-eighth royalty interest in the production therefrom. The following schedules provide summaries of both Peter's share of production for March 1980, and the WPT related thereto:

CRUDE OIL PRODUCTION, REVENUE AND TAX

Well/Oil	Bbl	Royalty	Price	Revenue	Severance	WPT
TWO-Stripper	248	31	$34	$1054	$52.70	$334.49
SEVEN-Old	2480	310	7	2170	108.50	N/A
SEVEN-New*1	744	93	15	1395	69.75	119.97
SEVEN-Market*2	74.4	9.3	34	316	15.80	129.46
EIGHT-New	4960	620	15	9300	465.00	799.80
EIGHT-Market*2	744	93	34	3162	158.10	1294.56
TEN-Newly discovered (3/80)	2480	310	39	12,090	604.50	1946.80
TOTALS	11,730.4	1466.3	$20*3	$29,487	$1474.35	$4625.08

***1** Reflects a 3-1/3 percent per month lowering of base production control level since June 1, 1979, thereby converting lower tier (or old oil) to upper tier (new oil) classification for pricing purposes.

***2** Reflects the 4.6 percent per month conversion of upper tier (or new oil) to uncontrolled (or market) pricing for the twenty month period January 1, 1980 to October 1, 1981.

***3** Weighted average price.

COMPUTATION OF WINDFALL PROFIT TAX

Well	Removal Price	Base Price	Inflation Adjustment	State Tax Adjustment	Tax Rate	Roy.	WPT
TWO	$34	$14.77[a]	$.29	$.95	60%	31	$10.79
SEVEN	7	12.81	N/A	N/A	70%	310	N/A
	15	12.81	.25	.10	70%	93	1.29
	34	12.81	.25	1.05	70%	9.3	13.92
EIGHT	15	12.81	.25	.10	70%	620	1.29
	34	12.81	.25	1.05	70%	93	13.92
TEN	39	16.55[b]	.41	1.10	30%	310	6.28

[a] $34.00 × 15.20/35.00 = 14.77; assumes 12/79 price was also $34.00.

[b] $35.00 × 16.55/35.00 = 16.55; assumes 12/79 price would have been $35.00.

In summary, Peter incurred WPT of $4,625.14 on gross revenue of $29,487; and therefore, after deductions for the Texas severance tax of $1474.35, Peter receives a check from the operator for $23,387.51.

If one assumes production results for the prior month were virtually the same as those for March 1980, then Peter's royalties would decrease by the amount of the WPT, *i.e.,* from $28,012.65 to $23,387.51. Thus, the effective rate of the WPT in this example is apparently 15.7 percent; however, insofar as the WPT is deductible for income tax purposes, the real effective rate is closer to 5 percent if we assume that Peter is in the 70 percent marginal tax bracket. The real effective rate would, of course, be higher if we assume Peter is in a lower marginal-rate income tax bracket, *e.g.,* by filing a joint return or after deducting percentage depletion.

As lower tier oil and upper tier oil are reclassified, Peter's gross revenue from his royalty interest increases because the operator can sell the crude oil at higher prices. However, almost seventy cents of each additional dollar of revenue will be withheld by the purchaser (or operator where elected) for payment of the WPT to the Federal government. Inasmuch as the WPT is deductible for income tax purposes, one could argue that the marginal WPT rate for the higher priced Tier Three oil is effectively 9 percent if the taxpayer is in the 70 percent income tax bracket. The effective marginal WPT rate would increase if Peter were in an income tax bracket where the marginal rate is less than 70 percent.

If Peter filed a joint return or incurred significant ordinary losses (*e.g.,* drought decimates the herd and feed crop on his ranch) in any one tax year, the marginal rate at which his income from royalties is taxed could be considerably lower than 70 percent. In addition, one could argue that the marginal income tax rate is never higher than about 55 percent (56 percent in 1981) insofar as the

fective marginal WPT rate remains at 9 to 21 percent. depletion allowance on gross revenues. However, the effective marginal WPT rate remains at 9 percent (to 21).

Until October 1981 Peter's gross revenue from royalties should increase for two reasons—decontrol of prices for domestic crude oil and increases in market price for crude oil. After October 1981 royalty revenues should only increase because market prices increase. No matter what the origin of the increase in gross revenues, Peter's WPT liability will increase both absolutely, and relatively, insofar as the bulk of his royalty income is from wells producing Tier One oil and the WPT is imposed at a 70 percent rate thereon. However, if Tier One oil production decreases relative to Tier Three oil, *i.e.,* newly discovered oil, Peter would pay relatively less WPT although the total WPT he pays may continue to increase. Moreover, any relative decrease in WPT would be partially offset by an increase in the relative amount of income tax paid on royalty income because of a relatively lower deduction for the WPT.

If another hypothetical royalty owner, Ima N. Vestor, held an overriding royalty interest of one-eighth of the revenue from each of the four producing wells, there would be no difference in the WPT liability assuming the same production and revenue as delineated in the above two schedules. In the case of any royalty owners with a net profits interest in Peter's four producing wells, royalty income earned and WPT incurred would depend on the specific contractual arrangement between the holder of the working interest and the lessee who assigned the working interest while retaining a net profits interest.

Income Tax Deduction for WPT

As explained above, the deductibility of the WPT for Federal income tax purposes mitigates somewhat the high marginal WPT rates, especially for those taxpayers whose income places them in the higher marginal income tax rate brackets. The Crude Oil Windfall Profit Tax Act of 1980 added Section 164(a)(5) which authorizes the deduction of the Section 4986 windfall profit tax. Without specific authority for deduction of the WPT, it could have been argued that Section 275(a) which prohibits the deduction of federal excess profits taxes and selected federal excise taxes disallowed deduction of the excise tax on windfall profit from the sale of crude oil.

In the case of an individual, the WPT paid or accrued is deductible in determining adjusted gross income,[36] and therefore, the WPT is deductible although the individual does not itemize deductions because the total thereof is less than the zero bracket amount. Inasmuch as most individuals are cash-basis taxpayers, there may be some question as to the amount of WPT deductible for 1980 when royalties and withheld taxes are not paid until January 1981 by the purchaser (or operator where elected).

For corporate taxpayers, the WPT is deductible as a business expense. In the case of a fiduciary that does not currently distribute all income to beneficiaries, the WPT is deductible as investment expense in determining distributable income, *i.e.,* before the deduction for distributions to beneficiaries, exemptions, capital gain deduction, etc. In the case of fiduciaries that are required to currecently distribute net income to beneficiaries and of partnerships, a WPT deduction may be taken by the reporting entity or the taxable person—beneficiary or partner—depending on the trust or partnership agreement and other local law considerations.

The amount of WPT deductible for income tax purposes in a particular year depends upon the amount of

36 I.R.C. § 62(5).

that tax paid or accrued by the taxpayer. Inasmuch as most corporations are accrual basis taxpayers, the amount of WPT applicable to the amount of royalty income accrued determines the accrual basis corporation's deduction for WPT. In the case of fiduciaries and partnerships, the cash method is the predominant accounting method choice; and the amount of WPT withheld from royalty income received during the calendar year determines the amount of WPT deductible by the fiduciary, beneficiaries or partners.

Tax Accounting for the Royalty Owner's WPT

Insofar as the purchaser of crude oil is responsible for withholding the WPT from the royalty owner's share of oil production revenue, the tax accounting problems for the latter do not ensue until after he (she or it) receives the final calendar year payment and the annual production statement from the former, on or before January 31 of the following year. In most cases, the WPT withheld will approximate the royalty owner's actual liability. As explained above, the purchaser is responsible for informing the royalty owner (and the IRS) of both the former's under- or over-withholding and the total WPT withheld during the calendar year.

In those situations where over-withholding has occurred, the royalty owner can take a tax credit (or refund) when he (she or it) files a Federal income tax return. To correct an under-withholding situation, the royalty owner may be required to file an annual WPT return (Form 6248) accompanied by payment of the liability due on or before the last day of the second month following the calendar year, *i.e.,* February 29 (or 28). Alternatively, the royalty owner may, on or before the last day for filing the annual WPT return, deposit the amount of the underpayment accompanied by a deposit form (FTD Form

504) with a financial institution that is an authorized federal depositary.

Tax Planning for Royalty Owners

Inasmuch as the WPT is an excise tax on domestic crude oil production, there are few tax planning opportunities for producers who are not exempt from the tax. The most obvious opportunity is found in the Section 4988 ninety-percent-of-net-income limitation; however, royalty owners by the very nature of their economic interest in oil production can neither incur additional production expenses nor accelerate the payment of production expenses on low-profit oil properties to take advantage of the 90 percent limitation. Even if a royalty owner could actively take advantage of the "ninety-percent-of-net-income limitation," he (she or it) would be constrained somewhat by the "fifty-percent-of-taxable-income limitation" of Section 613 which limits the percentage depletion deduction.

As explained in the introduction, royalty owners aware of the "windfall profits" tax legislation just assumed it would not apply to them because President Carter had characterized the exaction as a levy on the large oil companies and since royalty owners (and independent producers) were spared in 1975 when percentage depletion was repealed. Although the efforts of Senators and Congressmen from oil producing states to exempt royalty owners from the WPT were not fruitful, one of the pending (December 1980) Congressional proposals to provide tax relief for royalty owners is probably going to be enacted insofar as Senators and Congressmen from the nonproducing states now realize that the majority of royalty owners are not oil companies or wealthy individuals, but farmers and ranchers, as well as retirees who invested in oil and gas as a hedge against inflation. Temporary tax relief in the form of a $1,000 income tax credit for tax year 1980 will probably be enacted by Congress.[37]

In anticipation of an impending $1,000 income tax credit for the WPT, a traditional family tax planning strategy would seem to dictate the giving of a portion of the royalty interest to family members assuming each family member would qualify for an income tax credit of $1,000. However, the proposed legislation limits the $1,000 credit to one for each group of related parties, *e.g.,* family members.

Insofar as the incremental state severance tax is deductible in determining the windfall profit, a cash basis taxpayer should encourage the operator of a well in which the former has a royalty interest to speed up state severance tax payments if the latter is contemplating incurring greater production costs or accelerating payment thereof in an effort to take advantage of the ninety-percent-of-net-income limitation.

Inasmuch as the proposed $1,000 income tax credit would only be available for the 1980 tax year, the tax planner may, by anticipating the nature of the permanent tax relief for royalty owners, be able to plan for 1981 (and years thereafter) to minimize the WPT. Bills to exempt the first ten barrels per day of production for royalty owners have been introduced in the Senate (S.B. 2521) by Senator Lloyd Bentsen (D-Texas) and Senator Robert Dole (R-Kansas) and the House (H.R. 7481) by Congressman J.J. Pickle (D-Texas). However, these bills limit the exemption to one per related group, *i.e.,* one per family or one per controlled group of entities.[38]

In summary, there seem to be no current opportunities for tax planning available to royalty owners. Moreover,

---

37 "Reconciliations: Substantial Obstacles Face Efforts to Increase FY1981 Revenues," *Daily Tax Report,* July 18, 1980, p. K2.

38 S.B. 2521 and H.R. 7481, 96th Congress, 2d Sess., June 3, 1980.

the tax relief pending in Congress does not offer any obvious tax planning opportunities because the proposed legislation has been designed to preclude more than one taxpayer among a group of taxable persons who are related from qualifying for a specific tax relief provision. In conclusion, the royalty owner's nonoperating, economic interest in oil production normally places him (her or it) at the mercy of the independent producer, integrated oil company, or other operator in respect to the level of production from a well where the use of more technology or the incurring of greater production costs could result in more production and royalty income.

Oil and gas royalty owners may be entitled to $1,000 credit for windfall profit tax payments

As a temporary relief for the unexpected impact of the Windfall Profit Tax on royalty owners, Congress enacted a $1,000 credit for 1980 only. This article reviews the qualifications for the credit, the restrictions on its availability, and presents an example of its operation.

by **ROBERT L. BLACK, CPA,** *and* **CRAIG E. REESE, Ph.D.,** *Austin, Texas*

Although taxpayers who receive oil and gas royalties are permitted by Section 164(a)(5) to deduct the Windfall Profit Tax (WPT)[1] allocable to such income, Section 6429 permits a credit of up to $1,000, in lieu of such a deduction for the WPT tax.

The Royalty Owners Credit (ROC) applies only to the WPT "paid" by qualified royalty owners during the period from March 1, 1980 to December 31, 1980.

Technically, the amount paid is an overpayment of WPT, which may be credited on behalf of the taxpayer or refunded. Most individual taxpayers will use the credit method by claiming the qualifying amount on their Federal income tax return (Form 1040).

Determining the ROC for individuals may be difficult in many situations. Given the last minute enactment of this statute, there are no Regulations or Revenue Rulings to clarify Section 6429 and the brief explanation provided in the Conference Committee Report. In addition, the IRS neither includes a line on Form 1040 indicating the amount of ROC to be claimed nor refers to it in the accompanying instructions. Consequently, many eligible taxpayers may overlook the availability of this credit, although they could demand the amount later by filing a claim for refund. At this time, the IRS is suggesting that taxpayers insert the amount of ROC claimed on line 62 ("total payments") of their Form 1040. This must be accompanied by a completed Form 6249-A (Royalty Owner's Credit for Overpaid Windfall Profit Tax) or Form 6249.

Form 6249-A is generally for individual taxpayers whose WPT liability and WPT withheld are less than the maximum amount of the ROC for which they are eligible. Individuals or their relatives who are shareholders in family farm corporations must use Form 6249 to claim a Section 6429 credit. If an individual must share the ROC with family members, Form 6249 must be used except where the only family member with whom a ROC must be shared is a spouse with whom the individual is filing a joint return. Individual royalty owners eligible for the ROC have an extension for the filing of Form 1040s for 1980. Such individuals may defer filing their Form 1040s until June 15, 1981, without being subject to a penalty for underpayment of Federal income tax for the period April 15-June 15. However, such taxpayers will be subject to the payment of interest at the current 12% annual rate on any underpayment of tax for that two-month period.

Including the ROC in the payment section rather than the credit section of Form 1040 page 2 would seem to minimize any conflict concerning its parity with or precedence over other credits, some of which, *e.g.*, investment credits, can be carried back or forward. While the ROC is not transferable to other years, its refundability is insured by its treatment as a payment; when combined with other payments, any amount of ROC in excess of the tax liability will be automatically refunded to a taxpayer or applied against 1981 estimated tax. Nevertheless, the ROC is considered a "credit" for 1040 purposes, and lacking specific instructions (except line 3, Form 6249-A), one would be inclined to list it in the credit section (lines 38-47) of Form 1040. This must be guarded against because to do so could lead to losing the credit if, when combined with other credits, the total exceeds the income tax due. Such an action would become even more confusing as the

Article reprinted courtesy of *Taxation for Accountants*, March 1981, pp. 170-175 priority for crediting each separate credit would then come into play.

Qualifications

Owners. The above discussion concentrated on individuals, because they constitute the majority of eligible royalty owners. There are, nevertheless, two other types of royalty owners qualifying for the $1,000 credit or refund—estates and qualified family-farm corporations, each of which also are permitted a credit on their 1980 returns or a payment by filing a refund claim.

To be eligible, an estate must have been in existence at any time during the period March 1, 1980, to December 31, 1980, and during the same time have received qualifying royalty income. Qualifying estates that have since terminated should either (1) claim a credit on their final return if unfiled, (2) amend the final return, or (3) file a claim for refund. Active estates can claim the credit on their 1980 returns, as long as some portion of the period covered by the return overlaps the March to December period.

Family farm corporations (hereinafter FFC) must meet a restrictive set of criteria to qualify. In general, the statute refers to Section 2032A (regarding estate tax valuations) for the definition of an FFC. Eligibility requires that: (1) the corporation was in existence on June 25, 1980; (2) all outstanding shares of stock were held by members of the same family (defined in Section 2032(e)(2)) at all times after June 24, 1980 and before 1981; and (3) the corporation held 80% in value of its assets (other than qualified royalty interests) on such date for use for farming purposes (according to Section 2032A(e)(5)).

Section 6429(d)(4)(C) is unclear concerning the relevant date. The term "such date" is used in this subparagraph but has no antecedent date in subparagraph (4) or subsection (d). Furthermore, both of the two preceding subparagraphs to which it might apply have dates in them. Subparagraph (B) refers to June 24, 1980 and January 1, 1981, and subparagraph (A) refers to June 25, 1980. Apparently June 25 was intended to be the applicable date; yet the 80% test of subparagraph (C) could be more easily performed at December 31, for which these corporations would more likely have financial statements available.

Production. A qualified royalty owner is entitled to the credit on crude oil removed between March 1 and December 31, 1980, and attributable to an economic interest of such royalty owner except for an operating mineral interest. For definition of "operating mineral interest," Section 6429 refers to Section 614(d), which limits an operating interest to: ". . . an interest in respect of which the costs of production of the mineral are required to be taken into account by the taxpayer for purposes of computing the 50 percent limitation provided for in Section 613, or would be so required if the mine, well, or other natural deposit were in the production stage."

Under Reg. 1.614-2(b), the term "operating mineral interest" does not include royalty interests or similar interests such as production payments or net profits interests. Consequently, what is typified as a royalty owner's credit is, in fact, applicable to a broader spectrum of economic interests in oil. Similarly, by referring to Section 614(d), the question of whether certain "carried interests" would be eligible for the ROC is raised. Specifically, the carried party in some arrangements might be eligible for the ROC by not being considered the holder of an operating interest for these purposes.

Limits on ROC

Section 6429(c) limits the availability of the $1,000 credit among related taxpayers. It is designed both to prevent an individual from splitting qualified economic interests so as to reap greater benefits and to limit the benefits received by individuals and corporations linked by certain kinship or common ownership.

Allocation within a family. An individual and the spouse and minor children of such individual are treated as one unit for ROC purposes. Regardless of how much qualified royalty production they own as separate interests or the number of individuals and returns involved, these family members must share a single $1,000 ROC. Allocation among the family members is determined "in proportion to their respective qualified royalty production" according to Section 6429(c)(2).

This mandatory allocation may cause particular problems, including instances of noncompliance, when spouses are separated but not yet divorced or when royalty-owning children reside with one of two separated or divorced parents. Separated spouses, especially those in community property states, must be alert to an automatic allocation if an economic interest in oil is held jointly or as community property.

Similarly, control over ROC filing by minor children not living with a qualifying taxpayer and limited availability of production information for ROC computations will create difficulty. For instance, how should such minor children be included in the allocation computation if their divorced parents both have eligible royalty income? Are they to be counted in both computations, the principal one, or neither? Section 6429 would seem to imply that they should be included in both computations, but this seems unfair because they could hardly claim a credit or refund determined by combining the two households. It should not be forgotten that minor children with no Federal income tax liability can still benefit from the ROC provision by filing a claim for refund.

Allocation between FFC corporations. An individual owning stock in two or more qualified family farm corporations must allocate the $1,000 maximum credit among them. Such allocation is, under Section 6429(c)(4), "in proportion to their respective qualified royalty production."

Interestingly, there is no mention of any proration between corporations according to the differing ownership interests of the individual who, because of common ownership, triggers the allocation. Thus, for example, it would seem that two FFCs with the same production for the ROC period must split the $1,000 evenly. That is, each would be entitled to a $500 ROC, even if the shareholder causing the split owns 100% of the one and only 1% of the other (99% of which is owned by other family members as defined by Section 2032A(e)(2)).

Allocation between FFC and individuals. For taxpayers with both individual and FFC interests, Section 6429(c)(3) establishes a hierarchy for allocating an available $1,000 between them. First, the credit is allocated between FFCs (as above), which may absorb the full credit or restrict the remaining amount depending on the proportionate interests—as explained next—of the individual. Then, each FFC amount (after allocation to other FFCs owned by the taxpayer) is multiplied by the ratio of fair market value of shares owned by the individual in the present FFC to the fair market value of all of the FFC's shares. According to the IRS Fact Sheet (Document 6671), June 25, 1980 should be used to determine the FMV of FFC shares. Finally, the resulting amount reduces the $1,000 ROC available to an individual and his family. The remaining ROC available to the individual is calculated as follows:

$$\$1{,}000 - \left[\text{FFC Amount} \times \frac{\text{FMV of Individual's Shares in the FFC}}{\text{FMV of Total Shares of the FFC}}\right]$$

CRAIG E. REESE, Ph.D., and ROBERT L. BLACK, Ph.D., are Assistant Professors, Taxation/Accounting, at Texas A&M University, College Station, Texas. They have written on the Windfall Profit Tax for the Oil and Gas Tax Quarterly and a previous article on this subject by Prof. Reese appeared in the May, 1980 issue of TAXATION FOR ACCOUNTANTS.

The individual's family and their respective FFC amounts and ownership interests are to be treated as if *one* individual held them. Application to multiple FFCs is implied by a reference to corporations in the Section 6429(c)(3) paragraph heading and by the reference within paragraph (3) to paragraph (4) concerning multiple FFCs. Therefore, it seems that the above bracketed amount is determined for each separate FFC, if more than one, but on the basis of all family-owned shares in each FFC and applied to all FFC interests. These bracketed formula amounts would then be added to determine the balance of $1,000 still available. As a last step, the allocation procedures for sharing the ROC among family members, if applicable, must be applied to the unused portion of the credit.

Qualified royalty production. Although this analysis refers to "qualified royalty production," nowhere is this term defined. As already discussed, Section 6429(d)(2) defines the term only insofar as the types of eligible owners of crude oil interests and the relevant period of production are concerned. Nowhere in the statute is there an explanation of how to compute "qualified royalty production." It may be that the paragraph intends any measurement to be according to the number of barrels of taxable crude oil removed during the period March 1 to December 31, 1980. This inference follows from the definition of a similar term in Sections 4992(d) "qualified production of oil," used for allocating within related groups the 1,000 barrels per day of independent producers, who receive favorable WPT treatment on such production. Nevertheless, until administrative guidance is received, this term might be assumed, among several interpretations, to mean the removal or selling price of extracted production or the WPT paid thereon.

WPT deduction adjustment. Section 280D, "Portion of Chapter 45 Taxes for Which Credit or Refund is Allowable Under Section 6429" requires a *mandatory* reduction of the WPT paid and claimed as a deduction in computing taxable income from these economic interests in oil. The reduction is required *regardless* of whether the taxpayer actually receives a tax benefit by taking the credit or even files a return claiming the credit or a refund.

Comprehensive example of ROC

Several aspects of calculating the $1,000 credit available to royalty owners will be illustrated in the following comprehensive example.

Example. Xavier paid $5,000 of WPT in connection with $45,000 in gross royalty income on 15,000 barrels of production. Xavier owns 50% of Apples Farm, Inc., ("Apples") and his wife, Yvonne, owns the other 50%. Xavier also owns 33⅓% of the FMV of shares in Oranges Farm, Inc., ("Oranges"); the remaining shares are owned equally by Xavier's two brothers. Finally, Yvonne owns 25% of Nuts Farm, Inc., ("Nuts") which is owned by her family and their unrelated lawyer. Allocations of the ROC allowed Xavier, Yvonne and the FFCs would depend on the following factors:

	1980 WPT paid	*Barrels of qualified royalty prod.*	*% of FMV owned by Xavier (X) or Yvonne (Y)*
Apples Farm, Inc.	$2,000	4,000	100% (X & Y)
Oranges Farm, Inc.	$4,000	6,000	33⅓% (X)
Nuts Farm, Inc.	$8,000	10,000	25% (Y)

First, qualification as a family farm corporation must be determined. Apples and Oranges are 100% owned by the spouses or Xavier's brothers (lineal descendants of his grandparents per Section 2032A (e)(2)); thus, assuming at least 80% of the non-royalty farming assets were held on June 25, 1980, Apples and Oranges would be qualified family farm corporations. Nuts is not an FFC: some of its shares are held by an unrelated lawyer, so it does not meet the test in Section 6429(d)(4)(B) requiring *all* shares to be held by family members.

Having determined eligibility, our next step is to allocate a single $1,000 credit between the two FFCs, presumably according to the number of barrels of qualified royalty production by each. This allocation is required because Xavier owns shares in each FFC. Since Apples and Oranges had production of 4,000 and 6,000 barrels, respectively, the potential credits would be $400 (4/10 × $1,000) for Apples and $600 (6/10 × $1,000) for Oranges.

A strict interpretation of Section 6429(c)(4) would not have required an allocation of the $1,000 ROC between the FFCs if Yvonne owned the only "family" interest in Apples and similarly Xavier owned the only interest in Oranges. This follows from Section 6429(c)(3)(B)(i), which imputes treatment as one "individual" for all family members only to the division between individuals and corporations in subparagraph (A). That is, paragraph (4) seems to be outside this redefinition of an individual for purposes of the statute. Nevertheless, this may be contrary to the intent of the statute, which generally attempts to aggregate interests within a paragraph (c)(2) type of family.

Furthermore, nowhere does the statute suggest how the credit should be divided, if at all, when several farm families own many FFCs in interlocking arrangements. For instance, in the present example, how would Oranges' credit be calculated if at least one of Xavier's brothers (who together own 66⅔%) also owns an interest(s) in one or more other qualifying FFCs?

For purposes of determining Xavier and Yvonne's joint ROC as family members, the maximum $1,000 must be reduced by the proportionate ROC benefit they realize through Apples and Oranges. According to the formula earlier presented, all of Apples' $400 credit will offset their potential $1,000 ROC, because they jointly own 100% of the corporation. Xavier owns only 33⅓% of Oranges; assuming the FMV is proportionately the same, the formula reduction would equal $200 (33⅓% of the $600 allocated to Oranges). Total reductions from FFC interests in both Apples and Oranges would therefore equal $600.

The remaining $400 ($1,000 maximum ROC less $600 attributed to FFCs) could be used as a credit by Xavier on a married filing separate return or Xavier and Yvonne on a joint return. However, if Xavier and Yvonne's minor child, Zeon, had a qualified royalty interest with $1,200 of WPT paid and 5,000 barrels of qualified royalty production, their available ROC would be scaled down even further. Specifically, the remaining $400 would be allocated $100 (¼ × $400) to Zeon and $300 (¾ × $400) to Xavier. These amounts are calculated according to each family member's respective share of total qualified royalty production. Zeon's 5,000 barrels plus Xavier's 15,000 barrels equal ¼ and ¾ respectively. If for some reason Zeon had less than $100 of WPT paid, then the applicable ROC would be limited to this lesser amount (with Xavier apparently unable to use the residual).

Finally, taxable royalty income would be affected by the mandatory adjustment to the WPT deduction for the allowable ROC that could be claimed as a credit or refunded. Results of this adjustment for each taxpayer in the example are set out in the following schedule.

Taxpayer	*1980 WPT paid*	*Allowable ROC*	*Adjusted WPT deductible*
Apples (FFC)	$2,000	$400	$1,600
Oranges (FFC)	$4,000	$600	$3,400
Nuts (not FFC)	$8,000	None	$8,000
Xavier (individual)	$5,000	$300	$4,700
Yvonne (spouse)	None	None	None
Zeon (minor child)	$1,200	$100	$1,100

In summary, Apples and Oranges have split a $1,000 family farm ROC between them: Nuts was

CITATIONS

1 See Reese, *New windfall profit tax on crude oil: How it works and whom it affects*, 24 TA 291 (May, 1980).
2 Reg. 150.4997-a(c)(2).
3 Reg. 150.6402-1.
4 Ibid.
5 Reg. 150.4995-3(e).
6 Reg. 150.4996-1(b)(2).
7 Williams and Myers, *Manual Oil and Gas Terms*, 4th ed. (Matthew Bender, 1976), p. 362.
8 *Kirby Petroleum Co.*, 326 U.S. 599, 46-1 USTC ¶9149, 34 AFTR 526 (S. Ct., 1946).
9 Reg. 1.614-2(b).
10 Reg. 150.4996-1(b)(3).
11 See Reg. 51.4988-2(b).
12 See Reg. 150.4996-1(b).

not allowed an ROC because it is not an FFC; and Xavier and Zeon, as members of a family which also owns qualifying FFCs, have divided an ROC within their family after reducing the potential $1,000 for their proportionate benefit from interests in FFCs.

Withholding adjustments

The withholding problems for the royalty owner do not ensue until after receipt of the final calendar-year payment and the final monthly or annual production statement in January or February of the following year. A royalty owner is treated as having paid any amount of WPT withheld on the last day of the first February after the calendar year in which the oil was removed from the premises, *i.e.*, February 28, 1981, for 1980. In most cases, the WPT withheld will be identical to the royalty owner's actual liability. Where there is a discrepancy, the first purchaser (or operator) is responsible for informing the royalty owner and the IRS of both the former's overwithholding or underwithholding and the total WPT withheld during the calendar year.[2] In practice, the royalty owner is notified of withholding problems by the purchaser (or operator) on March 31 or earlier with a WPT Information Return (on WPT Form 6248 or similar statement containing information required by Reg. 150.4997-2(c)).

Where *overwithholding* has occurred, the royalty owner can either (1) take a credit when filing a Federal income tax or WPT return, or (2) file a claim for refund of overpayment of Federal tax. Therefore, if a royalty owner's WPT liability is less than the WPT withheld by the first purchaser (or operator), the royalty owner may file a claim for refund (with WPT Form 6249 or 6249-A attached) as of the last day of the first February following the tax year. On the other hand, an overpayment of WPT as of the last day of the first February following a tax year may be credited upon the royalty owner's filing of either a Federal income tax return (with WPT Form 6249 or 6249-A attached) or a Federal Excise Tax Return (Forms 720 and 6047 with WPT Form 6249). Thus, royalty owners may reduce their Federal income tax liability by the amount of overwithheld WPT, including that amount resulting from the $1,000 ROC, on 1980 crude oil production on a 1980 Federal income tax return.[3]

To correct an *underwithholding* situation, the royalty owner can either (1) file an annual WPT Return (Form 720 along with WPT Form 6248) accompanied by payment of the liability due on or before the last day of the second month following the calendar year in which the crude oil was produced, or (2) deposit the amount of the underpayment accompanied by a deposit form (FTD Form 504) with a financial institution that is an authorized Federal depository on or before the last day for filing the annual WPT Return.[4] Thus, a royalty owner may not defer payment of a WPT liability until a timely Federal income tax return is filed, because a royalty owner's WPT liability is due on the last day of the second month following a calendar year.[5] However, the ROC should offset the WPT underpayment of most individuals and estates with royalty income.

Other considerations

Partnerships, estates and trusts. For WPT purposes, a partnership holding an economic interest in crude oil is not treated as a producer; rather, under Section 4996(a)(1)(B), the partnership crude oil production and royalty income is allocated among the partners and the partners are treated as the producers of partnership crude oil. Therefore, partnerships must furnish to their partners any information related to the production of crude oil, including WPT payments and liability, within 15 days after receipt thereof from a purchaser or operator. Partnerships with both operating and royalty (nonoperating) interests will need to be cautious of the way their WPT is reported to partners. If WPT for royalty interests were less than $1,000, then a partner might inadvertently attempt to claim an ROC, based on the combined WPT, in excess of the eligible royalty amount.

Trusts and estates are treated similarly in respect to both the determination of WPT payments and liability and the computation of percentage depletion for Federal income purposes. A trust or estate, rather than its beneficiaries, is considered the producer of oil for WPT purposes.[6] In contrast, grantor trusts whose income is taxable to the grantor would not be considered the producer of oil because transfers of oil producing property interests thereto are revocable. While individuals (including partners), estates and family farm corporations may qualify for the $1,000 ROC, trusts, when treated as separate entities, and the individual benefiiciaries thereof, would not be eligible for the ROC on WPT paid by trusts because they are not among the three eligible types of producers specified by Section 6429.

Generally, a tax-exempt group's share of the revenue from crude oil production is subject to the WPT unless the net revenue from the crude oil produced therefrom is dedicated to specified educational or medical purposes, or is dedicated to a public purpose. Certainly, non-qualifying religious and charitable institutions were surprised by the imposition of the WPT on their share of the revenue from crude oil production just because they do not satisfy the rather restrictive requirements established for exemption from the WPT. Ironically, their tax-exempt status for Federal income tax purposes precludes their benefiting from the Section 164(a)(5) income tax deduction for WPT paid or accrued, except where the tax-exempt group has a working interest in an oil-producing property, *i.e.,* earns unrelated business income. Finally, the Section 6429 $1,000 income tax credit for WPT paid or accrued in 1980 is unavailable to tax-exempt groups.

Net profits interests. A net profits interest (NPI) is a share of gross production from a mineral property measured as a stated percentage of net profit from the operation of that property.[7] An NPI is a royalty interest if it reflects a part of the price, rent or consideration that a lessee pays to a lessor as remuneration for the use of a mineral producing property.[8] An NPI is unlike an overriding or fee royalty because income accruing to the former is net of certain development and operating costs specified in a net profits agreement. Consequently, it is only a royalty economic interest, rather than an operating economic interest, in mineral producing property insofar as the net profits agreement provides that a stated percentage of the operator's net profit accrues to the lessor and that only the lessee is directly liable for operating costs. That is, the lessor can not be liable for any share of operating losses, but such losses may reduce the lessor's future net profits.[9]

Inasmuch as the WPT reduces the net profit from the operation of a crude oil producing property, the net royalty of a lessor with an NPI is reduced by a portion of the total WPT paid on the gross production of the leased property. However, owners of NPIs compute, for WPT purposes, their share of production without regard to any reduction in profits for the WPT paid thereon.[10]

Example. X holds hold the entire working interest in a property subject to a 20% net profits interest held by Y. Before the division of net profits, X is to recover from oil production all costs, including taxes. The property produces 40 barrels of taxable crude oil sold at $30 per barrel. Expenses total $450 (exclusive of windfall profit tax). Regardless of whether under the contract the term "taxes" includes the windfall profit tax, Y is taxable as the producer of five barrels, the number of barrels attributable to 20% of the net profit computed without regard to the windfall profit tax ($1,200 gross proceeds less expenses of $450 equals $750 net profit: 20% equals $150 or five barrels at $30 per barrel). X is the producer of 35 barrels.

If oil were regular WPT Tier 1 and WPT paid thereon equaled $460, Y would receive a net royalty of $58, which apparently represents $150 gross income less WPT paid of $92. Therefore, it seems that the Section 4988 net income limitation would, when applied, result in an overpayment of WPT.[11]

Advanced royalties and lease bonuses. Although lease bonuses are considered royalties for depletion purposes, WPT would not seem to be payable thereon inasmuch as such payments are made upon execution of the lease and before any oil production occurs. In addition, the lessee must capitalize such payments. In contrast, in the case of advanced royalties recoupable from subsequent production, WPT could be incurred by the royalty owner but only to the extent it is recouped by the lessee payor in the year paid; this results from the treatment of production payments as an economic interest for WPT purposes as provided in Section 636.[12]

Tax preference implications. There is perhaps an unforeseen benefit of the ROC for some taxpayers subject to the minimum tax on excess intangible drilling costs of Section 57(a)(11). Because taxpayers are required to reduce their WPT deduction by the amount of ROC allowable, the resulting increased net income from oil will eliminate dollar for dollar the IDC tax preference. Where there is minimum tax due, this will mitigate somewhat this provision that frequently applies to passive investors in oil drilling ventures, *e.g.,* oil tax shelter partnerships.

More specifically, any amount of IDC tax preference may be decreased by a taxpayer's net income from oil properties. This determination is made by aggregating all oil properties of the taxpayer. Consequently, a taxpayer can shift the "lost" portion of a WPT deduction, which resulted from an allowable ROC adjustment, to offset an unrelated IDC tax preference from another oil property.

Example. Partner P in TX oil drilling partnership receives an IDC tax preference of $27,000. P also is a producer eligible for the ROC by having paid $3,500 in WPT on different property(s). P's net income from oil would increase by the $1,000 allowable ROC; this increase would cause the IDC tax preference to decrease by $1,000 to $26,000 (saving $150 in minimum tax) because of this ROC adjustment.

Moreover, if a taxpayer also is eligible for the 50% maximum tax on personal service income, the reduction in an IDC tax preference will cause a dollar-for-dollar increase in personal service taxable income, thus saving tax.

Interest limitations. While the tax preference rules permit recovery of part of the WPT deduction replaced by the ROC, no adjustment need be made for excess investment interest (Section 163(d)). WPT paid is not expressly part of the net investment income computation, so there is no adjustment for the ROC, and thus no detrimental effect to potential excess investment interest. ★

Part VII

Withholding Adjustments and Refunds

Generally, the WPT is withheld by the first purchaser of oil from the property. By special arrangement, the operator, the producer, or an agent called a *qualified disburser* can act as the withholding agent. Frequently, due to estimations, incorrect information, or a change in a producer's status, errors in withholding are made.

Errors in withholding may result in either over- or underwithholding. Full adjustment of errors in withholding should be made through under- or overwithholding in the next payment to the same producer. Where the next payment after discovery of a withholding error is inadequate to make the withholding adjustment, then the adjustment by over- or underwithholding must be made in subsequent payments to the same producer. This look-back adjustment does not go on forever. All withholding adjustments must be made through payments for crude oil removed during the same calendar year in which the withholding error occurred and prior to furnishing the annual statement or return (on or before March 31 following the calendar year of removal).

How the claim for credit or refund of overpaid windfall profit tax is filed depends on the situation under which the overpayment occurred. If the overpayment is attributable to oil subject to withholding (some oil is not subject to withholding), a claim for refund is filed on Form 843 after the February following the end of the taxable year. Credit for the tax applied in reduction of future liability can be claimed on the producer's federal tax return —excise or income.

If the overpayments are attributable to oil not subject to withholding, a claim for refund, applied for on Form 843, may be filed on or after the date for filing the quarterly return for such taxable period (last day of the second month following a taxable period). A claim for credit should be made on the quarterly WPT return. Whenever an overpayment is due to the net income limitation, the claim for credit or refund must be applied for on the federal income tax return for the year.

Generally where underwithholding has occurred and was not corrected in subsequent payments, the additional tax must be paid either by filing the annual WPT return or depositing the monies at a Federal Reserve Bank or other authorized financial institution.

LITIGATING THE WINDFALL PROFIT TAX

Robert L. Moore, II
James W. Midgley*

The legislative history of the Crude Oil Windfall Profit Tax Act indicates that Congress was aware of what it called "enforcement difficulties" encountered by the Department of Energy (DOE) in administering price controls.[1] Congress sought to avoid such perceived difficulties with respect to the Windfall Profit Tax, by imposing strict requirements for filing tax returns and for certifying information, by adding restrictions in anticipation of potential areas of abuse, and by subjecting noncomplying persons to civil and criminal penalties. As a result, industry now faces the problem of complying with extremely complex legislation. Already described by many as an administrative nightmare, the Windfall

---

* Robert L. Moore, II and James W. Midgley are partners in the law firm of Miller & Chevalier, Washington, D.C.

1 See H.R. Rep. No. 96-304, 96th Cong., 1st Sess. 43 (1979); S. Rep. No. 96-394, 96th Cong., 1st Sess. 66 (1979).

Article reprinted courtesy of *Oil & Gas Tax Quarterly*, March 1981, pp. 443–458

Profit Tax seems likely to result in litigation in numerous areas.[2]

This article presents an overview of the enforcement and litigation framework of the Windfall Profit Tax Act as applied to taxpayer/producers, and highlights some of the substantive legal issues which are likely to arise in proceedings under the Act, particularly in regard to the problems of incorporating DOE price control concepts. Additionally, this article discusses some of the considera tions involved in selecting the forum in which to contest a windfall profit tax liability.

The Enforcement and Litigation Framework

The Act, together with long-standing provisions of the Internal Revenue Code, provides specific rules for when a taxpayer/producer may commence a contest of its windfall profit tax liability. Where oil is subject to withholding, the producer of such oil is deemed to have paid withheld taxes as of the last day of February of the following calendar year,[3] and no deficiency may be assessed, or claim for refund commenced, prior to that date.[4]

Integrated oil companies required to make periodic deposits of tax must file quarterly returns of windfall profit tax by the end of the second month following each quarter.[5] As to oil covered by an integrated oil company's quarterly return, a deficiency may be assessed or a claim

2 The constitutionality of the Windfall Profit Tax is presently in litigation in Energy Consumers & Producers Ass'n v. Miller, Civil No. 80-132-C (E.D. Okla., April 3, 1980). Additionally, the Independent Petroleum Association of America and others have recently filed suit challenging the constitutionality of the tax. See Independent Petroleum Ass'n of Am., et al. v. United States of America, No. C80-0302 (D. Wyo., October 14, 1980).

3 I.R.C. § 4995(a)(4).

4 I.R.C. § 4995(a)(8).

5 I.R.C. § 6076(a).

for refund filed at any time after the filing of the quarterly return.[6]

Litigation of windfall profit tax liability can be commenced either by contesting a deficiency assessment or by filing suit for refund. The deficiency procedures are the same as those applicable to income, estate, and gift taxes. Thus, upon the assessment of a deficiency, a producer may pay the tax assessed or, within ninety days after notice of a deficiency, petition the United States Tax Court for a redetermination of the deficiency. Decisions of the Tax Court are appealable to the United States Court of Appeals for the judicial circuit in which the taxpayer/producer is located.

Producers seeking to institute suits for refund must first file a claim for refund with the Internal Revenue Service.[7] A claim for refund must be filed either within three years after a return of windfall profit tax is filed, or two years after payment of the tax, whichever occurs later.[8] Where no return of windfall profit tax is filed by a producer because the tax is collected through withholding, then the "return" used for computing the time for filing a refund claim will be the producer's income tax return for the year in which oil is removed.[9]

The time for filing a claim for refund (and for assessing a deficiency) will be longer with respect to any tax resulting from a so-called "Department of Energy change." If the DOE reclassifies a particular property or crude oil from a property, the period of limitations for tax attributable to the reclassification is extended until one year after the DOE action becomes final.[10]

---

6 Prop. Treas. Reg. § 150.6402-1(b)(1).

7 I.R.C. § 7422(a).

8 I.R.C. § 6511(a).

9 I.R.C. § 6511(h)(1).

10 I.R.C. §§ 6501(a)(2), 6511(h)(2).

If a claim for refund is denied (or deemed to have been denied by the passage of six months), a producer is entitled to file suit for refund either in the United States Court of Claims or in the United States District Court for the judicial district in which the taxpayer/producer is located. Such a suit must be filed within two years in the event of an actual (rather than deemed) denial of a claim for refund.[11]

Likely Areas of Controversy

The Windfall Profit Tax incorporates both DOE price control concepts and income tax concepts and attempts to blend them into an excise tax. A number of these borrowed concepts are controversial, however, and thus are likely to create further controversy and litigation.

Controversial DOE Concepts

The Windfall Profit Tax incorporates the DOE energy regulations[12] and utilizes those regulations in the two basic steps necessary to calculate the amount of tax owed: (i) the determination of the amount of "windfall profit" subject to the tax; and (ii) the determination of the tax rate to be applied to particular crude oil. By incorporating the energy regulations, the tax in turn incorporates a variety of existing disputes concerning the meaning and proper interpretation of the energy regulations.

A threshold question under the tax is how much deference should (or must) the Secretary of the Treasury give to the DOE's interpretations of the energy regulations, or to judicial decisions interpreting the energy regulations in litigation between DOE and the industry. Congress has implicitly addressed this question in the legislative history relating to the definitions of removal price and newly

11 I.R.C. § 6532.

12 § 4996(b)(8) of the tax incorporates the DOE regulations in effect on either March 1, 1979, or June 1, 1979.

discovered crude oil, and in the treatment of multiple completion wells. In each of these instances, the DOE's interpretation of the energy regulations was in litigation at the time the tax was pending before Congress.

The tax generally defines "removal price" as the sales price for crude oil.[13] The Conference Report specifically invites the Secretary to further define removal price by regulation.[14] The Conference Report also notes that the term "removal price" is meant to signify the same concept as the term "produced and sold," which is used in the energy regulations for purposes of calculating base production control levels.

The term "produced and sold" was recently clarified in *Tenneco Oil Co.* v. *FEA*,[15] where the Temporary Emergency Court of Appeals determined that the term "sale" is to be given its ordinary meaning, *i.e.*, a transfer of title for valuable consideration. Under the facts of that case, beneficial use or consumption of crude oil by the producer in the production process (for example, to power a steam generator located on the property) would not be deemed a "sale" and thus would not be included as part of the property's base production control level. Similarly, the Conference Report states that for purposes of the tax, crude oil reinjected into the producing property or used in the powering of production is not sold or removed, and therefore will not be taxed. The Conference Report thus incorporates the *Tenneco* holding in the Windfall Profit Tax.[16]

13 I.R.C. § 4988(c).

14 See H.R. Rep. No. 96-817, 96th Cong., 2d Sess. 114 (1980).

15 4 CCH Energy Mgt. Para. 26,174 (Em. App. December 3, 1979).

16 See H.R. Rep. No. 96-817, *supra* at 105-06. Recently, DOE issued a notice of proposed rulemaking in which it proposes to adopt a definition of "produced and sold" that is contrary to *Tenneco.* See 45 Fed. Reg. 42,222, 42,225-26 (June 23, 1980). If the proposal is adopted, any disposition of crude oil for which value or benefit is directly or indirectly received, including its use as a powerhouse fuel or for reinjection, would constitute production and sale from the property. Hence, if the proposal is adopted, the DOE and tax definitions will be different.

The second interpretive issue addressed by Congress is the definition of "newly discovered" crude oil. The tax defines newly discovered oil according to the June 1979 energy regulation's definition:[17] domestic crude oil which is either produced from a new lease on the Outer Continental Shelf, or from a property not on the Outer Continental Shelf from which no crude oil was produced in calendar year 1978.

Even though the definition of newly discovered oil is identical for purposes of the tax and the DOE pricing regulations, the interpretation of the definition is significantly different for the two purposes. The Conference Report states that for purposes of the Windfall Profit Tax, a property is disqualified only if it had commercial production during 1978.[18] Production incident to exploration or testing will not disqualify a property's production from newly discovered status. In contrast, the Department of Energy in Ruling 1980-3 has interpreted the definition of newly discovered oil to exclude *all* crude oil from properties which had *any* production during 1978. In the Ruling, DOE states that irrespective of the interpretation given to the definition by the Conference Report, that interpretation is only for windfall profit tax purposes and "cannot retroactively change the meaning of the term . . . for DOE pricing purposes . . . ."[19]

---

17 I.R.C. § 4991(e)(2).

18 H.R. Rep. No. 96-817, *supra* at 98.

19 3 CCH Energy Mgt. Para. 16,077 n.3. DOE has proposed to amend the definition of newly discovered crude oil for pricing purposes in a way that would bring its meaning closer to its windfall profit tax meaning. The proposal would define a newly discovered crude oil property in terms of a lack of "production and sales" in commercial quantities in 1978. But the proposal would also define "production and sales" as any disposition which directly or indirectly benefits the producer. See 45 Fed. Reg. 42,222 (June 23, 1980). The notice of proposed rulemaking asked for comments on "the degree of need for uniformity in the definition of 'newly discovered crude oil' for purposes of DOE's pricing regulations and for purposes of the windfall profit tax." *Id.* at 42,223 n.l.

The third interpretation of the energy regulations in the legislative history involves the proper treatment of multiple completions within a single well. DOE took the position in Rulings 1975-42 and 1977-2 that multiple completions can be counted as separate wells for purposes of determining stripper well status, but only if each completion is produced through a separate tubing string. In discussing heavy oil, the Conference Report adopted this interpretation for purposes of the Windfall Profit Tax even though this interpretation had been held invalid for DOE pricing purposes by a district court.[20]

These examples demonstrate that the interpretation of the DOE energy regulations by DOE or even by the courts, when done for purposes of the DOE pricing scheme, are influential but not necessarily binding on the Treasury for purposes of the Windfall Profit Tax. Indeed, the legislative history of the Windfall Profit Tax Act shows that Congress intended for the Secretary of the Treasury to have ultimate interpretive authority. The Senate Finance Committee Report states:

> Since the energy regulations adopted by the tax do not purport to embody a comprehensive compilation of rules pertaining to all relevant crude oil matters, it is anticipated that the Secretary will give due consideration to the various administrative rulings and judicial decisions which have interpreted or which construe those regulations. To the extent such rulings and decisions are consistent with the provisions of the committee substitute, it is anticipated they will be followed by the Secretary; to the extent they are not consistent entirely with the committee's substitute, it is antici-

---

20 See H.R. Rep. No. 96-817, *supra* at 102. The district court was reversed by the Temporary Emergency Court of Appeals subsequent to the Conference Report's publication. See Energy Consumers & Producers Ass'n, Inc. v. DOE, 4 CCH Energy Mgt. Para. 26,198 (Em. App., April 4, 1980).

pated that the Secretary will attempt to reconcile them with the least change feasible.[21]

Thus, Congress expected the Secretary of the Treasury to follow the energy regulations, and interpretations of those regulations, to the extent they are consistent with the purposes of the Act. The Act even empowers the Secretary to prescribe regulations which change the application of the energy regulations to the tax if necessary.[22]

As noted above, by incorporating the DOE regulations into the Windfall Profit Tax, the tax in turn incorporates a variety of disputes concerning the meaning of those regulations. One such dispute involves the DOE definition of "property," which is expressly incorporated in the Proposed Regulations under the Windfall Profit Tax.[23]

"Property" was originally defined by the energy regulations as "the right which arises from a lease or from a fee interest to produce domestic crude petroleum."[24] This definition was adopted as part of the two-tier pricing system of old and new oil. Like the two-tier system, it was intended to be part of a short-lived, temporary system of price controls. It was also intended to be consistent with normal accounting practices so as to minimize disruption to normal business practices.[25]

Virtually no guidance was given to producers on the meaning of this definition until two years later, when

---

21 S. Rep. No. 96-394, *supra* at 57.

22 I.R.C. § 4997(b).

23 Prop. Treas. Reg. § 150.4996-1(i). "Except as otherwise provided in section 4988 (b) (relating to the net income limitation on windfall profit), the term "property" has the same meaning as that term is given by the energy regulations. See 10 C.F.R. § 212.72(a); FEA Rul. 1977-1, 42 Fed. Reg. 3268 (1977)."

24 38 Fed. Reg. 22,536, 22,538 (August 22, 1973).

25 See 41 Fed. Reg. 16,179, 16,180 (April 16, 1976).

Ruling 1975-15 was issued.[26] Moreover, despite Ruling 1975-15, the definition remained uncertain. As late as November 1976, the Deputy Administrator of the Federal Energy Administration (FEA) admitted that the exact meaning of the definition had never been clear, not even to the agency itself.[27] As a result, in late August 1976, FEA issued a notice entitled "Clarifications to Mandatory Petroleum Price Regulations Applicable to Domestic Crude Oil."[28] These Clarifications were subsequently published as FEA Ruling 1977-1.[29] Six days later, FEA issued Ruling 1977-2, which further interpreted the "property" definition.[30]

DOE's interpretations as set forth in Rulings 1975-15, 1977-1, and 1977-2 have resulted in intense litigation. The Rulings are presently under judicial challenge as arbitrary and capricious, and for failure to comply with rulemaking requirements. Moreover, DOE's present interpretation of the "property" definition, especially Ruling 1977-2, is being challenged as inconsistent with some or all of the original definition or earlier Rulings. The areas of major disagreement with DOE appear to include the effects of various types of multi-lease and single-lease unitizations, the requirements for royalty owner accountability and severance tax accountability, the proper treatment of noncontiguous tracts, the question whether separate state reporting of production is ever required for

---

26 40 Fed. Reg. 40,832 (September 4, 1975).

27 Hearings on Crude Oil Pricing Compliance Problems Before the Subcommittee on Energy and Power of the House Committee on Interstate and Foreign Commerce, Serial No. 94-162, 94th Cong., 2d Sess. 103 (November 11, 1976).

28 41 Fed. Reg. 36,172 (August 26, 1976).

29 42 Fed. Reg. 3,628 (January 19, 1977).

30 42 Fed. Reg. 4,409 (January 25, 1977).

separate property treatment, and the propriety of pre-September 1, 1976, reservoir recognition.[31]

In addition, on September 1, 1976, the property definition was amended to allow producers to elect to treat individual crude oil reservoirs as separate properties. The following sentence was added to the definition:

> A producer may treat as a separate property each separate and distinct producing reservoir subject to the same right to produce crude oil, provided that such reservoir is recognized by the appropriate governmental regulatory authority as a producing formation that is separate and distinct from, and not in communication with, any other producing formation.[32]

DOE's interpretation of this amendment to the property definition is also under attack. Virtually all of DOE's requirements for state recognition are being challenged in various proceedings.

There are other significant disputes over the meaning of the energy regulations which have a direct impact on the Windfall Profit Tax. For example, the energy regulations define "stripper" well oil as oil and associated condensate produced on any property whose average daily production per well did not exceed ten barrels during any consecutive twelve-month period beginning after December 31, 1972. The definition is important under the Windfall Profit Tax for purposes of classifying oil as "Tier 2" oil. What constitutes a stripper property for

31 See, *e.g., The Crude Oil Cluster Proceedings,* Case Nos. DRO-0193-0197 and 0199. (On May 1, 1979, DOE initiated enforcement proceedings before the DOE Office of Hearings and Appeals against seven major producers seeking $1.7 billion in alleged overcharges. The cases involve the meaning and validity of virtually all aspects of the "property" concept and the rulings relating thereto, the definition of posted price, and the treatment of injection wells for purposes of qualifying stripper well properties.) Some of the issues are discussed in Atlantic Richfield Co., *et al.,* 5 DOE Para. 82,521 (January 25, 1980).

32 10 C.F.R. § 212.72.

purposes of the energy regulations is currently at issue in various actions including major, multi-district litigation consolidated in the United States District Court in Kansas.[33]

Various issues concerning the proper determination of "posted price" are also currently in litigation, including what constitutes public circulation of a posted price, what defines the geographic limits to a field, and what constitutes equivalent quality. The "posted price" concept of the energy regulations is incorporated in the Windfall Profit Tax's definition of "base price." Recently, the Secretary of the Treasury interpreted the definition of posted price for purposes of determining the highest posted price as of December 31, 1979, and presumably for other purposes of the Tax as well.[34] The Secretary's interpretation, which substantially adopted DOE's interpretation of the term, is as follows:

> a written statement of crude oil prices constituting an offer to purchase oil at that price circulated publicly among sellers and buyers of crude oil in a particular field in accordance with historic practices.

The Secretary's clarification also states that a posted price must be an offer to purchase at a specific price; offers to buy at a price not specified as a sum certain do not qualify.

In light of differing interpretations of the DOE regulations, a basic question arising from their incorporation into the Windfall Profit Tax is how a taxpayer must treat contested DOE regulations for Windfall Profit Tax purposes. To lessen the possibility of assessment of penalties, a taxpayer following his own interpretation of contested DOE regulations may want to note that fact specifically

33 See Dkt MDL No. 378.

34 See Treas. Reg. § 150.4989-1(c)(2)(ii)(B) (temporary), 45 Fed. Reg. 63,263 (September 24, 1980).

in filing a return or providing a certification. A taxpayer might also consider paying the Windfall Profit Tax in accordance with the DOE's interpretation of a contested DOE regulation, and then institute a refund proceeding in accordance with the taxpayer's interpretation of the regulation.

Other Controversial Concepts

The Windfall Profit Tax also incorporates controversial income tax concepts. The tax generally applies only to producers having an economic interest in property.[35] What constitutes an "economic interest" has been the subject of numerous court decisions involving the allowability of percentage depletion; nevertheless, the concept of "economic interest" remains unclear.

Another depletion concept incorporated in the Windfall Profit Tax is the concept of "taxable income from the property," which is incorporated in the net income limitation of Section 4988(b). Under the Code, percentage depletion is limited to 50 percent of taxable income from the property.[36] The regulations and the case law prescribe rules for determining gross income from the property, allowable deductions attributable to the property, and the apportionment of overhead. These rules will be as difficult to administer for Windfall Profit Tax purposes as for depletion purposes.

The Windfall Profit Tax itself creates a number of conceptual and controversial problems which seem destined for litigation. One repeated complaint about the tax is the extent to which the Secretary of the Treasury has been delegated authority. For example, the Secretary may adjust the removal price paid in "any transaction" in order to reflect the fair market value of oil removed.[37] The

---

35 I.R.C. § 4996(a)(1).

36 I.R.C. § 613(a).

37 I.R.C. § 4996(f).

Secretary also has the authority to prescribe the method for determining base prices applicable to Tier 2 Oil and Tier 3 Oil.[38] And importantly, as noted above, the Secretary may prescribe regulations changing the application of the DOE regulations to the Windfall Profit Tax.[39]

Certain types of transactions cause conceptual problems in administering the Windfall Profit Tax. For example, neither the Act nor the proposed regulations address the proper treatment of crude oil exchange transactions. Is each party a "first purchaser" required to withhold? Are the constructive sales price rules under Section 613 applicable?

The definition of a qualifying severance tax may also present questions in that the tax must be determined on the "gross value" of the extracted oil. This introduces a new, undefined standard that may disqualify some commonly recognized severance taxes as offsets in computing taxable windfall profit.[40]

Practical Considerations in Contesting Tax Liability

Under Section 7421 of the Internal Revenue Code, the courts are denied jurisdiction to entertain suits to restrain assessment or collection of taxes. Accordingly, even if you consider the Windfall Profit Tax unconstitutional, you must nevertheless follow the usual enforce-

---

38 I.R.C. § 4989(d)(1).

39 I.R.C. § 4997(b).

40 The Internal Revenue Service has already issued a revenue ruling holding that a particular severance tax does not qualify for the severance tax adjustment provided by § 4988(a)(2). In Rev. Rul. 80-217, 1980-32 I.R.B. 11 (Aug. 11, 1980), a state imposed a severance tax based on the gross value of oil removed, but also provided certain state income tax credits to the producer which ameliorated the effect on the producer of the severance tax. The Internal Revenue Service held that in substance the severance tax was not determined on the basis of the gross value of the oil removed and thus does not qualify for the § 4988(a)(2) adjustment.

ment procedures by either contesting a deficiency in Tax Court or suing for a refund in the United States District Court or the United States Court of Claims. As a practical matter, the Tax Court may not be a viable alternative if a taxpayer/producer is eager to file suit quickly. The taxpayer will have to wait for the Internal Revenue Service to assess a deficiency, which conceivably could take years. Moreover, if the oil the taxpayer produced was subject to withholding, there may not be a tax "deficiency" to be assessed. Therefore, a refund suit may be the most practical means of contesting the application of the tax.

As noted above, before filing suit for refund, a taxpayer must first file a claim for refund. Under the usual procedures, if a claim for refund is not acted upon within six months, the claim will be deemed to have been denied for purposes of filing suit. It is possible, however, to accelerate the refund claim process and get to court in much less time than six months. The Internal Revenue Service has a special "quick denial" procedure that producers may be able to use to obtain prompt rejection of a claim for refund.[41]

Once a claim for refund has been denied, a taxpayer/producer may file suit for refund either in United States District Court or in the United States Court of Claims. In either case, the tax assessed for the period in controversy must have been paid in full.[42]

Deciding upon the court in which to file suit may depend on several practical considerations. In the district court, the taxpayer will be in a local forum, which could be advantageous depending on the location. The taxpayer may also request a jury trial (as may the government),

---

41 See IR-1600, 769 CCH Standard Fed. Tax Rptr. Para. 6609 (April 23, 1976).

42 See H.R. Rep. No. 96-817, *supra* at 115.

which may or may not be advantageous. In the Court of Claims, on the other hand, no jury trial is available.

Choosing the appropriate court may also depend on how complicated the case is from a technical standpoint, and how much trial preparation will be involved. The Court of Claims "specializes" in tax cases and other claims against the Government, and is well accustomed to long, complex cases. On the other hand, if the case involves an issue of interpretation of DOE regulations, the United States District Court may have prior experience (and perhaps favorable precedent) from past price control litigation.

There are other practical court considerations. Given the comprehensive discovery process in the district courts, a producer involved in a Windfall Profit Tax dispute may want to be in district court rather than in Tax Court or in the Court of Claims. This is especially true if the producer intends to seek discovery against third persons such as the DOE or first purchasers.

Choosing the appropriate forum to contest windfall profit tax liability becomes more complicated by the fact that persons other than the taxpayer/producer and the Internal Revenue Service may have a stake in the outcome of the litigation. In fact, other persons may be or may have been involved in the same issues in another court and in another context. For example, suppose that the DOE brings an enforcement action asserting that the operator of a particular property overcharged for oil from the property, on the ground that the oil was "old" oil subject to price controls, and not uncontrolled, stripper well oil as claimed by the operator. If the DOE is successful, the operator may be liable for the difference between the ceiling price for old oil and the uncontrolled market price for which the oil was sold. Also, if the DOE is successful, the outcome may have a direct effect on the windfall profit tax liability of the producer of the property; presumably, the producer paid taxes based on a "windfall profit" equal to the difference between the market price and the adjusted base price for Tier 2 Oil, as provided by Section 4989 of the Windfall Profit Tax. However, if the operator is required to make a refund as a result of the DOE enforcement action, the producer may then be in a position to file a refund claim asserting an overpayment of windfall profit tax.

In this hypothetical situation, should the taxpayer/producer consider intervening in the suit between the DOE and the operator? If the outcome is favorable to the taxpayer/producer, would the Internal Revenue Service be bound by the decision even though it was, arguably, not a party to the controversy? And what are the relative rights and obligations in this situation between the operator and the producer?

The multiplicity of potential forums and litigants, as well as the possibility that litigants seemingly on the same side may advocate inconsistent positions, raise numerous practical problems that need to be evaluated prior to deciding where and when to file suit to challenge the Windfall Profit Tax. Given the amounts of money at stake and the complexity of the issues involved, litigation in this area seems inevitable.

APPLICATION OF SECTION 111 TO THE WINDFALL PROFIT TAX REFUND

Terry L. Crain, CPA
Donald J. Hupp, CPA

The Crude Oil Windfall Profit Tax Act of 1980[1] provides that a taxpayer may apply for a refund of his windfall profit tax if it was overwithheld. Although the tax treatment of the refund was not discussed in the 1980 Act, it appears that the provisions of Section 111 may apply to the refund. The computation associated with the taxation of the refund under Section 111, which may be very involved, will be discussed in this article.

Overwithholding of the Windfall Profit Tax

A windfall profit tax refund may be available with respect to a property for one of two reasons. First, an excess of windfall profit tax may have been withheld due to a withholding error. A withholding error is one in which an incorrect amount of windfall profit tax was withheld from the property, computed without regard to the net income limitation.[2] This type of error may have been common in 1980 when purchasers were modifying their revenue accounting systems to cope with the windfall profit tax. Also, certifications of independent producer status, which provided for reduced rates on Tier 1 and Tier 2 oil, may not have been timely received by the

---

* Terry L. Crain and Donald J. Hupp are partners in the accounting firm of Jarratt, Hupp, and Thompson in Wichita Falls, Texas.

1 The Crude Oil Windfall Profit Tax Act, Pub. L. No. 96-223, April 2, 1980.

2 I.R.C. § 4995(a)(3)(B).

Article reprinted courtesy of *Oil & Gas Tax Quarterly*, March 1981, pp. 479–502

purchaser.[3] Corrections of withholding errors must be made as soon as possible by adjusting amounts withheld in later payments. However, no adjustment may be made to the amount withheld from oil removed in a later calendar year, or from payments made after Form 6248 has been issued to the producer.[4] Therefore, a correction for an overwithheld amount for 1980 cannot be made from oil removed in 1981.

A second cause for a windfall profit tax refund is a statutory one, provided by the net income limitation. Although not taken into consideration for withholding purposes in most cases, the windfall profit attributable to any barrel of taxable crude oil cannot exceed 90 percent of the net income attributable to the barrel.[5] Net income attributable to a barrel is computed by dividing taxable income from the property attributable to taxable crude oil by the number of barrels of taxable crude oil removed from the property for the taxable year.[6] Taxable income is determined under Section 613(a), with certain modifications. Depletion, windfall profit tax, and productive intangible development costs are not allowed as deductions. However, the taxpayer is allowed to deduct cost depletion computed as though productive intangible development costs had been capitalized.[7] A taxpayer who purchases a proven property after 1978 may not be allowed to compute cost depletion on the entire purchase amount. He

---

3 I.R.C. § 4987 provides reduced rates for independent producer oil attributable to a qualified working interest as follows:

	Independent Working Interest	All Other
Tier 1	50%	70%
Tier 2	30%	60%
Tier 3	30%	30%

4 Treas. Reg. § 150.4995-1(c).

5 I.R.C. § 4988(b)(1).

6 I.R.C. § 4988(b)(2).

7 I.R.C. § 4988(b)(3).

may only use an amount equal to the costs allowable with respect to the transferor plus any costs incurred after the purchase.[8]

Applying for the Refund

A taxpayer may apply for a refund when he files his income tax return, or by filing a claim on Form 843. The refund may not be applied for until after the last day of February following the close of the calendar year. In the case of a refund due to the net income limitation, the claim may not be filed until the income tax return is filed for the taxable year that includes the last day of the last taxable period of such calendar year.[9]

Taxation of the Refund

If Section 111 applies to the overwithheld windfall profit tax, then the refund is an item of income, not a reduction in current year expenses.[10] Section 111 provides that income during any taxable year attributable to the recovery of bad debts, prior taxes, and delinquency amounts shall be excluded from gross income to the extent of the "recovery exclusion" with respect to such items.[11] The windfall profit tax refund, net of the recovery exclusion, is an item of income. The refund should not be used to reduce current windfall profit tax expense. The recovery exclusion is the amount of windfall profit tax expense deducted in the prior year, which did not result in a reduction of any tax.

The concept of the recovery exclusion, as it applies to percentage depletion, has been discussed in Revenue Rul-

8 I.R.C. § 4988(b)(4).

9 Treas. Reg. § 150.6402-1(c).

10 I.R.C. § 111.

11 Treas. Reg. § 111-1(a).

ing 77-79.[12] In this ruling, the taxpayer was notified by a state that additional severance taxes were due on minerals produced within the state. In 1974, the taxpayer paid the tax and sued the state. In 1976, the court found in favor of the taxpayer and the state refunded 1,500x dollars to the corporation. In computing percentage depletion for 1974, the 50 percent of taxable income limitation applied to the property. Without the additional 1,500x dollars of severance tax, percentage depletion would have been increased by 500x dollars. Applying the rule of Section 111, the taxpayer must include 1,000x dollars in gross income in 1976 for the severance tax refund. That is, the 1,500x dollar refund in 1976 may be reduced by the 500x dollar recovery exclusion. The ruling also held that the taxpayer must reduce his basis in the property by the 500x dollar recovery exclusion in 1976.

Example

Assume a calendar year taxpayer has a windfall profit tax refund in 1981 of $10,000. His income and expenses for that property for 1980 were as follows:

Income and Expense as Originally Filed

Gross income		$100,000
Expenses:		
Severance Tax	$ 5,000	
Lease operating expense	32,000	
Depreciation	8,000	
Windfall profit tax	20,000	65,000
Net income		$ 35,000
Depletion:		
22% of Gross Income		$ 22,000
50% of Net income		$ 17,500

12 Rev. Rul. 77-79, 1977-1 C.B. 34.

Recomputed Excluding Section 111 Items

Gross income		$100,000
Expenses:		
Severance Tax	$ 5,000	
Lease operating expense	32,000	
Depreciation	8,000	
Windfall profit tax	10,000	55,000
Net income		$ 45,000
Depletion:		
22% of Gross Income		$ 22,000
50% of Net income		$ 22,500

Percentage depletion for 1980 was limited to 50 percent of taxable income, or $17,500. When depletion is recomputed for 1980 excluding the Section 111 item of $10,000 windfall profit tax, allowable depletion is $22,000. Therefore the recovery exclusion is $4,500. The taxpayer must include $5,500 of the windfall profit tax refund in gross income in 1981. That is, the $10,000 refund less the $4,500 recovery exclusion.

Reduction in Basis

In Revenue Ruling 77-79, the Internal Revenue Service held that the basis in the property must be reduced to the extent of the recovery exclusion. A question arises as to what happens if the basis in the property has already been reduced to zero. Should the "recovery exclusion" constitute a tax preference item to the extent it is in excess of the basis in the property? It is likely that such an issue will arise if the windfall profit tax refund comes under the purview of Section 111.

Conclusion

Implementation of the windfall profit tax will create many additional computations. In the example, the simplest facts were assumed. However, a taxpayer who receives refunds on several properties, and who also has to contend with the 65 percent limit of Section 613A, may face a complex mathematical task in computing the recovery exclusion.

Administrative and Accounting Aspects of the WPT: Withholding, Depositary, Certification, Reporting and Recordkeeping Requirements

Prof. Craig E. Reese and
Ron R. Roberts, CPA*

When Congress passed and President Carter signed into law the Windfall Profit Tax (hereinafter WPT), an immediate administrative and accounting burden was imposed on the oil industry that has no equal in the recent history of this country. The WPT's administrative and accounting requirements were not only time-consuming and costly to implement, but they also resulted in incomplete, confusing, and often transitory guidelines for taxpayer compliance. The law was enacted on April 2, 1980, retroactive to March 1, 1980; temporary Treasury regulations were initially proposed on April 4, 1980. Subsequently, the original temporary regulations have been amended and augmented by additional temporary regulations as well as by various revenue rulings, revenue procedures, IRS notices, and IRS announcements. In addition, several new IRS forms have been created to ease somewhat the administrative and accounting burden of the WPT.

Finally, the WPT law has been amended twice since its enactment: first, to provide a one-time credit to qualified royalty owners of $1,000 or WPT paid in 1980 (the Omnibus Reconciliation Act of 1980), and second, to provide credits and exemptions with the Economic Recovery Tax Act of 1981. This second amendment provided a royalty-owner credit of $2,500 on WPT paid in 1981 and the exemption of the first two barrels per day of royalty-owner qualified daily production from the WPT for the years 1982 through 1984. For 1985 and thereafter, the exemption is increased to three barrels per day of royalty-owner qualified daily production. In addition to the amendment relating to royalty owners, the tax rate on Tier III (newly discovered production) will be reduced from 30 percent to 15 percent beginning in 1982 through 1986, and certain independent producer stripper-oil wells will be completely exempt from the WPT beginning with oil removed in 1983.† Such amendments to the statute also affect administrative and accounting problems for the oil industry.

The following text is a summary and analysis of the administrative and accounting aspects of the WPT as of mid-April 1981. The text begins with an explanation of the withholding requirements. Then depositary, certification, reporting, and recordkeeping requirements are explained.

Withholding Requirements

In general, the first purchaser is the party responsible for collection of the WPT. First purchaser (hereinafter purchaser) is the first person—defined in Section 7701a-1 as an individual, a trust, estate, partnership, association, company, or corporation—purchasing domestic crude oil.

The amount that the purchaser must deduct and withhold is computed on the basis of information contained in an operator's certification.‡ Purchasers may rely on an operator's certification of the type of oil produced unless they have reason to believe the information contained therein is incorrect. Guidelines for determining the meaning of "reason to believe" have not been promulgated.

*Tax Partner, Touche Ross & Co., San Antonio, Texas.

† Several bills were proposed early in the 97th Congress. For example, the Senate Finance Committee Chairman, Sen. Robert Dole (R-Kan.), introduced a bill (5.19) on January 5, 1981, to exempt the first 10 b/d from the WPT. Bill 5.19 was cosponsored by 30 other senators.

‡ Sec. 4995a-2A. Operator is defined in Temp. Reg. Sec. 150.4996-1d. Hereafter, all references to sections will be noted by suffix only in the text.

A purchaser's computation of the amount withheld from a payment to a producer is based on the general rules for determining the WPT for crude oil production as certified by an operator; however, the net income limitation (NIL) is not considered in determining the amount to be withheld. More specifically, the WPT withheld or WPT deposit is the product of windfall profit and the producer's tax rate, where the "profit" is determined by subtracting the sum of the applicable base price adjusted for inflation and the severance tax adjustment from the removal price.[1]

Where purchasers have not received an operator's certification or have received a certification but have reason to believe that any information contained therein either is incorrect or is not complete and accurate information reflecting permanent base prices, such purchasers may compute withholding based upon the information they believe to be correct and applicable and on the assumptions explained below.

Where the tax tier is not known, Tier 1 should be assumed, and the oil is subject to the 70% rate or 50% rate in the case of an independent producer. Where the adjusted base price is not known, the following adjusted base price should be assumed:

- If Tier 1 oil, $11.01 plus the applicable inflation adjustment;
- If Tier 2 oil, $12.11 plus the applicable inflation adjustment; or
- If Tier 3 oil, $13.21 plus the applicable inflation adjustment.
- Where the severance tax adjustment is not known, it is assumed to be inapplicable, unless the actual severance tax adjustment is known by the purchaser.

These withholding rules were effective in respect to payments made after November 30, 1980, for oil removed on or after March 1, 1980, unless the purchaser chose to apply at an earlier date. If the purchaser did not receive an operator's certification or if the purchaser had reason to believe that any information contained in any certification was incorrect, the purchaser must have deducted and withheld the following amounts from payments made before December 1, 1980, for crude oil removed after February 29, 1980:

1. None if the purchaser paid the lower-tier ceiling price for oil
2. An amount equal to 70% of the excess of the removal price over the sum of the Tier 1 base price of $11.01 adjusted for inflation and the severance tax adjustment.

Responsibilities of the Operator

Generally, the operator has no WPT withholding requirements; however, the operator and purchaser may elect jointly to have the operator withhold (4995a-7). More specifically, the election may be made in respect to either the entire property or a portion thereof, and all requirements generally imposed on the purchaser under the WPT law will be imposed on the operator. In addition, the operator must notify all those with an economic interest in production from the property (or a portion thereof) that the election has been made and that all information required to be sent to the purchaser should be sent to the operator (4995-4a).

The election must be in writing, signed by both the operator and the purchaser, and must state that both parties have agreed that the operator of the property will be responsible for all requirements imposed on the purchaser under the WPT law. Each party must file the election statement (Form 6458) within 10 days of execution with the Austin IRS Service Center. Formerly, WPT documents were filed at the IRS Center where the party files its federal income tax return.

The election remains in effect until terminated by either party executing a document, signed, dated, and delivered to the other party. The termination takes effect 60 days after execution of the termination document (Form 6458) unless both agree to an earlier date. The terminating party must notify all affected producers promptly and the parties must file a copy of the document with the Austin IRS Service Center within 10 days of termination. Parties receiving a termination document (Form 6458) must forward a copy within 20 days of receipt to the Austin IRS Service Center (4995-4b).

The election is allowed only when substitution of operator makes administration of the WPT more practical, (4995a-7B). Therefore, the election is allowable only if the operator is otherwise required to make deposits as a purchaser of oil produced from a different oil reservoir. Inasmuch as such a limitation severely restricts the flexibility implicit in IRB Sec. 4995a-7B, the final regulations may be more permissive. For example, substitution would seem advantageous where the operator rather than the first purchaser holds the basic division order.

Responsibilities of Qualified Disbursers

In deference to the multitude of comments received by the IRS from representatives of the oil industry during 1980, the withholding and depositary regulations originally promulgated in April 1980 were amended in January 1981 to permit more flexibility in determining the withholding agent for the WPT on payments to producers. Additional flexibility was deemed necessary to permit the holder of a basic division order (e.g., the operator of a property or a designated disburser) rather than a purchaser (e.g., a gathering company or refinery) to act as a withholding agent, inasmuch as the division order holder has the responsibility for distributing sales proceeds to the various producers as specified in the division order. In summary, the qualified disburser designation has been created to allow those holding basic division orders or other disbursers of payments for oil to elect to act as the withholding agent for those producers to whom they disburse payments for oil (TD 7755, IRB 1981-8).

Generally, a disburser or partnership of producers has no withholding responsibility (4996-1j). However, a qualified disburser, who is either (1) a disburser who distributes 10 percent or more of the entire proceeds from the sale of oil from a property (or portion thereof, if that portion constituted a separate property prior to a unitization or aggregation), exclusive of that person's own share of the proceeds (if any), or (2) a federally registered partnership, as defined in Section 6501-0-4, may make an election to act as a withholding agent in respect to the oil, the sales proceeds of which are distributed by that disburser or partnership and to treat as excepted from withholding its own production. In general, a qualified disburser electing to act as a withholding agent is treated as a purchaser for WPT purposes and thereby is subject to the same withholding, depositary, reporting and recordkeeping requirements otherwise applicable to a purchaser (4995-5a).

A qualified disburser election must be in writing, must be dated, must be signed by the qualified disburser, must provide facts that establish the person making the election is a qualified disburser, and must state the person has assumed complete responsibility for meeting all of the requirements otherwise imposed on the purchaser to whom the election statement is furnished. The qualified disburser must furnish a separate election statement (Form 6458) for each property in respect to which an election is made (4995-5c). In addition, the disburser must notify the operator of the oil producing property and every payee of any portion of its disbursements that a qualified disburser election has been made and that all information otherwise required to be sent to the purchaser should be sent to the qualified disburser (4995-5a). Finally, the purchaser must forward a copy of the qualified disburser's election statement (Form 6458) to the IRS Service Center in Austin within 10 days of receipt (4995-5c).

In general, the election becomes effective on the date the election statement is furnished to the purchaser; however, the election statement may specify a later effective date. Alternatively, the election could have been made effective retroactively in respect to all oil removed after December 31, 1980, if the purchaser and qualified disburser agreed in writing on or before March 1, 1981.

Any qualified disburser election remains in effect until 60 days after the disburser furnishes the purchaser with a signed and dated statement declaring that the election is terminated unless the purchaser agrees to an earlier termination date for the election in a written statement to the disburser. Alternatively, the disburser may specify a later effective date for terminating its qualified disburser election in the termination statement it sends the purchaser. In addition, the disburser must notify promptly the operator and all the producers affected by the change in withholding agents of the termination and the related alteration in responsibilities, not only for withholding but also for deposits of WPT withheld, reporting of WPT, recordkeeping, etc. Furthermore, the disburser must forward a copy of the termination statement to the IRS Service Center, Austin, within 10 days of furnishing such document to the purchaser. Finally, where a qualified disburser electing to act as a withholding agent receives purchase payments through an intermediate disburser (rather than directly from a purchaser), any statements otherwise required to be furnished to the purchaser should be provided for the intermediate disburser. Consequently, the latter person receiving such statements assumes the responsibility for furnishing a copy to those persons from whom it receives payment for the sales proceeds of oil (and so on) (4995-5c).

One must ask why a qualified disburser would undertake the arduous task of withholding and reporting for the WPT. Due to the overly burdensome reporting requirements imposed on some producers downstream from the first purchaser (i.e., operators who hold basic division orders and partnerships) in the WPT paperflow, the additional cost associated with a qualified disburser election in some cases will be more than offset by the effect of increased cash flow resulting from determining the WPT to be withheld by taking into account the effect of the NIL. In certain cases, a qualified disburser can obtain cash flow resulting from the NIL, which would be deferred for as long as thirteen months if the election were not made. This election should be particularly useful to qualifying partnerships and could, in fact, reduce their reporting burden in some cases even where the NIL does not come into play. A similar result may be achieved by some operators. Last, in some rather isolated and unique situations, some qualified disbursers may be able to achieve the use of interest-free money for up to 25 days. However, the election must be considered only after weighing all of the applicable facts in each situation.

Responsibilities of the Producer

In general, producers have no responsibility to withhold WPT because they typically sell their production. In contrast, a producer is responsible for depositing WPT in respect to oil not subject to withholding. More specifically, the producer must pay its own WPT in the following four cases (4995-1a):

(1) Where oil is removed from the premises before sale
(2) Where manufacture or conversion of oil into refined products begins before removal from the premises
(3) Where the producer makes a qualified disburser election
(4) Where the producer of oil is an integrated oil company that has furnished an integrated oil company certificate to the purchaser.

Insofar as the lion's share of domestic crude-oil production either is purchased by or its production is controlled by integrated oil companies, the responsibilities of the integrated oil-company purchaser to make deposits of WPT are explained first. Then the depositary requirements for nonintegrated oil-company purchasers are provided. Finally, the limited responsibilities of producers, qualified disbursers, and operators to deposit WPT are delineated for completeness.

Responsibilities of the Integrated Oil Company

As indicated above, the first purchaser of domestic crude oil is generally required to withhold WPT from payments to producers (operators or qualified disbursers where the operator or disburser then transfers such payments to persons with an economic interest). The deposits of integrated oil-company purchasers must be made semimonthly. In other words, there must be a deposit for the first 15 days of a calendar month following the 15th day of that month. The deposits are due by the 24th day of the month for production payments made during the first 15-day period of the month and by the ninth day of the following month for production payments made during the portion of the month following the 15th (4995-3a). There are also "safe-harbor" rules whereby depositary requirements are considered to have been met in respect to estimated deposits for a semimonthly period.

These depositary requirements are considered to have been met for a semimonthly period in respect to estimated deposits only if one of the four conditions explained below are satisfied by the integrated oil company. If the company's deposit for the semimonthly period is not less than 90 percent of the total amount otherwise required to be deposited by it for such period, then the depositary requirements would be satisfied if such period occurs in a month other than the last month in a taxable period (calendar quarter) and the company deposits any underpayment for such month by the ninth day of the second month following such month.

Alternatively, if its deposit for each semimonthly period in the month is not less than 45 percent of the total amount otherwise required to be deposited by it for the month, then the depositary requirements would be fulfilled if such month is other than the last month in a taxable period and the company deposits any underpayment for such month by the ninth day of the second month following. Moreover, if its deposit for each semimonthly period in the month is not less than 50 percent of the total amount required to be deposited by it for the second preceding calendar month (determined without regard to the four safe-harbor conditions), then the depositary requirements would be met if such month is other than the last month in a calendar quarter and the company deposits any underpayment for such month by the ninth day of the second month following such month.

If the requirements of any of the above three safe-harbor conditions are satisfied for the first semimonthly period of a calendar month and the company's deposit for the second semimonthly period of that calendar month is, when added to the deposit for the first semimonthly period, not less than 90 percent of the total amount otherwise required to be deposited by it for the month, then the depositary requirements would be discharged if such period occurs in a month other than the last month in a calendar quarter and the company deposits any underpayment for such month by the ninth day of the second month following such month. However, the second and third safe-harbor conditions do not apply to any company that normally incurs in the first semimonthly period in each month more than 75 percent of its total liability for deposit for the month (determined without regard to the four safe-harbor conditions explained above). Finally, if the aggregate amount of deposit liability for a taxable period (determined without regard to the four safe-harbor conditions explained above) exceeds the total amount deposited by an integrated oil company for such taxable period (calendar quarter), then the company is required, on or before the last day of the first month following the close of the taxable period, to deposit an amount equal to the amount by which the deposit liability exceeds the total deposits made for the taxable period (4995-3a1).

Responsibilities of Other Purchasers

The nonintegrated oil-company purchaser, which includes independent refiners and all purchasers other than integrated oil companies, are required to make deposits for monthly periods, i.e., on a monthly rather than semimonthly basis. In general, deposits are due not later than 45 days after the close of the month in which oil is removed from the premises (4995-3c). There is an exception for an independent refiner who purchases oil pursuant to a deferred-payment contract with no payment to be made before the 46th day after the end of the month of purchase. For such refiners, deposits are due not later than the last day of the second calendar month after the month of removal (4995-3b). Insofar as the regulations specify no safe-harbor rules for deposits made by the nonintegrated oil-company purchaser, it would seem that the more general rules for underpayment of WPT implicitly provide guidance for such depositors.

Responsibilities of the Operator

Generally, the operator is subject to no depositary requirements. However, an operator is required to make deposits if the joint election has been made for the operator to assume the duties of the purchaser (4995-3d). Where the operator is an integrated oil company, the rules for integrated oil-company purchasers explained above apply. Similarly, the safe-harbor rules applicable to deposits made by integrated first purchasers would apply to deposits made by integrated operators.

Where the operator is not an integrated oil company but the joint election is with an integrated oil-company purchaser, the rules for integrated oil-company purchasers explained above are also applicable to the operator. Thus, the safe-harbor rules for the integrated first purchaser would apply to the nonintegrated operator jointly electing with an integrated oil company.

Finally, where neither the operator nor the purchaser is an integrated oil company, the rules for other purchasers (as explained above) are applicable to the operator. In other words, deposits are due not later than 45 days after the close of the month in which oil is removed from the premises. The exception for independent refiners would apply. However, there are no safe-harbor rules for deposits made by the nonintegrated oil-company operator jointly electing with a nonintegrated oil-company purchaser.

Insofar as the operator jointly elects with each first purchaser, it is not unusual that the former may be a party to elections with both integrated and nonintegrated purchasers. Presumably, where the operator is not an integrated oil company and there is a joint election with two or more purchasers, including both integrated and nonintegrated oil companies, the operator's depositary responsibilities would encompass the rules applicable to both integrated and nonintegrated purchasers. The applicability thereof would depend upon the relative proportion of each type of the purchaser's acquisition of production.

Responsibilities of Qualified Disbursers

As explained above, any qualified disburser electing to act as a withholding agent assumes the WPT responsibilities otherwise imposed on the purchaser. Consequently, although disbursers and partnerships of producers generally are not subject to depositary responsibilities, an electing qualified disburser is required to make deposits in respect to oil payments from which it is withholding WPT and for its own production from the property covered by the qualified disburser election. Thus, that portion of a qualified disburser's production subject to its own election is not subject to withholding.

In general, the special deposit rules applicable to operators are also pertinent to qualified disbursers. However, where some of the qualified disburser's own production is from property covered by the election, the deposit rules for producers not subject to withholding are applicable (4995-5e). Inasmuch as the qualified disburser election is in addition to the operator election, persons eligible for both must choose one. Where an operator prefers the qualified disburser election, it must properly terminate its operator election before making a new election as a qualified disburser (TP 7755, IRB 1981-8).

If a qualified disburser is neither an integrated oil company nor a producer of oil from property encompassed by its election, it must make deposits according to rules applicable to other purchasers as explained above. However, where on December 31, 1980, an integrated oil company (other than an independent refiner) was a disburser in respect to an oil-producing property, a qualified disburser that subsequently undertakes any portion of the distribution responsibility of that integrated oil company must make deposits according to the rules applicable to integrated oil companies as explained above (4995-3d2).

Where a qualified disburser is a producer of oil from a property subject to its election but is not an integrated oil company, that disburser must make deposits in respect to all oil encompassed by its election as if the oil production were oil not subject to withholding (4995-3d1). Finally, if a qualified disburser is an integrated oil company (other than an independent refiner), it must make deposits according to the rules applicable to such integrated oil companies (4995-3d2).

Responsibilities of the Producer

Although the producer generally is not required to deposit the WPT, a producer must make deposits in respect to its crude-oil production that is not subject to withholding. The specific depositary requirements, i.e., the timing and proper amount of the deposits that are applicable, depend on the type of producer—integrated or nonintegrated. If the producer is an integrated oil company, the rules explained above for integrated oil-company purchasers would generally be applicable, including the safe-harbor rules in respect to estimated deposits for semimonthly periods. However, integrated oil-company producers may adjust deposits on their production for an estimate of the effect of the Section 4988b net income limitation on their WPT liability.

Where a producer is not an integrated oil company, basically the same rules that apply to the nonintegrated purchaser are applicable. However, in determining the amount of their monthly deposits, such producers may consider the net income limitation of Section 4988b. Moreover, there is a separate set of safe-harbor rules for the monthly estimated deposits of such producers. Thus, nonintegrated producers' depositary requirements are considered to have been met for a month in respect to their estimated deposits, including deposits based on their estimate of the effect of the net income limitation if one of the four safe-harbor rules are satisfied.

A producer has met the depositary requirements where the producer's aggregate deposit liability in respect to oil not subject to withholding for the three months of a taxable period is less than $100, and the producer deposits the amount of tax owed on or before the last day for filing the return required by Temp. Reg. Sec. 150.4997-1 for that taxable period or remits the tax owed with that return. The depositary requirements would also be satisfied if the producer's deposit for the month is not less than 90 percent of the total amount otherwise required by Temp. Reg. Sec. 150.4995-3 to be deposited by it for the month and the producer complies with the requirements of Temp. Reg. Sec. 150.4995-3f2. Subparagraph 2 requires the producer to deposit the difference between the total WPT liability for a taxable period (calendar quarter) and the total amount deposited by the producer (in respect to oil not subject to withholding) for such period within 45 days after the close of the last month in the taxable period.

A third way producers can satisfy their depositary requirements establishes a minimum level for monthly deposits. More specifically, where the producer's deposit for each month of the taxable period is not less than 30 percent of the total amount otherwise required by Temp. Reg. Sec. 150.4995-3 to be deposited by it for the three months of the taxable period, the depositary requirements are met if the producer also complies with the requirements of Temp. Reg. Sec. 150.4995-3f2. Finally, if the producer's deposit for the month is not less than 100 percent of the amount required by Section 4995 (Temp. Reg. Sec. 150.4995-3) to be deposited by it for the third preceding month (determined without regard to the four safe-harbor rules), and if the producer also complies with the requirements of Temp. Reg. Sec. 150.4995-3f2, then the depositary requirements have been satisfied by the producer. However, the third and fourth safe-harbor rules are not applicable to any producer that normally incurs in the first month in each taxable period more than 45 percent of its total liability for deposit for the taxable period (determined without regard to the second, third, and fourth safe-harbor rules).

The Net Income Limitation

In general, a producer who deposits for a taxable period an amount that exceeds the tax imposed by Section 4986 but does not exceed the tax imposed by Section 4986 computed without regard to the Section 4988 net income limitation may not claim a credit or refund of the overpayment or excess until the end of the producer's federal income tax year for which the limitation is computed (4995-3g2i). However, the excess (if any) of an integrated oil-company producer's deposits for a semimonthly period (or calendar month, in the case of nonintegrated oil-company producers) over the tax imposed by Section 4986 computed with regard to the net income limitation for that period (or month) is to be applied in order of time to each of the producer's succeeding semimonthly periods (or months), to the extent that the amount by which the taxes for that period (or month) exceed the deposit for such subsequent period (or month) until such excess is exhausted. The preceding rule, however, does not apply to any amount for which the producer files a claim for credit or refund of overpayment of WPT as provided in Section 6402. Furthermore, no amount of the excess may be applied to a deposit for a subsequent semimonthly period (or month) that occurs in a taxable period beginning in a different federal income tax year (4995-3f1).

Depositary Procedures

Deposits are made either with a Federal Reserve Bank or, at the election of the depositor, with an authorized financial institution, i.e., a financial institution authorized in accordance with Treasury Department Circular No. 1079 (31 CFR Part 214) to accept remittances of the taxes for transmission to a Federal Reserve Bank. Although a person required to make deposits of the WPT may make one or more remittances of the amount required to be deposited, a deposit(s) for one taxable period must be made separately from any deposit(s) for another taxable period.

WPT deposits are supposed to be accompanied by a Federal Tax Deposit Form 504 when remitted to a Federal Reserve Bank or other authorized financial institution. As explained above, the timing of a depositor's obligation to remit WPT depends on the identity of the depositor. The timeliness of a deposit is determined by the date the deposit is received (or deemed received pursuant to Section 7502e) either by a Federal Reserve Bank or by another authorized financial institution, whichever is earlier (4995-3h).

Withholding Adjustments

Errors in withholding may result in either over- or underwithholding. Withholding adjustments are necessary in at least the following four cases: incorrect determination of the WPT by the first purchaser, disburser, or operator; the correction of a producer's or operator's certification, e.g., where certification of independent-producer oil is later revoked; the receipt of a retroactively effective producer's certification after the purchaser or operator has withheld WPT without the benefit of such certification; and receipt of a retroactively effective operator's certification (or qualified disburser's election) after the purchaser has withheld WPT without the benefit of such certification (or election).

Full adjustment of errors in withholding should be made through under- or overwithholding in the next payment to the same producer. Where the next payment after discovery of a withholding error is inadequate to make the withholding adjustment, then the adjustment by over- or underwithholding must be made in subsequent payments to the same producer.

In adjusting for underwithholding, the total amount withheld by the purchaser, operator, or disburser from any payment is limited to the windfall profit on the oil for which the producer receives the payment. However, a producer may authorize any purchaser, operator, or disburser to withhold additional amounts from payments to the producer for oil to correct errors resulting in underwithholding. All withholding adjustments must be made through payments for crude oil removed during the same calendar year in which the withholding error occurred and prior to furnishing the annual statement or return, i.e., on or before the March 31 following the calendar year of removal (4995-1c).

Credit or Refund for Overpayment

In general, any producer who pays, or is deemed to have paid, more than the correct amount of the WPT for either a taxable year or a taxable period may file for a refund of the overpayment or may claim credit for such overpayment, in the manner and subject to the conditions explained below as well as those prescribed by Temp. Reg. Sec. 301.6402-2. The specific procedures for credit or refund of WPT differ somewhat for overpayments attributable to amounts deducted and withheld as contrasted with overpayments attributable to oil production that is not subject to withholding. In addition, Temp. Reg. Sec. 150.6402-1 regulates amounts deducted and withheld on tax exempt oil.

Overpayments Attributable to Oil Subject to Withholding

The producer generally is treated as having paid any amount withheld on the last day of the first February after the calendar year in which the oil is removed from the premises. Consequently, a claim for credit or refund generally should be applied for after such last day of February. There is, however, an important exception that applies in the case of an overpayment due to application of the net income limitation in respect to fiscal-year producers and oil not subject to withholding. Thus, a calendar-year producer could file a claim for refund due to overwithholding and the net income limitation on or after March 1, following the calendar year in which the production occurred. However, a producer who uses a tax year ending on other than December 31 will find the rules somewhat more complex.

A producer using a fiscal tax year other than December 31 can file a claim for refund due to the net income limitation only after the later of the last day of the first February after the end of the taxable period or the last day of the producer's taxable year (6402-1c). Accordingly, a producer who uses a taxable year ending April 30 could file a claim for refund for the period March 1, 1980, to April 30, 1980, on or after March 1, 1981. A claim for refund for the period May 1, 1980, to December 31, 1980, could only be filed on or after May 1, 1981, and a claim for refund for the period January 1, 1981, to April 30, 1981, could only be filed on or after March 1, 1982.

The amount of the claim is the excess of the amount deducted and withheld from the producer in respect to oil removed during the calendar year over the amount of the producer's liability for WPT on oil subject to withholding for all taxable periods of the calendar year. A claim for refund is applied for on Form 843. Alternatively, a claim for credit is applied for on the producer's federal income tax return for the taxable year in which the producer is deemed to have paid the tax. A copy of all forms 6248, Annual WPT Information Returns (explained in greater detail below) furnished to the producer by the first purchaser or operator, must be attached to the claim for credit or refund. The overpayment of WPT due either to incomplete withholding adjustments or application of the net income limitation is calculated on Form 6249, Computation of Overpaid Windfall Profit Tax.

Overpayments Attributable to Oil Not Subject to Withholding

If the amount of the claim for refund or credit is the overpayment of WPT attributable only to WPT paid on crude oil not subject to withholding removed during a taxable period (calendar quarter), a claim for refund, which is applied for on Form 843, may be filed on or after the date for filing the quarterly return for such taxable period. Inasmuch as the quarterly return must be filed not later than the last day of the second month following the close of the taxable period, a refund claim can be filed on or after such quarterly return filing date. A claim for credit should be made through an adjustment on the Quarterly WPT Return (Form 720 with WPT Form 6047 attached) for either the current or subsequent taxable periods in accordance with Form 720 instructions.

As noted above, there is an exception applicable to situations where an overpayment is due to the application of the net income limitation. In such cases, the claim for credit (on an excise or income tax return) or refund (on Form 843) of overpayment of WPT for any taxable period may not be filed until the end of the producer's taxable year that includes the last day of that taxable period. However, producers not subject to withholding may adjust their deposits for periods ending after their taxable year to reflect the effect of the net income limitation, using an estimate of the net income limitation and adjusting succeeding deposits.

Procedures for Correcting Underpayments

As implied above, it is possible that underwithholding the WPT will not be corrected through overwithholding sometime during the tax (calendar) year. Generally, where the producer's actual WPT liability for crude oil removed during the calendar year is greater than the amount of WPT withheld, the producer must either remit the WPT owed with an Annual WPT Excise Tax Return (Form 720 with Form 6248 attached) or deposit the amount of WPT owed along with an FTD Form 504 at a Federal Reserve Bank or other authorized financial institution (4995-3e). Either the annual return with payment due or the deposit is due on or before the last day of the fifth month following the close of the calendar year (6076-1).

Underpayments Attributable to Oil Not Subject to Withholding

It is also possible that the WPT deposits of producers who are not subject to the withholding thereof may amount to less than their WPT liability for a taxable period (calendar quarter). Where the deposits for a calendar quarter are less than the producer's liability, the procedure for correcting such an underpayment depends on whether the producer is an integrated oil company or some other type of producer.

Where the WPT liability of an integrated oil-company producer for a calendar quarter is greater than the total amount deposited by such producer for the taxable period, the integrated oil company must deposit the underpayment on or before the last day of the first month following the close of the calendar quarter (4995-3a2). In contrast, nonintegrated oil-company producers must deposit an underpayment of WPT for a taxable period not later than 45 days after the close of the last month in such taxable period (4995-3f2).

Certification of Production

In general, certification of production by a producer provides the first purchaser, operator, disburser or partnership producer with the necessary information to determine the proper WPT rate or exemption from the WPT. Thus, the certificate should identify both the type of oil produced—independent producer or the tax-exempt status of the oil—and the producer by name, address, and federal employer identification (or social security) number. As implied above, the certificate must be delivered to the purchaser of the oil, to the operator of the property from which the oil is produced, to a qualified disburser, or, if the producer is a partner in a partnership which produced the oil, to the partnership (4995-2a). The IRS has provided Form 6458 for use in certifying production or the revocation thereof.

After discovering the oil is not eligible for certification, the producer must furnish notice of revocation within ten days to the person to whom the certificate was furnished (4995-2d). Although a certificate is signed under the penalties of perjury, revocation is not made under penalties of perjury (4995-2a).

Exemption Certificate

An exemption certificate is a written statement that certifies a producer's oil is exempt from WPT because the oil is exempt Indian oil or the oil is from a qualified governmental interest or a qualified charitable interest. As indicated above, Form 6458 may be used either to certify or revoke certification of exempt status. The exemption certificate must be filed with the IRS Service Center in Austin rather than with the region in which the producer files its federal income tax return. The certificate must be filed with the IRS within 10 days after it is furnished to the purchaser or operator. Only one Form 6458 need be filed with the IRS, although the producer furnishes certificates to more than one purchaser, operator, or disburser (4995-2b, amended by TD 7755, IRB 1981-8).

Independent Producer's Certificate

An independent producer's certificate is a written statement certifying that the entire amount of the producer's oil expected to be sold to the purchaser is subject to the lower rates of tax because the oil constitutes independent-producer oil. An independent producer's certificate should not be furnished in respect to oil if it is reasonable to believe that the number of barrels to be affected by the certificate, when taken together with all other oil in respect to which an independent producer's certificate has been furnished by the producer, will exceed the producer's independent-producer amount, i.e., 1,000 barrels per day of production.

As in the case of an exemption certificate, Form 6458 may be used either to certify or revoke certification of independent-producer status. The instructions for IRS Form 6458 require the producer to certify that all of its production from the property qualifies as independent-producer oil. Treasury regulations require that all of the producer's oil production expected to be sold to the purchaser receiving the certification qualifies as independent-producer oil (4995-2c). This inconsistency should be corrected when the final regulations are issued. Finally, an independent producer's certificate does not have to be filed with the IRS.

Integrated Oil-Company Certificate

An integrated oil-company certificate is a written statement certifying that the producer is an integrated oil company that will deposit WPT, so the purchaser should not withhold WPT on the integrated producer's share of production. The certificate is effective for all payments made after the date on which the purchaser receives the certificate. Mandatory certificates must be furnished to the purchaser by an integrated oil company that is a producer of oil from a property of which that producer is also the operator. Optional certificates may be furnished to the purchaser by an integrated oil company that is not also the operator (4995-2c).

Certification by Partnership Producers

Where a partner is exempt from WPT, an independent producer, or an integrated oil company, the partnership should certify its partners' status. However, the partnership may only certify its partners' production to the extent it has received certification from them. In reflecting each partner's certification, the partnership must state the percentage of oil certified as exempt, subject to lower independent producer tax rates, or not subject to withholding insofar as the producer is an integrated oil company. To support the partnership certification, the partnership must retain a copy of each partner's certification in its records for as long as material in the administration of any federal tax law (4995-2e). In addition, partnership producers must furnish monthly certification where a producing property has no operator. Apparently, the general requirements applicable to a partner producer's certification are transferred to the partnership, including signature under penalties of perjury.

Certification Responsibilities of Operators

The operator (or producer if there is no operator) must furnish monthly certifications to be used in determining the amount of WPT withheld and/or deposited. The certificate must be furnished by the 15th day of the month following the month in which the oil is removed from the premises to one of the following (6050C-1c): the purchaser or disburser in the case of oil subject to withholding or the producer in the case of oil not subject to withholding. In the case of oil not subject to withholding, there is an exception that applies where the producer is a partner in a partnership. If the producer and the partnership elect, the monthly statement may be furnished to the partnership. The partnership must then furnish the information to the partner (with respect to that partner's share of oil) within 15 days of receipt (6050C-1a).

The monthly statement must include the following information: the tier of the oil and, if it is Tier 3 oil, whether the oil is newly discovered, heavy, or incremental tertiary oil; the total amounts of oil removed and the amounts by tier and category; the adjusted base price for each tier of oil removed; the state severance tax adjustment, if any, for each tier of oil; and the property from which the oil was removed. In respect to Alaskan oil produced from Sadlerochit Reservoir, the monthly statement must include the average removal price for the month and any adjustment for the TAPS (Trans-Alaskan Pipeline System) tariff as provided in Section 4996d. If the oil is exempt Alaskan oil, the statement should certify that it is exempt from WPT, in which case the detailed information included in monthly statements is not required.

An agreement may be made between the operator and the recipient of the monthly statements relieving the operator of the duty to furnish some or all of the information that must usually be included. Such an agreement must be in writing and be signed by both parties. The recipient must otherwise have the information necessary to compute WPT. Finally, any such agreement will terminate immediately upon notification by either party to the other party in a written signed statement that the agreement is terminated (6050C-1d).

In addition, operators are relieved of their obligation to furnish monthly statements when the purchaser has elected not to withhold and deposit. More specifically, if the operator has agreed in a joint election with the purchaser (as explained above) to assume the responsibilities of that purchaser, the monthly statement is not required in respect to oil subject to withholding (6050C-1e).

Finally, where the operator receives a producer's certificate certifying a share of production to be exempt from tax, subject to a lower rate of tax, or not to be withheld upon, the operator is also relieved of the obligation to furnish monthly statements. However, the operator either must furnish a copy of the producer's certificate to each purchaser of oil from the property by the 15th day of the month following the month in which the certificate is received or must furnish a certificate summarizing the contents of one or more producer's certificates received and stating that such certificates are available for inspection if the payment is to be received by the operator on behalf of the producers (6050C-1f).

Certification Under the Economic Recovery Tax Act of 1981

As mentioned earlier, the Economic Recovery Tax Act of 1981 amended the WPT law; two of these changes will affect these certification requirements. These are the amendments relating to the exemption of royalty-owner production and independent-producer stripper oil. While there are no current guidelines applicable to these changes that will go into effect in 1982 and 1983, respectively, each of these will certainly require certification in addition to that set forth above.

Reporting and Recordkeeping

Although the primary responsibility for reporting and recordkeeping would seem to fall on the first purchaser, operators, qualified disbursers, and producers—especially in integrated oil companies—may often bear reporting and recordkeeping responsibilities. In addition, partnerships with oil production may be required to report WPT information to and maintain supporting records for their partners, first purchasers, operators, qualified disbursers, and the federal government.

Reporting Responsibilities of First Purchasers

Each crude oil purchaser who is required to deduct and withhold WPT from payments to producers must file a Quarterly Federal Excise Tax Return (Form 720) along with a Windfall Profit Tax Return (Form 6047) by the last day of the second month following the end of the taxable period (calendar quarter) (6076-1). The instructions for WPT Form 6047 specify that only one Form 720 should be filed to report all excise taxes for the calendar quarter. If Form 720 reflects both the WPT and other excise taxes reportable on dates prior to that required for the WPT, the form will be considered timely filed by the later date if timely deposits of all excise taxes have been made (Rev. Proc. 80-23, IRB 1980-26).

Form 720 should reflect withholding adjustments to prior periods' returns. Where the entire adjustment is attributable to the same quarter as the withholding giving rise to the adjustment, Form 720 should reflect only the amount withheld as adjusted. Alternatively, where the adjustment is attributable to more than one quarter within a calendar year, the purchaser should attach to Form 720 a statement that includes the basis for the withholding adjustment; the amount of the adjustment; the return period to which the adjustment relates; and statements both that the required supporting evidence is included and that IRS No. 50 (Form 6047) on Form 720 is being adjusted (4995-1c1i).

The purchaser must also furnish a monthly statement to each producer, disburser, operator, or partnership to which the purchaser makes a payment for oil being removed during the month. These statements must be submitted by the end of the first month following the removal month to which each applies. Each monthly statement must include either a summary of the total amount of WPT withheld by the purchaser from payments made to the producer, operator, or partnership with respect to oil removed during that month, or a declaration that no withholding was made because of the receipt of an exemption certificate with respect to the producer's oil (4997-2b). Apparently, there is no requirement that the purchaser furnish monthly statements in respect to payments made for oil not subject to withholding, e.g., the purchase of oil from an integrated oil company. The annual WPT Information Return (Form 6248) must be furnished by the purchaser to each producer, disburser, operator, or partnership to which it makes payment for oil. Form 6248 must be furnished on or before March 31 of the year immediately following the calendar year to which it applies. A copy of each Form 6248 must also be filed with the IRS on or before that last day of the fourth month following the end of the calendar year, i.e., April 30 (4997-2cc).

Each Form 6248 should include the following information:

1. The quantity, removal price, severance tax adjustment, TAPS adjustment (if any), adjusted base price, and WPT liability (computed without regard to net income limitation) for oil in each tier removed during the calendar year
2. Each category of Tier 3 oil treated as a separate tier
3. Independent producer oil withheld upon at 50% rate and at 30% rate treated as separate tiers
4. The total quantity of taxable crude oil removed during the calendar year
5. The total amount of WPT liability incurred during the year in respect to the oil
6. The amount of WPT withheld by the purchaser in respect to the oil removed during the calendar year on a month-by-month and an annual basis (4997-2c1)

For federal income tax purposes, the amount of WPT withheld from payments made to the producer, operator, disburser, or partnership during the calendar year without regard to when the oil was removed should be included on Form 6248 (4997-2c2). In addition, any other information as may be required by Form 6248 or its instructions should be included in the Annual WPT Information Return (4997-2c4).

Most of the information delineated above must also be provided annually for payments to persons exempt from the WPT. In respect to each exempt producer, the purchaser not only should provide the aforementioned information about the exempt production as if it were taxable crude oil but it also should identify the applicable exemption (4997-2c1).

In the case of withholding adjustments not completed during the course of the calendar year (as explained above), the purchaser should provide additional information, including the amount of WPT ascertained to have been underwithheld or overwithheld, the amount actually adjusted, and the amount remaining unadjusted. In the case of underwithholding, the information that the producer is liable for WPT in excess of the WPT withheld by the purchaser and that this information is being supplied to the IRS should be included on the annual return. For overwithholding, the information that the purchaser was unable to adjust the overpayment fully under Temp. Reg. Sec. 150.4995-1c and that the producer is eligible for a credit or refund should be provided with Form 6248 (4997-2c2).

Although there is no statutory requirement

for the purchaser to furnish a Form 6248 in respect to payments made for oil not subject to withholding, the regulations require every producer of oil not subject to withholding by the purchaser to file an Annual WPT Information Return (Form 6248) in respect to that oil (4997-2c3).

Reporting Responsibilities of Operators

There are two major exceptions to the general rule that the operator is not subject to reporting requirements, i.e., filing tax returns or information returns or providing information statements. First, where the operator and the first purchaser have made the joint election under Section 4995a-7 wherein the operator agrees to assume the responsibilities of the purchaser, the operator is subject to the same tax return and information requirements that would otherwise be imposed on the purchaser with whom the operator made an election.

If the operator receives payment from the purchaser on behalf of other producers with an interest in the property, the operator must file or furnish within 15 days of receipt most information provided by the purchaser in respect to the oil production of each producer, disburser, or partnership of producers. The operator must report within 15 days of receipt to each producer, disburser, or partnership of producers, both the information on the operator's monthly statement received from the purchaser relating to each producer's, disburser's, or partnership's share of the oil purchased, and the information on the operator's Form 6248 received from the purchaser relating to each producer's, disburser's, or partnership's share of the oil purchased for the taxable year.

The operator must also report to the IRS within 15 days of receipt the information on the operator's Form 6248 received from the purchaser relating to each producer's, disburser's or partnership's share of the oil purchased. Based on the information received from the purchaser on the operator's Form 6248, information should be furnished to each producer, disburser, or partnership of producers and filed with the IRS on a separate Form 6248 (for each producer, disburser, or partnership of producers) (4997-2a). Unfortunately, this requirement that the monthly and annual statements be furnished and filed within 15 days of receipt has imposed severe time constraints on many operators during 1981.

Reporting Responsibilities of Qualified Disbursers

Although disbursers and partnerships are generally not subject to reporting requirements (i.e., filing tax or information returns or furnishing information statements), a qualified disburser who elects to be a withholding agent assumes the reporting responsibilities of a purchaser, integrated oil company, or operator that formerly acted as a withholding agent. In addition, to the extent that a qualified disburser receives information as an intermediary between producers and purchasers, it is responsible for relaying promptly the information to the producer or the purchaser, whichever is appropriate.

Where the qualified disburser acts as a withholding agent as provided in Temp. Reg. Sec. 150.4995-5, it is subject to the identical tax return and information requirements that would have been imposed on the purchaser or operator from whom the qualified disburser has assumed withholding responsibilities. One should review the above explanations of the reporting responsibilities of both purchasers and operators for an understanding of the reporting requirements assumed by a qualified disburser, e.g., filing excise tax returns, and annual information and tax returns.

As an intermediary between the purchaser and the producer, the qualified disburser is required to forward to each producer within 15 days of receipt the information on the monthly statement received from the purchaser (or operator) relating to that producer's (or partnership's) share of oil purchased. Similarly, the qualified disburser would be required to furnish to both producers and the IRS within 15 days of receipt the information on a Form 6248 received from a purchaser.

Reporting Responsibilities of Partnerships of Producers

In general, a partnership of producers has no reporting responsibilities. Of course, if a partnership is also a first purchaser or integrated oil company, an operator electing to act as a withholding agent, or a qualified disburser electing to be a withholding agent, then that partnership assumes the reporting responsibilities of its alter ego. If a partnership of producers receives payments from a purchaser, an operator, or a qualified disburser on behalf of the partners in the partnership, the partnership must furnish to each partner or file with the IRS, as is appropriate, certain information within 15 days of receipt. To each partner, the partnership must relay both the information on the partnership's monthly statement received from the purchaser (disburser or operator) relating to that partner's share of the oil purchased and the information on the partnership's Form 6248 received from the purchaser (disburser or operator) relating to that partner's share of the oil purchased. To the IRS, the partnership must forward the information on the partnership's Form 6248 received from the purchaser (disburser or operator) relating to each partner's share of the oil purchased (4997-2a).

Reporting Responsibilities of Producers

Insofar as payments for its crude oil production are subject to the withholding of WPT by purchasers (operators or qualified disbursers), a producer's reporting requirements are limited to those resulting from over- or underwithholding that are not corrected by the withholding agent during the taxable year. As explained above, underwithholding of the WPT not corrected by the withholding agent sometime during the calendar year through over withholding is treated as an underpayment of WPT for the tax year. Consequently, the producer must file an Annual WPT Federal Excise Return (Form 720 with WPT Form 6047 attached) along with payment of the WPT due on or before May 31, i.e., the last day of the fifth month following the tax year for which the underpayment of WPT occurred (4997-1a2, 4995-3e). Alternatively, the amount of the underpayment may be deposited with a Federal Reserve Bank or other authorized financial institution on or before May 31, relieving the producer of the responsibility to remit the WPT balance due with the annual WPT return.

As explained above, any withholding of WPT that is not corrected by underwithholding sometime during the calendar year is treated as an overpayment of WPT, which can be either refunded or credited against the producer's federal income tax or WPT liability. In applying for a WPT refund, a producer should file a claim for refund (Form 843 with WPT Forms 6248 and 6249 or 6249-A attached) on or after the last day of the first February after the close of the calendar year for which the WPT was overpaid but presumably not before the receipt by the producer of the annual WPT information statement (WPT Form 6248) from the withholding agent.

Alternatively, a producer may claim a credit for overpaid WPT when filing either its federal income tax return or its federal excise tax return. The producer's income tax return (along with WPT Forms 6248 and 6249 or 6249-A) is filed according to the due date (with properly filed extensions) for such return but not before the last day of the first February following the close of the calendar year in respect to which the overpayment occurred (6402-1e). Similarly, where the producer is otherwise required to pay the WPT and file the federal quarterly WPT excise tax return within a month after the end of the taxable period (calendar quarter), the producer may reduce the amount of WPT payable by the amount of WPT overpaid when filing a WPT excise tax return (Form 720 with both WPT forms 6248 and 6249 attached) on or before the due date for such return but not before the last day of the first February following the close of the calendar year for which the overpayment was made. In practice, producers would not file a claim for refund or claim an income tax or WPT credit until receiving their annual WPT information return (Form 6248) on or before March 31.

Responsibilities of Producers Not Subject to Withholding

Although purchasers (operators or disbursers) are generally responsible for withholding WPT from payments to producers, at least four types of producers are excepted from such withholding requirements: producers of crude oil removed from the premises before it is sold; producers of crude oil manufactured or converted into refined products before the oil is removed from the premises; producers of crude oil who have made a qualified disburser election; and producers who have furnished an integrated oil-company certificate to the first purchaser (4995-1a).

Insofar as such producers are exempted from withholding, they must make timely deposits of their WPT and file quarterly federal excise tax returns (Form 720 with WPT Form 6047 attached) (4997-1a1iii). As explained above, all of the other requirements applicable to the purchaser in both filing the WPT excise tax return and making WPT deposits are essentially assumed by the producer whose oil production is not subject to withholding.

Recordkeeping

In general, the regulations require that each person liable for the WPT, each producer or purchaser of domestic crude oil, each operator of a property from which domestic crude oil is produced, each disburser, and each partnership or other person receiving on behalf of or providing information to producers keep records of all documents, material, and information necessary in determining and administering the WPT for as long as the records may be material in administering the federal tax law. More specifically, these persons are required to maintain all information to support a DOE property categorization, including land files, base period data, stripper property determinations; all certifications, returns, and information statements; all information used in determining base prices, severance tax adjustments, and removal prices; and all information used to calculate the net income for purposes of the net income limitation, including reserves and historical costs (4997-1b).

Needless to say, the administrative and accounting requirements of the WPT are among the most complicated found in the federal tax system. When one considers the short notice that the oil industry was given, the WPT may have been the single most burdensome piece of tax legislation in the history of the U.S. In summary, if the temporary WPT regulations are finalized with only minor changes, the administrative and accounting aspects of the WPT will soon be integrated with the other paperwork requirements of the energy business so the industry can concentrate on its more socially desirable role in the development of increased energy production.

Part VIII

Postscript

Needless to say, the first year that any tax is imposed will always be replete with administrative and interpretive difficulties. The windfall profit tax by its very design was destined to be difficult to implement. The most obvious initial problem resulted from its retroactivity and the designation of the first purchaser as a withholding agent for the WPT of a taxpayer producer, i.e., the person with an economic interest in crude-oil production. Another major problem for first purchasers and the taxpayer producer resulted from the unusual definition of income for determining the net income limitation and the overlapping of DOE and IRS authority in respect to the definition of property for WPT purposes. In time, of course, such difficulties have been or will be resolved.

Although a windfall profit tax of one type or another was proposed during the Nixon and Ford administrations and earlier in the Carter administration, the final form of the WPT is an excise tax on crude oil and not a tax on excess profits. A political economist would probably describe the tax as a sharing of the marginal revenue resulting from the decontrol of crude-oil prices with the federal government. This sharing allegedly is necessary because the oil industry could not digest fully such a massive increase in cash flow through the rapid expansion of exploration for and development of crude-oil production.

During the 1980 presidential campaign, the WPT was a significant political issue in oil-producing states such as Texas, Louisiana, and California. However, former President Carter either ignored the issue or promised only to repeal the WPT on small-volume royalty owners when he campaigned in oil-producing states. In contrast, President Reagan promised to work for the repeal of the entire WPT. In practice, the Reagan administration's Economic Recovery Act (ERA) of 1981 included only limited changes in the WPT because repeal of the tax could add up to a $25 billion loss in revenue. There is currently no Reagan administration proposal to repeal the WPT.

Based on the Reagan administration's own estimates, the federal government is already facing a budget deficit of between $40 and $60 billion for fiscal year 1982 because of its tax cuts, high interest rates, and the economic recession. So it cannot afford to repeal the WPT without either imposing another tax or further reducing budget outlays — either of which requires congressional approval. After the first round of budget cuts, the latter would seem to be impossible and the former is not only inconsistent with the political and economic philosophy of our President but also politically risky in a congressional election year. However, the WPT changes in ERA should only cost a few billion dollars in revenue. Such changes could pacify most royalty owners and independent producers while encouraging oil production from stripper wells and newly discovered wells.

Generally, the IRS has been willing to accommodate the constructive criticism of the proposed regulations by oil industry critics as well as by their representatives from the accounting and legal professions. Moreover, inadequacies in DOE regulations should be corrected as the IRS writes its own regulations pertinent to the definitions of property and the determination of crude-oil base prices. One should anticipate more changes in the regulations as the IRS carries out audits of first purchasers, operators, and producers who withheld and/or paid WPT during the 1980 tax year. The IRS will learn much about the implementation of their regulations from WPT audits, and their knowledge will most certainly be translated into a refinement of their WPT regulations and the issuance of revenue rulings and procedures. Finally, the body of law on windfall profit taxation should also be expanded by the litigation that results from disputes that are not resolved within the IRS audit and appeals process.

On January 28, 1981, President Reagan delivered on his campaign promise to decontrol the price of crude oil immediately, although the decontrol thereof was already assured by June of 1981. The Reagan administration has also been considering an acceleration of the decontrol of natural gas prices, which are due to be decontrolled completely sometime during 1985. If inflation mitigates by the end of 1981, it seems likely that the administration would ask Congress to enact legislation to accelerate the decontrol of natural gas prices.

Unfortunately, the price for accelerated decontrol may again be a WPT on the marginal revenue from increased prices for natural gas. Inasmuch as there are over 25 different categories of oil under the current system of price controls, any differential tax rate structure for a WPT on natural gas would create classification problems similar to (and maybe worse than) those experienced with the WPT on crude oil. In addition, determining the impact of a net income limitation on the producer's WPT liability would also result in a set of recordkeeping and computational problems similar to those that have plagued the WPT on crude oil. Hopefully, the oil and gas industry's experience with the WPT on crude oil would provide a basis for minimizing other administrative and interpretive difficulties associated with a WPT on natural gas.

Although the oil and gas industry should work to influence Congress to impose the least amount of WPT on natural gas, it must also ensure that the statutory provisions authorizing such taxation do not create the same compliance problems that resulted from the WPT law for crude oil. Similarly, the IRS and Department of Treasury should have the benefit of the oil and gas industry's experience with the proposed regulations for the WPT on crude oil. There is always a danger that the industry's advice will include self-serving recommendations; therefore, the accounting and legal professions should contribute to the policy-making process both in the Congress and during the regulation writing period.

Of course, these professional representatives for the tax-paying oil and gas producers may also exhibit self-serving tendencies in advising the Congress, IRS, and Treasury. Therefore, opposing groups representing consumers and utilities and research groups representing no particular interest except their individual disciplinary bias should take part in the tax legislative process, as well as the subsequent administrative/regulatory process for which the IRS and Department of Treasury are responsible.

In response to criticism of the WPT on crude oil, a few statutory changes therein were included in the Economic Recovery (Tax) Act of 1981. These changes are explained in detail below. One should not anticipate any major changes in the WPT on crude oil; however, the IRS will continue to refine its administrative law—regulations, rulings, procedures, and information releases. Another potential cause of change in the WPT law would be judicial decisions, especially the constitutional case initiated by several oil-producing states and independent producers.

Economic Recovery Tax Act of 1981

To ensure enactment of his tax program of lower tax rates and increased incentives for capital investment, President Reagan had to accept provisions sponsored by parochial and reform interests in the Congress. As noted above, the Reagan administration's concession on the WPT should pacify both small royalty owners and independent producers without sacrificing billions in revenue from the WPT. More specifically, the Economic Recovery Act (hereinafter ERA) expands the definition of exempt oil to encompass the stripper-well oil of independent producers (beginning in 1983), a specified amount of the oil of royalty owners (beginning in 1982), and the production of oil from the economic interest of a Section 170c-2 organization caring for delinquent, dependent, orphaned, neglected or handicapped children. It also extends the royalty owner credit (now $2,500) for one year (1981) and lowers the tax rate for newly discovered (Tier III) oil from 30% to 15% over a five-year period.

Stripper Oil

Although much of the oil from stripper wells had been relieved from price controls before the decontrol of crude oil prices began, it was not exempt from windfall profit taxation in the Crude Oil Windfall Profit Tax Act when the law was passed by the Congress in 1980. Such an inconsistency in energy policy was criticized immediately by the oil industry. In response to such criticism, the Congress has amended Sections 4991, 4992, and 4994 to provide for exempting oil produced from stripper wells by independent producers beginning in 1983. Based on DOE price-control regulations, a stripper well is a well located on a property from which the average daily per well production has been 10 barrels or less for any consecutive twelve-month period after 1972. Under the WPT law, oil from such wells is classified as Tier II oil; therefore, it is subject to a WPT rate of 60%. If an independent producer has an economic interest in a stripper well, then the WPT rate may be 30%, inasmuch as independent producers are eligible for reduced WPT rates on up to 1,000 barrels per day of tiers I and II oil.

During 1980, 1981, and 1982, an independent producer would pay WPT on stripper oil at a rate of 60% or 30%, depending on the allocation of the 1,000 barrel per day independent producer amount between Tier I and Tier II production. Starting in 1983, the production from stripper wells would be exempt to the extent of an independent producer's operating interest therein; however, royalty owners and other producers would continue to pay WPT on stripper oil at the regular Tier II rate of 60%. Of course, a royalty owner's stripper oil may also be exempt to the extent covered by the 2 (or 3) barrel per day exemption. Finally, an independent producer's 1,000 barrel per day independent producer amount is not reduced by the amount to which the exemption for stripper-well oil applies.

To ensure independent producers do not traffic in stripper wells to take advantage of their exemption from the WPT, Section 4994g-2 provides for a limitation on the transfer of stripper well properties between nonindependent producers and independent producers. Thus, an independent producer's exempt stripper-well oil does not include production from a working interest in any property that, at any time after July 22, 1981, was owned by a person other than an independent producer (within the meaning of Section 4992b-1).

Royalty Owners

As a result of considerable criticism from hundreds of thousands of royalty owners, the Omnibus Reconciliation Act of 1980 included a provision that entitled most royalty owners to a $1,000 credit on their WPT liability for 1980. This royalty owner's credit (hereinafter ROC) for individuals, estates and family farm corporations is increased to $2,500 and extended for one year (1981) by the Economic Recovery Act.

For tax years after 1981, royalty owners are entitled to an exemption from the WPT of two barrels per day (in 1982 through 1984) or three barrels per day (after 1984). In addition, ERA clarifies several of the questions that had arisen in the interpretation of the Section 6429 ROC as enacted in the Omnibus Reconciliation Act, especially those related to allocating the ROC between family members, family farm corporations, estates and beneficiaries of estates.

Essentially, the Section 4991b definition of exempt oil is expanded for years after 1981 to include the first few (two or three) barrels of daily production for individuals, estates, and family farm corporations with royalty interests. Just as with the ROC, family members, family farm corporations, estates, and beneficiaries must share the exempt royalty oil amount, i.e., two barrels in 1982–1984 and three after 1984. Similarly, the limitation (6429d-3) on the transfer of royalty interests is continued, although revised, to reflect the fact that persons with economic interests in oil producing property could not have known there would be continuing preferential treatment for royalty owners before June 10, 1981.

Section 4995, withholding and depositary requirements, has also been amended to authorize adjustments in withholding by first purchasers, operators, or qualified disbursers to reflect exempt royalty oil. At this time, it is not certain how such adjustments and the certification will be made because Section 4995a-9 instructs the IRS to promulgate the regulations necessary to implement withholding adjustments for exempt royalty oil. However, Section 4994f-2B makes it clear that a qualified royalty owner may allocate the royalty limit, i.e., two or three barrels per day multiplied by the number of days in any quarter, to any qualified royalty production he selects where the qualified royalty owner's qualified royalty production for any quarter exceeds the royalty limit. Thus, royalty owners apparently have been given the opportunity to plan the allocation of their exempt royalty oil to qualified royalty production to minimize the WPT.

Newly Discovered Oil

Currently, the lowest WPT rate of 30% is applicable to Tier III oil, which includes newly discovered oil, heavy oil, and incremental tertiary oil. In deference to oil-industry critics who argue that newly discovered oil should be exempt from the WPT to encourage exploration, development, and production, Congress included a provision in ERA that amends Section 4987 to lower the WPT rate on newly discovered oil, i.e., crude oil from a property that did not begin production until after 1978 from 30% to 15% over a five-year period. Section 4987b-3 now provides for the following WPT rate structure applicable to newly discovered oil:

For taxable periods beginning in	*WPT rate %*
1982	27½
1983	25
1984	22½
1985	20
1986, etc.	15

Tax Exemption for Qualified Charitable Interests

In general, the exemption of eleemosynary organizations from income taxation is much broader than the exemption of such organizations from windfall profit taxation. Most certainly in response to complaints from a few charitable and/or educational child-care organizations with economic interests in oil-producing property, the Section 4994b definition of a qualified charitable interest has been expanded to encompass oil produced from interests held by or for the benefit of a Section 170c-2 charitable organization that is organized and operated primarily for the residential placement, care, or treatment of delinquent, dependent, orphaned, or handicapped children.

DIFFERENTIAL IMPACT OF THE WINDFALL PROFIT TAX ON THE CASH FLOWS OF OIL COMPANIES

Dr. James W. Kolari
Dr. John C. Groth*

Although the "windfall profit tax" (WPT) has been passed, it will be a period of time before its final form, implications, and nuances are fully understood. For example, one question that arises is, What is the impact of the WPT on the cash flow of an oil company? This issue is important for two reasons. First, a large proportion of cash generated in oil firms is normally reinvested in energy related investments. Second, when cash flows in oil firms are reinvested, there is a compounding effect. This compounding effect is important because it makes a great impact on a firm's ability to finance itself from internal sources. The natural consequence is an effect on investment opportunities a firm may undertake and, in turn, on its growth.[1]

The purpose of this article is to show the differential impact of the WPT on the cash flows of independent oil companies as compared to integrated companies. As we shall see, the presence of the differential impact coupled with the compounding effect leads to some interesting

---

* Professors J.W. Kolari and J.C. Groth are, respectively, Assistant and Associate Professors of Finance at Texas A&M University.

1 Recall that internally generated funds are a "cheaper" source of capital than equity funds. A decrease in the availability of internally generated funds thus causes the cost of future financial resources to increase if a greater proportion of future capital needs is obtained from "new" equity. The impact of the WPT on cost of capital and the firm is the subject of another paper in preparation.

Article reprinted courtesy of *Oil & Gas Tax Quarterly*, March 1981, pp. 513–527

implications concerning the future growth of firms subject to the WPT. Additionally, the differential impact of the WPT on independent and integrated oil companies leads to a number of significant implications of interest to practitioners, researchers, policy makers, and legislators.

The WPT has multiple and sometimes interrelated effects on a firm. To avoid confusion we specifically center attention on cash flows. Thus, we address only the impact of WPT on cash flows, and not the impact of various tax exposures and strategies with respect to corporate and other taxes. We also refrain from discussing the effect the tax will have on the supply of oil and subsequent price. Furthermore, the effects of the tax on earnings per share, cost of capital, dividend policy, and investment are reserved for other mediums.

The intricacies and often uniqueness of tax legislation, plus our desire to focus on key concepts and relationships, suggest the need for some simplifications and assumptions in our discussion. Making these assumptions allows us to isolate and grasp relevant issues without altering our main conclusions.

Background/Assumptions

The WPT act classifies firms as either independent or integrated oil producers. This classification affects the tax rate as shown in Table 1.

TABLE 1
WPT Rates on Crude Oil

	Independent	Integrated
Tier I Oil	50%	70%
Tier II Oil	30%	60%
Tier III Oil	30%	30%

The lower rate for independents applies only to the first 1000 barrels per day (BPD). Beyond this minimum limit, independents are taxed at rates identical to those of integrated producers. Thus, a lower tax on independent firms occurs when Tier I or Tier II oil is produced and the firm's production is less than 1000 BPD. Robert Shattuck [*Oil & Gas Tax Q.* (June 1980)] previously addressed in detail the independent versus integrated classification and issues related to the WPT in this journal. Essentially, to qualify as an independent producer, activities must be mainly in exploration and production, although limited refining and retailing operations are permissible.

The simplifying assumptions we make are

— A dollar not paid in WPT would be reinvested by the firm if the tax did not exist;

— The firm only uses internally generated funds as equity funds for reinvestment;

— Cash flows occur at the end of the year; and

— Cash flows are immediately reinvested and the expected rate of return on the reinvested flows is the same in each year and for each firm.

These simplifications prevent unnecessary confusion in the calculation of cash flows over time. Indeed, real world factors may make these assumptions appear too simplistic. It is worth reiterating, therefore, that they are intended to enhance our ability to focus on cash flows; and, their use does not affect the relationships and conclusions we want to highlight. We certainly recognize that all firms do not reinvest at the same expected rates of return, that some do pay out part of cash generated, and that other real world factors exist. But we want to hold certain variables constant so that attention is centered on the differential impact of the WPT on cash flows.

Differential Impact on Cash Flows

Cash flow available in the current period is related to after-tax cash flows generated last period. Those after-tax cash flows depend on the amount invested at the beginning of last period, the cash flow rate of return earned during last period, and the taxes paid. Obviously, then, cash flow in each successive period is related to the previous periods and the differential impact of taxes on cash flows available for investment. If one assumes that all after-tax cash flows are reinvested, then the differential impact of any taxes on the flows in the current period and all successive periods will differentially affect all future cash flows. Moreover, these differences will be amplified by a compounding effect operating on cash returns generated on the additional funds that could be invested resulting from lower tax payments in current and future periods.

As an illustration, the differential impact in the current period of the WPT on independents producing less than 1000 barrels per day versus integrated oil producers can be seen with a simple example. Suppose that the world price of oil is $30 per barrel, the base price per barrel for Tier I oil is $13, and the severance tax rate is 7 percent. The WPT and net value per barrel of oil after the WPT for Tier I oil is calculated as shown in Table 2. Thus this example shows that the independent pays $3.16 per barrel less in taxes as long as production does not exceed 1000 BPD. That is $3.16 more that can be reinvested by the independent producer to generate additional cash flows in the next period that the integrated producer will not have to invest to generate cash flows. This continues to happen in successive periods except that the "extra cash flow" is greater than $3.16 because of the compounding effect of the rate of return earned on the differential investment made by the independent.

TABLE 2
WPT Calculations[1]

	Independent Producer	Integrated Producer
1. World Price Per Barrel of Oil	\$30.00	\$30.00
2. Base Price Per Barrel of Oil	13.00	13.00
3. Value of Oil Exposed to Severance Tax	17.00	17.00
4. Severance Tax (\$17.00 × 7%)	1.19	1.19
5. Value of Oil Exposed to Windfall Profit Tax (\$17.00 − \$1.19)	15.81	15.81
6. Tier I Windfall Profit Tax Rates	50%	70%
7. Tier I Windfall Profit Taxes[2] Per Barrel of Oil (\$15.81 × #6)	7.91	11.07
8. Value Per Barrel of Oil After Severance and Windfall Profit Taxes (\$30 - #4 - #7)	20.90	17.74

1 The WPT is limited to 90% of net income per barrel. Again, for simplicity, we assume that the companies are within this net income limitation.

2 Ignoring other taxes and expenses.

For instance, at a \$30 per barrel price, a small independent currently producing 100 BPD for thirty days will have \$9,480 more cash retained for reinvestment at the end of the first quarter. More importantly, this incremental cash flow will compound itself over time. And, if production increases as a result of reinvestment, the differential amount paid in taxes and the increased production leads to a greater growth in cash flow for the independent versus integrated producer — even assuming that production for an integrated firm grows at the same rate.

Since we wish to focus attention on the impact of the WPT, let us see the differential impact on cash flows of the WPT and how the difference is magnified over time, with other things held constant. Column One of Table 3 shows the effect on differential cash flows over time assuming a 4 percent per quarter rate of return. The numbers represent the amount by which cash flow is greater in the independent firm because of the different WPT treatment, compared to how the integrated firm is taxed on 100 barrels of production. By the end of nine years, which is the term of the windfall profit tax excluding the phase-out period, the $9,480 differential cash flow has grown to a total differential cash flow of $735,600.

Although this figure is large, it is even greater for Tier II oil. Furthermore, it increases as the world price of oil escalates to $40 or $50 per barrel. At $50 per barrel for Tier II oil, for example, an independent having a constant production level of 100 BPD will have a total cash flow advantage of $2,273,600 over integrated producers. For the 1000 BPD producer, it is $22.76 million.

Figure 1 contains two graphs depicting the cash flows over time of the independent and integrated producer shown in Table 3. From these graphs it is easy to see that as world prices escalate, the effect of compounding exacerbates the differential in cash flows.

So far we have assumed that oil production by both independent and integrated producers does not increase in future quarters. Obviously, this is unrealistic in a world of rising energy demands. If production grew at an effective annual rate of 10.4 percent (or 2.5 percent per quarter) and beginning production was 100 BPD, the firm would produce 237 BPD at the end of nine years. Translating this growth in production into differential cash flows for Tier I oil means that an independent producer, starting at a cash flow advantage of $9,480 (100 BPD $30 oil) as

TABLE 3

The Differential Impact of the WPT on Cash Flows Over Time: Independent vs. Integrated Oil Producers*
(in thousands)

World Price/ Quarter	Tier I $30	Tier I $40	Tier I $50	Tier II $30	Tier II $40	Tier II $50
1	9.5	15.1	20.6	12.5	20.9	29.3
2	19.3	30.7	42.1	25.6	42.7	59.8
3	29.6	47.0	64.4	39.1	65.3	91.5
4	40.3	64.0	87.6	53.3	88.8	124.4
--1st year						
5	51.3	81.9	111.8	67.9	113.3	158.7
6	62.9	99.9	136.9	79.4	132.4	194.3
7	74.9	118.9	163.0	99.0	165.2	231.4
8	87.4	138.8	190.2	115.5	192.7	270.0
--2nd year						
9	100.3	159.4	218.4	132.7	221.3	310.1
10	113.8	180.8	247.8	150.6	251.0	351.8
11	127.8	203.1	278.4	169.1	282.0	395.1
12	142.4	226.3	310.1	188.4	314.2	440.2
--3rd year						
13	157.6	250.4	343.2	208.5	347.7	487.1
14	173.4	275.5	377.5	229.4	382.5	535.9
15	189.8	301.5	413.3	251.1	418.7	586.7
16	206.9	328.7	450.4	273.7	456.3	639.4
--4th year						
17	224.6	356.9	489.1	297.2	495.5	694.3
18	243.1	386.2	529.3	321.6	536.2	751.4
19	262.3	416.7	571.1	347.0	578.6	810.8
20	282.3	448.5	614.6	373.4	622.7	872.5
--5th year						
21	303.1	481.5	659.8	400.9	668.3	936.7
22	324.7	515.8	706.9	404.4	716.1	1,003.5
23	347.1	551.5	755.8	459.2	765.7	1,072.9
24	370.5	588.6	806.7	490.1	817.2	1,145.1
--6th year						
25	394.8	627.2	859.6	522.2	870.8	1,220.2
26	420.1	667.3	914.6	555.7	926.5	1,298.3
27	446.4	709.1	971.8	590.4	984.5	1,379.6
28	473.7	752.5	1,031.3	626.6	1,044.8	1,464.0
--7th year						
29	502.1	797.7	1,093.2	664.2	1,107.5	1,551.9
30	521.7	844.6	1,157.6	703.3	1,172.7	1,643.3
31	562.4	893.5	1,224.5	742.7	1,238.5	1,738.3
32	594.4	944.3	1,294.2	786.3	1,311.1	1,837.2
--8th year						
33	627.7	997.1	1,336.6	830.3	1,384.4	1,939.9
34	662.3	1,052.1	1,441.9	876.0	1,460.7	2,046.8
35	698.2	1,109.2	1,520.2	922.6	1,540.1	2,158.0
36	735.6	1,168.6	1,601.6	973.1	1,622.6	2,273.6

*A constant return on investment of 4 percent per quarter is assumed, which corresponds to an effective compound annual rate of return of about 17 percent. Also a constant 100 BPD of production for 30 days per quarter is assumed.

Note: The amounts stated above are the compounded effects on cash flows resulting from the lower WPT (in thousands of dollars rounded to nearest tenth).

FIGURE 1

The Differential Impact of the WPT on Cash Flows Over Time: Independent vs. Integrated Oil Producers

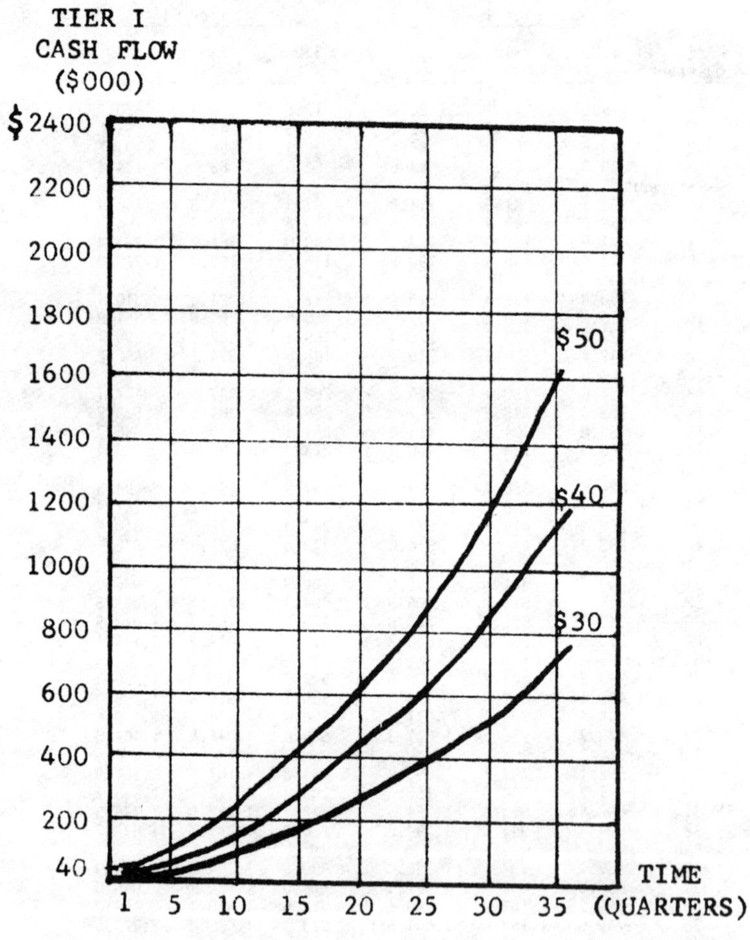

Figure 1
(continued)

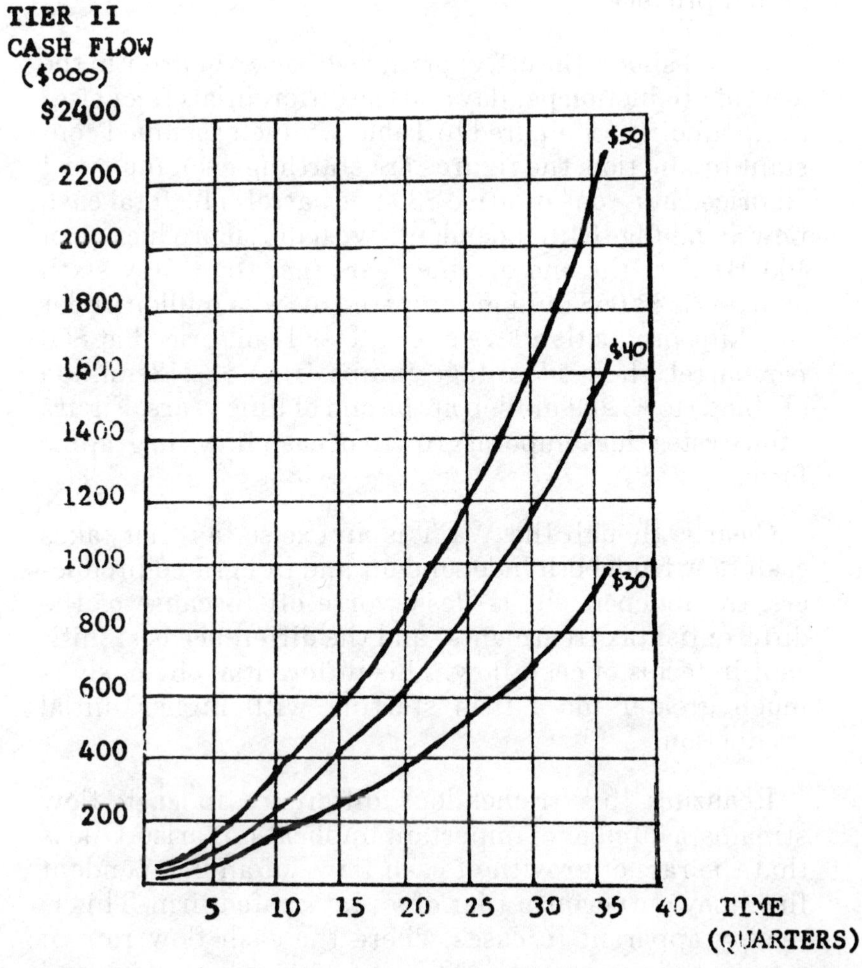

calculated previously, would end the nine year period with a cash flow advantage of about $1,068,200 over integrated producers.

Table 4 shows the effect of a growth each quarter in the level of production per day and the differential effect after compounding. Compared to Table 3, which assumed constant production, the figures are startling even for Tier I oil priced at a conservative $30 per barrel. The total cash flow advantage of independents with initial production of 100 BPD at the end of nine years (*i.e.,* the thirty-sixth quarter) is $1.068 million compared to $.735 million under constant production levels. For Tier II oil priced at $50 per barrel, their advantage jumps from $2.273 million (Table 2) to $3.299 million at the end of nine years. Figure 2 illustrates this temporal growth of cash flows in graphic form.

Clearly, though the WPT is an excise tax that takes cash flow from both independent and integrated producers, the independent is "less worse off" because of the differential tax treatment—and the difference is significant in terms of cash flow. This differential obviously is much greater for a firm starting with higher initial production.

Realizing this tremendous difference in cash flow streams, a number of important implications arise. One is that the rate of growth of cash flows of an independent firm may outperform that of an integrated firm. This is readily apparent in cases where the cash flow rate of return on investment is the same for independent and integrated producers. It may still be true even if the rate of return on investments for the independent is less than that for an integrated firm. Such a case can occur if the rate of return for independents is less but not enough to offset their post-tax cash flow advantage per barrel of Tier I and Tier II oil, due to the WPT. On the other hand,

TABLE 4
The Differential Impact of the WPT on Cash Flows Over Time Assuming Production Increases 2.5 Percent Per Quarter: Independent vs. Integrated Oil Producers*
(in thousands)

World Price/ Quarter	Tier I			Tier II		
	$30	$40	$50	$30	$40	$50
1	9.5	15.1	20.6	12.5	20.9	29.3
2	19.6	31.2	42.7	26.0	43.3	60.6
3	30.5	48.4	66.3	40.3	67.2	94.1
4	42.0	66.7	91.5	55.6	92.7	129.7
--1st year						
5	54.3	86.3	118.2	71.8	119.8	167.7
6	67.4	107.0	146.7	89.1	148.6	208.1
7	81.3	129.1	176.9	107.5	179.2	251.0
8	96.0	152.2	209.0	127.0	211.7	296.5
--2nd year						
9	111.6	177.3	242.9	147.6	246.1	344.6
10	128.1	203.5	278.9	169.4	282.5	395.6
11	145.5	231.2	316.8	192.5	321.0	449.5
12	164.0	260.5	357.0	216.9	361.6	506.4
--3rd year						
13	183.4	291.4	399.3	242.6	404.5	566.5
14	203.9	324.0	444.0	269.7	449.8	629.8
15	225.5	358.3	491.1	298.3	497.5	696.6
16	248.4	394.6	540.8	328.6	547.9	767.2
--4th year						
17	272.6	433.0	593.4	360.5	601.2	841.8
18	298.1	473.5	648.9	394.3	657.4	920.6
19	325.0	516.2	707.5	429.9	716.8	1003.7
20	353.3	561.3	769.2	467.4	799.3	1091.3
--5th year						
21	383.2	608.7	834.3	506.9	845.2	1183.5
22	414.6	658.7	902.7	548.5	914.5	1280.6
23	447.7	711.2	974.8	592.2	987.5	1382.8
24	482.5	766.5	1050.5	638.2	1064.2	1490.2
--6th year						
25	519.0	824.6	1130.1	686.6	1144.9	1603.1
26	556.5	886.6	1213.9	737.5	1229.8	1722.0
27	598.0	950.1	1302.1	791.1	1319.1	1847.1
28	640.6	1017.7	1394.8	847.4	1413.0	1978.7
--7th year						
29	685.4	1088.8	1492.3	906.7	1511.8	2117.0
30	732.5	1163.6	1594.7	968.9	1615.6	2262.3
31	781.8	1242.0	1702.2	1034.2	1724.5	2414.8
32	833.7	1324.4	1815.1	1102.8	1838.9	2574.9
--8th year						
33	888.1	1410.8	1933.5	1174.7	1958.8	2742.9
34	945.2	1501.6	2057.9	1250.3	2084.9	2919.4
35	1005.2	1596.9	2188.6	1329.7	2217.2	3104.7
36	1068.2	1696.9	2325.6	1413.0	2356.1	3299.2
--9th year						

*A constant return on investment of 4 percent per quarter is assumed, which corresponds to an annual rate of return of about 17 percent. Also, 100 BPD are produced in the first quarter. Thereafter production is assumed to grow at 2 1/2 percent per quarter.

Note: The amounts stated above are the compounded effects on cash flows resulting from the lower WPT (in thousands of dollars rounded to nearest tenth).

if independents have a greater cash flow rate of return on reinvested funds than integrated firms, the differential impact is compounded even more.

Since oil companies generally reinvest a large proportion of their cash, it seems inevitable that a difference in production growth will occur. That is, relative to its size, the independent will have more cash flow to invest unless its cost of exploration, production, and success ratio are significantly unfavorable compared to the integrated firm. This difference only serves to increase the cash flow advantage to independents beyond what our examples have shown—at least until the independent reaches 1000 BPD. Beyond this point, the incremental impact of additional barrels produced disappears.

Summary/Conclusion

The different WPT tax rate for independent producers with less than 1000 BPD impacts cash flows generated in a firm. Though the WPT clearly reduces cash flow available to both independent and integrated firms, the independent is "less worse off." The impact over time of the lower tax rate significantly affects after-tax cash flows for the independent, other things held constant. If production increases over time, the impact is substantially greater. The impact will affect several variables which are of interest to analysts and investors—*e.g.*, cash flow of the firm after taking account of other factors impinging on cash flow, earnings per share, growth in reserves, growth in equity, and more.

Understanding this differential impact can lead to a clearer understanding of true relationships. For example, an analyst calculating rates of growth in cash flow per share for various firms might conclude that one firm is performing better (in its business activities) than another because the rate of growth is greater. If the analyst failed

FIGURE 2

The Differential Impact of the WPT on Cash Flows Over Time Assuming Production Increases 2.5 Percent Per Quarter: Independent vs. Integrated Oil Producers

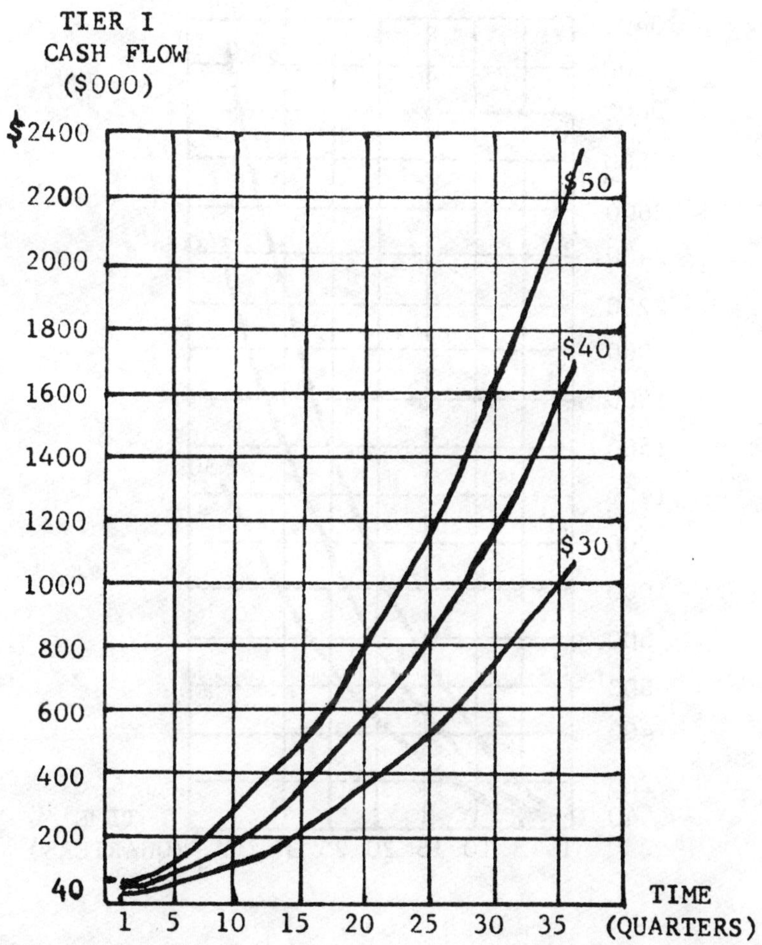

FIGURE 2
(continued)

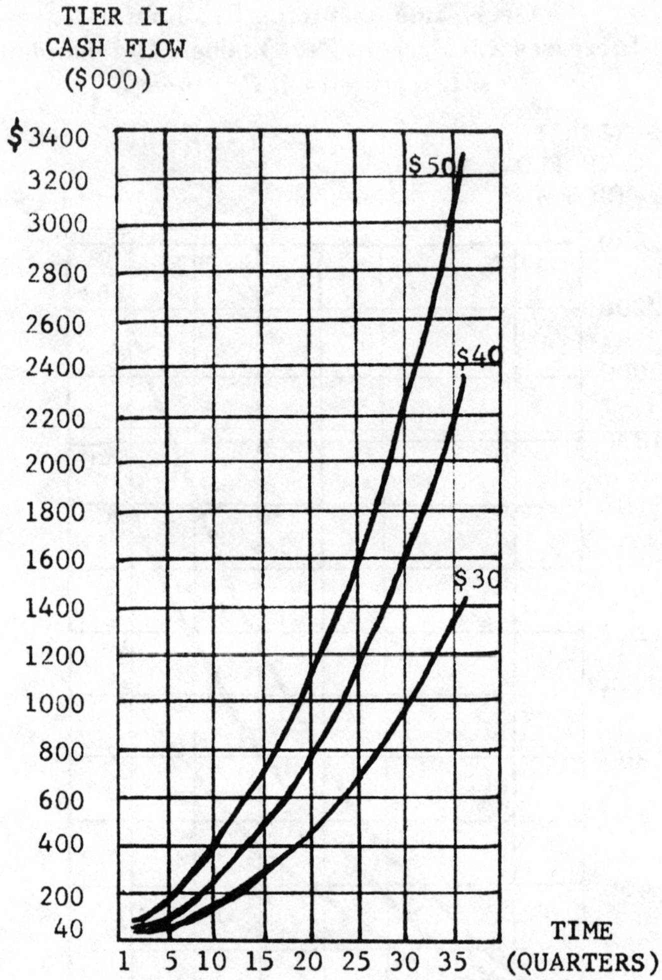

to adjust for the WPT differential impact that maps through to cash flow per share, the wrong conclusion might be made. The superior growth in cash flow relative to other firms might be due to being "less worse off tax-wise," and not because of superior exploration, production, management, etc.

There are a number of other variables commonly examined by users of financial information which will feel the influence of the WPT. The user who understands the WPT differential impact will at least have a chance at recognizing its changing impact on such variables. Adjustments can then be made prior to performing an analysis. We cannot say we have simplified the task of making such adjustments, but we hope to have prompted attention to this area. In fact, currently an article which seeks to identify the differential impact of the WPT on reported earnings is in preparation.